The Main Functional Groups (*continued*)

Structure	Class of Compound	Specific Example	Name	Use
C. Containing nitrogen				
$-NH_2$	primary amine	$CH_3CH_2NH_2$	ethylamine	intermediate for dyes, medicinals
$-NHR$	secondary amine	$(CH_3CH_2)_2NH$	diethylamine	pharmaceuticals
$-NR_2$	tertiary amine	$(CH_3)_3N$	trimethylamine	insect attractant
$-C{\equiv}N$	nitrile	$CH_2{=}CH-C{\equiv}N$	acrylonitrile	orlon manufacture
D. Containing oxygen and nitrogen				
$-\overset{+}{N}\overset{O}{\underset{O^-}{}}$	nitro compounds	CH_3NO_2	nitromethane	rocket fuel
$\overset{O}{-\overset{\|}{C}}-NH_2$	primary amide	$\overset{O}{H\overset{\|}{C}NH_2}$	formamide	softener for paper
E. Containing halogen				
$-X$	alkyl or aryl halide	CH_3Cl	methyl chloride	refrigerant, local anesthetic
$\overset{O}{-\overset{\|}{C}}-X$	acid (acyl) halide	$CH_3\overset{O}{\overset{\|}{C}}Cl$	acetyl chloride	acetylating agent
F. Containing sulfur				
$-SH$	thiol	CH_3CH_2SH	ethanethiol	odorant to detect gas leaks
$-S-$	thioether	$(CH_2{=}CHCH_2)_2S$	allyl sulfide	odor of garlic
$-\overset{O}{\underset{O}{\overset{\|}{\underset{\|}{S}}}}-OH$	sulfonic acid	$CH_3-\bigcirc-SO_3H$	*para*-toluenesulfonic acid	strong organic acid

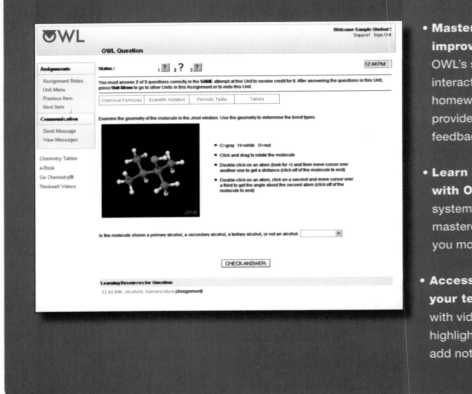

Organic Chemistry

A SHORT COURSE

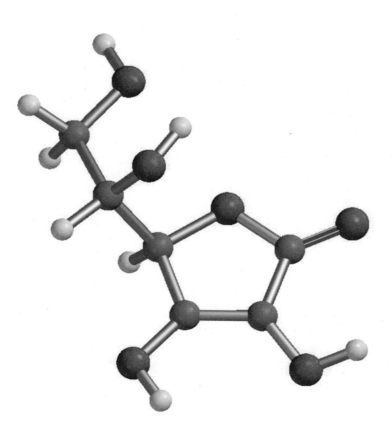

Organic Chemistry

University of Illinois Urbana Champaign Edition
13th Edition

Harold Hart | Christopher M. Hadad | Leslie E. Craine
David J. Hart

CENGAGE
Learning·

Australia • Brazil • Japan • Korea • Mexico • Singapore • Spain • United Kingdom • United States

**CENGAGE
Learning·**

**Organic Chemistry: University of Illinois
Urbana Champaign Edition, 13th Edition**

Organic Chemistry: A Short Course, 13th Edition
Harold Hart | Christopher M. Hadad | Leslie E. Craine | David J. Hart

© 2012, 2007 Cengage Learning. All rights reserved.

Executive Editors:
Maureen Staudt
Michael Stranz

Senior Project Development Manager:
Linda deStefano

Marketing Specialist:
Courtney Sheldon

Senior Production/Manufacturing Manager:
Donna M. Brown

Production Editorial Manager:
Kim Fry

Sr. Rights Acquisition Account Manager:
Todd Osborne

Cover Image:
Getty Images*

*Unless otherwise noted, all cover images used by Custom
Solutions, a part of Cengage Learning, have been supplied
courtesy of Getty Images with the exception of the Earthview
cover image, which has been supplied by the National
Aeronautics and Space Administration (NASA).

For product information and technology assistance, contact us at
Cengage Learning Customer & Sales Support, 1-800-354-9706

For permission to use material from this text or product,
submit all requests online at **cengage.com/permissions**
Further permissions questions can be emailed to
permissionrequest@cengage.com

This book contains select works from existing Cengage Learning resources and
was produced by Cengage Learning Custom Solutions for collegiate use. As such,
those adopting and/or contributing to this work are responsible for editorial
content accuracy, continuity and completeness.

Compilation © 2014 Cengage Learning
ISBN-13: 978-1-305-03353-5

ISBN-10: 1-305-03353-1

Cengage Learning
5191 Natorp Boulevard
Mason, Ohio 45040
USA
Cengage Learning is a leading provider of customized learning solutions with
office locations around the globe, including Singapore, the United Kingdom,
Australia, Mexico, Brazil, and Japan. Locate your local office at:
international.cengage.com/region.

Cengage Learning products are represented in Canada by Nelson Education, Ltd.
For your lifelong learning solutions, visit **www.cengage.com/custom.**
Visit our corporate website at **www.cengage.com.**

Printed in the United States of America

Brief Contents

Preface

Purpose

Over fifty years have passed since the first edition of this text was published. Although the content and appearance of the book have changed over time, our purpose in writing *Organic Chemistry: A Short Course* remains constant: to present a brief introduction to modern organic chemistry in a clear and engaging manner.

This book was written for students who, for the most part, will not major in chemistry, but whose main interest requires some knowledge of organic chemistry, such as agriculture, biology, human or veterinary medicine, pharmacy, nursing, medical technology, health sciences, engineering, nutrition, and forestry. To encourage these students to enjoy the subject as we do, we have made a special effort to relate the practical applications of organic chemistry to biological processes and everyday life. The success of this approach is demonstrated by the widespread use of this textbook by hundreds of thousands of students in the United States and around the world, via its numerous translations.

Organic Chemistry: A Short Course is designed for a one-semester introductory course, but it can be readily adapted to other course types. Often, it is used in a one- or two-quarter course. In some countries (France and Japan, for example), it serves as an introductory text for chemistry majors, followed by a longer and more detailed full-year text. It has even been used in the United States for a one-year science majors course (with suitable supplementation by the instructor). In many high schools, it is used as the text for a second-year course, following the usual introductory general chemistry course.

New to the 13th Edition

The text was critically revised to clarify difficult content and to improve the presentation. In addition to many small changes, major changes to this edition have focused on improving graphics throughout the text in a pedagogically useful manner. For example, (1) some new ball-and-stick structures have been added to help students visualize molecules in three dimensions; (2) many additional problems have been written, and many of these problems require students to develop their three-dimensional visualization skills; (3) in some locations, new graphics and some electrostatic potential maps have been added in order to help in discussions of acid–base chemistry; and (4) several energy diagrams are used to illustrate the structural changes that occur as reactions proceed from reactants to products.

Other changes include increased use of the arrow-pushing formalism to facilitate teaching and understanding of reaction mechanisms. Users of the last edition who enjoyed the "A Word About . . ." essays will enjoy the addition of five new activities, many of which cover topics related to green chemistry. Each essay references one or more related problem that will allow students to apply the knowledge they have gained from these features.

We are very conscious of the need to keep the book to a manageable size for the one-semester course. Outdated information has been deleted and, in some cases, replaced with new material. In the end, users will find this edition practically identical in length to the previous one.

Organization

The organization is fairly classical, with some exceptions. After an introductory chapter on bonding, isomerism, and an overview of the subject (Chapter 1), the next three chapters treat saturated, unsaturated, and aromatic hydrocarbons in sequence. The concept of reaction mechanism is presented early, and examples are included in virtually all subsequent chapters. Stereoisomerism is also introduced early, briefly in Chapters 2 and 3, and then given separate attention in a full chapter (Chapter 5). Halogenated compounds are used in Chapter 6 as a vehicle for introducing aliphatic substitution and elimination mechanisms and dynamic stereochemistry.

Chapters 7 through 10 cover oxygen functionality in order of the increasing oxidation state of carbon—alcohols and phenols, ethers and epoxides, aldehydes and ketones, and acids and their derivatives. Brief mention of sulfur analogs is made in these chapters. Chapter 11 deals with amines. Chapters 2 through 11 treat every main functional group and constitute the heart of the course. Chapter 12 then takes up spectroscopy, with an emphasis on nuclear magnetic resonance (NMR) and applications to structure determination. This chapter handles the student's question: How do you know that those molecules really have the structures you say they have?

Next come two chapters on topics not always treated in introductory texts but that are especially important in practical organic chemistry—Chapter 13 on heterocyclic compounds and Chapter 14 on polymers. The book ends with four chapters on biologically important substances—lipids; carbohydrates; amino acids, peptides, and proteins; and nucleic acids.

"A Word About . . ." Essays

Although relevant applications of organic chemistry are stressed throughout the text, short sections under the general rubric "A Word About . . ." emphasize applications to other branches of science and to human life. These sections, which have been a popular feature, appear at appropriate places within the text rather than as isolated essays. They stand out from the text so that instructors can easily refer to these sections, as desired. There are forty-one of these essays on topics ranging from polycyclic aromatic hydrocarbons and cancer to ether and anesthesia, water treatment and the chemistry of enols and enolates, green chemistry and ibuprofen, sweetness and sweeteners, and DNA and crime.

"A Closer Look At . . ." Online Activities

Many resources on topics relevant to organic chemistry have become readily available over the Internet. Each "A Closer Look At . . ." section features a guided tour of selected topics in organic chemistry through directed activities based on selected Web sites. Instructors may assign these activities as desired, using them as a basis for class discussion or as a springboard for projects. Eleven of these activities appear in this edition, covering topics such as mass spectrometry and carbon dating (Chapter 12), Nobel laureates and protein chemistry (Chapter 17), and the polymerase chain reaction (Chapter 18).

Examples and Problems

Problem solving is essential to learning organic chemistry. Examples (worked-out problems) appear at appropriate places within each chapter to help students develop these skills. These examples and their solutions are clearly marked. Unsolved problems that provide immediate learning reinforcement are included in each chapter and are supplemented with an abundance of end-of-chapter problems. The combined number of examples and problems is over 1,000—an average of almost 60 per chapter.

OWL for Organic Chemistry

Instant Access OWL with eBook for text (6 months) ISBN-10: 1-111-47131-2, ISBN-13: 978-1-111-47131-6

By Steve Hixson and Peter Lillya of the University of Massachusetts, Amherst, and William Vining of the State University of New York at Oneonta. End-of chapter questions by David W. Brown, Florida Gulf Coast University. **OWL** Online Web Learning offers more assignable, gradable content (including end-of chapter questions specific to this textbook) and more reliability and flexibility than any other system. OWL's powerful course management tools allow instructors to control due dates, number of attempts, and whether students see answers or receive feedback on how to solve problems. OWL includes the **YouBook**, a Flash-based eBook that is interactive and customizable. It features a text edit tool that allows instructors to modify the textbook narrative as needed. With YouBook, instructors can quickly re-order entire sections and chapters or hide any content they don't teach to create an eBook that perfectly matches their syllabus. Instructors can further customize the YouBook by publishing web links. The YouBook also includes animated figures, video clips, highlighting, notes, and more.

Developed by chemistry instructors for teaching chemistry, OWL is the only system specifically designed to support **mastery learning**, where students work as long as they need to master each chemical concept and skill. OWL has already helped hundreds of thousands of students master chemistry through a wide range of assignment types, including tutorials, interactive simulations, and algorithmically generated homework questions that provide instant, answer-specific feedback.

OWL is continually enhanced with online learning tools to address the various learning styles of today's students such as:

- **Quick Prep** review courses that help students learn essential skills to succeed in General and Organic Chemistry
- **Jmol** molecular visualization program for rotating molecules and measuring bond distances and angles

In addition, when you become an OWL user, you can expect service that goes far beyond the ordinary. For more information or to see a demo, please contact your Cengage Learning representative or visit us at www.cengage.com/owl.

Student Ancillaries

Study Guide and Solutions Manual Written by the authors of the main text, this guide contains chapter summaries and learning objectives, reaction summaries, mechanism summaries, answers to all text problems, and sample test questions. Download a sample chapter from the Student Companion Website, which is accessible from www. cengage.com ISBN-10: 1-111-42585-X, ISBN-13: 978-1-111-42585-2.

Laboratory Manual Written by Leslie Craine and T. K. Vinod, this manual contains thirty experiments that have been tested with thousands of students. Most of the preparative experiments contain procedures on both macroscale and microscale, thus adding considerable flexibility for the instructor and the opportunity for both types of laboratory experience for the student. Experiments involving molecular modeling now contain computer-modeling activities in addition to activities based on traditional modeling kits. The experiments, capable of being completed in a two- or three-hour lab period, are a good mix of techniques, preparations, tests, and applications. Hazardous chemicals on the OSHA list have been avoided, care has been taken to minimize contact with solvents, and updated caution notes and waste disposal instructions are included. ISBN-10: 1-111-42584-1, ISBN-13: 978-1-111-42584-8

Student Companion Website The Student Companion Website includes a glossary, flashcards, and an interactive periodic table, which are accessible from www.cengagebrain.com.

CengageBrain.com App Now, students can prepare for class anytime and anywhere using the CengageBrain.com application developed specifically for the Apple iPhone® and iPod touch®, which allows students to access free study materials—book-specific quizzes, flash cards, related Cengage Learning materials and more—so they can study the way they want, when they want to . . . even on the go. For more information about this complimentary application, please visit www.cengagebrain.com.

Visit CengageBrain.com To access these and additional course materials, please visit www.cengagebrain.com. At the CengageBrain.com home page, search for the ISBN (from the back cover of your book) using the search box at the top of the page. This will take you to the product page where these resources can be found. (Instructors can log in at login.cengage.com.)

Instructor Ancillaries

A complete suite of customizable teaching tools accompanies *Organic Chemistry: A Short Course*. Whether available in print, online, or on CD, these integrated resources are designed to save you time and help make class preparation, presentation, assessment, and course management more efficient and effective.

PowerLecture With ExamView® Instructor's CD/DVD Package
ISBN-10: 1-111-42587-6, ISBN-13: 978-1-111-42587-6
PowerLecture is a one-stop digital library and presentation tool that includes:

- Prepared **Microsoft® PowerPoint® Lecture Slides** that cover all key points from the text in a convenient format that you can enhance with your own materials or with the supplied interactive video and animations for personalized, media-enhanced lectures.

- Image libraries in PowerPoint and JPEG formats that contain **digital files for all text art, all photographs, and all numbered tables** in the text. These files can be used to create your own transparencies or PowerPoint lectures.

- *Instructor's Resource Manual* written by Christopher M. Hadad that offers a transition guide, tables suggesting the approximate number of lectures to devote to each chapter, summaries of the worked examples and problems, a chapter-by-chapter outline listing those sections that are most important, and answers to the review problems on synthesis that are featured in the Study Guide and Solutions Manual.

- **Instructor's Resource Guide** for the *Laboratory Manual* written by Christopher M. Hadad of The Ohio State University, that contains detailed discussions of experiments and answers to all of the prelab exercise questions and most of the questions in the report sheets contained in the Laboratory Manual.

- **Sample chapters from the *Study Guide and Solutions Manual.*** We provide sample chapters of this in Adobe Acrobat PDF format as a courtesy to instructors who may wish to recommend it to students.

- **ExamView Computerized Testing** that enables you to create customized tests of up to 250 items in print or online using more than 700 questions carefully matched to the corresponding text sections. Tests can be taken electronically or printed for class distribution.

Faculty Companion Website

Accessible from www.cengagebrain.com. this Web site provides downloadable files for the Instructor's Resource Guide for the Lab Manual, Instructor's Resource Manual, as well as WebCT and Blackboard versions of Exam*View*® Computerized Testing.

Cengage Learning Custom Solutions develops personalized solutions to meet your course needs. Match your learning materials to your syllabus and create the perfect learning solution—your customized text will contain the same thought-provoking, scientifically sound content, superior authorship, and stunning art that you've come to expect from Cengage Learning Brooks/Cole texts, yet in a more flexible format. Visit www.cengage.com/custom to start building your book today.

Signature Labs . . . for the customized laboratory. Signature Labs is Cengage Learning's digital library of tried-and-true labs that help you take the guesswork out of running your chemistry laboratory. Select just the experiments you want from hundreds of options and approaches. Provide your students with only the experiments they will conduct so that you will get the results you seek. Visit www.signaturelabs.com to begin building your manual today.

Acknowledgments

We would like to thank the following reviewers for diligently contributing their insights to this edition of *Organic Chemistry*:

Scott W. Cowley, *Colorado School of Mines*; Sarah A. Cummings, *University of Nevada, Reno*; J. Brent Friesen, *Dominican University*; Michael Harmata, *University of Missouri-Columbia*; Marjorie J. Hummel, *Governors State University*; and Barbara Oviedo Mejia, *California State University, Chico*.

We have incorporated many of their recommendations, and the book is much improved as a result.

One pleasure of authorship is receiving letters from students (and their teachers) who have benefited from the book. We thank all who have written to us, from all parts of the world, since the last edition; many of the suggestions have been incorporated into this revision. We are happy to hear from users and nonusers, faculty and students, who have suggestions for further improvement.

David J. Hart
Department of Chemistry, The Ohio State University

Christopher M. Hadad
Department of Chemistry, The Ohio State University

Leslie E. Craine
Department of Chemistry, Central Connecticut State University

Harold Hart
Emeritus Professor of Chemistry, Michigan State University

A WORD ABOUT...   Oranges and the Cover of This Book

Recent editions of this book featured apples, limes, and onions. Continuing with the theme of edible fruits and organic chemistry, the cover of this edition features a photograph of an orange peel and the chemical structure of the ester, octyl acetate. Many esters (Chapter 10) are rather pleasant-smelling substances and are responsible for the flavor and fragrance of many fruits. Among the

and a few other vertebrates lack an enzyme that is essential for the biosynthesis of L-ascorbic acid from D-glucose (Chapter 16). L-Ascorbic acid is needed for collagen synthesis (collagen is the structural protein of skin, connective tissue, tendon, cartilage, and bone; Chapter 17). Hence, ascorbic acid must be included in the diet of humans and these other species. The lack of

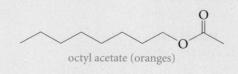

octyl acetate (oranges)

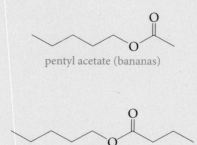

pentyl acetate (bananas)

ethyl butanoate (pineapples)

pentyl butanoate (apricots)

more common are octyl acetate (oranges), pentyl acetate (bananas), ethyl butanoate (pineapples), and pentyl butanoate (apricots). Natural flavors can be exceedingly complex. For example, no fewer than 53 esters have been identified among the volatile constituents of Bartlett pears! In the chemical industry, mixtures of esters are used as perfumes and artificial flavorings.

The therapeutic properties of oranges are legendary, due to the fact that oranges, like other citrus fruit, contain vitamin C, L-ascorbic acid. Humans, monkeys, guinea pigs,

L-ascorbic acid in one's diet leads to diseases that plagued sailors for centuries. These included scurvy, a disease that results in weak blood vessels, hemorrhaging, loosening of teeth, lack of ability to heal wounds, and eventual death.

L-Ascorbic acid resembles a monosaccharide (Chapter 16), but its structure has several unusual features. The compound has a five-membered unsaturated lactone ring (Chapter 10) with two hydroxyl groups (Chapter 7) attached to a carbon-carbon double bond (Chapter 3), an enediol structure.

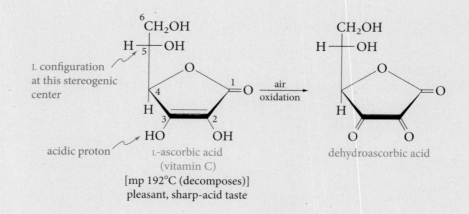

L configuration at this stereogenic center

acidic proton

L-ascorbic acid
(vitamin C)
[mp 192°C (decomposes)]
pleasant, sharp-acid taste

dehydroascorbic acid

As a consequence of this structural feature, L-ascorbic acid is easily oxidized to dehydroascorbic acid. Both forms are biologically effective as a vitamin. There is no

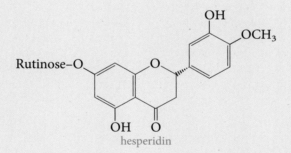

resonance stabilized ascorbate anion

carboxyl group in L-ascorbic acid; nevertheless, vitamin C is an acid with a pK_a of 4.17.

An orange peel is a rich source of organic compounds, including lipids and flavonoids. In order to prevent water loss, the orange peel wax is composed of esters of unsaturated fatty acids (Chapter 15) and long-chain alcohols. The unsaturated fatty acids are dominated by linoleic, oleic, linolenic, arachidic and

aid in the retention of water inside the fruit. Orange peel wax also contains other fatty acid conjugates, including glycolipids and phospholipids (Chapter 15). The orange peel is also a source of flavonoids, including hesperidin. Many of these flavonoid compounds have been studied for their biological properties, including potential effectiveness as anti-cancer, anti-inflammatory, and anti-allergy effects.

As you read this book, you will come across numerous "A Word About . . ." sections that relate the chemistry you are studying to our world. We encourage

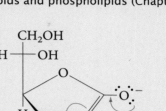

hesperidin

erucic acids (Chapter 15), and the long-chain alcohols (Chapter 7) contain typically thirty-two or thirty-four carbons. The large hydrocarbon units in the orange peel

you to return to this "A Word About . . ." with greater understanding after you have completed your course in organic chemistry.

Natural and synthetic organic compounds are everywhere in the environment and in our material culture.

To the Student

In this introduction, we will briefly discuss organic chemistry and its importance in a technological society. We will also explain how this course is organized and give you a few hints that may help you to study more effectively.

What Is Organic Chemistry About?

The term *organic* suggests that this branch of chemistry has something to do with *organisms,* or living things. Originally, organic chemistry did deal only with substances obtained from living matter. Years ago, chemists spent much of their time extracting, purifying, and analyzing substances from animals and plants. They were motivated by a natural curiosity about living matter and also by the desire to obtain from nature ingredients for medicines, dyes, and other useful products.

It gradually became clear that most compounds in plants and animals differ in several respects from those that occur in nonliving matter, such as minerals. In particular, most compounds in living matter are made up of the same few elements: carbon, hydrogen, oxygen, nitrogen, and sometimes sulfur, phosphorus, and a few others. Carbon is virtually always present. This fact led to our present definition: **Organic chemistry** is the chemistry of carbon compounds. This definition broadens the scope of the subject to include not only compounds from nature but also synthetic compounds—compounds invented by organic chemists and prepared in their laboratories.

Organic chemistry is the chemistry of carbon compounds.

Synthetic Organic Compounds

Scientists used to believe that compounds occurring in living matter were different from other substances and that they contained some sort of intangible vital force that imbued them with life. This idea discouraged chemists from trying to make organic compounds in the laboratory. But in 1828, the German chemist Friedrich Wöhler, then 28 years old, accidentally prepared urea, a well-known constituent of urine, by heating the inorganic (or mineral) substance ammonium cyanate. He was quite excited about this result, and in a letter to his former teacher, the Swedish chemist Jöns Jacob Berzelius, he wrote, "I can make urea without the necessity of a kidney, or even of an animal, whether man or dog." This experiment and others like it gradually discredited the vital-force theory and opened the way for modern synthetic organic chemistry.

Synthesis usually consists of piecing together small, relatively simple molecules to make larger, more complex ones. To make a molecule that contains many atoms from molecules that contain fewer atoms, one must know how to link atoms to each other—that is, how to make and break chemical bonds. Wöhler's preparation of urea was accidental, but synthesis is much more effective when it is carried out in a controlled and rational way so that when all the atoms are assembled, they will be connected to one another in the correct manner to give the desired product.

Chemical bonds are made or broken during chemical reactions. In this course, you will learn about quite a few reactions that can be used to make new bonds and that are therefore useful in the synthesis of pharmaceuticals and industrial chemicals.

Synthesis consists of piecing together small simple molecules to make larger, more complex molecules.

Why Synthesis?

At present, the number of organic compounds that have been synthesized in research laboratories is far greater than the number isolated from nature. Why is it important to know how to synthesize molecules? There are several reasons. For one, it might be important to synthesize a natural product in the laboratory to make the substance more widely available at lower cost than it would be if the compound had to be extracted from its natural source. Some examples of compounds first isolated from nature but now produced synthetically for commercial use are vitamins, amino acids, dyes for clothing, fragrances, and the moth-repellent camphor. Although the term *synthetic* is sometimes frowned upon as implying something artificial or unnatural, these synthetic natural products are in fact identical to the same compounds extracted from nature.

Another reason for synthesis is to create new substances that may have new and useful properties. Synthetic fibers such as nylon and Orlon, for example, have properties that make them superior for some uses to natural fibers such as silk, cotton, and hemp. Most pharmaceutical drugs used in medicine are synthetic (including aspirin, ether, Novocain, and ibuprofen). The list of synthetic products that we take for granted is long indeed—plastics, detergents, insecticides, and oral contraceptives are just a few. All of these are compounds of carbon; all are organic compounds.

Finally, organic chemists sometimes synthesize new compounds to test chemical theories—and sometimes they synthesize compounds just for the fun of it. Certain geometric structures, for example, are aesthetically pleasing, and it can be a challenge to make a molecule in which the carbon atoms are arranged in some regular way. One example is the hydrocarbon cubane, C_8H_8. First synthesized in 1964, its molecules have eight carbons at the corners of a cube, each carbon with one hydrogen and three other carbons connected to it. Cubane is more than just aesthetically pleasing. The bond angles in cubane are distorted from normal because of its geometry. Studying the chemistry of cubane therefore gives chemists information about how the distortion of carbon–carbon and carbon–hydrogen bonds affects their chemical behavior.

Although initially of only theoretical interest, the special properties of cubane may eventually lead to its practical use in medicine and in explosives.

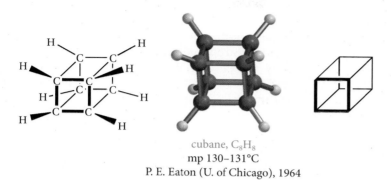

cubane, C_8H_8
mp 130–131°C
P. E. Eaton (U. of Chicago), 1964

Organic Chemistry in Everyday Life

Organic chemistry touches our daily lives. We are made of and surrounded by organic compounds. Almost all of the reactions in living matter involve organic compounds, and it is impossible to understand life, at least from the physical point of view, without knowing some organic chemistry. The major constituents of living matter—proteins, carbohydrates, lipids (fats), nucleic acids (DNA and RNA), cell membranes, enzymes, hormones—are organic, and later in the book, we will describe their chemical structures. These structures are quite complex. To understand them, we will first have to discuss simpler molecules.

Other organic substances include the gasoline, oil, and tires for our cars; the clothing we wear; the wood for our furniture; the paper for our books; the medicines we take; and plastic containers, camera film, perfume, carpeting, and fabrics. Name it, and the chances are good that it is organic. Daily, in the paper, on the Internet, or on television, we encounter references to polyethylene, epoxys, Styrofoam, nicotine, polyunsaturated fats, and cholesterol. All of these terms refer to organic substances; we will study them and many more like them in this book.

In short, organic chemistry is more than just a branch of science for the professional chemist or for the student preparing to become a physician, dentist, veterinarian, pharmacist, nurse, or agriculturist. It is part of our technological culture.

Organization

Organic chemistry is a vast subject. Some molecules and reactions are simple; others are quite complex. We will proceed from the simple to the complex by beginning with a chapter on bonding, with special emphasis on bonds to carbon. Next, there are three chapters on organic compounds containing only two elements: carbon and hydrogen (called hydrocarbons). The second of these chapters (Chapter 3) contains an introduction to organic reaction mechanisms and a discussion of reaction equilibria and rates. These are followed by a chapter that deals with the three-dimensionality of organic compounds. Next, we add other elements to the carbon and hydrogen framework, halogens in Chapter 6, oxygen and sulfur in Chapters 7 through 10, and nitrogen in Chapter 11. At that point, we will have completed an introduction to all the main classes of organic compounds.

Spectroscopy is a valuable tool for determining organic structures—that is, the details of how atoms and groups are arranged in organic molecules. We take up this topic in Chapter 12. Next comes a chapter on heterocyclic compounds, many of which are important in medicine and in natural products. It is followed by a chapter on polymers, which highlights one of the most important industrial uses of organic chemistry. The last four chapters deal with the organic chemistry of four major classes of biologically important molecules: the lipids, carbohydrates, proteins, and nucleic acids. Because the structures of these molecules of nature are rather complex, we leave them for last. But with the background knowledge of simpler molecules that you will have acquired by then, these compounds and their chemistry will be clearer and more understandable.

To help you organize and review new material, we have placed a *Reaction Summary* and a *Mechanism Summary* at the end of each chapter in which new reactions and new reaction mechanisms are introduced.

"A Word About . . ."

In each chapter after the first, you will find special sections under the general heading "A Word About . . ." These are short, self-contained articles that expand on the main subject of the chapter. They may deal with intellectual curiosities (the first one, on impossible organic structures); industrial applications (petroleum, gasoline, and octane number in Chapter 3 and industrial alcohols in Chapter 7); organic chemistry in biology or medicine (polycyclic aromatic hydrocarbons and cancer in Chapter 4 and morphine and other nitrogen-containing drugs in Chapter 13); or just fun topics (sweetness and sweeteners in Chapter 16). They provide a convenient break at various points in each chapter, and we hope that you will enjoy them.

"A Closer Look At . . ."

Throughout the text, there are several sections titled "A Closer Look At . . ." These sections feature various online activities on selected topics of organic chemistry. *A Closer Look At* activities provide a wonderful basis for classroom discussion, as well as offer a springboard for potential projects.

The Importance of Problem Solving

One key to success in studying organic chemistry is problem solving. Each chapter in this book contains numerous facts that must be digested. Also, the subject matter builds continuously so that to understand each new topic, it is essential to have the preceding information clear in your mind and available for recall. To learn all these materials, careful study of the text is necessary, but it is *not sufficient*. Practical knowledge of how to use the facts is required, and such skill can be obtained only through the solving of problems and mastery of the concepts.

This book contains several types of problems. Some, called *Examples*, contain a *Solution*, so you can see how to work such problems. Throughout a chapter, examples are usually followed by similar *Problems*, designed to reinforce your learning immediately by allowing you to be sure that you understand the new material just presented. These *Problems* will be of most value if you work them when you come across them as you read the book. At the end of each chapter, *Additional Problems* enable you to practice your problem-solving skills and evaluate your retention of material. The end-of-chapter problems are grouped by topics. In general, problems that simply test your knowledge come first and more challenging problems follow.

Try to work as many problems as you can. If you have trouble, two sources of help we suggest are your instructor and the *Study Guide and Solutions Manual* that accompanies this text. If you visit your instructors with your questions, you are likely to find that they are thrilled to be asked to help, and they may provide you with the insight you need to better understand a concept or problem. The study guide provides answers to the problems and explains how to solve them. It also provides you with review materials and additional problems that do not appear in the textbook. Problem solving is time-consuming, but it will pay off in an understanding of the subject.

And now, let us begin.

Methyl butyrate and propyl acetate, organic flavor and fragrance molecules found in apples and pears, respectively, are structural isomers (Sec. 1.8).

$$CH_3CH_2CH_2\overset{\overset{\displaystyle O}{\|}}{C}OCH_3$$
methyl butyrate

$$CH_3\overset{\overset{\displaystyle O}{\|}}{C}OCH_2CH_2CH_3$$
propyl acetate

1

Jerry Howard/Positive Images

Bonding and Isomerism

Why does sucrose (table sugar) melt at 185°C, while sodium chloride (table salt)—melts at a much higher temperature, 801°C? Why do both of these substances dissolve in water, while olive oil does not? Why does the molecule methyl butyrate smell like apples, while the molecule propyl acetate, which contains the same number and kind of atoms, smells like pears? To answer questions such as these, you must understand how atoms bond with one another and how molecules interact with one another. Bonding is the key to the structure, physical properties, and chemical behavior of different kinds of matter.

Perhaps you have already studied bonding and related concepts in a beginning chemistry course. Browse through each section of this chapter to see whether it is familiar, and try to work the problems. If you can work the problems, you can safely skip that section. But if you have difficulty with any of the problems within or at the end of this chapter, study the entire chapter carefully because we will use the ideas developed here throughout the rest of the book.

UWL

Online homework for this chapter can be assigned in OWL, an online homework assessment tool.

1.1   How Electrons Are Arranged in Atoms

An **atom** consists of a small, dense **nucleus** containing positively charged **protons** and neutral **neutrons** and surrounded by negatively charged **electrons**. The **atomic number** of an element equals the number of protons in its nucleus; its **atomic weight** is the sum of the number of protons and neutrons in its nucleus.

Atoms contain a small, dense **nucleus** surrounded by **electrons**. The nucleus is positively charged and contains most of the mass of the atom. The nucleus consists of **protons**, which are positively charged, and **neutrons**, which are neutral. (The only exception is hydrogen, whose nucleus consists of only a single proton.) In a neutral atom, the positive charge of the nucleus is exactly balanced by the negative charge of the electrons that surround it. The **atomic number** of an element is equal to the number of protons in its nucleus (and to the number of electrons around the nucleus in a neutral atom). The **atomic weight** is approximately equal to the sum of the number of protons and the number of neutrons in the nucleus; the electrons are not counted because they are very light by comparison. The periodic table on the inside back cover of this book shows all the elements with their atomic numbers and weights.

We are concerned here mainly with the atom's electrons because their number and arrangement provide the key to how a particular atom reacts with other atoms to form molecules. Also, we will deal only with electron arrangements in the lighter elements because these elements are the most important in organic molecules.

Electrons are located in **orbitals**. Orbitals are grouped in **shells**. An orbital can hold a maximum of two electrons.

Electrons are concentrated in certain regions of space around the nucleus called **orbitals**. Each orbital can contain a maximum of two electrons. The orbitals, which differ in shape, are designated by the letters *s, p,* and *d.* In addition, orbitals are grouped in **shells** designated by the numbers 1, 2, 3, and so on. Each shell contains different types and numbers of orbitals, corresponding to the shell number. For example, shell 1 contains only one type of orbital, designated the 1*s* orbital. Shell 2 contains two types of orbitals, 2*s* and 2*p,* and shell 3 contains three types, 3*s,* 3*p,* and 3*d.* Within a particular shell, the number of *s, p,* and *d* orbitals is 1, 3, and 5, respectively (Table 1.1). These rules permit us to count how many electrons each shell will contain when it is filled (last column in Table 1.1). Table 1.2 shows how the electrons of the first 18 elements are arranged.

The first shell is filled for helium (He) and all elements beyond, and the second shell is filled for neon (Ne) and all elements beyond. Filled shells play almost no role in chemical bonding. Rather, the outer electrons, or **valence electrons**, are mainly involved in chemical bonding, and we will focus our attention on them.

Valence electrons are located in the outermost shell. The **kernel** of the atom contains the nucleus and the inner electrons.

Table 1.3 shows the valence electrons, the electrons in the outermost shell, for the first 18 elements. The element's symbol stands for the **kernel** of the element (the nucleus plus the filled electron shells), and the dots represent the valence electrons. The elements are arranged in groups according to the periodic table, and (except for helium) these group numbers correspond to the number of valence electrons.

Armed with this information about atomic structure, we are now ready to tackle the problem of how elements combine to form chemical bonds.

Table 1.1 ◢ **Numbers of Orbitals and Electrons in the First Three Shells**

Shell number	Number of orbitals of each type			Total number of electrons when shell is filled
	s	*p*	*d*	
1	1	0	0	2
2	1	3	0	8
3	1	3	5	18

Table 1.2 ■ Electron Arrangements of the First 18 Elements

Atomic number	Element	Number of electrons in each orbital				
		$1s$	$2s$	$2p$	$3s$	$3p$
1	H	1				
2	He	2				
3	Li	2	1			
4	Be	2	2			
5	B	2	2	1		
6	C	2	2	2		
7	N	2	2	3		
8	O	2	2	4		
9	F	2	2	5		
10	Ne	2	2	6		
11	Na	2	2	6	1	
12	Mg	2	2	6	2	
13	Al	2	2	6	2	1
14	Si	2	2	6	2	2
15	P	2	2	6	2	3
16	S	2	2	6	2	4
17	Cl	2	2	6	2	5
18	Ar	2	2	6	2	6

Table 1.3 ■ Valence Electrons of the First 18 Elements

Group	I	II	III	IV	V	VI	VII	VIII
	H·							He:
	Li·	Be·	·B·	·C·	·N:	·O:	:F:	:Ne:
	Na·	Mg·	·Al·	·Si·	·P:	·S:	:Cl:	:Ar:

1.2 Ionic and Covalent Bonding

An early, but still useful, theory of chemical bonding was proposed in 1916 by Gilbert Newton Lewis, then a professor at the University of California, Berkeley. Lewis noticed that the **inert gas** helium had only two electrons surrounding its nucleus and that the next inert gas, neon, had 10 such electrons (2 + 8; see Table 1.2). He concluded that atoms of these gases must have very stable electron arrangements *because these elements do not combine with other atoms.* He further suggested that other atoms might react in such a way in order to achieve these stable arrangements. This stability could be achieved in one of two ways: by complete transfer of electrons from one atom to another or by sharing of electrons between atoms.

An **inert gas** has a stable electron configuration.

1.2.a Ionic Compounds

Ionic compounds are composed of positively charged **cations** and negatively charged **anions**.

Ionic bonds are formed by the transfer of one or more valence electrons from one atom to another. Because electrons are negatively charged, the atom that gives up electrons becomes positively charged, a **cation**. The atom that receives electrons becomes negatively charged, an **anion**. The reaction between sodium and chlorine atoms to form sodium chloride (ordinary table salt) is a typical electron-transfer reaction.*

$$\text{Na}\cdot \;+\; \cdot\ddot{\underset{..}{\text{Cl}}}: \;\longrightarrow\; \text{Na}^+ \;+\; :\ddot{\underset{..}{\text{Cl}}}:^-$$

sodium   chlorine   sodium   chloride
atom   atom   cation   anion

(1.1)

The sodium atom has only one valence electron (it is in the third shell; see Table 1.2). By giving up that electron, sodium achieves the electron arrangement of neon. At the same time, it becomes positively charged, a sodium cation. The chlorine atom has seven valence electrons. By accepting an additional electron, chlorine achieves the electron arrangement of argon and becomes negatively charged, a chloride anion. Atoms, such as sodium, that tend to give up electrons are said to be **electropositive**. Often such atoms are metals. Atoms, such as chlorine, that tend to accept electrons are said to be **electronegative**. Often such atoms are nonmetals.

Electropositive atoms give up electrons and form cations.

Electronegative atoms accept electrons and form anions.

EXAMPLE 1.1

Write an equation for the reaction of magnesium (Mg) with fluorine (F) atoms.

$$\text{Mg}\cdot \;+\; \cdot\ddot{\underset{..}{\text{F}}}: \;+\; \cdot\ddot{\underset{..}{\text{F}}}: \;\longrightarrow\; \text{Mg}^{2+} + 2\,:\ddot{\underset{..}{\text{F}}}:^-$$

Solution Magnesium has two valence electrons. Since each fluorine atom can accept only one electron (from the magnesium) to complete its valence shell, two fluorine atoms are needed to react with one magnesium atom.

PROBLEM 1.1 Write an equation for the reaction of sodium atoms (Na) with chlorine atoms (Cl).

The product of eq. 1.1 is sodium chloride, an ionic compound made up of equal numbers of sodium and chloride ions. In general, ionic compounds form when strongly electropositive atoms and strongly electronegative atoms interact. The ions in a crystal of an ionic substance are held together by the attractive force between their opposite charges, as shown in Figure 1.1 for a sodium chloride crystal.

In a sense, the ionic bond is not really a bond at all. Being oppositely charged, the ions attract one another like the opposite poles of a magnet. In the crystal, the ions are packed in a definite arrangement, but we cannot say that any particular ion is bonded or connected to any other particular ion. And, of course, when the substance is dissolved, the ions separate and are able to move about in solution relatively freely.

◼ **Figure 1.1**
Sodium chloride, NaCl, is an ionic crystal. The purple spheres represent sodium ions, Na^+, and the green spheres are chloride ions, Cl^-. Each ion is surrounded by six oppositely charged ions, except for those ions that are at the surface of the crystal.

---

*The curved arrow in eq. 1.1 shows the movement of one electron from the valence shell of the sodium atom to the valence shell of the chlorine atom. The use of curved arrows to show the movement of electrons is explained in greater detail in Section 1.13.

EXAMPLE 1.2

What charge will a beryllium ion carry?

Solution As seen in Table 1.3, beryllium (Be) has two valence electrons. To achieve the filled-shell electron arrangement of helium, it must lose both of its valence electrons. Thus, the beryllium cation will carry two positive charges and is represented by Be^{2+}.

PROBLEM 1.2 Using Table 1.3, determine what charge the ion will carry when each of the following elements reacts to form an ionic compound: Al, Li, S, and O.

Generally speaking, within a given horizontal row in the periodic table, the more electropositive elements are those farthest to the left, and the more electronegative elements are those farthest to the right. Within a given vertical column, the more electropositive elements are those toward the bottom, and the more electronegative elements are those toward the top.

EXAMPLE 1.3

Which atom is more electropositive?
a. lithium or beryllium
b. lithium or sodium

Solution
a. The lithium nucleus has less positive charge ($+3$) to attract electrons than the beryllium nucleus ($+4$). It takes less energy, therefore, to remove an electron from lithium than it does to remove one from beryllium. Since lithium loses an electron more easily than beryllium, lithium is the more electropositive atom.
b. The valence electron in the sodium atom is shielded from the positive charge of the nucleus by two inner shells of electrons, whereas the valence electron of lithium is shielded by only one inner shell. It takes less energy, therefore, to remove an electron from sodium; so, sodium is the more electropositive element.

PROBLEM 1.3 Using Table 1.3, determine which is the more electropositive element: sodium or aluminum, carbon or nitrogen, carbon or silicon.

PROBLEM 1.4 Using Table 1.3, determine which is the more electronegative element: fluorine or chlorine, oxygen or fluorine, nitrogen or phosphorus.

PROBLEM 1.5 Judging from its position in Table 1.3, do you expect carbon to be electropositive or electronegative?

1.2.b The Covalent Bond

Elements that are neither strongly electronegative nor strongly electropositive, or that have similar electronegativities, tend to form bonds by sharing electron pairs rather than completely transferring electrons. A **covalent bond** involves the mutual sharing of one or more electron pairs between atoms. Two (or more) atoms joined by covalent bonds constitute a **molecule**. When the two atoms are identical or have

A **covalent bond** is formed when two atoms share one or more electron pairs. A **molecule** consists of two or more atoms joined by covalent bonds.

equal electronegativities, the electron pairs are shared equally. The hydrogen molecule is an example.

$$H \cdot + H \cdot \longrightarrow H : H + \text{heat} \qquad (1.2)$$

hydrogen   hydrogen
atoms   molecule

Each hydrogen atom can be considered to have filled its first electron shell by the sharing process. That is, each atom is considered to "own" all of the electrons it shares with the other atom, as shown by the loops in these structures.

$$(\text{H} : \text{H} \qquad \text{H} : \text{H})$$

EXAMPLE 1.4

Write an equation similar to eq. 1.2 for the formation of a chlorine molecule from two chlorine atoms.

$$: \overset{..}{\underset{..}{Cl}} \cdot + \cdot \overset{..}{\underset{..}{Cl}} : \longrightarrow : \overset{..}{\underset{..}{Cl}} : \overset{..}{\underset{..}{Cl}} : + \text{heat}$$

Solution One electron pair is shared by the two chlorine atoms. In that way, each chlorine completes its valence shell with eight electrons (three unshared pairs and one shared pair).

PROBLEM 1.6 Write an equation similar to eq. 1.2 for the formation of a fluorine molecule from two fluorine atoms.

When two hydrogen atoms combine to form a molecule, heat is liberated. Conversely, this same amount of heat (energy) has to be supplied to a hydrogen molecule to break it apart into atoms. To break apart 1 mole (2 g) of hydrogen molecules into atoms requires 104 kcal (or 435 kJ*) of heat, quite a lot of energy. This energy is called the **bond energy**, or **BE**, and is different for bonds between different atoms (see Table A in the Appendix).

> **Bond energy (BE)** is the energy necessary to break a mole of covalent bonds. The amount of energy depends on the type of bond broken.

The H—H bond is a very strong bond. The main reason for this is that the shared electron pair is attracted to *both* hydrogen nuclei, whereas in a hydrogen atom, the valence electron is associated with only one nucleus. But other forces in the hydrogen molecule tend to counterbalance the attraction between the electron pair and the nuclei. These forces are the repulsion between the two like-charged nuclei and the repulsion between the two like-charged electrons. A balance is struck between the attractive and the repulsive forces. The hydrogen atoms neither fly apart nor do they fuse together. Instead, they remain connected, or bonded, and vibrate about some equilibrium distance, which we call the **bond length**. For a hydrogen molecule, the bond length (that is, the average distance between the two hydrogen nuclei) is 0.74 Å.** The length of a covalent bond depends on the atoms that are bonded and the number of electron pairs shared between the atoms. Bond lengths for some typical covalent bonds are given in Table B in the Appendix.

> The **bond length** is the average distance between two covalently bonded atoms.

---

*Although most organic chemists use the kilocalorie as the unit of heat energy, the currently used international unit is the kilojoule; 1 kcal = 4.184 kJ. In this text, the kilocalorie will be used. If your instructor prefers to use kJ, multiply kcal $\times$ 4.184 (or $\times$ 4 for a rough estimate) to convert to kJ.

**Å, or angstrom unit, is 10^{-8} cm, so the H—H bond length is 0.74 $\times$ 10^{-8} cm. Although the angstrom is commonly used by organic chemists, another unit often used for bond lengths is the picometer (pm; 1 Å = 100 pm). To convert the H—H bond length from Å to pm, multiply 0.74 $\times$ 100. The H—H bond length is 74 pm. In this text, the angstrom will be used as the unit for bond lengths.

1.3 Carbon and the Covalent Bond

Now let us look at carbon and its bonding. We represent atomic carbon by the symbol $\cdot \overset{\cdot}{\underset{\cdot}{C}} \cdot$ where the letter C stands for the kernel (the nucleus plus the two $1s$ electrons) and the dots represent the valence electrons.

With four valence electrons, the valence shell of carbon is half filled (or half empty). Carbon atoms have neither a strong tendency to lose all their electrons (and become C^{4+}) nor a strong tendency to gain four electrons (and become C^{4-}). Being in the middle of the periodic table, *carbon is neither strongly electropositive nor strongly electronegative.* Instead, it usually forms covalent bonds with other atoms by sharing electrons. For example, carbon combines with four hydrogen atoms (each of which supplies one valence electron) by sharing four electron pairs.* The substance formed is known as methane. Carbon can also share electron pairs with four chlorine atoms, forming tetrachloromethane.**

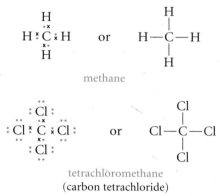

methane

tetrachloromethane
(carbon tetrachloride)

By sharing electron pairs, the atoms complete their valence shells. In both examples, carbon has eight valence electrons around it. In methane, each hydrogen atom completes its valence shell with two electrons, and in tetrachloromethane, each chlorine atom fills its valence shell with eight electrons. In this way, all valence shells are filled and the compounds are quite stable.

The shared electron pair is called a covalent bond because it bonds or links the atoms by its attraction to both nuclei. The single bond is usually represented by a dash, or a single line, as shown in the structures above for methane and tetrachloromethane.

EXAMPLE 1.5

Draw the structure for chloromethane (also called methyl chloride), CH_3Cl.

Solution

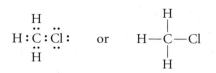

PROBLEM 1.7 Draw the structures for dichloromethane (also called methylene chloride), CH_2Cl_2, and trichloromethane (chloroform), $CHCl_3$.

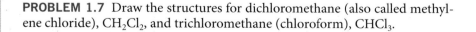

*To designate electrons from different atoms, the symbols · and x are often used. But the electrons are, of course, identical.

**Tetrachloromethane is the systematic name, and carbon tetrachloride is the common name. We discuss how to name organic compounds later.

1.4 Carbon–Carbon Single Bonds

The unique property of carbon atoms—that is, the property that makes it possible for millions of organic compounds to exist—is their ability to share electrons not only with different elements but also with other carbon atoms. For example, two carbon atoms may be bonded to one another, and each of these carbon atoms may be linked to other atoms. In ethane and hexachloroethane, each carbon is connected to the other carbon *and* to three hydrogen atoms or three chlorine atoms. Although they have two carbon atoms instead of one, these compounds have chemical properties similar to those of methane and tetrachloromethane, respectively.

$$
\begin{array}{ccc}
\text{H H} & & \text{H H} \\
\text{H:C:C:H} & \text{or} & \text{H—C—C—H} \\
\text{H H} & & \text{H H}
\end{array}
\qquad
\begin{array}{ccc}
:\text{Cl}: \ :\text{Cl}: & & \text{Cl Cl} \\
:\text{Cl:C : C:Cl}: & \text{or} & \text{Cl—C—C—Cl} \\
:\text{Cl}: \ :\text{Cl}: & & \text{Cl Cl}
\end{array}
$$

ethane   hexachloroethane

The carbon–carbon bond in ethane, like the hydrogen–hydrogen bond in a hydrogen molecule, is a purely covalent bond, with the electrons being shared *equally* between the two identical carbon atoms. As with the hydrogen molecule, heat is required to break the carbon–carbon bond of ethane to give two CH_3 fragments (called methyl radicals). A **radical** is a molecular fragment with an odd number of unshared electrons.

A **radical** is a molecular fragment with an odd number of unshared electrons.

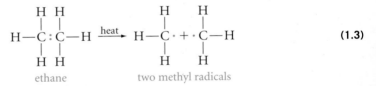

$$
\begin{array}{ccccc}
\text{H H} & & & \text{H} & \text{H} \\
\text{H—C:C—H} & \xrightarrow{\text{heat}} & \text{H—C·} & + & \text{·C—H} \\
\text{H H} & & \text{H} & & \text{H}
\end{array}
\qquad (1.3)
$$

ethane   two methyl radicals

However, less heat is required to break the carbon–carbon bond in ethane than is required to break the hydrogen–hydrogen bond in a hydrogen molecule. The actual amount is 88 kcal (or 368 kJ) per mole of ethane. The carbon–carbon bond in ethane is longer (1.54 Å) than the hydrogen–hydrogen bond (0.74 Å) and also somewhat weaker. Breaking carbon–carbon bonds by heat, as represented in eq. 1.3, is the first step in the *cracking* of petroleum, an important process in the manufacture of gasoline (see "A Word About Petroleum, Gasoline, and Octane Number" on pages 102–103).

EXAMPLE 1.6

What do you expect the length of a C—H bond (as in methane or ethane) to be?

Solution It should measure somewhere between the H—H bond length in a hydrogen molecule (0.74 Å) and the C—C bond length in ethane (1.54 Å). The actual value is about 1.09 Å, close to the average of the H—H and C—C bond lengths.

PROBLEM 1.8 The Cl—Cl bond length is 1.98 Å. Which bond will be longer, the C—C bond in ethane or the C—Cl bond in chloromethane?

There is almost no limit to the number of carbon atoms that can be linked, and some molecules contain as many as 100 or more carbon–carbon bonds. This ability of an element to form chains as a result of bonding between the same atoms is called **catenation**.

Catenation is the ability of an element to form chains of its own atoms through covalent bonding.

> **PROBLEM 1.9** Using the structure of ethane as a guide, draw the structure for propane, C_3H_8.

1.5 Polar Covalent Bonds

As we have seen, covalent bonds can be formed not only between identical atoms (H—H, C—C) but also between different atoms (C—H, C—Cl), provided that the atoms do not differ too greatly in electronegativity. However, if the atoms are different from one another, the electron pair may not be shared equally between them. Such a bond is sometimes called a **polar covalent bond** because the atoms that are linked carry a partial negative and a partial positive charge.

A **polar covalent bond** is a covalent bond in which the electron pair is not shared equally between the two atoms.

The hydrogen chloride molecule provides an example of a polar covalent bond. Chlorine atoms are more electronegative than hydrogen atoms, but even so, the bond that they form is covalent rather than ionic. However, the shared electron pair is attracted more toward the chlorine, which therefore is slightly negative with respect to the hydrogen. This bond polarization is indicated by an arrow whose head is negative and whose tail is marked with a plus sign. Alternatively, a partial charge, written as $\delta+$ or $\delta-$ (read as "delta plus" or "delta minus"), may be shown:

$$\overset{\text{\tiny +}\longrightarrow}{\text{H :Cl:}} \quad \text{or} \quad \overset{\delta+ \quad \delta-}{\text{H :Cl:}} \quad \text{or} \quad \overset{\delta+ \quad \delta-}{\text{H—Cl:}}$$

The bonding electron pair, which is shared *unequally,* is displaced toward the chlorine.

You can usually rely on the periodic table to determine which end of a polar covalent bond is more negative and which end is more positive. As we proceed from left to right across the table within a given period, the elements become *more* electronegative, owing to increasing atomic number or charge on the nucleus. The increasing nuclear charge attracts valence electrons more strongly. As we proceed from the top to the bottom of the table within a given group (down a column), the elements become *less* electronegative because the valence electrons are shielded from the nucleus by an increasing number of inner-shell electrons. From these generalizations, we can safely predict that the atom on the right in each of the following bonds will be negative with respect to the atom on the left:

$$\overset{+\longrightarrow}{\text{C—N}} \qquad \overset{+\longrightarrow}{\text{C—Cl}} \qquad \overset{+\longrightarrow}{\text{H—O}} \qquad \overset{+\longrightarrow}{\text{Br—Cl}}$$
$$\text{C—O} \qquad\quad \text{C—Br} \qquad\quad \text{H—S} \qquad\quad \text{Si—C}$$

The carbon–hydrogen bond, which is so common in organic compounds, requires special mention. Carbon and hydrogen have nearly identical electronegativities, so the C—H bond is almost purely covalent. The electronegativities of some common elements are listed in Table 1.4.

Table 1.4 ▰ Electronegativities of Some Common Elements

Group

I	II	III	IV	V	VI	VII
H 2.2						
Li 1.0	Be 1.6	B 2.0	C 2.5	N 3.0	O 3.4	F 4.0
Na 0.9	Mg 1.3	Al 1.6	Si 1.9	P 2.2	S 2.6	Cl 3.2
K 0.8	Ca 1.0					Br 3.0
						I 2.7

▰ < 1.0	▰ 1.5–1.9
▰ 1.0–1.4	▰ 2.0–2.4

▰ 2.5–2.9	
▰ 3.0–3.4	

EXAMPLE 1.7

Indicate any bond polarization in the structure of tetrachloromethane.

Solution

Chlorine is more electronegative than carbon. The electrons in each C—Cl bond are therefore displaced toward the chlorine.

PROBLEM 1.10 Predict the polarity of the N—Cl bond and of the S—O bond.

PROBLEM 1.11 Draw the structure of the refrigerant dichlorodifluoromethane, CCl_2F_2 (CFC-12), and indicate the polarity of the bonds. (The C atom is the central atom.)

PROBLEM 1.12 Draw the formula for methanol, CH_3OH, and (where appropriate) indicate the bond polarity with an arrow, ⟢⟶. (The C atom is bonded to three H atoms and the O atom.)

1.6 Multiple Covalent Bonds

To complete their valence shells, atoms may sometimes share more than one electron pair. Carbon dioxide, CO_2, is an example. The carbon atom has four valence electrons, and each oxygen has six valence electrons. A structure that allows each atom to complete its valence shell with eight electrons is

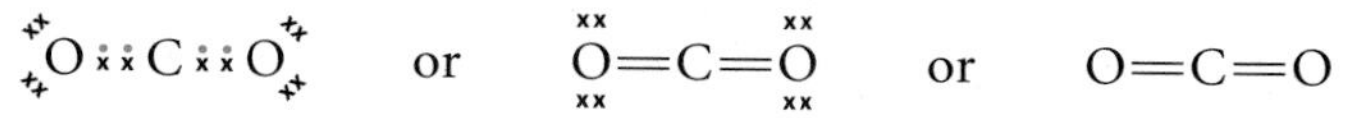

:Ö::C::Ö: or   O=C=O   or   O=C=O
   A   B   C

In structure A, the dots represent the electrons from carbon, and the x's are the electrons from the oxygens. Structure B shows the bonds' and oxygens' unshared electrons, and structure C shows only the covalent bonds. Two electron pairs are shared between carbon and oxygen. Consequently, the bond is called a **double bond**. Each oxygen atom also has two pairs of **nonbonding electrons**, or **unshared electron pairs**. The loops in the following structures show that each atom in carbon dioxide has a complete valence shell of eight electrons:

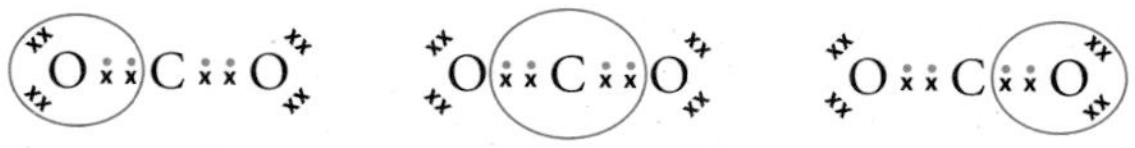

> In a **double bond**, two electron pairs are shared between two atoms.
>
> Nonbonding electrons, or **unshared electron pairs**, reside on one atom.

Hydrogen cyanide, HCN, is an example of a simple compound with a **triple bond**, a bond in which three electron pairs are shared.

H:C:::N: or   H—C≡N: or   H—C≡N

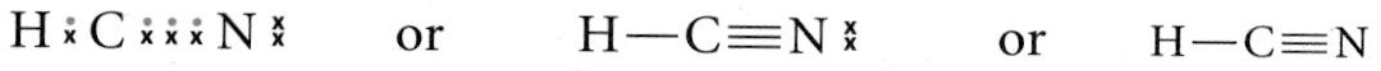

hydrogen cyanide

> In a **triple bond**, three electron pairs are shared between two atoms.

PROBLEM 1.13 Show with loops how each atom in hydrogen cyanide completes its valence shell.

EXAMPLE 1.8

Determine what, if anything, is wrong with the following electron arrangement for carbon dioxide:

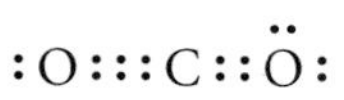

:O:::C::Ö:

Solution The formula contains the correct total number of valence electrons (16), and each oxygen is surrounded by 8 valence electrons, which is correct. However, what is wrong is that the carbon atom has 10 valence electrons, 2 more than is allowable.

PROBLEM 1.14 Show what is wrong with each of the following electron arrangements for carbon dioxide:

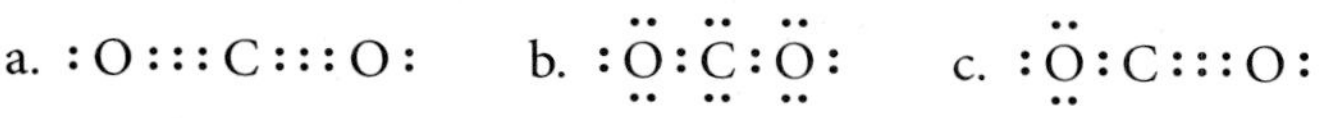

a. :O:::C:::O: b. :Ö:C:Ö: c. :Ö:C:::O:

PROBLEM 1.15 Methanal (formaldehyde) has the formula H_2CO. Draw a structure that shows how the valence electrons are arranged.

PROBLEM 1.16 Draw an electron-dot structure for carbon monoxide, CO.

Hydrocarbons are compounds
composed of just hydrogen and
carbon atoms.

Carbon atoms can be connected to one another by double bonds or triple bonds, as well as by single bonds. Thus, there are three **hydrocarbons** (compounds with just carbon and hydrogen atoms) that have two carbon atoms per molecule: ethane, ethene, and ethyne.

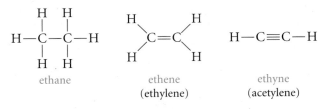

ethane   ethene (ethylene)   ethyne (acetylene)

They differ in that the carbon–carbon bond is single, double, or triple, respectively. They also differ in the number of hydrogens. As we will see later, these compounds have different chemical reactivities because of the different types of bonds between the carbon atoms.

EXAMPLE 1.9

Draw the structure for C_3H_6 having one carbon–carbon double bond.

Solution First, draw the three carbons with one double bond.

$$C=C-C$$

Then add the hydrogens in such a way that each carbon has eight electrons around it (or in such a way that each carbon has four bonds).

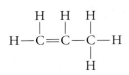

PROBLEM 1.17 Draw three different structures that have the formula C_4H_8 and have one carbon–carbon double bond.

1.7 Valence

The **valence** of an element is the
number of bonds that an atom of
the element can form.

The **valence** of an element is simply the number of bonds that an atom of the element can form. The number is usually equal to the *number of electrons needed to fill the valence shell*. Table 1.5 gives the common valences of several elements. Notice the difference between the number of valence electrons and the valence. Oxygen, for example, has six valence electrons but a valence of only 2. The *sum* of the two numbers is equal to the number of electrons in the filled shell.

The valences in Table 1.5 apply whether the bonds are single, double, or triple. For example, carbon has four bonds in each of the structures we have written so far: methane, tetrachloromethane, ethane, ethene, ethyne, carbon dioxide, and so on. These common valences are worth remembering, because they will help you to write correct structures.

Table 1.5 ◾ Valences of Common Elements						
Element	H·	·C·	·N:	·O:	:F:	:Cl:
Valence	1	4	3	2	1	1

EXAMPLE 1.10

Using dashes for bonds, draw a structure for C_3H_4 that has the proper valence of 1 for each hydrogen and 4 for each carbon.

Solution There are three possibilities:

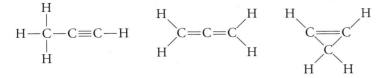

A compound that corresponds to each of these three different arrangements of the atoms is known.

PROBLEM 1.18 Use dashes for bonds and use the valences given in Table 1.5 to write a structure for each of the following:

a. CH_3F b. CH_5N

PROBLEM 1.19 Does C_2H_5 represent a stable molecule?

In Example 1.10, we saw that three carbon atoms and four hydrogen atoms can be connected to one another in three different ways, each of which satisfies the valences of both kinds of atoms. Let us take a closer look at this phenomenon.

1.8 / Isomerism

The **molecular formula** of a substance tells us the numbers of different atoms present, but a **structural formula** tells us how those atoms are arranged. For example, H_2O is the molecular formula for water. It tells us that each water molecule contains two hydrogen atoms and one oxygen atom. But the structural formula H—O—H tells us

> The **molecular formula** of a substance gives the number of different atoms present; the **structural formula** indicates how those atoms are arranged.

A CLOSER LOOK AT... / Green Chemistry

Conduct research on the Internet to find more information on green chemistry and to answer the following questions.

Green Chemistry

1. What is green chemistry?

2. What are the 12 principles of green chemistry?

3. What is the Pollution Prevention Act of 1990?

4. What are some organizations involved in promoting green chemistry? How are these organizations promoting green chemistry?

Hangers Cleaners

1. How does Hangers Cleaners make use of carbon dioxide?

2. What are the advantages of using CO_2 over traditional dry cleaning solvents? Explain why you think so.

Ionic Liquids and Their Uses

1. What are some of the advantages of using ionic liquids as solvents in chemical reactions?

2. What environmental problems posed by traditional solvents are avoided by using ionic liquids?

more than that. The structural formula gives us the connectivity between atoms and tells us that the hydrogens are connected to the oxygen (and not to each other).

It is sometimes possible to arrange the same atoms in more than one way and still satisfy their valences. Molecules that have the same kinds and numbers of atoms but different arrangements are called **isomers**, a term that comes from the Greek (*isos,* equal, and *meros,* part). **Structural** (or **constitutional**) **isomers** are compounds that have the same molecular formula, but different structural formulas. Let us look at a particular pair of isomers.

> Isomers are molecules with the same number and kinds of atoms but different arrangements of the atoms. **Structural** (or **constitutional**) isomers have the same molecular formula but different structural formulas.

Two very different chemical substances are known, each with the molecular formula C_2H_6O. One of these substances is a colorless liquid that boils at 78.5°C, whereas the other is a colorless gas at ordinary temperatures (boiling point (bp) −23.6°C). The only possible explanation is that the atoms must be arranged differently in the molecules of each substance and that these arrangements are somehow responsible for the fact that one substance is a liquid and the other is a gas.

For the molecular formula C_2H_6O, two (and only two) structural formulas are possible that satisfy the valence requirement of 4 for carbon, 2 for oxygen, and 1 for hydrogen. They are:

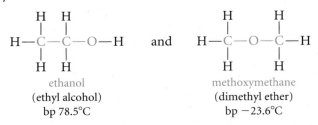

In one formula, the two carbons are connected to one another by a single covalent bond; in the other formula, each carbon is connected to the oxygen. When we complete the valences by adding hydrogens, each arrangement requires six hydrogens. Many kinds of experimental evidence verify these structural assignments. We leave for later chapters (Chapters 7 and 8) an explanation of why these arrangements of atoms produce substances that are so different from one another.

Ethanol and methoxymethane are structural isomers. They have the same molecular formula but different structural formulas. Ethanol and methoxymethane differ in physical and chemical properties as a consequence of their different molecular structures. In general, structural isomers are different compounds. They differ in physical and chemical properties as a consequence of their different molecular structures.

> **PROBLEM 1.20** Draw structural formulas for the three possible isomers of C_3H_8O.

1.9 Writing Structural Formulas

You will be writing structural formulas throughout this course. Perhaps a few hints about how to do so will be helpful. Let's look at another case of isomerism. Suppose we want to write out all possible structural formulas that correspond to the molecular formula C_5H_{12}. We begin by writing all five carbons in a **continuous chain**.

> In a **continuous chain**, atoms are bonded one after another.

$$C—C—C—C—C$$
a continuous chain

This chain uses up one valence for each of the end carbons and two valences for the carbons in the middle of the chain. Each end carbon therefore has three valences left for bonds to hydrogens. Each middle carbon has only two valences for bonds to hydrogens. As a consequence, the structural formula in this case is written as:

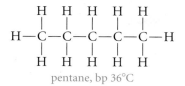

pentane, bp 36°C

To find structural formulas for the other isomers, we must consider **branched chains**. For example, we can reduce the longest chain to only four carbons and connect the fifth carbon to one of the middle carbons, as in the following structural formula:

In a **branched chain**, some atoms form branches from the longest continuous chain.

C—C—C—C
　　|
　　C

a branched chain

If we add the remaining bonds so that each carbon has a valence of 4, we see that three of the carbons have three hydrogens attached, but the other carbons have only one or two hydrogens. The molecular formula, however, is still C_5H_{12}.

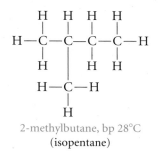

2-methylbutane, bp 28°C
(isopentane)

Suppose we keep the chain of four carbons and try to connect the fifth carbon somewhere else. Consider the following chains:

C—C—C—C　　　C—C—C—C　　　C—C—C—C
|　　　　　　　　　　　|　　　　　　　　|
C　　　　　　　　　　　C　　　　　　　　C

Do we have anything new here? *No!* The first two structures have five-carbon chains, exactly as in the formula for pentane, and the third structure is identical to the branched chain we have already drawn for 2-methylbutane—a four-carbon chain with a one-carbon branch attached to the second carbon in the chain (counting now from the right instead of from the left). Notice that for every drawing of pentane, you can draw a line through all five carbon atoms without lifting your pencil from the paper. For every drawing of 2-methylbutane, a continuous line can be drawn through exactly four carbon atoms.*

But there is a third isomer of C_5H_{12}. We can find it by reducing the longest chain to only three carbons and connecting two one-carbon branches to the middle carbon.

*Using a molecular model kit (see note on p. 37) to construct the carbon chains as drawn will help you to see which representations are identical and which are different.

If we fill in the hydrogens, we see that the middle carbon has no hydrogens attached to it.

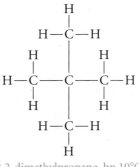

2,2-dimethylpropane, bp 10°C
(neopentane)

So we can draw three (and only three) different structural formulas that correspond to the molecular formula C_5H_{12}, and in fact, we find that only three different chemical substances with this formula exist. They are commonly called *n*-pentane (*n* for normal, with an unbranched carbon chain), isopentane, and neopentane.

PROBLEM 1.21   To which isomer of C_5H_{12} does each of the following structural formulas correspond?

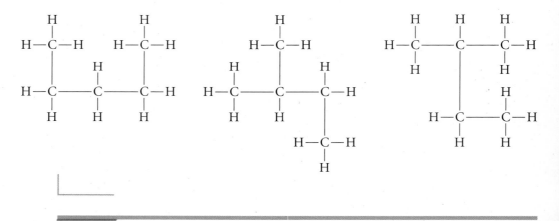

1.10 Abbreviated Structural Formulas

Structural formulas like the ones we have written so far are useful, but they are also somewhat cumbersome. They take up a lot of space and are tiresome to write out. Consequently, we often take some shortcuts that still convey the meaning of structural formulas. For example, we may abbreviate the structural formula of ethanol (ethyl alcohol) from:

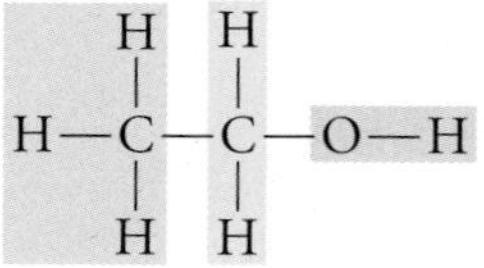

$$H-\overset{\displaystyle H}{\underset{\displaystyle H}{C}}-\overset{\displaystyle H}{\underset{\displaystyle H}{C}}-O-H \qquad \text{to} \qquad CH_3-CH_2-OH \qquad \text{or} \qquad CH_3CH_2OH$$

Each formula clearly represents ethanol rather than its isomer methoxymethane (dimethyl ether), which can be represented by any of the following structures:

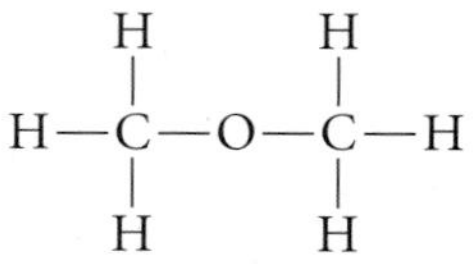

$$H-\overset{\displaystyle H}{\underset{\displaystyle H}{C}}-O-\overset{\displaystyle H}{\underset{\displaystyle H}{C}}-H \qquad \text{to} \qquad CH_3-O-CH_3 \qquad \text{or} \qquad CH_3OCH_3$$

The structural formulas for the three pentanes can be abbreviated in a similar fashion.

$$CH_3CH_2CH_2CH_2CH_3 \qquad CH_3CHCH_2CH_3 \qquad CH_3-\underset{\underset{CH_3}{|}}{\overset{\overset{CH_3}{|}}{C}}-CH_3$$

$$\underset{\underset{CH_3}{|}}{}$$

n-pentane   isopentane   neopentane

Sometimes these formulas are abbreviated even further. For example, they can be printed on a single line in the following ways:

$$CH_3(CH_2)_3CH_3 \qquad (CH_3)_2CHCH_2CH_3 \qquad (CH_3)_4C$$

n-pentane   isopentane   neopentane

EXAMPLE 1.11

Write a structural formula that shows all bonds for each of the following:

a. $CH_3CCl_2CH_3$

b. $(CH_3)_2C(CH_2CH_3)_2$

Solution

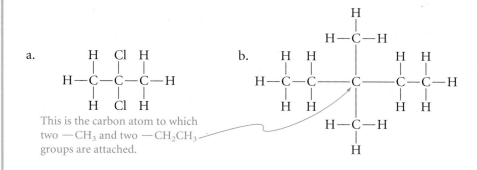

a.

$$H-\underset{\underset{H}{|}}{\overset{\overset{H}{|}}{C}}-\underset{\underset{Cl}{|}}{\overset{\overset{Cl}{|}}{C}}-\underset{\underset{H}{|}}{\overset{\overset{H}{|}}{C}}-H$$

This is the carbon atom to which two —CH_3 and two —CH_2CH_3 groups are attached.

PROBLEM 1.22 Write a structural formula that shows all bonds for each of the following:

a. $(CH_3)_3CCH_2CH_2OH$

b. $Cl_2C{=}CCl_2$

Perhaps the ultimate abbreviation of structures is the use of lines to represent the carbon framework:

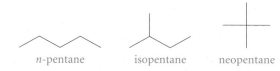

n-pentane   isopentane   neopentane

In these formulas, *each line segment is understood to have a carbon atom at each end.* The hydrogens are omitted, but we can quickly find the number of hydrogens on each carbon by subtracting from four (the valence of carbon) the number of line segments that emanates from any point. Multiple bonds are represented by multiple line segments. For example, the hydrocarbon with a chain of five carbon atoms and a double bond between the second and third carbon atoms (that is, $CH_3CH{=}CHCH_2CH_3$) is represented as follows:

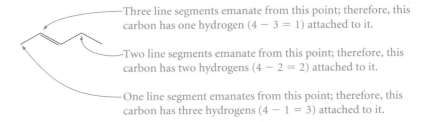

Three line segments emanate from this point; therefore, this carbon has one hydrogen (4 − 3 = 1) attached to it.
Two line segments emanate from this point; therefore, this carbon has two hydrogens (4 − 2 = 2) attached to it.
One line segment emanates from this point; therefore, this carbon has three hydrogens (4 − 1 = 3) attached to it.

EXAMPLE 1.12

Write a more detailed structural formula for .

Solution

CH2
CH3—C—CH2—CH3
or
H H
H C H H
H—C—C—C—C—H
H H H

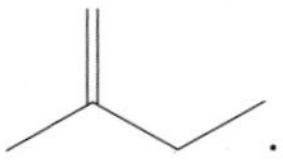

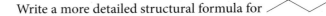

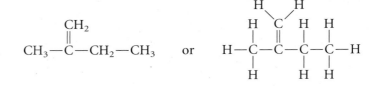

PROBLEM 1.23 Write a more detailed structural formula for .

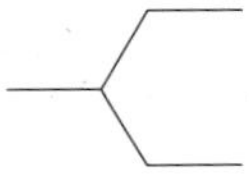

EXAMPLE 1.13

Write a line-segment formula for $CH_3CH_2CH{=}CHCH_2CH(CH_3)_2$.

Solution

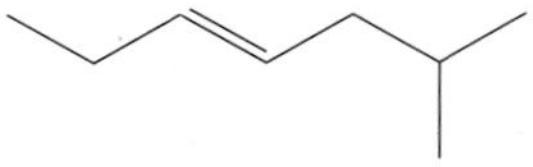

PROBLEM 1.24 Write a line-segment formula for $(CH_3)_2C{=}CHCH(CH_3)_2$.

1.11 Formal Charge

So far, we have considered only molecules whose atoms are neutral. But in some molecules, one or more atoms may be charged, either positively or negatively. Because such charges usually affect the chemical reactions of such molecules, it is important to know how to tell where the charge is located.

Consider the formula for hydronium ion, H_3O^+, the product of the reaction of a water molecule with a proton.

$$\mathrm{H{-}\ddot{\underset{\cdot\cdot}{O}}{-}H + H^+ \longrightarrow \left[H{-}\underset{\cdot\cdot}{\overset{\overset{H}{|}}{O}}{-}H\right]^+} \qquad (1.4)$$

hydronium ion

The structure has eight electrons around the oxygen and two electrons around each hydrogen, so that all valence shells are complete. Note that there are eight valence electrons altogether. Oxygen contributes six, and each hydrogen contributes one, for a total of nine, but the ion has a single positive charge, so one electron must have been given away, leaving eight. Six of these eight electrons are used to form three O—H single bonds, leaving one unshared electron pair on the oxygen.

Although the entire hydronium ion carries a positive charge, we can ask, "Which atom, in a formal sense, bears the charge?" To determine **formal charge**, we consider each atom to "own" *all* of its unshared electrons plus only *half* of its shared electrons (one electron from each covalent bond). We then subtract this total from the number of valence electrons in the neutral atom to get the formal charge. This definition can be expressed in equation form as follows:

> The **formal charge** on an atom in a covalently bonded molecule or ion is the number of valence electrons in the neutral atom minus the number of covalent bonds to the atom and the number of unshared electrons on the atom.

$$\frac{\text{Formal}}{\text{charge}} = \frac{\text{number of valence electrons}}{\text{in the neutral atom}} - \left(\frac{\text{unshared}}{\text{electrons}} + \frac{\text{half the shared}}{\text{electrons}}\right) \qquad (1.5)$$

or, in a simplified form,

$$\frac{\text{Formal}}{\text{charge}} = \frac{\text{number of valence electrons}}{\text{in the neutral atom}} - (\text{dots} + \text{bonds})$$

Let us apply this definition to the hydronium ion.

For each hydrogen atom:
Number of valence electrons in the neutral atom $= 1$
Number of unshared electrons $= 0$
Half the number of the shared electrons $= 1$
Therefore, the formal charge $= 1 - (0 + 1) = 0$

For the oxygen atom:
Number of valence electrons in the neutral atom $= 6$
Number of unshared electrons $= 2$
Half the number of the shared electrons $= 3$
Therefore, the formal charge $= 6 - (2 + 3) = +1$

Thus, it is the oxygen atom that formally carries the $+1$ charge in the hydronium ion.

EXAMPLE 1.14

On which atom is the formal charge in the hydroxide ion, OH^-?

Solution The electron-dot formula is

$$\left[:\overset{..}{\underset{..}{O}}:H \right]^-$$

Oxygen contributes six electrons, hydrogen contributes one, and there is one more for the negative charge, for a total of eight electrons. The formal charge on oxygen is $6 - (6 + 1) = -1$, so the oxygen carries the negative charge. (So instead, you might see hydroxide written as HO^- to reflect the negative charge on oxygen.) The hydrogen is neutral.

PROBLEM 1.25 Calculate the formal charge on the nitrogen atom in ammonia, NH_3; in the ammonium ion, NH_4^+; and in the amide ion, NH_2^-.

Now let us look at a slightly more complex situation involving electron-dot structures and formal charge.

1.12 Resonance

In electron-dot structures, a pair of dots or a dash represents a bond between just two atoms. But sometimes, an electron pair is involved with more than two atoms in the process of forming bonds. Molecules and ions in which this occurs cannot be adequately represented by a single electron-dot structure. As an example, consider the structure of the carbonate ion, CO_3^{2-}.

The total number of valence electrons in the carbonate ion is 24 (4 from the carbon, $3 \times 6 = 18$ from the three oxygens, *plus* 2 more electrons that give the ion its negative charge; these 2 electrons presumably have been donated by some metal, perhaps one each from two sodium atoms). An electron-dot structure that completes the valence shell of eight electrons around the carbon and each oxygen is

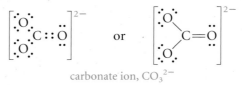

carbonate ion, CO_3^{2-}

The structure contains two carbon–oxygen *single* bonds and one carbon–oxygen *double* bond. Application of the definition for formal charge shows that the carbon is formally neutral, each singly bonded oxygen has a formal charge of -1, and the doubly bonded oxygen is formally neutral.

> **PROBLEM 1.26** Show that the last sentence of the preceding paragraph is correct.

When we wrote the electron-dot structure for the carbonate ion, our choice of which oxygen atom would be doubly bonded to the carbon atom was purely arbitrary. There are in fact *three exactly equivalent* structures that we might write.

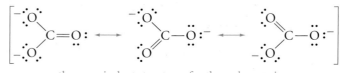

three equivalent structures for the carbonate ion

In each structure there is one $C{=}O$ bond and there are two $C{-}O$ bonds. These structures have the same arrangement of the atoms. They differ from one another *only* in the arrangement of the electrons.

The three structures for the carbonate ion are redrawn below, with curved arrows to show how electron pairs can be moved to convert one structure to another:

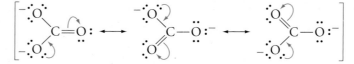

Chemists use curved arrows to keep track of a change in the location of electrons. A detailed explanation of the use of curved arrows is given in Section 1.13.

Physical measurements tell us that *none of the foregoing structures accurately describes the real carbonate ion*. For example, although each structure shows two different types of bonds between carbon and oxygen, we find experimentally that *all three carbon–oxygen bond lengths are identical: 1.31 Å*. This distance is intermediate between the normal $C{=}O$ (1.20 Å) and $C{-}O$ (1.41 Å) bond lengths. To explain this fact, we usually say that the real carbonate ion has a structure that is a **resonance hybrid** of the three contributing **resonance structures**. It is as if we could take an average

Resonance structures of a molecule or ion are two or more structures with identical arrangements of the atoms but different arrangements of the electrons. If resonance structures can be written, the true structure of the molecule or ion is a **resonance hybrid** of the contributing resonance structures.

of the three structures. In the real carbonate ion, the two formal negative charges are spread *equally* over the three oxygen atoms, so that each oxygen atom carries two-thirds of a negative charge. It is important to note that the carbonate ion does not physically alternate among three resonance structures but has in fact one structure—a *hybrid* of the three resonance structures.

Whenever we can write two or more structures for a molecule with different arrangements of the electrons but identical arrangements of the atoms, we call these structures *resonance structures*. Resonance is very different from isomerism, for which the atoms themselves are arranged differently. When resonance is possible, the substance is said to have a structure that is a resonance hybrid of the various contributing structures. We use a double-headed arrow (⟷) between contributing structures to distinguish resonance from an equilibrium between different compounds, for which we use ⇌.

Each carbon–oxygen bond in the carbonate ion is neither single nor double, but something in between—perhaps a one-and-one-third bond (any particular carbon–oxygen bond is single in two contributing structures and double in one). Sometimes we represent a resonance hybrid with one formula by writing a solid line for each full bond and a dotted line for each partial bond (in the carbonate ion, the dots represent one-third of a bond).

carbonate ion
resonance hybrid

PROBLEM 1.27 Draw the three equivalent contributing resonance structures for the nitrate ion, NO_3^-. What is the formal charge on the nitrogen atom and on each oxygen atom in the individual structures? What is the charge on the oxygens and on the nitrogen in the resonance hybrid structure? Show with curved arrows how the structures can be interconverted.

1.13 / Arrow Formalism

Arrows in chemical drawings have specific meanings. For example, in Section 1.12 we used curved arrows to move electrons to show the relatedness of the three resonance structures of the carbonate ion. Just as it is important to learn the structural representations and names of molecules, it is important to learn the language of arrow formalism in organic chemistry.

1. **Curved arrows** are used to show how electrons are moved in resonance structures and in reactions. Therefore, curved arrows always start at the initial position of electrons and end at their final position. In the example given below, the arrow that points from the C=O bond to the oxygen atom in the structure on the left indicates that the two electrons in one of the covalent bonds between carbon and oxygen are moved onto the oxygen atom:

> **Curved arrows** show how electrons are moved in resonance structures and in reactions.

Note that the carbon atom in the structure on the right now has a formal positive charge, and the oxygen has a formal negative charge. Notice also that when a pair of electrons in a polar covalent bond is moved to one of the bonded atoms, *it is moved to the more electronegative atom,* in this case oxygen. In the following example, the arrow that points from the unshared pair of electrons on the oxygen atom to a point between the carbon and oxygen atoms in the structure on the left indicates that the unshared pair of electrons on the oxygen atom moves between the oxygen and carbon atoms to form a covalent bond:

Note that both carbon and oxygen have formal charges of 0 in the structure on the right.

Fishhook arrows indicate the movement of only a single electron.

A curved arrow with half a head is called a **fishhook**. This kind of arrow is used to indicate the movement of a single electron. In eq. 1.6, two fishhooks are used to show the movement of each of the two electrons in the C—C bond of ethane to a carbon atom, forming two methyl radicals (see eq. 1.3):

$$
\begin{array}{ccc}
\text{H—C} & \text{C—H} & \longrightarrow \quad \text{H—C·+·C—H}
\end{array}
\tag{1.6}
$$

Straight arrows point from reactants to products in chemical reaction equations.

2. **Straight arrows** point from reactants to products in chemical reaction equations. An example is the straight arrow pointing from ethane to the two methyl radicals in eq. 1.6. Straight arrows with half-heads are commonly used in pairs to indicate that a reaction is *reversible*.

$$A + B \rightleftharpoons C + D$$

A double-headed straight arrow between two structures indicates resonance structures.

A **double-headed straight arrow** ($\longleftrightarrow$) between two structures indicates that they are resonance structures. Such an arrow does not indicate the occurrence of a chemical reaction. The double-headed arrows between resonance structures (Sec. 1.12) for the C=O bond are shown above.

EXAMPLE 1.15

Using correct arrow formalism, write the contributors to the resonance hybrid structure of the acetate ion, $CH_3CO_2^-$. Indicate any formal charges.

Solution There are two equivalent resonance structures for the acetate ion. Each one has a formal negative charge on one of the oxygen atoms.

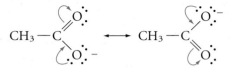

Notice that when one pair of electrons from oxygen is moved to form a covalent bond with carbon, a pair of electrons in a covalent bond between carbon and the other oxygen atom is moved to oxygen. This is necessary to ensure that the carbon atom does not exceed its valence of 4.

PROBLEM 1.28 Using correct arrow formalism, write the contributors to the resonance hybrid of azide ion, a linear ion with three connected nitrogens, N_3^-. Indicate the formal charge on each nitrogen atom.

We will use curved arrows throughout this text as a way of keeping track of electron movement. Several curved-arrow problems are included at the end of this chapter to help you get used to drawing them.

1.14 The Orbital View of Bonding; the Sigma Bond

Although electron-dot structures are often useful, they have some limitations. The Lewis theory of bonding itself has some limitations, especially in explaining the three-dimensional geometries of molecules. For this purpose in particular, we will discuss how another theory of bonding, involving orbitals, is more useful.

The atomic orbitals named in Section 1.1 have definite shapes. The *s* orbitals are spherical. The electrons that fill an *s* orbital confine their movement to a spherical region of space around the nucleus. The three *p* orbitals are dumbbell shaped and mutually perpendicular, oriented along the three coordinate axes, *x*, *y*, and *z*. Figure 1.2 shows the shapes of these orbitals.

▪ **Figure 1.2**

The shapes of the *s* and *p* orbitals used by the valence electrons of carbon. The nucleus is at the origin of the three coordinate axes.

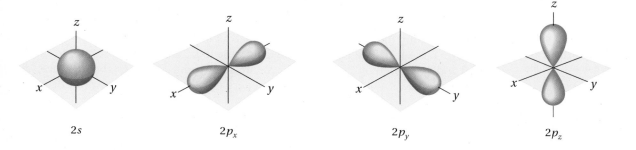

$2s$ $2p_x$ $2p_y$ $2p_z$

In the orbital view of bonding, atoms approach each other in such a way that their atomic orbitals can *overlap* to form a bond. For example, if two hydrogen atoms form a hydrogen molecule, their two spherical 1*s* orbitals combine to form a new orbital that encompasses both of the atoms (see Figure 1.3). This orbital contains both valence electrons (one from each hydrogen). Like atomic orbitals, each **molecular orbital** can contain no more than two electrons. In the hydrogen molecule, these electrons mainly occupy the space between the two nuclei.

A **molecular orbital** is the space occupied by electrons in a molecule.

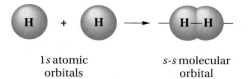

1*s* atomic   *s-s* molecular
orbitals   orbital

▪ **Figure 1.3**

The molecular orbital representation of covalent bond formation between two hydrogen atoms.

The orbital in the hydrogen molecule is cylindrically symmetric along the H—H internuclear axis. Such orbitals are called **sigma (σ) orbitals**, and the bond is referred to as a **sigma bond**. Sigma bonds may also be formed by the overlap of an *s* and a *p* orbital or of two *p* orbitals, as shown in Figure 1.4.*

A **sigma (σ) orbital** lies along the axis between two bonded atoms; a pair of electrons in a sigma orbital is called a **sigma bond**.

---

*Two properly aligned *p* orbitals can also overlap to form another type of bond, called a π (pi) bond. We discuss this type of bond in Chapter 3.

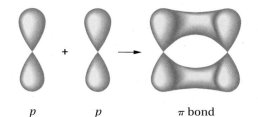

p   *p*   π bond

■ **Figure 1.4**

Orbital overlap to form σ bonds.

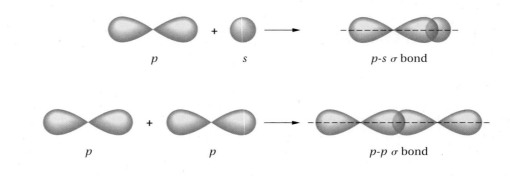

Let us see how these ideas apply to bonding in carbon compounds.

1.15 / Carbon sp^3 Hybrid Orbitals

■ **Figure 1.5**

Distribution of the six electrons in a carbon atom. Each dot stands for an electron.

An *sp^3* **hybrid orbital** is a *p*-shaped orbital that is one part *s* and three parts *p* in character.

In a carbon atom, the six electrons are arranged as shown in Figure 1.5 (compare with carbon in Table 1.2). The 1s shell is filled, and the four valence electrons are in the 2s orbital and two different 2p orbitals. There are a few things to notice about Figure 1.5. The energy scale at the left represents the energy of electrons in the various orbitals. The farther the electron is from the nucleus, the greater its potential energy, because it takes energy to keep the electron (negatively charged) and the nucleus (positively charged) apart. The 2s orbital has a slightly lower energy than the three 2p orbitals, which have equal energies (they differ from one another only in orientation around the nucleus, as shown in Figure 1.2). The two highest energy electrons are placed in different 2p orbitals rather than in the same orbital, because this keeps them farther apart and thus reduces the repulsion between these like-charged particles. One p orbital is vacant.

We might get a misleading idea about the bonding of carbon from Figure 1.5. For example, we might think that carbon should form only two bonds (to complete the partially filled 2p orbitals) or perhaps three bonds (if some atom donated two electrons to the empty 2p orbital). But we know from experience that this picture is wrong. Carbon usually forms *four* single bonds, and often these bonds are all equivalent, as in CH_4 or CCl_4. How can this discrepancy between theory and fact be resolved?

One solution, illustrated in Figure 1.6, is to mix or combine the four atomic orbitals of the valence shell to form four identical hybrid orbitals, each containing one valence electron. In this model, the hybrid orbitals are called *sp^3* **hybrid orbitals** because each one has one part *s* character and three parts *p* character. As shown in Figure 1.6, each sp^3 orbital has the same energy: less than that of the 2p orbitals but greater than that of the 2s orbital. The shape of sp^3 orbitals resembles the shape of p orbitals, except that the dumbbell is lopsided, and the electrons are more likely to be found in the lobe that extends out the greater distance from the nucleus, as shown in Figure 1.7. The four sp^3 hybrid orbitals of a single carbon atom are directed toward the corners of a regular tetrahedron, also shown in Figure 1.7. This particular geometry puts each orbital as far from the other three orbitals as it can be and thus minimizes repulsion when the orbitals are filled with electron pairs. The angle between any two of the four bonds formed from sp^3 orbitals is approximately 109.5°, the angle made by lines drawn from the center to the corners of a regular tetrahedron.

■ **Figure 1.6**

Unhybridized vs. sp^3 hybridized orbitals on carbon. The dots stand for electrons. (Only the electrons in the valence shell are shown; the electrons in the 1s orbital are omitted because they are not involved in bonding.)

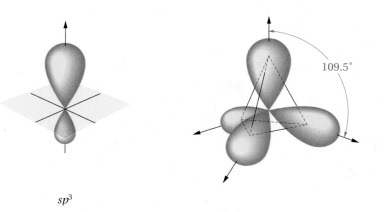

Hybrid orbitals can form sigma bonds by overlap with other hybrid orbitals or with nonhybridized atomic orbitals. Figure 1.8 shows some examples.

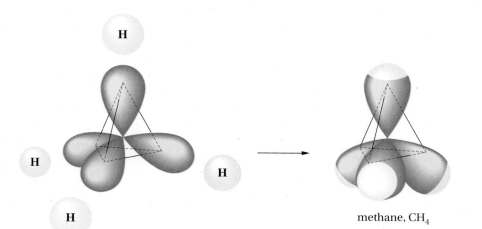

■ **Figure 1.8**

Examples of sigma (σ) bonds formed from sp^3 hybrid orbitals.

1.16 Tetrahedral Carbon; the Bonding in Methane

We can now describe how a carbon atom combines with four hydrogen atoms to form methane. This process is pictured in Figure 1.9. The carbon atom is joined to each hydrogen atom by a sigma bond, which is formed by the overlap of a carbon sp^3 orbital with a hydrogen $1s$ orbital. The four sigma bonds are directed from the carbon nucleus to the corners of a regular tetrahedron. In this way, the electron pair in any one bond experiences minimum repulsion from the electrons in the other bonds. Each H—C—H **bond angle** is the same, 109.5°. To summarize, in methane, there are four sp^3–s C—H sigma bonds, each directed from the carbon atom to one of the four corners of a regular tetrahedron.

A **bond angle** is the angle made by two covalent bonds to the same atom.

■ **Figure 1.9**

A molecule of methane, CH_4, is formed by the overlap of the four sp^3 carbon orbitals with the $1s$ orbitals of four hydrogen atoms. The resulting molecule has the geometry of a regular tetrahedron and contains four sigma bonds of the sp^3–s type.

methane, CH_4

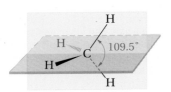

▬ Figure 1.10

The carbon and two of the hydrogens in methane form a plane that perpendicularly bisects the plane formed by the carbon and the other two hydrogens.

PROBLEM 1.29 Considering the repulsion that exists between electrons in different bonds, give a reason why a planar geometry for methane would be less stable than the tetrahedral geometry.

Because the tetrahedral geometry of carbon plays such an important role in organic chemistry, it is a good idea to become familiar with the features of a regular tetrahedron. One feature is that *the center and any two corners of a tetrahedron form a plane that is the perpendicular bisector of a similar plane formed by the center and the other two corners.* In methane, for example, any two hydrogens and the carbon form a plane that perpendicularly bisects the plane formed by the carbon and the other two hydrogens. These planes are illustrated in Figure 1.10.

The geometry of carbon with four single bonds, as in methane, is commonly represented as shown in Figure 1.11a, in which the **solid lines** lie in the plane of the page, the **dashed wedge** goes behind the plane of the paper, and the **solid wedge** extends out of the plane of the paper toward you. Structures drawn in this way are sometimes called **3D** (that is, three-dimensional) **structures**.

Two other 3D representations commonly used are the ball-and-stick model (Figure 1.11b) and the space-filling model (Figure 1.11c). The ball-and-stick model emphasizes the bonds that connect the atoms, while the space-filling model emphasizes the space occupied by the atoms.

In addition, a 3D representation, called an **electrostatic potential map**, is sometimes used to show the distribution of electrons in a molecule (Figure 1.11d). Red indicates partial negative charge (greater electron density), and blue indicates partial positive

(a) In a **3D structure, solid lines** lie in the plane of the page (C and H in C—H lie in the plane). **Dashed wedges** extend behind the plane (H in C⬤⬤H lies behind the plane). **Solid wedges** project out toward you (H in C➔H is in front of the plane).

(b) A **ball-and-stick model** of a molecule emphasizes the bonds that connect atoms.

(c) A **space-filling model** emphasizes the space occupied by the atoms.

(d) An **electrostatic potential map** shows the distribution of electrons in a molecule. Red indicates partial negative charge, and blue indicates partial positive charge.

▬ Figure 1.11

Four representations of methane.

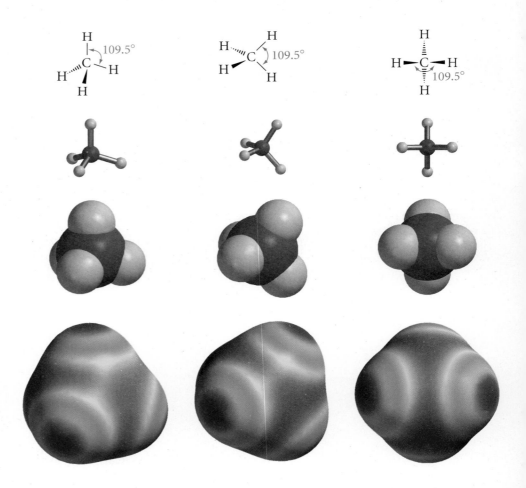

charge (less electron density). This representation is useful for showing whether a molecule is polar or nonpolar (see Sec. 2.7) and can give us insight into the chemical behavior of a molecule, as we will see when we look at the chemistry of functional groups in later chapters.

Now that we have described single covalent bonds and their geometry, we are ready to tackle, in the next chapter, the structure and chemistry of saturated hydrocarbons. But before we do that, we present a brief overview of organic chemistry, so that you can see how the subject will be organized for study.

Because carbon atoms can be linked to one another or to other atoms in so many different ways, the number of possible organic compounds is almost limitless. Literally millions of organic compounds have been characterized, and the number grows daily. How can we hope to study this vast subject systematically? Fortunately, organic compounds can be classified according to their structures into a relatively small number of groups. Structures can be classified both according to the molecular framework (sometimes called the carbon *skeleton*) and according to the groups that are attached to that framework.

1.17 Classification According to Molecular Framework

The three main classes of molecular frameworks for organic structures are acyclic, carbocyclic, and heterocyclic compounds.

1.17.a Acyclic Compounds

By **acyclic** (pronounced a´-cyclic), we mean *not cyclic*. Acyclic organic molecules have chains of carbon atoms but no rings. As we have seen, the chains may be unbranched or branched.

Acyclic compounds contain no rings. **Carbocyclic compounds** contain rings of carbon atoms. **Heterocyclic compounds** have rings containing at least one atom that is *not* carbon.

unbranched chain of eight carbon atoms

branched chain of eight carbon atoms

Pentane is an example of an acyclic compound with an unbranched carbon chain, whereas isopentane and neopentane are also acyclic but have branched carbon frameworks (Sec. 1.9). Figure 1.12 shows the structures of a few acyclic compounds that occur in nature.

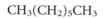

geraniol
(oil of roses)
bp 229–230°C

A branched chain compound used in perfumes

$CH_3(CH_2)_5CH_3$

heptane
(petroleum)
bp 98.4°C

A hydrocarbon present in petroleum, used as a standard in testing the octane rating of gasoline

$CH_3\overset{\overset{\displaystyle O}{\|}}{C}(CH_2)_4CH_3$

2-heptanone
(oil of cloves)
bp 151.5°C

A colorless liquid with a fruity odor, in part responsible for the "peppery" odor of blue cheese

Foodcollection/Getty Images

2-Heptanone contributes to the "peppery" odor of blue cheese.

■ **Figure 1.12**
Examples of natural acyclic compounds, their sources (in parentheses), and selected characteristics.

1.17.b Carbocyclic Compounds

Carbocyclic compounds contain rings of carbon atoms. The smallest possible carbocyclic ring has three carbon atoms, but carbon rings come in many sizes and shapes. The rings may have chains of carbon atoms attached to them and may contain multiple bonds. Many compounds with more than one carbocyclic ring are known. Figure 1.13 shows the structures of a few carbocyclic compounds that occur in nature. Five- and six-membered rings are most common, but smaller and larger rings are also found.

■ Figure 1.13

Examples of natural carbocyclic compounds with rings of various sizes and shapes. The source and special features of each structure are indicated below it.

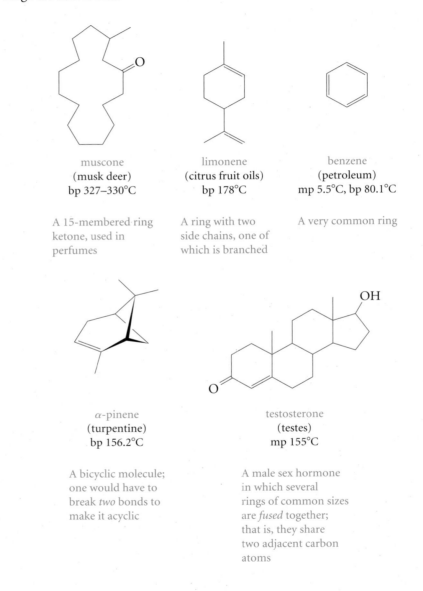

muscone
(musk deer)
bp 327–330°C

A 15-membered ring ketone, used in perfumes

limonene
(citrus fruit oils)
bp 178°C

A ring with two side chains, one of which is branched

benzene
(petroleum)
mp 5.5°C, bp 80.1°C

A very common ring

α-pinene
(turpentine)
bp 156.2°C

A bicyclic molecule; one would have to break *two* bonds to make it acyclic

testosterone
(testes)
mp 155°C

A male sex hormone in which several rings of common sizes are *fused* together; that is, they share two adjacent carbon atoms

Musk deer, source of muscone.

1.17.c Heterocyclic Compounds

Heterocyclic compounds make up the third and largest class of molecular frameworks for organic compounds. In heterocyclic compounds, at least one atom in the ring must be a heteroatom, an atom that is *not* carbon. The most common heteroatoms are oxygen, nitrogen, and sulfur, but heterocyclics with other elements are also known. More than one heteroatom may be present and, if so, the heteroatoms may be alike or different. Heterocyclic rings come in many sizes, may contain multiple bonds, may have carbon chains or rings attached to them, and in short may exhibit a great variety of structures. Figure 1.14 shows the structures of a few natural products that contain heterocyclic rings. In these abbreviated structural formulas, the symbols for the heteroatoms are shown, but the carbons are indicated using lines only.

The structures in Figures 1.12 through 1.14 show not only the molecular frameworks, but also various groups of atoms that may be part of or attached to the frameworks. Fortunately, these groups can also be classified in a way that helps simplify the study of organic chemistry.

Clover, a source of coumarin.

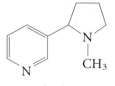

nicotine
bp 246°C

Present in tobacco, nicotine has two heterocyclic rings of different sizes, each containing one nitrogen.

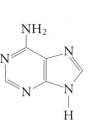

adenine
mp 360–365°C
(decomposes)

One of the four heterocyclic bases of DNA, adenine contains two fused heterocyclic rings, each of which contains two heteroatoms (nitrogen).

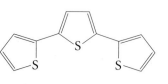

penicillin-G
(amorphous solid)

One of the most widely used antibiotics, penicillin has two heterocyclic rings, the smaller of which is crucial to biological activity.

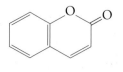

coumarin
mp 71°C

Found in clover and grasses, coumarin produces the pleasant odor of new-mown hay.

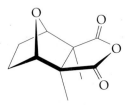

α-terthienyl
mp 92–93°C

This compound, with three linked sulfur-containing rings, is present in certain marigold species.

cantharidin
mp 218°C

This compound, an oxygen heterocycle, is the active principle in cantharis (also known as Spanish fly), a material isolated from certain dried beetles of the species *Cantharis vesicatoria* and incorrectly thought by some to increase sexual desire.

▬ **Figure 1.14**

Examples of natural heterocyclic compounds having a variety of heteroatoms and ring sizes.

1.18 / Classification According to Functional Group

Functional groups are groups of atoms that have characteristic chemical properties regardless of the molecular framework to which they are attached.

Certain groups of atoms have chemical properties that depend only moderately on the molecular framework to which they are attached. These groups of atoms are called **functional groups**. The hydroxyl group, —OH, is an example of a functional group, and compounds with this group attached to a carbon framework are called alcohols. In most organic reactions, some chemical change occurs at the functional group, but the rest of the molecule keeps its original structure. This maintenance of most of the structural formula throughout a chemical reaction greatly simplifies our study of organic chemistry. It allows us to focus attention on the chemistry of the various functional groups. We can study classes of compounds instead of having to learn the chemistry of each individual compound.

Some of the main functional groups that we will study are listed in Table 1.6, together with a typical compound of each type. Although we will describe these classes of compounds in greater detail in later chapters, it would be a good idea for you to become familiar with their names and structures now. If a particular functional group is mentioned before its chemistry is discussed in detail, and you forget what it is, you can refer to Table 1.6 or to the inside front cover of this book.

> **PROBLEM 1.30** What functional groups can you find in the following natural products? (Their formulas are given in Figures 1.12, 1.13, and 1.14.)
>
> a. testosterone   b. penicillin-G   c. muscone   d. α-pinene

Table 1.6 ▪ The Main Functional Groups

	Structure	Class of compound	Specific example	Common name of the specific example
A. Functional groups that are a part of the molecular framework	—C—C—	alkane	CH_3—CH_3	ethane, a component of natural gas
	C=C	alkene	CH_2=CH_2	ethylene, used to make polyethylene
	—C≡C—	alkyne	HC≡CH	acetylene, used in welding
	⬡	arene	⬡	benzene, raw material for polystyrene and phenol
B. Functional groups containing oxygen				
1. With carbon–oxygen single bonds	—C—OH	alcohol	CH_3CH_2OH	ethyl alcohol, found in beer, wines, and liquors
	—C—O—C—	ether	$CH_3CH_2OCH_2CH_3$	diethyl ether, once a common anesthetic

(continued)

Table 1.6 continued

	Structure	Class of compound	Specific example	Common name of the specific example
2. With carbon–oxygen double bonds*	$\overset{\displaystyle O}{\underset{\displaystyle \shortparallel}{}}$ —C—H	aldehyde	$CH_2{=}O$	formaldehyde, used to preserve biological specimens
	—C—C—C— with O double bond on middle C	ketone	CH_3CCH_3 (with O)	acetone, a solvent for varnish and rubber cement
3. With single and double carbon–oxygen bonds	—C—OH (with O double bond)	carboxylic acid	$CH_3C{-}OH$ (with O)	acetic acid, a component of vinegar
	—C—O—C— (with O double bond)	ester	$CH_3C{-}OCH_2CH_3$ (with O)	ethyl acetate, a solvent for nail polish and model airplane glue
C. Functional groups containing nitrogen**	—C—NH$_2$	primary amine	$CH_3CH_2NH_2$	ethylamine, smells like ammonia
	—C≡N	nitrile	$CH_2{=}CH{-}C{\equiv}N$	acrylonitrile, raw material for making Orlon
D. Functional group with oxygen and nitrogen	—C—NH$_2$ (with O double bond)	primary amide	$H{-}C{-}NH_2$ (with O)	formamide, a softener for paper
E. Functional group with halogen	—X	alkyl or aryl halide	CH_3Cl	methyl chloride, refrigerant and local anesthetic
F. Functional groups containing sulfur†	—C—SH	thiol (also called mercaptan)	CH_3SH	methanethiol, has the odor of rotten cabbage
	—C—S—C—	thioether (also called sulfide)	$(CH_2{=}CHCH_2)_2S$	diallyl sulfide, has the odor of garlic

*The $>$C$=$O group, present in several functional groups, is called a **carbonyl group**. The $-\overset{\displaystyle O}{\underset{\displaystyle \shortparallel}{C}}-$OH group of acids is called a **carboxyl group** (a contraction of *carb*onyl and hydr*oxyl*).

The —NH$_2$ group is called an **amino group.

†Thiols and thioethers are the sulfur analogs of alcohols and ethers.

ADDITIONAL PROBLEMS

⦿WL Interactive versions of these problems are assignable in OWL.

Valence, Bonding, and Lewis Structures

1.31 Show the number of valence electrons in each of the following atoms. Let the element's symbol represent its kernel, and use dots for the valence electrons.

a. chlorine   b. nitrogen   c. sulfur
d. carbon   e. oxygen   f. potassium

1.32 Use the relative positions of the elements in the periodic table (Table 1.3 or inside back cover) to classify the following substances as ionic or covalent:

a. F_2 b. SiF_4 c. CH_4
d. O_2 e. $CaCl_2$ f. NaI
g. NaBr   h. ClF

1.33 When a solution of salt (sodium chloride) in water is treated with a silver nitrate solution, a white precipitate forms immediately. When tetrachloromethane is shaken with aqueous silver nitrate, no such precipitate is produced. Explain these facts in terms of the types of bonds present in the two chlorides.

1.34 For each of the following elements, determine (1) how many valence electrons it has and (2) what its common valence is:

a. N   b. C   c. F
d. O   e. P   f. S

1.35 Write a structural formula for each of the following compounds, using a line to represent each single bond and dots for any unshared electron pairs:

a. CH_3OH b. CH_3CH_2Cl c. C_3H_8
d. $CH_3CH_2NH_2$ e. C_2H_5F f. CH_2O

1.36 Draw a structural formula for each of the following covalent molecules. Which bonds are polar? Indicate the polarity by proper placement of the symbols $\delta+$ and $\delta-$.

a. BF_3 b. CH_3F c. CO_2
d. Cl_2 e. SF_6 f. CH_4
g. SO_2 h. CH_3OH

1.37 Consider the X—H bond, in which X is an atom other than H. The H in a polar bond is more acidic (more easily removed) than the H in a nonpolar bond. Considering bond polarity, which hydrogen in acetic acid,

$$CH_3\overset{\displaystyle O}{\overset{\displaystyle \|}{C}}-OH,$$

do you expect to be most acidic? Write an equation for the reaction between acetic acid and potassium carbonate.

Structural Isomers

1.38 Draw structural formulas for all possible isomers having the following molecular formulas:

a. C_3H_8 b. C_3H_7F c. $C_2H_2Br_2$
d. C_3H_6 e. C_4H_9Cl f. $C_3H_6Cl_2$
g. C_3H_8S h. $C_2H_4F_2$

1.39 Draw structural formulas for the five isomers of C_6H_{14}. As you write them out, try to be systematic, starting with a consecutive chain of six carbon atoms.

Structural Formulas

1.40 For each of the following abbreviated structural formulas, write a structural formula that shows all of the bonds:

a. $CH_3(CH_2)_4CH_3$ b. $(CH_3)_3CCH_2CH_2CH_3$ c. $(CH_3CH_2)_2NH$
d. $CH_3CH_2SCH_2CH_3$ e. $ClCH_2CH_2OH$ f. $(CH_3CH_2)_2CHOH$

1.41 Write structural formulas that correspond to the following abbreviated structures, and show the correct number of hydrogens on each carbon:

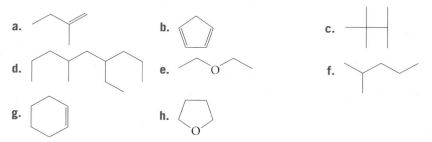

a.   b.   c.

d.   e.   f.

g.   h.

1.42 For each of the following abbreviated structural formulas, write a line-segment formula (like those in Problem 1.41).

a. $CH_3(CH_2)_4CH_3$ b. $(CH_3)_2CHCH_2CH_2\overset{\displaystyle O}{\overset{\displaystyle \|}{C}}CH_3$

c. $CH_3CHCH_2C(CH_3)_3$ d. $CH_3-CH\overset{H_2C}{\underset{H_2C}{<}}\overset{CH}{\underset{CH}{\|}}$
   $\quad\quad |$
   $\quad\quad OH$

1.43 An abbreviated formula of 2-heptanone is shown in Figure 1.12.

a. How many carbons does 2-heptanone have?
b. What is its molecular formula?
c. Write a more detailed structural formula for it.

1.44 What is the *molecular formula* for each of the following compounds? Consult Figures 1.13 and 1.14 for the abbreviated structural formulas.

a. nicotine   b. adenine
c. limonene   d. coumarin
e. benzene

Formal Charge, Resonance, and Curved-Arrow Formalism

1.45 Write electron-dot formulas for the following species. Show where the formal charges, if any, are located.

a. cyanide ion, CN^- b. nitric acid, $HONO_2$
c. dimethyl ether, CH_3OCH_3 d. ammonium ion, NH_4^+
e. nitrous acid, HONO   f. carbon monoxide, CO
g. boron trifluoride, BF_3 h. hydrogen peroxide, H_2O_2
i. bicarbonate ion, HCO_3^-

1.46 Draw electron-dot formulas for the two contributors to the resonance hybrid structure of the nitrite ion, NO_2^-. (Each oxygen is connected to the nitrogen.) What is the charge on each oxygen in each contributor and in the hybrid structure? Show by curved arrows how the electron pairs can relocate to interconvert the two structures.

1.47 Write the structure obtained when electrons move as indicated by the curved arrows in the following structure:

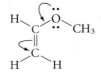

Does each atom in the resulting structure have a complete valence shell of electrons? Locate any formal charges in each structure.

1.48 Consider each of the following highly reactive carbon species. What is the formal charge on carbon in each of these structures?

$$
\begin{array}{cccc}
\text{H} & \text{H} & \text{H} & \text{H} \\
| & | & | & | \\
\text{H}-\text{C} & \text{H}-\text{C}\cdot & \text{H}-\text{C}\colon & \text{H}-\text{C}\cdot \\
| & | & | & \\
\text{H} & \text{H} & \text{H} & \\
\end{array}
$$

1.49 Add curved arrows to the following structures to show how electron pairs must be moved to interconvert the structures, and locate any formal charges.

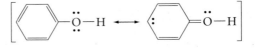

1.50 Add curved arrows to show how electrons must move to form the product from the reactants in the following equation, and locate any formal charges.

$$
\text{CH}_3-\overset{..}{\underset{..}{\text{O}}}\text{H} + \text{CH}_3-\overset{\overset{\displaystyle :\overset{..}{\text{O}}}{\|}}{\text{C}}-\text{OCH}_3 \longrightarrow \text{CH}_3-\overset{\overset{\displaystyle :\overset{..}{\text{O}}:}{|}}{\underset{\underset{..}{\text{HO}-\text{CH}_3}}{\text{C}}}-\text{OCH}_3
$$

Electronic Structure and Molecular Geometry

1.51 Fill in any unshared electron pairs that are missing from the following formulas:

a. $(\text{CH}_3\text{CH}_2)_2\text{NH}$

b. $\text{CH}_3\overset{\overset{\displaystyle O}{\|}}{\text{C}}-\text{OH}$

c. $\text{CH}_3\text{CH}_2\text{SCH}_2\text{CH}_3$

d. $\text{CH}_3\text{OCH}_2\text{CH}_2\text{OH}$

1.52 Make a drawing (similar to the right-hand part of Figure 1.6) of the electron distribution that will be expected in nitrogen atoms if the *s* and *p* orbitals are hybridized to *sp*³. Based on this model, predict the geometry of the ammonia molecule, NH_3.

1.53 The ammonium ion, NH_4^+, has a tetrahedral geometry analogous to that of methane. Explain this structure in terms of atomic and molecular orbitals.

1.54 Use lines, dashed wedges, and solid wedges to show the geometry of CF_4 and CH_3SH.

1.55 Silicon is just below carbon in the periodic table. Predict the geometry of silicon tetrafluoride, SiF_4.

1.56 Examine the three ball-and-stick models shown below:

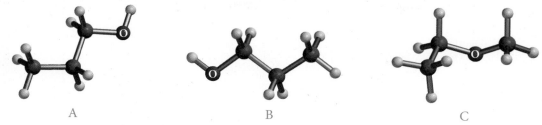

A   B   C

a. Redraw the three structures using solid lines, dashed wedges, and solid wedges (see Figure 1.11).
b. What is the relationship, identical or isomers, between structures A and B? Between structures A and C?

Classification of Organic Compounds

1.57 Write a structural formula that corresponds to the molecular formula C_3H_6O and is

a. acyclic   b. carbocyclic   c. heterocyclic

1.58 Draw a chemical structure for diacetyl (2,3-butanedione), a diketone (see Table 1.6) with the $C_4H_6O_2$ chemical formula. Diacetyl is used as a flavoring for microwave popcorn, but has been under scrutiny of late as a possible causative agent for bronchiolitis obliterans, often referred to as popcorn lung disease.

1.59 Divide the following compounds into groups that might be expected to exhibit similar chemical behavior:

a. C_4H_{10}
d. C_8H_{18}
g. $CH_3CH_2CH_3$
j. C_3H_7OH

b. CH_3OCH_3
e. $HOCH_2CH_2CH_2OH$
h. CH_3OH
k. $CH_3CH_2OCH_3$

c. C_3H_7OH
f. CH_3NH_2
i. $(CH_3)_2CHNH_2$
l. $H_2NCH_2CH_2NH_2$

1.60 Using Table 1.6, write a structural formula for each of the following:

a. an alcohol, C_3H_8O
c. an aldehyde, C_3H_6O
e. a carboxylic acid, $C_3H_6O_2$

b. an ether, $C_4H_{10}O$
d. a ketone, C_3H_6O
f. an ester, $C_5H_{10}O_2$

1.61 Many organic compounds contain more than one functional group. An example is phenylalanine (shown below), one of the simple building blocks of proteins (Chapter 17).

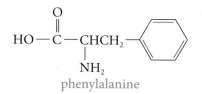

phenylalanine

a. What functional groups are present in phenylalanine?
b. Redraw the structure, adding all unshared electron pairs.
c. What is the molecular formula of phenylalanine?
d. Draw another structural isomer that has this formula. What functional groups does this isomer have?

Refining of petroleum, a major natural source of alkanes (see "A Word about Petroleum, Gasoline, and Octane Number," pp. 102–103).

$$CH_3(CH_2)_nCH_3$$

Sami Sarkis/Photodisc/Getty images

Alkanes and Cycloalkanes; Conformational and Geometric Isomerism

The main components of petroleum and natural gas, resources that now supply most of our fuel for energy, are **hydrocarbons**, compounds that contain only carbon and hydrogen. There are three main classes of hydrocarbons, based on the types of carbon–carbon bonds present. **Saturated hydrocarbons** contain only carbon–carbon *single* bonds. **Unsaturated hydrocarbons** contain carbon–carbon *multiple* bonds—double bonds, triple bonds, or both. **Aromatic hydrocarbons** are a special class of cyclic compounds related in structure to benzene.*

Saturated hydrocarbons are known as **alkanes** if they are acyclic, or as **cycloalkanes** if they are cyclic. Let us look at their structures and properties.

*Unsaturated and aromatic hydrocarbons are discussed in Chapters 3 and 4, respectively.

2.1 The Structures of Alkanes

The simplest alkane is methane. Its tetrahedral three-dimensional structure was described in the previous chapter (see Figure 1.9). Additional alkanes are constructed by lengthening the carbon chain and adding an appropriate number of hydrogens to complete the carbon valences (for examples, see Figure 2.1* and Table 2.1).

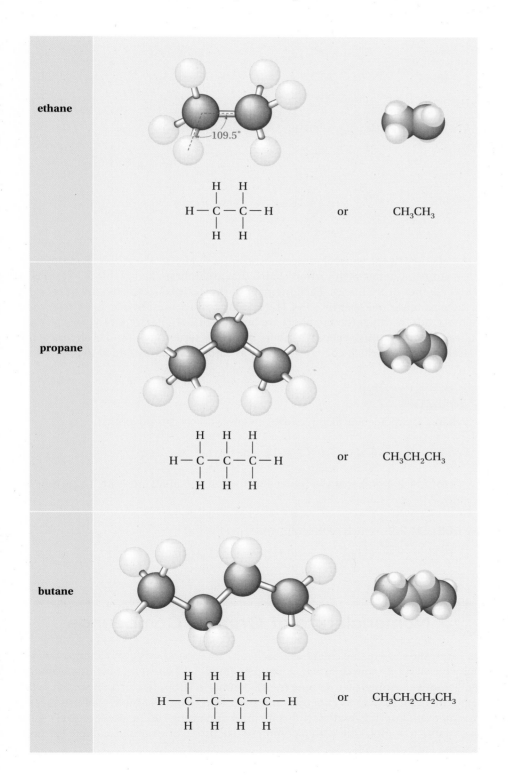

■ Figure 2.1

Three-dimensional models of ethane, propane, and butane. The ball-and-stick models at the left show the way in which the atoms are connected and depict the correct bond angles. The space-filling models at the right are constructed to scale and give a better idea of the molecular shape, though some of the hydrogens may appear hidden.

*Molecular models can help you visualize organic structures in three dimensions. They will be extremely useful to you throughout this course, especially when we consider various types of isomerism. Relatively inexpensive sets are usually available at stores that sell textbooks, and your instructor can suggest which kind to buy. If you cannot locate or afford a set, you can create models that are adequate for most purposes from toothpicks (for bonds) and marshmallows, gum drops, or jelly beans (for atoms).

Alkanes are **saturated hydrocarbons**, containing only carbon–carbon single bonds. **Cycloalkanes** contain rings. **Unsaturated hydrocarbons** contain carbon–carbon double or triple bonds. **Aromatic hydrocarbons** are cyclic compounds structurally related to benzene.

Table 2.1 ▪ Names and Formulas of the First Ten Unbranched Alkanes

Name	Number of carbons	Molecular formula	Structural formula	Number of structural isomers
methane	1	CH_4	CH_4	1
ethane	2	C_2H_6	CH_3CH_3	1
propane	3	C_3H_8	$CH_3CH_2CH_3$	1
butane	4	C_4H_{10}	$CH_3CH_2CH_2CH_3$	2
pentane	5	C_5H_{12}	$CH_3(CH_2)_3CH_3$	3
hexane	6	C_6H_{14}	$CH_3(CH_2)_4CH_3$	5
heptane	7	C_7H_{16}	$CH_3(CH_2)_5CH_3$	9
octane	8	C_8H_{18}	$CH_3(CH_2)_6CH_3$	18
nonane	9	C_9H_{20}	$CH_3(CH_2)_7CH_3$	35
decane	10	$C_{10}H_{22}$	$CH_3(CH_2)_8CH_3$	75

All alkanes fit the general molecular formula C_nH_{2n+2}, where n is the number of carbon atoms. Alkanes with carbon chains that are unbranched (Table 2.1) are called **normal alkanes** or n-alkanes. Each member of this series differs from the next higher and the next lower member by a —CH_2— group (called a **methylene group**). A series of compounds in which the members are built up in a regular, repetitive way like this is called a **homologous series**. Members of such a series have similar chemical and physical properties, which change gradually as carbon atoms are added to the chain.

Unbranched alkanes are called **normal alkanes**, or n-alkanes.

A —CH_2— group is called a **methylene group**.

Compounds of a **homologous series** differ by a regular unit of structure and share similar properties.

EXAMPLE 2.1

What is the molecular formula of an alkane with six carbon atoms?

Solution If $n = 6$, then $2n + 2 = 14$. The formula is C_6H_{14}.

PROBLEM 2.1 What is the molecular formula of an alkane with 12 carbon atoms?

PROBLEM 2.2 Which of the following are alkanes?
a. C_7H_{16} b. C_7H_{12} c. C_8H_{16} d. $C_{29}H_{60}$

2.2 Nomenclature of Organic Compounds

In the early days of organic chemistry, each new compound was given a name that was usually based on its source or use. Examples (Figs. 1.13 and 1.14) include limonene (from lemons), α-pinene (from pine trees), coumarin (from the tonka bean, known to South American natives as *cumaru*), and penicillin (from the mold that produces it, *Penicillium notatum*). Even today, this method of naming can be used to give a short, simple name to a molecule with a complex structure. For example, cubane (p. xxvii) was named after its shape.

It became clear many years ago, however, that one could not rely only on common or trivial names and that a systematic method for naming compounds was needed. Ideally, the rules of the system should result in a unique name for each compound. Knowing the rules and seeing a structure, one should be able to write the systematic name. Seeing the systematic name, one should be able to write the correct structure.

Eventually, internationally recognized systems of nomenclature were devised by a commission of the International Union of Pure and Applied Chemistry; they are known as the IUPAC (pronounced "eye-you-pack") systems. In this book, we will use mainly IUPAC names. However, in some cases, the common name is so widely used that we will ask you to learn it (for example, formaldehyde [common] is used in preference to methanal [systematic], and cubane is much easier to remember than its systematic name, pentacyclo$[4.2.0.0^{2,5}.0^{3,8}.0^{4,7}]$octane).

2.3 IUPAC Rules for Naming Alkanes

1. The general name for acyclic saturated hydrocarbons is *alkanes*. The *-ane* ending is used for all saturated hydrocarbons. This is important to remember because later other endings will be used for other functional groups.

2. Alkanes without branches are named according to the *number of carbon atoms*. These names, up to ten carbons, are given in the first column of Table 2.1.

3. For alkanes with branches, the **root name** is that of the longest continuous chain of carbon atoms. For example, in the structure

> The **root name** of an alkane is that of the longest continuous chain of carbon atoms.

$$CH_3\text{—}CH\text{—}CH\text{—}CH_2\text{—}CH_3 \quad \text{or} \quad CH_3\text{—}CH\text{—}CH\text{—}CH_2\text{—}CH_3$$

(with CH_3 substituents above the second and third carbons)

the longest continuous chain (in color) has five carbon atoms. The compound is therefore named as a substituted *pent*ane, even though there are seven carbon atoms altogether.

4. Groups attached to the main chain are called **substituents**. Saturated substituents that contain only carbon and hydrogen are called **alkyl groups**. An alkyl group is named by taking the name of the alkane with the same number of carbon atoms and changing the *-ane* ending to *-yl*.

> **Substituents** are groups attached to the main chain of a molecule. Saturated substituents containing only C and H are called **alkyl groups**.

In the previous example, each substituent has only one carbon. Derived from methane by removing one of the hydrogens, a one-carbon substituent is called a **methyl group**.

> The one-carbon alkyl group derived from methane is called a **methyl group**.

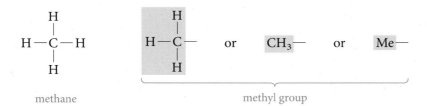

methane   methyl group

The names of substituents with more than one carbon atom will be described in Section 2.4.

5. The main chain is numbered in such a way that the first substituent encountered along the chain receives the lowest possible number. Each substituent is then located by its name and by the number of the carbon atom to which it is attached. When two or more identical groups are attached to the main chain, prefixes such

as *di-*, *tri-*, and *tetra-* are used. *Every substituent must be named and numbered, even if two identical substituents are attached to the same carbon of the main chain.* The compound

$$
\begin{array}{ccccc}
 & \overset{2}{C}H_3 & \overset{3}{C}H_3 & & \\
\overset{1}{C}H_3 & -\overset{2}{C}H & -\overset{3}{C}H & -\overset{4}{C}H_2 & -\overset{5}{C}H_3
\end{array}
$$

is correctly named 2,3-dimethylpentane. The name tells us that there are two methyl substituents, one attached to carbon-2 and one attached to carbon-3 of a five-carbon saturated chain.

6. If two or more different types of substituents are present, they are listed alphabetically, except that prefixes such as *di-* and *tri-* are not considered when alphabetizing.

7. Punctuation is important when writing IUPAC names. IUPAC names for hydrocarbons are written as one word. Numbers are separated from each other by commas and are separated from letters by hyphens. There is no space between the last named substituent and the name of the parent alkane that follows it.

To summarize and amplify these rules, we take the following steps to find an acceptable IUPAC name for an alkane:

1. Locate the longest continuous carbon chain. This gives the name of the parent hydrocarbon. For example,

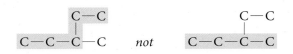

2. Number the longest chain beginning at the end nearest the first branch point. For example,

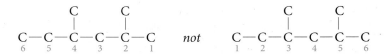

If there are two equally long continuous chains, select the one with the most branches. For example,

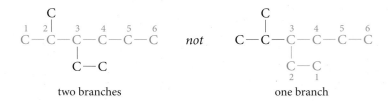

If there is a branch equidistant from each end of the longest chain, begin numbering nearest to a third branch:

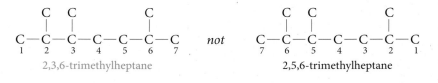

If there is no third branch, begin numbering nearest the substituent whose name has alphabetic priority:

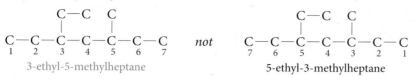

3-ethyl-5-methylheptane   5-ethyl-3-methylheptane

3. Write the name as one word, placing substituents in alphabetic order and using proper punctuation.

EXAMPLE 2.2

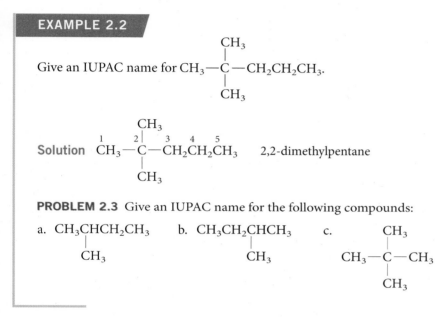

Give an IUPAC name for $CH_3-\overset{\underset{|}{CH_3}}{\underset{|}{CH_3}}C-CH_2CH_2CH_3$.

Solution $\overset{1}{CH_3}-\overset{\overset{CH_3}{|}}{\underset{\underset{CH_3}{|}}{C}}-\overset{3}{C}H_2\overset{4}{C}H_2\overset{5}{C}H_3$ 2,2-dimethylpentane

PROBLEM 2.3 Give an IUPAC name for the following compounds:

a. $CH_3CHCH_2CH_3$ b. $CH_3CH_2CHCH_3$ c.
         | |
        CH_3 CH_3

$$CH_3-\overset{\overset{CH_3}{|}}{\underset{\underset{CH_3}{|}}{C}}-CH_3$$

2.4 Alkyl and Halogen Substituents

As illustrated for the methyl group, alkyl substituents are named by changing the *-ane* ending of alkanes to *-yl*. Thus the two-carbon alkyl group is called the **ethyl group**, from ethane.

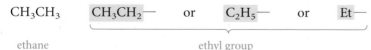

CH_3CH_3 CH_3CH_2- or C_2H_5- or $Et-$

ethane   ethyl group

The two-carbon alkyl group is the **ethyl group**. The **propyl group** and the **isopropyl group** are three-carbon groups attached to the main chain by the first and second carbons, respectively.

When we come to propane, there are two possible alkyl groups, depending on which type of hydrogen is removed. If a *terminal* hydrogen is removed, the group is called a **propyl group**.

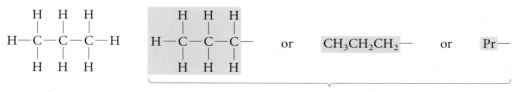

propyl group

But if a hydrogen is removed from the *central* carbon atom, we get a different isomeric propyl group, called the **isopropyl** (or 1-methylethyl)* **group.**

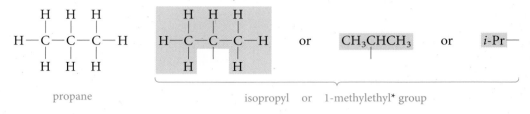

propane   isopropyl   or   1-methylethyl* group

There are four different butyl groups. The butyl and *sec*-butyl groups are based on *n*-butane, while the isobutyl and *tert*-butyl groups come from isobutane.

$CH_3CH_2CH_2CH_2—$ and $CH_3CHCH_2CH_3$

butyl   sec-butyl
(or 1-methylpropyl)

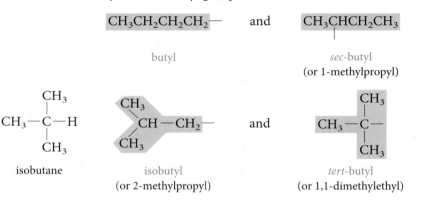

isobutane   isobutyl   tert-butyl
(or 2-methylpropyl)   (or 1,1-dimethylethyl)

These names for the alkyl groups with up to four carbon atoms are very commonly used, so you should memorize them.

R is the general symbol for an alkyl group.

The letter **R** is used as a general symbol for an alkyl group. The formula R—H therefore represents any alkane, and the formula R—Cl stands for any alkyl chloride (methyl chloride, ethyl chloride, and so on).

Halogen substituents are named by changing the -*ine* ending of the element to -*o*.

F—   Cl—   Br—   I—
fluoro-   chloro-   bromo-   iodo-

EXAMPLE 2.3

Give the common and IUPAC names for $CH_3CH_2CH_2Br$.

Solution The common name is propyl bromide (the common name of the alkyl group is followed by the name of the halide). The IUPAC name is 1-bromopropane, the halogen being named as a substituent on the three-carbon chain.

PROBLEM 2.4 Give an IUPAC name for CH_2ClF.

PROBLEM 2.5 Write the formula for each of the following compounds:

a. isobutyl chloride   b. isopropyl bromide
c. 2-chlorobutane   d. *tert*-butyl iodide
e. propyl fluoride   f. general formula for an alkyl bromide

---

*The name 1-methylethyl for this group comes about by regarding it as a substituted ethyl group.

ethyl   1-methylethyl

2.5 Use of the IUPAC Rules

The examples given in Table 2.2 illustrate how the IUPAC rules are applied for particular structures. Study each example to see how a correct name is obtained and how to avoid certain pitfalls.

It is important not only to be able to write a correct IUPAC name for a given structure, but also to do the converse: Write the structure given the IUPAC name. In this case, first write the longest carbon chain and number it, then add the substituents to the correct carbon atoms, and finally fill in the formula with the correct number of hydrogens at each carbon. For example, to write the formula for 2,2,4-trimethylpentane, we go through the following steps:

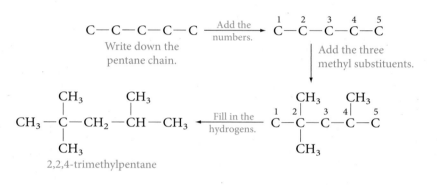

Table 2.2 ■ Examples of Use of the IUPAC Rules

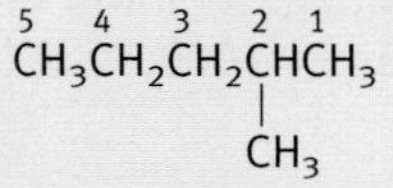

$\overset{5}{C}H_3\overset{4}{C}H_2\overset{3}{C}H_2\overset{2}{C}H\overset{1}{C}H_3$
  |
  CH_3

2-methylpentane
(*not* 4-methylpentane)

The ending -*ane* tells us that all the carbon–carbon bonds are single; *pent*- indicates five carbons in the longest chain. We number them from right to left, starting closest to the branch point.

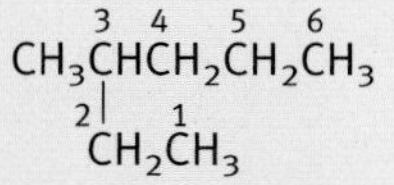

$\overset{3}{C}H_3\overset{4}{C}H\overset{5}{C}H_2\overset{6}{C}H_2CH_3$
     $\overset{2}{|}\overset{1}{|}$
     CH_2CH_3

3-methylhexane
(*not* 2-ethylpentane
or 4-methylhexane)

This is a six-carbon saturated chain with a methyl group on the third carbon. We would usually write the structure as $CH_3CH_2CHCH_2CH_2CH_3$.
                                                          |
                                                         CH_3

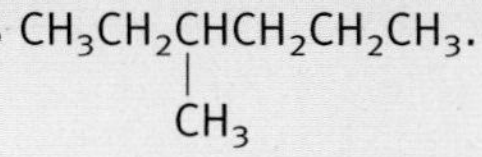

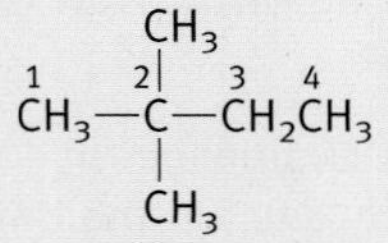

         CH_3
          |
$\overset{1}{C}H_3-\overset{2}{C}-\overset{3}{C}H_2\overset{4}{C}H_3$
          |
         CH_3

2,2-dimethylbutane
(*not* 2,2-methylbutane
or 2-dimethylbutane)

There must be a number for each substituent, and the prefix *di*- says that there are two methyl substituents.

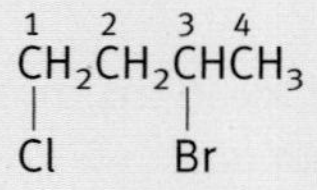

$\overset{1}{C}H_2\overset{2}{C}H_2\overset{3}{C}H\overset{4}{C}H_3$
  | |
  Cl   Br

3-bromo-1-chlorobutane
(*not* 1-chloro-3-bromobutane
or 2-bromo-4-chlorobutane)

First, we number the butane chain from the end closest to the first substituent. Then we name the substituents in alphabetical order, regardless of position number.

PROBLEM 2.6 Name the following compounds by the IUPAC system:

a. $CH_3CHFCH_2CH_3$

b.
$$(CH_3)_3CCHCH(CH_3)_2$$
with Br attached:

b.
Br
|
$(CH_3)_3CCHCH(CH_3)_2$

PROBLEM 2.7 Write the structure for 3,3-dimethyloctane.

PROBLEM 2.8 Explain why 1,3-difluorobutane is a correct IUPAC name, but 1,3-dimethylpentane is *not* a correct IUPAC name.

2.6 / Sources of Alkanes

Petroleum and natural gas are the two most important natural sources of alkanes.

The two most important natural sources of alkanes are **petroleum** and **natural gas**. Petroleum is a complex liquid mixture of organic compounds, many of which are alkanes or cycloalkanes. For more details about how petroleum is refined to obtain gasoline, fuel oil, and other useful substances, read "A Word about Petroleum, Gasoline, and Octane Number" on pages 102–103.

Natural gas, often found associated with petroleum deposits, consists mainly of methane (about 80%) and ethane (5% to 10%), with lesser amounts of some higher alkanes. Propane is the major constituent of liquefied petroleum gas (LPG), a domestic fuel used mainly in rural areas and mobile homes. Butane is the gas of choice in some areas. Natural gas is becoming an energy source that can compete with and possibly surpass oil. In the United States, there are about a million miles of natural gas pipelines distributing this energy source to all parts of the country. Natural gas is also distributed worldwide via huge tankers. To conserve space, the gas is liquefied ($-160°C$), because 1 cubic meter (m^3) of liquefied gas is equivalent to about 600 m^3 of gas at atmospheric pressure. Large tankers can carry more than 100,000 m^3 of liquefied gas.

A CLOSER LOOK AT... Natural Gas

Conduct research on the Internet to find more information and answer questions about natural gas.

Natural Gas as a Fossil Fuel

1. What are the physical properties of natural gas?

2. Why does natural gas used for home heating (or from the Bunsen burner in your chemistry lab) have an odor?

3. Why do the physical properties of natural gas make it safer to use than most other fossil fuels?

4. How is natural gas produced in nature? What keeps it from escaping to the surface of the earth? How is it obtained from its natural source?

5. How many miles (or kilometers) of pipeline for transporting natural gas currently exist in the United States?

6. What percent of U.S. energy needs are supplied by natural gas?

7. What are the major geographic locations of natural gas in the United States and Canada?

2.7 Physical Properties of Alkanes and Nonbonding Intermolecular Interactions

Alkanes are insoluble in water. This is because water molecules are *polar,* whereas alkanes are *nonpolar* (all the C—C and C—H bonds are nearly purely covalent). The O—H bond in a water molecule is strongly polarized by the high electronegativity of oxygen (Sec. 1.5). This polarization places a partial positive charge on the hydrogen atom and a partial negative charge on the oxygen atom (Figure 2.2(a)). As a result, the hydrogen atoms in one water molecule are strongly attracted to the oxygen atoms in other water molecules, and the small size of the H atoms allows the molecules to approach each other very closely. This special attraction is called **hydrogen bonding** (Figure 2.2(b)).* To intersperse alkane and water molecules, we would have to break up the hydrogen bonding interactions between water molecules, which would require considerable energy. Alkanes, with their nonpolar C—H bonds, cannot replace hydrogen bonding among water molecules with attractive alkane–water interactions that are comparable in strength, so mixing alkane molecules and water molecules is *not* an energetically favored process.

The mutual insolubility of alkanes and water is used to advantage by many plants. Alkanes often constitute part of the protective coating on leaves and fruits. If you have ever polished an apple, you know that the skin, or cuticle, contains waxes. Constituents of these waxes include the normal alkanes $C_{27}H_{56}$ and $C_{29}H_{60}$. The leaf wax of cabbage and broccoli is mainly n-$C_{29}H_{60}$, and the main alkane of tobacco leaves is n-$C_{31}H_{64}$. Similar hydrocarbons are found in beeswax. The major function of plant waxes is to prevent water loss from the leaves or fruit.

Alkanes have lower boiling points for a given molecular weight than most other organic compounds. This is because they are nonpolar molecules. They are constantly

(a)   (b)

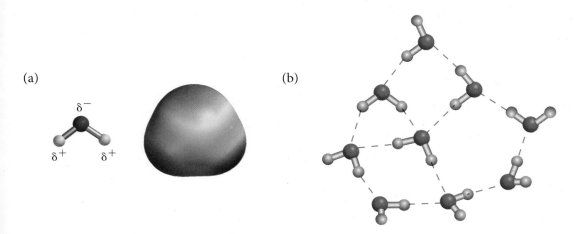

■ **Figure 2.2**
(a) Electrostatic potential map for a water molecule, showing the partial negative charge (red) for the oxygen atom and partial positive charge (blue) for the hydrogens. (b) Interaction of partial positive and negative charges in a network of water molecules via bridging hydrogen bonds.

*Molecules that contain N—H and F—H covalent bonds also have hydrogen bonding interactions with molecules containing N, O, or F atoms.

A CLOSER LOOK AT...   Hydrogen Bonding

Conduct research on the Internet to find more information about hydrogen bonding and to answer the following questions.

Water and Ice

1. What is the partial charge on the O atom? On each H atom?

2. If the water molecule were linear (H—O—H) instead of bent $\underset{H \quad H}{O}$, would it still be polar?

3. What is the average length (in angstroms) of a hydrogen bond between two water molecules?

4. How is a hydrogen bond different from a covalent bond?

Water, Ice, and Hydrogen Bonding

1. Search online for information on water, ice, and hydrogen bonds.

    a. How many hydrogen bonds does a water molecule make in liquid water? In ice?

    b. Why is ice less dense than liquid water? How is this related to hydrogen bonding?

2. One property of alkanes is that they are not soluble in water. This is related to interactions between molecules. Let us explore the connection to hydrogen bonding.

    a. What is required for hydrogen bonding between molecules?

    b. Can alkane molecules form hydrogen bonds to each other or to water molecules?

    c. When the oil tanker Exxon *Valdez* broke apart near the Alaskan coast, the oil (composed mostly of alkanes) that spilled did not dissolve in the water. It floated on top. Explain these facts in terms of intermolecular interactions and the properties of alkanes and water molecules.

---

moving, and the electrons in a nonpolar molecule can become unevenly distributed within the molecule, causing the molecule to have partially positive and partially negative ends. The *temporarily* polarized molecule causes its neighbor to become temporarily polarized as well, and these molecules are weakly attracted to each other. Such interactions between molecules are called **van der Waals attractions**.

Because they are weak attractions, the process of separating molecules from one another (which is what we do when we convert a liquid to a gas) requires relatively little energy, and the boiling points of these compounds are relatively low. Figure 2.3 shows the boiling points of some alkanes. Since these attractive forces can only operate over short distances between the surfaces of molecules, *the boiling points of alkanes rise as the chain length increases and fall as the chains become branched and more nearly spherical in shape.* Figure 2.4 illustrates the effect of molecular shape on van der Waals attractions.

▬ **Figure 2.3**

As shown by the curve, the boiling points of the normal alkanes rise smoothly as the length of the carbon chain increases. Note from the table, however, that chain branching causes a decrease in boiling point (each compound in the table has the same number of carbons and hydrogens, C_5H_{12}).

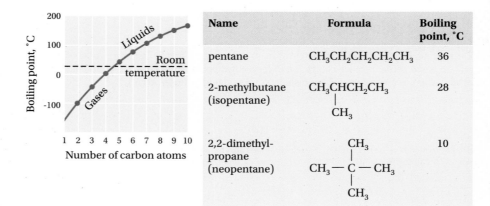

Name	Formula	Boiling point, °C
pentane	$CH_3CH_2CH_2CH_2CH_3$	36
2-methylbutane (isopentane)	$CH_3CHCH_2CH_3$ CH_3	28
2,2-dimethyl-propane (neopentane)	$CH_3-\overset{\displaystyle CH_3}{\underset{\displaystyle CH_3}{C}}-CH_3$	10

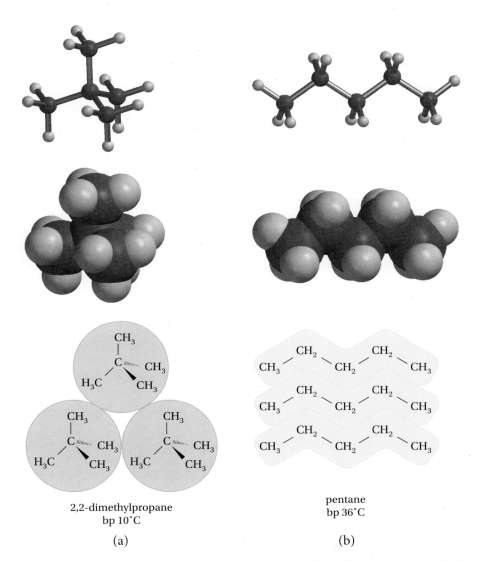

■ **Figure 2.4**
Ball-and-stick (top) and space-filling (middle) representations for 2,2-dimethylpropane (a) and pentane (b) showing the relatively spherical nature of 2,2-dimethylpropane as compared to the rod-shaped nature of pentane (bottom).

2,2-dimethylpropane
bp 10°C

(a)

pentane
bp 36°C

(b)

Despite having the same molecular weight, the rod-shaped pentane molecules have more surface area available for contact between them than the spherical 2,2-dimethylpropane molecules. Pentane molecules, therefore, experience more van der Waals attractions (hence, higher boiling point) than do 2,2-dimethylpropane molecules.

Hydrogen bonding and van der Waals attractions are examples of **nonbonding intermolecular interactions**. These kinds of interactions have important consequences for the properties and behavior of molecules, and we will encounter more examples as we continue to explore the chemistry of different classes of organic compounds.

Hydrogen bonding and **van der Waals attractions** are **nonbonding intermolecular interactions**.

2.8 Conformations of Alkanes

The shapes of molecules often affect their properties. A simple molecule like ethane, for example, can have an infinite number of shapes as a consequence of rotating one carbon atom (and its attached hydrogens) with respect to the other carbon atom. These arrangements are called **conformations** or **conformers**. Conformers are **stereoisomers**, isomers in which the atoms are connected in the same order but are arranged differently in space. Two possible conformers for ethane are shown in Figure 2.5.*

Different **conformations** (shapes) of the same molecule that are interconvertible by rotation around a single bond are called **conformers** or **rotamers**. Conformers are **stereoisomers**, isomers with the same atom connectivity but different spatial arrangements of atoms.

*Build a 3D model of ethane (using a molecular model kit) and use it as you read this section to model the staggered and eclipsed conformations shown in Figure 2.5.

In the staggered conformation of ethane, each C—H bond on one carbon bisects an H—C—H angle on the other carbon. In the eclipsed conformation, C—H bonds on the front and back carbons are aligned. By rotating one carbon 60° with respect to the other, we can interconvert staggered and eclipsed conformations. Between these two extremes are an infinite number of intermediate conformations of ethane.

The staggered and eclipsed conformations of ethane can be regarded as **rotamers** because each is convertible to the other by rotation about the carbon–carbon bond. Such rotation about a single bond occurs easily because the amount of overlap of the sp^3 orbitals on the two carbon atoms is unaffected by rotation about the sigma bond (see Figure 1.8). Indeed, there is enough energy available at room temperature for the staggered and eclipsed conformers of ethane to interconvert rapidly. Consequently, the conformers cannot be separated from one another. We know from various types of physical evidence, however, that both forms are not equally stable. The staggered conformation is the most stable (has the lowest potential energy) of all ethane conformations, while the eclipsed conformation is the least stable (has the highest potential energy). At room temperature, the staggered conformation is practically the only conformation present.

(2.1)

staggered   eclipsed

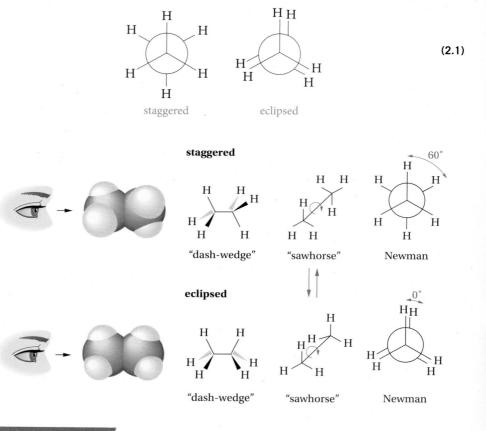

■ **Figure 2.5**
Two of the possible conformations of ethane: staggered and eclipsed. Interconversion is easy via a 60° rotation about the C—C bond, as shown by the curved arrows. The structures at the left are space-filling models. In each case, the next structure is a "dash-wedge" structure, which, if viewed as shown by the eyes, converts to the "sawhorse" drawing, or the Newman projection at the right, an end-on view down the C—C axis. In the Newman projection, the circle represents two connected carbon atoms. Bonds on the "front" carbon go to the center of the circle, and bonds on the "rear" carbon go only to the edge of the circle.

EXAMPLE 2.4

Draw the Newman projections for the staggered and eclipsed conformations of propane.

Solution

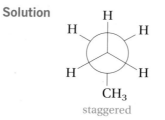

staggered

The projection formula is similar to that of ethane, except for the replacement of one hydrogen with methyl.

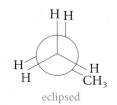

eclipsed

Rotation of the "rear" carbon of the staggered conformation by 60° gives the eclipsed conformation shown.

We are looking down the C_1—C_2 bond.

PROBLEM 2.9 Draw Newman projections for two different *staggered* conformations of butane (looking end-on at the bond between carbon-2 and carbon-3), and predict which of the two conformations is more stable. (If you have a model kit, build a model of butane to help you visualize the Newman projections.)

The most important thing to remember about conformers is that they are just different forms of a single molecule that can be interconverted by rotational motions about single (sigma) bonds. More often than not, there is sufficient thermal energy for this rotation at room temperature. Consequently, at room temperature, it is usually not possible to separate conformers from one another.

Now let us look at the structures of cycloalkanes and their conformations.

2.9 Cycloalkane Nomenclature and Conformation

Cycloalkanes are saturated hydrocarbons that have at least one ring of carbon atoms. A common example is cyclohexane.

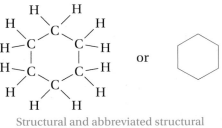

Structural and abbreviated structural
formulas for cyclohexane

Cycloalkanes are named by placing the prefix *cyclo-* before the alkane name that corresponds to the number of carbon atoms in the ring. The structures and names of the first six unsubstituted cycloalkanes are as follows:

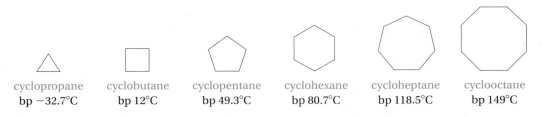

| cyclopropane | cyclobutane | cyclopentane | cyclohexane | cycloheptane | cyclooctane |
| bp −32.7°C | bp 12°C | bp 49.3°C | bp 80.7°C | bp 118.5°C | bp 149°C |

Alkyl or halogen substituents attached to the rings are named in the usual way. If only one substituent is present, no number is needed to locate it. If there are several substituents, numbers are required. One substituent is always located at ring carbon number 1, and the remaining ring carbons are then numbered consecutively in a way that gives the other substituents the lowest possible numbers. With different substituents, the one with highest alphabetic priority is located at carbon 1. The following examples illustrate the system:

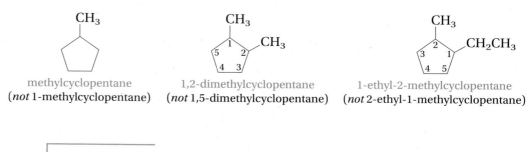

methylcyclopentane
(*not* 1-methylcyclopentane)

1,2-dimethylcyclopentane
(*not* 1,5-dimethylcyclopentane)

1-ethyl-2-methylcyclopentane
(*not* 2-ethyl-1-methylcyclopentane)

PROBLEM 2.10 The general formula for an alkane is C_nH_{2n+2}. What is the corresponding formula for a cycloalkane with one ring?

PROBLEM 2.11 Draw the structural formulas for

a. 1,3-dimethylcyclohexane
b. 1,2,3-trichlorocyclopropane
c. 1,2-diethylcyclobutane
d. 1-ethyl-3-fluorocyclopentane

PROBLEM 2.12 Give IUPAC names for

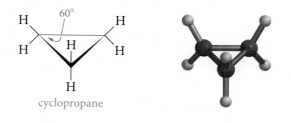

What are the conformations of cycloalkanes? Cyclopropane, with only three carbon atoms, is necessarily planar (because three points determine a plane). The C—C—C angle is only 60° (the carbons form an equilateral triangle), much less than the usual sp^3 tetrahedral angle of 109.5°. The hydrogens lie above and below the carbon plane, and hydrogens on adjacent carbons are eclipsed.

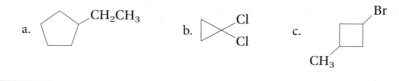

cyclopropane

EXAMPLE 2.5

Explain why the hydrogens in cyclopropane lie above and below the carbon plane.

Solution Refer to Figure 1.10. The carbons in cyclopropane have a geometry similar to that shown there, except that the C—C—C angle is "squeezed" and is smaller than tetrahedral. In compensation, the H—C—H angle is expanded and is larger than tetrahedral, approximately 120°.

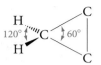

The H—C—H plane perpendicularly bisects the C—C—C plane, which, as drawn here, lies in the plane of the paper.

Cycloalkanes with more than three carbon atoms are nonplanar and have "puckered" conformations. In cyclobutane and cyclopentane, puckering allows the molecule to adopt the most stable conformation (with the least strain energy). Puckering introduces strain by making the C—C—C angles a little smaller than they would be if the molecules were planar; however, less eclipsing of the adjacent hydrogens compensates for this.

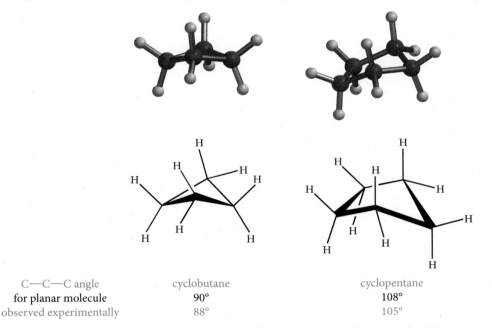

C—C—C angle	cyclobutane	cyclopentane
for planar molecule	90°	108°
observed experimentally	88°	105°

Six-membered rings are rather special and have been studied in great detail because they are very common in nature. If cyclohexane were planar, the internal C—C—C angles would be those of a regular hexagon, 120°—quite a bit larger than the normal tetrahedral angle (109.5°). The resulting strain prevents cyclohexane from being planar (flat). Its most favored conformation is the **chair conformation**, an arrangement in which all of the C—C—C angles are 109.5° and all of the hydrogens on adjacent carbon atoms are perfectly staggered. Figure 2.6 shows models of the cyclohexane chair conformation.* (If a set of molecular models is available, it would be a good idea

In the **chair conformation** of cyclohexane, the six **axial** hydrogen atoms lie above and below the mean plane of the ring, while the six **equatorial** hydrogens lie in the plane.

---

*Diamond is one naturally occurring form of carbon. In the diamond crystal, the carbon atoms are connected to one another in a structure similar to the chair form of cyclohexane, except that all of the hydrogens are replaced by carbon atoms, resulting in a continuous network of carbon atoms. The hydrocarbons **adamantane** and **diamantane** show the beginnings of the diamond structure in their fusing of chair cyclohexanes. For a fascinating article on diamond structure, see "Diamond Cleavage" by M. F. Ansell in *Chemistry in Britain,* **1984,** 1017–1021.

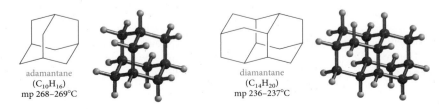

adamantane
($C_{10}H_{16}$)
mp 268–269°C

diamantane
($C_{14}H_{20}$)
mp 236–237°C

▪ Figure 2.6

The chair conformation of cyclohexane, shown in ball-and-stick (left) and space-filling (center) models. The axial hydrogens, depicted in green, lie above or below the mean plane of the carbons, and the six equatorial hydrogens, depicted in red, lie approximately in that mean plane. The carbon atoms are depicted in gray. The origin of the chair terminology is illustrated at the right.

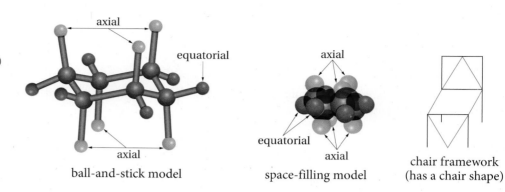

ball-and-stick model   space-filling model   chair framework (has a chair shape)

for you to construct a cyclohexane model to better visualize the concepts discussed in this and the next two sections.)

> **PROBLEM 2.13** How are the H—C—H and C—C—C planes at any one carbon atom in cyclohexane related? (Refer, if necessary, to Example 2.5.)

In the chair conformation, the hydrogens in cyclohexane fall into two sets, called **axial** and **equatorial**. Three axial hydrogens lie above and three lie below the average plane of the carbon atoms; the six equatorial hydrogens lie approximately in that plane. By a motion in which alternate ring carbons (say, 1, 3, and 5) move in one direction (down) and the other three ring carbons move in the opposite direction (up), one chair conformation can be converted into another chair conformation in which all axial hydrogens have become equatorial, and all equatorial hydrogens have become axial.

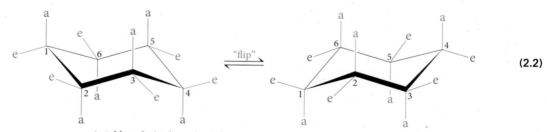

(2.2)

Axial bonds (red) in the left structure become equatorial bonds (red) in the right structure when the ring "flips."

At room temperature, this flipping process is rapid, but at low temperatures (say, −90°C), it slows down enough that the two different types of hydrogens can actually be detected by proton nuclear magnetic resonance (NMR) spectroscopy (see Chapter 12).

Cyclohexane conformations have another important feature. If you look carefully at the space-filling model of cyclohexane (Figure 2.6), you will notice that *the three axial hydrogens on the same face of the ring are close to each other*. If an axial hydrogen is replaced by a larger substituent (such as a methyl group), the axial crowding is even worse. Therefore, the preferred conformation is the one in which the larger substituent, in this case the methyl group, is equatorial (Figure 2.7).

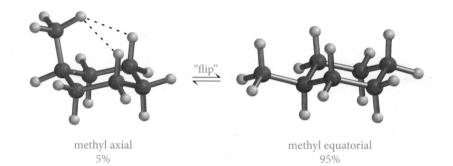

methyl axial
5%

methyl equatorial
95%

▬ **Figure 2.7**
Conformational equilibrium between the axial (left) and equatorial (right) isomers of methylcyclohexane. The steric interactions between the axial methyl and the 1,3-diaxial hydrogens are evident in the left ball-and-stick structure.

PROBLEM 2.14 Another puckered conformation for cyclohexane, one in which all C—C—C angles are the normal 109.5°, is the boat conformation.

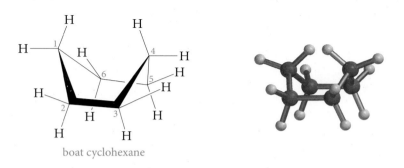

boat cyclohexane

Explain why this conformation is very much less stable than the chair conformation. (*Hint:* Note the arrangement of hydrogens as you sight along the bond between carbon-2 and carbon-3; a molecular model will help you answer this problem.)

PROBLEM 2.15 For *tert*-butylcyclohexane, only one conformation, with the *tert*-butyl group equatorial, is detected experimentally. Explain why this conformational preference is greater than that for methylcyclohexane (see Figure 2.7).

The six-membered ring in the chair conformation is a common structural feature of many organic molecules, including sugar molecules (Sec. 16.7) like glucose, where one ring carbon is replaced by an oxygen atom.

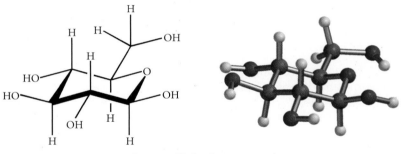

glucose (β-D-glucopyranose)

Notice that the bulkier group on each carbon is in the equatorial position. The conformations of sugars will be studied in greater detail in Chapter 16.

Before we proceed to reactions of alkanes and cycloalkanes, we need to consider a type of isomerism that may arise when two or more carbon atoms in a cycloalkane have substituents.

2.10 | *Cis–Trans* Isomerism in Cycloalkanes

Cis–trans isomers of cycloalkanes are a type of stereoisomer, also called **geometric** stereoisomers, in which substituents are on the same side (*cis*) or on the opposite sides (*trans*) of the ring.

Stereoisomerism deals with molecules that have the same order of attachment of the atoms, but different arrangements of the atoms in space. ***Cis–trans* isomerism** (sometimes called **geometric isomerism**) is one kind of stereoisomerism, and it is most easily understood with a specific case. Consider, for example, the possible structures of 1,2-dimethylcyclopentane. For simplicity, let us neglect the slight puckering of the ring and draw it as if it were planar. The two methyl groups may be on the same side of the ring plane or they may be on the opposite sides.

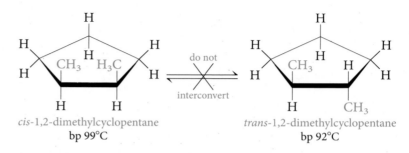

cis-1,2-dimethylcyclopentane
bp 99°C

trans-1,2-dimethylcyclopentane
bp 92°C

The methyl groups are said to be *cis* (Latin, on the same side) or *trans* (Latin, across) to each other.

Cis–trans isomers differ from one another only in the way that the atoms or groups are positioned in space. Yet this difference is sufficient to give them different physical and chemical properties. (Note, for example, the boiling points for the two 1,2-dimethylcyclopentane structures.) Therefore, *cis–trans* isomers are unique compounds. Unlike conformers, they are not readily interconverted by rotation around carbon–carbon bonds. In this example, the cyclic structure limits rotation about the ring bonds. To interconvert these dimethylcyclopentanes, one would have to break open, rotate, and re-form the ring, or carry out some other bond-breaking process.

Cis–trans isomers can be separated from each other and kept separate, usually without interconversion at room temperature. *Cis–trans* isomerism can be important in determining the biological properties of molecules. For example, a molecule in which two reactive groups are *cis* will interact differently with an enzyme or biological receptor site than will its isomer with the same two groups *trans*.

PROBLEM 2.16 Draw the structure for the *cis* and *trans* isomers of

a. 1,3-dibromocyclopentane
b. 1-chloro-2-methylcyclopropane

A WORD ABOUT... Isomers—Possible and Impossible

Table 2.1 shows that there are 75 structural isomers of the alkane $C_{10}H_{22}$. How many such isomers do you think there might be if we double the number of carbons ($C_{20}H_{42}$)? The answer is 366,319! And if we double the number of carbons again ($C_{40}H_{82}$)? Exactly 62,481,801,147,341. Of course, no one sits down with pencil and paper or molecular models and determines these numbers by constructing all the possibilities; it could take a lifetime. Complex mathematical formulas have been developed to compute these numbers.

Although we can write some isomers' formulas on paper, they are structurally impossible and cannot be synthesized. Consider, for example, the series of alkanes obtained by replacing the hydrogens of methane with methyl groups and then repeating that process on the product indefinitely. You can see from the following drawings that we build up molecules in this way with a central core of carbon atoms and a surface of hydrogen atoms.

$$CH_4 \longrightarrow C(CH_3)_4 \longrightarrow$$

$$C[C(CH_3)_3]_4 \longrightarrow C\{C[C(CH_3)_3]_3\}_4$$

$$CH_4 \longrightarrow C_5H_{12} \longrightarrow C_{17}H_{36} \longrightarrow C_{53}H_{108}$$

In three dimensions, the molecules are nearly spherical. Of these compounds, only the first two are known (methane and 2,2-dimethylpropane). The $C_{17}H_{36}$ hydrocarbon (tetra-*t*-butylmethane or, more accurately, 3,3-di-*t*-butyl-2,2,4,4-tetramethylpentane) has not yet been synthesized, and if it ever is, it will be an exceptionally strained molecule. The reason is simply that there is not enough room for all the methyl groups on the surface of the molecule.

Repetitive branching in compounds can lead to molecular shapes that resemble this tree.

Martial Colomb/Digital Vision/Getty Images

Therefore, if this $C_{17}H_{36}$ isomer is ever prepared, its bond angles and bond lengths are likely to be severely distorted from the normal. There is almost no possibility of synthesizing the $C_{53}H_{108}$ isomer in this series; its structure is too strained. It is interesting to note that, like these hydrocarbons, the growth of trees, sponges, and other biological structures is similarly limited by the ratio of surface area to volume. (For more on this subject, see the article by R. E. Davies and P. J. Freyd, *J. Chem. Educ.* **1989**, *66*, 278–281.)

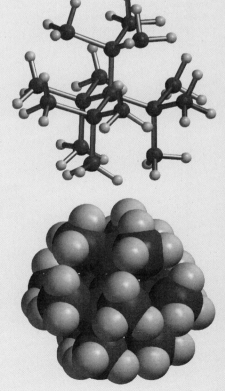

methane

2,2-dimethylpropane

tetra-*t*-butylmethane
($C_{17}H_{36}$)

2.11 / Summary of Isomerism

At this point, it may be useful to summarize the relationships of the several types of isomers we have discussed so far. These relationships are outlined in Figure 2.8.

■ **Figure 2.8**
The relationships of the various types of isomers.

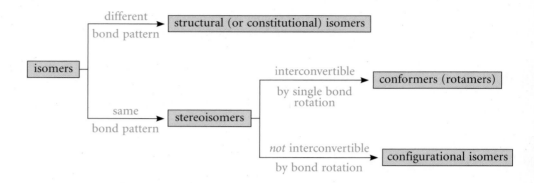

The first thing to look at in a pair of isomers is their bonding patterns (or atom connectivities). If the bonding patterns are *different,* the compounds are structural (or constitutional) isomers. But if the bonding patterns are the *same,* the compounds are stereoisomers. Examples of structural isomers are ethanol and methoxymethane (page 14) or the three isomeric pentanes (page 15). Examples of stereoisomers are the staggered and eclipsed forms of ethane (page 48) or the *cis* and *trans* isomers of 1,2-dimethylcyclopentane (page 54).

If compounds are stereoisomers, we can make a further distinction as to isomer type. If *single-bond rotation* easily interconverts the two stereoisomers (as with staggered and eclipsed ethane), we call them conformers. If the two stereoisomers can be interconverted only by breaking and remaking bonds (as with *cis-* and *trans-*1,2-dimethylcyclopentane), we call them **configurational isomers.***

Configurational isomers (such as *cis–trans* isomers) are stereoisomers that can only be interconverted by breaking and remaking bonds.

PROBLEM 2.17 Classify each of the following isomer pairs according to the scheme in Figure 2.8.

a. *cis-* and *trans-*1,2-dimethylcyclohexane
b. chair and boat forms of cyclohexane
c. 1-fluoropropane and 2-fluoropropane

2.12 / Reactions of Alkanes

All of the bonds in alkanes are single, covalent, and nonpolar. Hence alkanes are relatively inert. Alkanes ordinarily do not react with most common acids, bases, or oxidizing and reducing agents. Because of this inertness, alkanes can be used as solvents for extraction or crystallization as well as for carrying out chemical reactions of other substances. However, alkanes do react with some reagents, such as molecular oxygen and the halogens. We will discuss those reactions here.

---

*Remember that conformers are different conformations of the same molecule, whereas configurational isomers are different molecules. Geometric isomers (*cis–trans* isomers) are one type of configurational isomer. As we will see in Chapter 3, geometric isomerism also occurs in alkenes. Also, we will see other types of configurational isomers in Chapter 5.

2.12.a Oxidation and Combustion; Alkanes as Fuels

The most important use of alkanes is as fuel. With excess oxygen, alkanes burn to form carbon dioxide and water. Most important, the reactions evolve considerable heat (that is, the reactions are **exothermic**).

Exothermic reactions evolve heat.

$$CH_4 \; + \; 2\,O_2 \longrightarrow CO_2 + 2\,H_2O + \text{heat (212.8 kcal/mol)} \qquad \textbf{(2.3)}$$
methane

$$C_4H_{10} + \tfrac{13}{2}\,O_2 \longrightarrow 4\,CO_2 + 5\,H_2O + \text{heat (688.0 kcal/mol)} \qquad \textbf{(2.4)}$$
butane

These combustion reactions are the basis for the use of hydrocarbons for heat (natural gas and heating oil) and for power (gasoline). An initiation step is required—usually ignition by a spark or flame. Once initiated, the reaction proceeds spontaneously and exothermically.

In methane, all four bonds to the carbon atom are C—H bonds. In carbon dioxide, its combustion product, all four bonds to the carbon are C—O bonds. **Combustion** is an **oxidation reaction**, the replacement of C—H bonds by C—O bonds. In methane, carbon is in its most reduced form, and in carbon dioxide, it is in its most oxidized form. Intermediate oxidation states of carbon are also known, in which only one, two, or three of the C—H bonds are converted to C—O bonds. It is not surprising, then, that if insufficient oxygen is available for complete combustion of a hydrocarbon, *partial* oxidation may occur, as illustrated in eqs. 2.5 through 2.8.

Combustion of hydrocarbons is an **oxidation reaction** in which C—H bonds are replaced with C—O bonds.

$$2\,CH_4 + 3\,O_2 \longrightarrow \quad 2\,CO \quad + \quad 4\,H_2O \qquad \textbf{(2.5)}$$
carbon monoxide

$$CH_4 + O_2 \longrightarrow \quad C \quad + \quad 2\,H_2O \qquad \textbf{(2.6)}$$
carbon

$$CH_4 + O_2 \longrightarrow \quad CH_2O \quad + \quad H_2O \qquad \textbf{(2.7)}$$
formaldehyde

$$2\,C_2H_6 + 3\,O_2 \longrightarrow \quad 2\,CH_3CO_2H + 2\,H_2O \qquad \textbf{(2.8)}$$
acetic acid

Auto tailpipe exhaust fumes contain condensed water.

Toxic carbon monoxide in exhaust fumes (eq. 2.5), soot emitted copiously from trucks with diesel engines (eq. 2.6), smog resulting in part from aldehydes (eq. 2.7), and acid buildup in lubricating oils (eq. 2.8) are all prices we pay for being a motorized society.* However, incomplete hydrocarbon combustion is occasionally useful, as in the manufacture of carbon blacks (eq. 2.6) used for automobile tires, and lampblack, a pigment used in ink.

EXAMPLE 2.6

In which compound is carbon more oxidized, formaldehyde (CH_2O) or formic acid (HCO_2H)?

Solution Draw the structures:

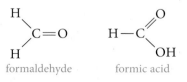

formaldehyde   formic acid

Formic acid is the more oxidized form (three C—O and one C—H bond, compared to two C—O and two C—H bonds in formaldehyde).

---

*You may have noticed white exhaust fumes coming from car tailpipes in cold weather. Combustion of hydrocarbons produces water (eqs. 2.3–2.8), so what you see is condensed water from the combustion of gasoline.

PROBLEM 2.18 Which of the following represents the more oxidized form of carbon?

a. methanol (CH_3OH) or formaldehyde (CH_2O)
b. methanol (CH_3OH) or dimethyl ether (CH_3OCH_3)
c. formaldehyde (CH_2O) or methyl formate (HCO_2CH_3)*

A WORD ABOUT...   Alternative Energy: The Benefits of Hydrogen

Our world's current dependence on petroleum and fossil fuels is significant. Besides burning these fossil fuels for energy, we use crude oil to prepare chemicals that are then used to make almost everything—the clothing we wear, the medicines we take, and the plastics, carpeting, and fabrics we use. Concerns about global warming, especially for carbon dioxide (CO_2) emissions, have further exacerbated worries about crude oil consumption and its impact on the environment and the world's population. Recently, a greater push has begun for finding alternative sources that can meet our energy demand and can provide for our chemical needs.

Alternative and renewable energy sources are being investigated, and these sources include solar energy, nuclear, biomass, wind, hydroelectric, and wave technology. Biomass, material obtained from living or recently lived organisms, provides an excellent source of carbohydrates (Chapter 16), lignins (Chapter 7), and lipids (Chapter 15). Much research has been expended into the conversion of carbohydrates, especially from corn and sugar beets, to value-added chemicals, including ethanol (CH_3CH_2OH, Chapter 7). Ethanol is used as a chemical to produce other products, as a fuel additive for gasoline-combustion engines, and for a myriad of other applications.

However, carbohydrates as precursors to chemical feedstocks present a conundrum with regard to our food supply. Should we take a food source and convert it to something that we burn in an engine instead of feeding the world's people? Moreover, due to its use in generating ethanol as a fuel additive (Chapter 8), the demand for corn caused the price of many food products to rise dramatically as corn is used to feed cattle as well as to make a host of consumed products.

Alternatively, lipids provide tremendous opportunities as they can be "harvested" from various sources, such as microbial, algal, vegetable, and animal origins, and there is significant current interest in preparing biofuels, such as biodiesel, from lipids (Chapter 15).

Another source of energy that is under investigation is hydrogen (H_2), particularly for mobile sources. Hydrogen offers many advantages over many alternative fuel sources. First, hydrogen (H_2) is a clean fuel that does not emit CO_2 when burned. A significant portion of the global CO_2 emissions comes from mobile sources, specifically cars and other transportation. When a carbon source, such as methane, is burned, CO_2 is generated (eq. 2.3). To minimize CO_2 emissions into the atmosphere, the fuel must not contain carbon. Thus, H_2 is a better choice. Second, the combustion of H_2 is very exothermic, releasing 68.4 kcal/mol of energy when one mole of H_2 is burned.

$$H_2 + \tfrac{1}{2}\,O_2 \;\longrightarrow\; H_2O + \text{heat (68.4 kcal/mol)}$$

Methane, on the other hand, releases 212.8 kcal/mol of energy. Most importantly, for H_2 as a fuel, the emissions are pretty simple, just water. No CO_2, NO, or NO_2 is generated—the latter two are related to formation of tropospheric ozone, which is deleterious to human health.

Our current combustion engines have to be modified for using H_2 as this fuel ignites rapidly, but this issue has been resolved by vehicle manufacturers. Transporting hydrogen, though, is a challenge. Gaseous H_2 takes up a lot of space. Tankers can liquefy H_2 to very low temperatures to reduce its volume for transport, but this is not so easy for a family sedan.

Hence, an emerging area of chemical research is how to make H_2 from easily transportable sources. For example, three units of H_2 could be generated from ethanol (CH_3CH_2OH). A person could fill up a vehicle at the "ethanol pump," and, as needed, some on-board catalyst could convert it into H_2 for combustion in the engine. This work is at the forefront of basic and applied research.

See Problems 2.49 and 2.53.

---

*See Table 1.6 for the generic structure of an ester.

2.12.b Halogenation of Alkanes

When a mixture of an alkane and chlorine gas is stored at low temperatures in the dark, no reaction occurs. In sunlight or at high temperatures, however, an exothermic reaction occurs. One or more hydrogen atoms of the alkane are replaced by chlorine atoms. This reaction can be represented by the general equation

$$R-H + Cl-Cl \xrightarrow[\text{heat}]{\text{light or}} R-Cl + H-Cl \qquad (2.9)$$

or, specifically for methane:

$$CH_4 + Cl-Cl \xrightarrow[\text{or heat}]{\text{sunlight}} CH_3Cl + HCl \qquad (2.10)$$

methane   chloromethane
(methyl chloride)
bp $-24.2°C$

The reaction is called **chlorination**. This process is a **substitution reaction**, as a chlorine is substituted for a hydrogen.

     An analogous reaction, called **bromination**, occurs when the halogen source is bromine.

$$R-H + Br-Br \xrightarrow[\text{heat}]{\text{light or}} R-Br + HBr \qquad (2.11)$$

> **Chlorination** of hydrocarbons is a **substitution reaction** in which a chlorine atom is substituted for a hydrogen atom. Likewise in **bromination** reactions, a bromine atom is substituted for a hydrogen atom.

If excess halogen is present, the reaction can continue further to give polyhalogenated products. Thus, methane and excess chlorine can give products with two, three, or four chlorines.*

$$CH_3Cl \xrightarrow{Cl_2} CH_2Cl_2 \xrightarrow{Cl_2} CHCl_3 \xrightarrow{Cl_2} CCl_4 \qquad (2.12)$$

          dichloromethane   trichloromethane   tetrachloromethane
       (methylene chloride)   (chloroform)   (carbon tetrachloride)
           bp $40°C$ bp $61.7°C$ bp $76.5°C$

By controlling the reaction conditions and the ratio of chlorine to methane, we can favor formation of one or another of the possible products.

> **PROBLEM 2.19** Write the names and structures of all possible products for the bromination of methane.

With longer chain alkanes, mixtures of products may be obtained even at the first step.** For example, with propane,

$$CH_3CH_2CH_3 + Cl_2 \xrightarrow[\text{or heat}]{\text{light}} CH_3CH_2CH_2Cl + CH_3\overset{\displaystyle |}{\underset{\displaystyle Cl}{C}}HCH_3 + HCl \qquad (2.13)$$

propane   1-chloropropane   2-chloropropane
                        (*n*-propyl chloride)   (isopropyl chloride)

When larger alkanes are halogenated, the mixture of products becomes even more complex; individual isomers become difficult to separate and obtain pure, so halogenation

---

*Note that we sometimes write the formula of one of the reactants (in this case Cl_2) over the arrow for convenience, as in eq. 2.12. We also sometimes omit obvious inorganic products (in this case, HCl).

**Note that we often do not write a balanced equation, especially when more than one product is formed from a single organic reactant. Instead, we show, on the right side of the equation, the structures of *all* of the important organic products, as in eq. 2.13.

A WORD ABOUT... Methane, Marsh Gas, and Miller's Experiment

Methane is commonly found in nature wherever bacteria decompose organic matter in the absence of oxygen, as in marshes, swamps, or the muddy sediment of lakes—hence, its common name, *marsh gas*. In China, methane has been collected from the mud at the bottom of swamps for use in domestic cooking and lighting. Methane is similarly formed from bacteria in the digestive tracts of certain ruminant animals, such as cows.

The scale of methane production by bacteria is considerable. The earth's atmosphere contains an average of 1 part per million of methane. Because our planet is small and because methane is light compared to most other air constituents (O_2, N_2), one would expect most of the methane to have escaped from our atmosphere, and it has been calculated that the equilibrium concentration should be very much less than is observed. The reason, then, for the relatively high observed concentration is that at the same time that methane escapes from the atmosphere, it is constantly replenished by bacterial decay of plant matter.

In cities, the amount of methane in the atmosphere reaches much higher levels, up to several parts per million. The peak concentrations come in the early morning and late afternoon, directly correlated with the peaks of automobile traffic. Fortunately, methane, which constitutes about 50% of urban atmospheric hydrocarbon pollutants, seems to have no direct harmful effect on human health.

Methane can accumulate in coal mines, where it is a hazard because, when mixed with 5% to 14% of air, it is explosive. Also, miners can be asphyxiated by it (due to lack of sufficient oxygen). Dangerous concentrations of methane can be detected readily by a variety of safety devices.

Hydrogen is the most common element in the solar system (it constitutes about 87% of the sun's mass). It therefore seemed reasonable to think that, when the planets were formed, other elements should have been present in reduced (not oxidized) forms: carbon as methane, nitrogen as ammonia, and oxygen as water. Indeed, some of the outer planets (Saturn and Jupiter) still have atmospheres that are rich in methane and ammonia.

A now-famous experiment by Stanley L. Miller (working in the laboratory of H. C. Urey at Columbia University)

Coal mining in Appalachia.

supports the idea that life could have arisen in a reducing atmosphere. Miller found that when mixtures of methane, ammonia, water, and hydrogen were subjected to electric discharges (to simulate lightning), some organic compounds (amino acids, for example) that are important to biology and necessary for life were formed. Similar results have since been obtained using heat or ultraviolet light in place of electric discharges (it seems likely that the earth's early atmosphere was subjected to much more ultraviolet radiation than it is now). When oxygen was added to these simulated primeval atmospheres, no amino acids were produced—strong evidence that the earth's original atmosphere did *not* contain free oxygen.

In the years since Miller's experiment, ideas about the chemistry of life's origin have become more precise as a consequence of much experimentation and of exploration in outer space. We now know that the earth's primary atmosphere was formed mainly by degassing the molten interior rather than by accretion from the solar nebula. It seems likely that the main carbon sources in the earth's early atmosphere were CO_2 and CO, *not* methane as assumed by Miller, and that nitrogen was present mainly as N_2 rather than as ammonia. Repetition of Miller-type experiments with these assumed primordial atmospheres again gave biomolecules.

Miller's experiment provided a model for much work in the branch of a science now called **chemical evolution** or **prebiotic chemistry**, the study of chemical events that may have taken place on earth or elsewhere in the universe leading to the appearance of the first living cell. For additional reading, you can consult *Chemical Evolution* by Stephen F. Mason, Clarendon Press, Oxford, 1991.

See Problem 2.54.

tends not to be a useful way to synthesize specific alkyl halides. With unsubstituted *cycloalkanes*, however, where all of the hydrogens are equivalent, a single pure organic product can be obtained:

$$\text{cyclopentane} + Br_2 \xrightarrow{\text{light}} \text{bromocyclopentane} + HBr \qquad (2.14)$$

cyclopentane

bromocyclopentane
(cyclopentyl bromide)

PROBLEM 2.20 Write the structures of all possible products of *monochlori-nation* of pentane. Note the complexity of the product mixture, compared to that from the corresponding reaction with *cyclo*pentane (eq. 2.14).

PROBLEM 2.21 How many organic products can be obtained from the monobromination of heptane? Of cycloheptane?

PROBLEM 2.22 Do you think that the bromination of 2,2-dimethylpropane might be synthetically useful?

2.13 The Free-Radical Chain Mechanism of Halogenation

One may well ask how halogenation occurs. Why is light or heat necessary? Equations 2.9 and 2.10 express the *overall* reaction for halogenation. They describe the structures of the reactants and the products, and they show necessary reaction conditions or catalysts over the arrow. But they do *not* tell us exactly how the products are formed from the reactants.

A **reaction mechanism** is a step-by-step description of the bond-breaking and bond-making processes that occur when reagents react to form products. In the case of halogenation, various experiments show that this reaction occurs in several steps, and not in one magical step. Indeed, halogenation occurs via a **free-radical chain** of reactions.

The **chain-initiating step** is the breaking of the halogen molecule into two halogen atoms.

A **reaction mechanism** is a step-by-step description of the bond-breaking and bond-making processes that occur when reagents react to form products.

A **free-radical chain reaction** includes a **chain-initiating step**, **chain-propagating steps**, and **chain-terminating steps**.

$$\textit{initiation} \qquad :\!\ddot{C}l\!:\!\ddot{C}l\!: \xrightarrow[\text{or heat}]{\text{light}} :\!\ddot{C}l\cdot + :\!\ddot{C}l\cdot \qquad (2.15)^*$$

chlorine molecule   chlorine atoms

The Cl—Cl bond is weaker than either the C—H bond or the C—C bond (compare the bond energies, Table A in the Appendix), and is therefore the easiest bond to break by supplying heat energy. When light is the energy source, molecular chlorine (Cl_2) absorbs visible light but alkanes do not. Thus, once again, the Cl—Cl bond would break first.

---

*Recall from Section 1.13 that we use a "fishhook," or half-headed arrow, ⌒, to show the movement of only *one* electron, whereas we use a complete (double-headed) arrow, ⌒, to describe the movement of an electron *pair*.

The **chain-propagating steps** are

propagation
$$R\!-\!H + \cdot\ddot{C}l\colon \longrightarrow R\cdot + H\!-\!Cl \qquad (2.16)$$
alkyl
radical

$$R\cdot + Cl\!-\!Cl \longrightarrow R\!-\!Cl + \cdot\ddot{C}l\colon \qquad (2.17)$$
alkyl
chloride

Chlorine atoms are very reactive, because they have an incomplete valence shell (seven electrons instead of the required eight). They may either recombine to form chlorine molecules (the reverse of eq. 2.15) or, if they collide with an alkane molecule, abstract a hydrogen atom to form hydrogen chloride and an alkyl radical R•. Recall from Section 1.4 that a radical is a fragment with an odd number of unshared electrons. The space-filling models in Figure 2.1 show that alkanes seem to have an exposed surface of hydrogens covering the carbon skeleton. So it is most likely that, if a halogen atom collides with an alkane molecule, it will hit the hydrogen end of a C—H bond.

Like a chlorine atom, the alkyl radical formed in the first step of the chain (eq. 2.16) is very reactive (note that the alkyl radical, like the halogen radical, has an incomplete octet). If the alkyl radical was to collide with a chlorine molecule (Cl_2), it could form an alkyl chloride molecule and a chlorine atom (eq. 2.17). The chlorine atom formed in this step can then react to repeat the sequence. When you add eq. 2.16 and eq. 2.17, you get the overall equation for chlorination (eq. 2.9). In each chain-propagating step, a radical (or atom) is consumed, but another radical (or atom) is formed and can continue the chain. Almost all of the reactants are consumed, and almost all of the products are formed in these steps.

Were it not for **chain-terminating steps**, all of the reactants could, in principle, be consumed by initiating a single reaction chain. However, because many chlorine molecules react to form chlorine atoms in the chain-initiating step, many chains are started simultaneously. Quite a few radicals are present as the reaction proceeds. If any two radicals combine, the chain will be terminated. Three possible chain-terminating steps are

termination
$$:\ddot{C}l\cdot + \cdot\ddot{C}l\colon \longrightarrow Cl - Cl \qquad (2.18)$$

$$R\cdot + \cdot R \longrightarrow R - R \qquad (2.19)$$

$$R\cdot + \cdot\ddot{C}l\cdot \longrightarrow R - Cl \qquad (2.20)$$

No new radicals are formed in these reactions, so the chain is broken or, as we say, terminated. Note that eq. 2.20 is a useful reaction as it leads to a desired product, but the other termination reactions lead to regeneration of the starting halogen (Cl_2, eq. 2.18) or a byproduct (eq. 2.19).

PROBLEM 2.23 Show that when eq. 2.16 and eq. 2.17 are added, the overall equation for chlorination (eq. 2.9) results.

PROBLEM 2.24 Write equations for all of the steps (initiation, propagation, and termination) in the free-radical chlorination of methane to form methyl chloride.

PROBLEM 2.25 Account for the experimental observation that small amounts of ethane and chloroethane are produced during the monochlorination of methane. (*Hint:* Consider the possible chain-terminating steps.)

REACTION SUMMARY

1. Reactions of Alkanes and Cycloalkanes

a. Combustion (Sec. 2.12a)

$$C_nH_{2n+2} + \left(\frac{3n+1}{2}\right)O_2 \longrightarrow nCO_2 + (n+1)H_2O$$

b. Halogenation (Sec. 2.12b)

$$R—H + X_2 \xrightarrow[\text{or light}]{\text{heat}} R—X + H—X \quad (X = Cl, Br)$$

MECHANISM SUMMARY

1. Halogenation (Sec. 2.13)

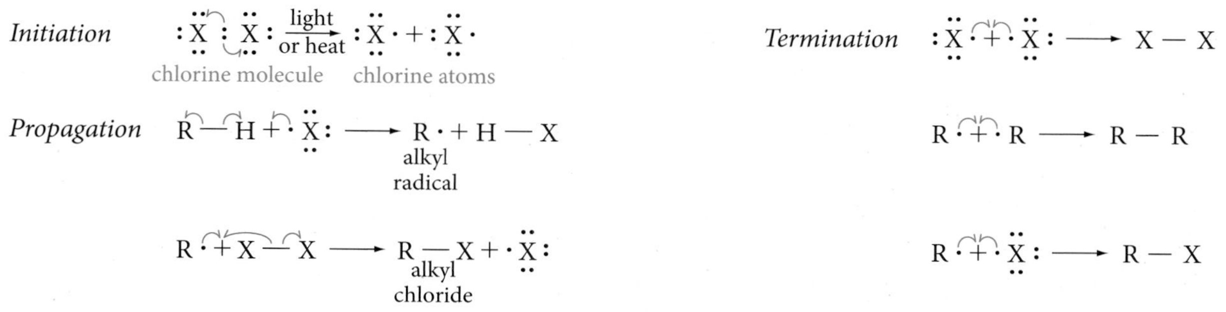

Initiation

$$:\ddot{X}—\ddot{X}: \xrightarrow[\text{or heat}]{\text{light}} :\ddot{X}· + :\ddot{X}·$$

chlorine molecule   chlorine atoms

Propagation

$$R—H + ·\ddot{X}: \longrightarrow R· + H—X$$
alkyl radical

$$R· + X—X \longrightarrow R—X + ·\ddot{X}:$$
alkyl chloride

Termination

$$:\ddot{X}· + ·\ddot{X}: \longrightarrow X—X$$

$$R· + ·R \longrightarrow R—R$$

$$R· + ·\ddot{X}: \longrightarrow R—X$$

$(X = Cl, Br)$

ADDITIONAL PROBLEMS

⏾WL Interactive versions of these problems are assignable in OWL.

Alkane Nomenclature and Structural Formulas

2.26 Write structural formulas for the following compounds:

a. 2-methylhexane
d. 2-bromo-4-methyloctane
g. 1-isopropyl-1,3-dimethylcyclohexane
b. 2,3-dimethylbutane
e. 1,1-diiodocyclobutane
h. 1,1,2-trifluoropropane
c. 4-ethyl-2,2-dimethylheptane
f. 2-chlorobutane
i. 1,1,3,3-tetrachlorocyclopropane

2.27 Write expanded formulas for the following compounds and name them using the IUPAC system:

a. $(CH_3)_3CCH_2CH_2CH_3$
d. $CH_3CCl_2CF_3$
g. EtBr
b. $CH_3(CH_2)_2CH_3$
e. $(CH_2)_4$
h. $ClCH_2CH_2Cl$
c. $(CH_3)_2CHCH_2CH_2CH_3$
f. $CH_3CH_2CHFCH_3$
i. *i*-PrCl

2.28 Give both common and IUPAC names for the following compounds:

a. CH_3Br
d. $(CH_3)_2CHBr$
g. $CH_3CH_2CH_2CH_2F$
b. CH_3CH_2Cl
e. CHI_3
c. CH_2Cl_2
f. $(CH_3)_3CCl$

2.29 Write a structure for each of the compounds listed. Explain why the name given here is incorrect, and give a correct name in each case.

   a. 2,3-fluoropropane
   d. 1-methyl-2-ethylcyclopropane
   g. 1,3-dimethylcyclopropane

   b. 1-methylbutane
   e. 1,1,3-trimethylhexane

   c. 2-ethylbutane
   f. 4-bromo-3-methylbutane

2.30 Chemical substances used for communication in nature are called *pheromones.* The pheromone used by the female tiger moth to attract the male is the 18-carbon-atom alkane 2-methylheptadecane. Write its structural formula.

2.31 Write the structural formulas for all isomers of each of the following compounds, and name each isomer by the IUPAC system. (The number of isomers is indicated in parentheses.)

   a. C_4H_{10} (2)
   d. $C_3H_6Br_2$ (4)

   b. C_4H_9Cl (4)
   e. $C_2H_2ClBr_3$ (3)

   c. C_3H_6FCl (5)
   f. C_5H_{12} (3)

2.32 Write structural formulas and names for all possible cycloalkanes having each of the following molecular formulas. Be sure to include *cis–trans* isomers when appropriate. Name each compound by the IUPAC system.

   a. C_5H_{10} (there are 6)

   b. C_6H_{12} (there are 16)

2.33 Write a correct IUPAC name for each of the following structures:

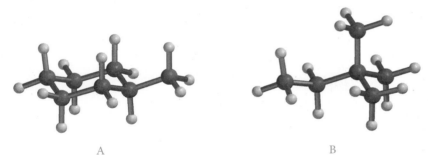

   A   B

2.34 Draw the tetra-ethyl analog of 2,2-dimethylpropane as discussed in "A Word About... Isomers—Possible and Impossible" on page 55. What is the correct IUPAC name for this compound? Make models of this compound and 2,2-dimethylpropane and compare how sterically congested they are.

Alkane Properties and Intermolecular Interactions

2.35 Without referring to tables, arrange the following five hydrocarbons in order of increasing boiling point. (*Hint:* Draw structures or make models of the five hydrocarbons to see their shapes and sizes.)

   a. 2-methylhexane
   d. hexane

   b. heptane
   e. 2-methylpentane

   c. 3,3-dimethylpentane

Explain your answer in terms of intermolecular interactions.

2.36 Arrange the following liquids in order from least soluble in hexane to most soluble in hexane:

   a.   **b.**   **c.**

Explain your answer in terms of intermolecular interactions.

Conformations of Alkanes

2.37 In Problem 2.9, you drew two staggered conformations of butane (looking end-on down the bond between carbon-2 and carbon-3). There are also two eclipsed conformations around this bond. Draw Newman projections for them. Arrange all four conformations in order of decreasing stability.

2.38 Draw the Newman projections for the unique staggered and eclipsed conformers of 2-methylbutane.

2.39 Draw all possible staggered and eclipsed conformations of 1-bromo-2-chloroethane (see the following ball-and-stick model), using Newman projections. Underneath each structure, draw the corresponding "dash-wedge" and "sawhorse" structures. Rank the conformations in order of decreasing stability.

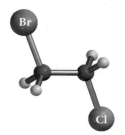

Conformations of Cycloalkanes; *Cis–Trans* Isomerism

2.40 Draw the formula for the preferred conformation of

    a. *cis*-1,4-dimethylcyclohexane   **b.** *trans*-1-isopropyl-3-methylcyclohexane
    c. 1,1-diethylcyclopentane   **d.** ethylcyclohexane

2.41 Name the following *cis–trans* pairs:

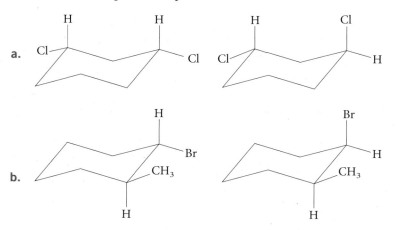

2.42 Explain with the aid of conformational structures why *cis*-1,3-dimethylcyclohexane is more stable than *trans*-1,3-dimethylcyclohexane, whereas the reverse order of stability is observed for the 1,2 and 1,4 isomers. (Constructing models will help you with this problem.)

2.43 Draw structural formulas for all possible dimethylcyclobutanes. Include *cis–trans* isomers.

2.44 Which will be more stable, *cis*- or *trans*-1,4-di-*tert*-butylcyclohexane? Explain your answer by drawing conformational structures for each compound.

2.45 Examine the relationships of isomers as described in Figure 2.8 (p. 56). Then classify the following pairs of structures as structural isomers, conformers, configurational (*cis–trans*) isomers, or identical.

a. the pairs of compounds in Problem 2.41

b.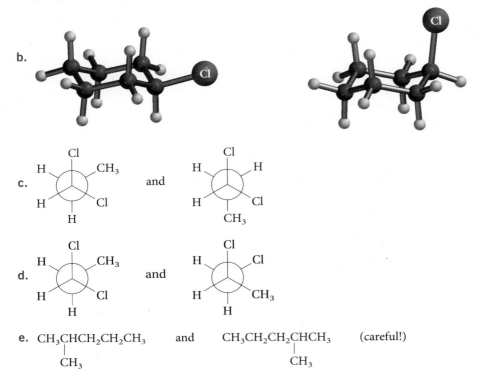

c.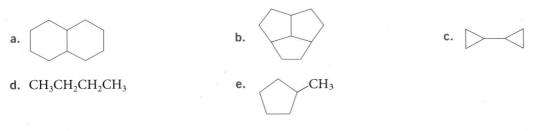

e. CH₃CHCH₂CH₂CH₃   and   CH₃CH₂CH₂CHCH₃   (careful!)
    | |
    CH₃   CH₃

2.46 Draw structural formulas for all possible difluorocyclohexanes. Include *cis–trans* isomers.

Reactions of Alkanes: Combustion and Halogenation

2.47 How many monobromination products can be obtained from each of the following polycyclic alkanes?

a.

b.

c.

d. CH₃CH₂CH₂CH₃

e. ⬠CH₃

2.48 Using structural formulas, write equations for each of the following combustion reactions (see Reaction Summary 1.a, p. 63):

   a. the complete combustion of propane
   b. the complete combustion of pentane
   c. the complete combustion of butane

2.49 Petroleum diesel is a complex fuel mixture, typically composed of alkanes with carbon chains containing 8 to 21 carbon atoms. Using a 10-carbon alkane as an example, write a balanced equation for the complete combustion of this fuel to CO_2 and H_2O.

2.50 Using structural formulas, write equations for the following halogenation reactions (see Reaction Summary 1.b, p. 63), and name each organic product:

   a. the monochlorination of propane
   b. the monobromination of cyclopentane
   c. the complete chlorination of butane
   d. the monobromination of methylcyclohexane

2.51 From the dichlorination of propane, four isomeric products with the formula $C_3H_6Cl_2$ were isolated and designated A, B, C, and D. Each was separated and further chlorinated to give one or more trichloropropanes, $C_3H_5Cl_3$. A and B gave three trichloro compounds, C gave one, and D gave two. Deduce the structures of C and D. One of the products from A was identical to the product from C. Deduce structures for A and B. (*Hint:* Start by drawing the structures of all four dichlorinated propane isomers.)

2.52 Write all of the steps in the free-radical chain mechanism for the monochlorination of ethane (see Mechanism Summary, p. 63).

$$CH_3CH_3 + Cl_2 \longrightarrow CH_3CH_2Cl + HCl$$

What trace by-products would you expect to be formed as a consequence of the chain-terminating steps?

2.53 Using methanol (CH_3OH) as a fuel source, write a balanced reaction for the formation of H_2. Do the same for $C_{10}H_{22}$ (a component of diesel fuel). For an H_2 fuel cell, why would it be better to use $C_{10}H_{22}$ rather than methanol? What would be a possible disadvantage?

2.54 As noted in the "A Word about...Methane, Marsh Gas, and Miller's Experiment" on page 60, methane can be formed in muddy sediments because of the reducing environment (i.e., lack of oxygen). Write a balanced reaction for the conversion of glucose ($C_6H_{12}O_6$, Sec. 2.9) with molecular hydrogen (H_2) to form methane and water.

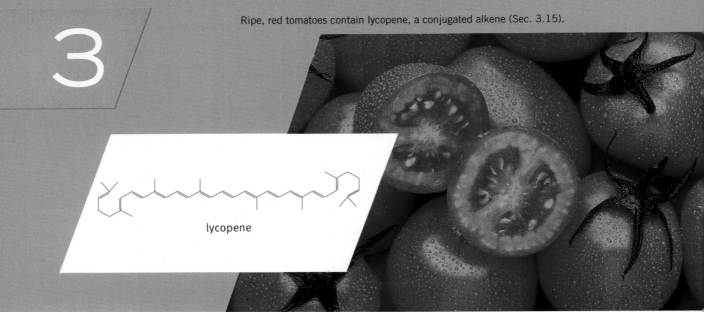

Ripe, red tomatoes contain lycopene, a conjugated alkene (Sec. 3.15).

lycopene

© Herminia Dosal/Photo Researchers

Alkenes and Alkynes

Alkenes are compounds containing carbon–carbon double bonds. The simplest alkene, ethene, is a plant hormone (see "A Word About . . . Ethylene," pp. 98–99) and an important starting material for the manufacture of other organic compounds (see Figure 3.13, p. 98). The alkene functional group is found in sources as varied as citrus fruits (limonene, Fig. 1.12), steroids (cholesterol, Sec. 15.9), and insect pheromones (muscalure; see "A Word about the Gypsy Moth's Epoxide," p. 245). Alkenes have physical properties similar to those of alkanes (Sec. 2.7). They are less dense than water and, being nonpolar, are not very soluble in water. As with alkanes, compounds with four or fewer carbons are colorless gases, whereas higher homologs are volatile liquids.

Alkynes, compounds containing carbon–carbon triple bonds, are similar to alkenes in their physical properties and chemical behavior. In this chapter, we will examine the structure and chemical reactions of these two classes of compounds. We will also examine briefly the relationship between chemical reactions and energy.

ʊWL

Online homework for this chapter can be assigned in OWL, an online homework assessment tool.

Hydrocarbons that contain a carbon–carbon double bond are called **alkenes**; those with a carbon–carbon triple bond are **alkynes**.* Their general formulas are

$$C_nH_{2n} \qquad C_nH_{2n-2}$$

alkenes   alkynes

Both of these classes of hydrocarbons are **unsaturated**, because they contain fewer hydrogens per carbon than alkanes (C_nH_{2n+2}). Alkanes can be obtained from alkenes or alkynes by adding 1 or 2 moles of hydrogen.

$$
\begin{array}{c}
RCH{=}CHR \\
\text{alkene}
\end{array}
\quad
\begin{array}{c}
\xrightarrow[\text{catalyst}]{H_2} \\[6pt]
\xrightarrow[\text{catalyst}]{2H_2}
\end{array}
\quad
\begin{array}{c}
RCH_2CH_2R \\
\text{alkane}
\end{array}
\qquad (3.1)
$$

$$
\begin{array}{c}
RC{\equiv}CR \\
\text{alkyne}
\end{array}
$$

Compounds with more than one double or triple bond exist. If two double bonds are present, the compounds are called **alkadienes** or, more commonly, **dienes**. There are also trienes, tetraenes, and even polyenes (compounds with *many* double bonds, from the Greek *poly*, many). Polyenes are responsible for the color of carrots (β-carotene, p. 76) and tomatoes (lycopene, p. 68). Compounds with more than one triple bond, or with double and triple bonds, are also known.

> Alkenes and alkynes are unsaturated hydrocarbons containing carbon–carbon double bonds and carbon–carbon triple bonds, respectively.

> Alkadienes, or dienes, contain two C—C double bonds that can be cumulated (next to each other), conjugated (separated by one C—C single bond), or nonconjugated (separated by more than one C—C single bond).

EXAMPLE 3.1

What are all of the structural possibilities for the compound C_3H_4?

Solution The formula C_3H_4 corresponds to the general formula C_nH_{2n-2}; thus, a C_3H_4 compound is four hydrogens less than the corresponding alkane (C_nH_{2n+2}), C_3H_8. The C_3H_4 compound could have one triple bond, two double bonds, or one ring and one double bond. For their structures, see the solution to Example 1.10 on page 13.

PROBLEM 3.1 What are all of the structural possibilities for C_4H_6? (Nine compounds, four acyclic and five cyclic, are known.)

When two or more multiple bonds are present in a molecule, it is useful to classify the structure further, depending on the relative positions of the multiple bonds. Double bonds are said to be **cumulated** when they are right next to one another. When multiple bonds *alternate* with single bonds, they are called **conjugated**. When more than one single bond comes between multiple bonds, the latter are isolated or **nonconjugated**.

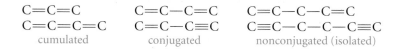

C=C=C	C=C—C=C	C=C—C—C=C
C=C=C=C	C=C—C≡C	C≡C—C—C—C≡C
cumulated	conjugated	nonconjugated (isolated)

---

*An old but still used synonym for alkenes is *olefins*. Alkynes are also called *acetylenes*, after the first member of the series.

PROBLEM 3.2 Which of the following compounds have conjugated multiple bonds?

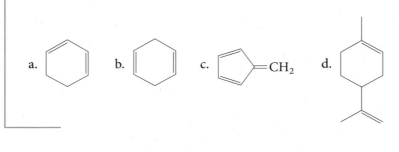

a.   b.   c. ═CH₂   d.

3.2 / Nomenclature

The IUPAC rules for naming alkenes and alkynes are similar to those for alkanes (Sec. 2.3), but a few rules must be added for naming and locating the multiple bonds.

1. The ending *-ene* is used to designate a carbon–carbon double bond. When more than one double bond is present, the ending is *-diene, -triene,* and so on. The ending *-yne* (rhymes with wine) is used for a triple bond (*-diyne* for two triple bonds and so on). Compounds with a double *and* a triple bond are *-enynes.*

2. Select the longest chain that includes *both* carbons of the double or triple bond. For example,

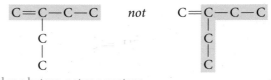

named as a butene, not as a pentene

3. Number the chain from the end nearest the multiple bond so that the carbon atoms in that bond have the lowest possible numbers.

$$\overset{1}{C}-\overset{2}{C}=\overset{3}{C}-\overset{4}{C}-\overset{5}{C} \quad not \quad \overset{5}{C}-\overset{4}{C}=\overset{3}{C}-\overset{2}{C}-\overset{1}{C}$$

If the multiple bond is equidistant from both ends of the chain, number the chain from the end nearest the first branch point.

$$\overset{1}{C}-\overset{2}{C}=\overset{3}{C}-\overset{4}{C} \quad not \quad \overset{4}{C}-\overset{3}{C}=\overset{2}{C}-\overset{1}{C}$$
with C branches on C-2 / C-3

4. Indicate the position of the multiple bond using the *lower numbered carbon atom* of that bond. For example,

$$\overset{1}{CH_2}=\overset{2}{CH}\overset{3}{CH_2}\overset{4}{CH_3} \quad \text{1-butene, } not \text{ 2-butene}$$

5. If more than one multiple bond is present, number the chain from the end nearest the first multiple bond.

$$\overset{1}{C}=\overset{2}{C}-\overset{3}{C}=\overset{4}{C}-\overset{5}{C} \quad not \quad \overset{5}{C}=\overset{4}{C}-\overset{3}{C}=\overset{2}{C}-\overset{1}{C}$$

If a double and a triple bond are equidistant from the end of the chain, the *double* bond receives the lowest numbers. For example,

$$\overset{1}{C}=\overset{2}{C}-\overset{3}{C}\equiv\overset{4}{C} \quad not \quad \overset{4}{C}=\overset{3}{C}-\overset{2}{C}\equiv\overset{1}{C}$$

Let us see how these rules are applied. The first two members of each series are

$$CH_3CH_3 \quad\quad CH_2{=}CH_2 \quad\quad HC{\equiv}CH$$
ethane   ethene   ethyne

$$CH_3CH_2CH_3 \quad\quad CH_2{=}CHCH_3 \quad\quad HC{\equiv}CCH_3$$
propane   propene   propyne

The root of the name (*eth-* or *prop-*) tells us the number of carbons, and the ending (*-ane, -ene,* or *-yne*) tells us whether the bonds are single, double, or triple. No number is necessary in these cases, because in each instance, only one structure is possible.

With four carbons, a number is necessary to locate the double or triple bond.

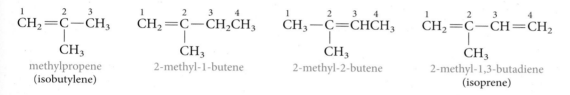

$$\overset{1}{C}H_2{=}\overset{2}{C}H\overset{3}{C}H_2\overset{4}{C}H_3 \quad \overset{1}{C}H_3\overset{2}{C}H{=}\overset{3}{C}H\overset{4}{C}H_3 \quad H\overset{1}{C}{\equiv}\overset{2}{C}\overset{3}{C}H_2\overset{4}{C}H_3 \quad \overset{1}{C}H_3\overset{2}{C}{\equiv}\overset{3}{C}\overset{4}{C}H_3$$

1-butene   2-butene   1-butyne   2-butyne

Branches are named in the usual way.

$$\overset{1}{C}H_2{=}\overset{2}{C}{-}\overset{3}{C}H_3$$
$$\underset{CH_3}{|}$$
methylpropene
(isobutylene)

$$\overset{1}{C}H_2{=}\overset{2}{C}{-}\overset{3}{C}H_2\overset{4}{C}H_3$$
$$\underset{CH_3}{|}$$
2-methyl-1-butene

$$\overset{1}{C}H_3{-}\overset{2}{C}{=}\overset{3}{C}H\overset{4}{C}H_3$$
$$\underset{CH_3}{|}$$
2-methyl-2-butene

$$\overset{1}{C}H_2{=}\overset{2}{C}{-}\overset{3}{C}H{=}\overset{4}{C}H_2$$
$$\underset{CH_3}{|}$$
2-methyl-1,3-butadiene
(isoprene)

Note how the rules are applied in the following examples:

$$\overset{1}{C}H_3{-}\overset{2}{C}H{=}\overset{3}{C}H{-}\overset{4}{C}H{-}\overset{5}{C}H_3$$
$$\underset{CH_3}{|}$$
4-methyl-2-pentene
(*Not* 2-methyl-3-pentene; the chain is numbered so that the double bond gets the lower number.)

$$\overset{1}{C}H_2{=}\overset{2}{C}{-}\overset{3}{C}H_2\overset{4}{C}H_3$$
$$\underset{CH_2CH_3}{|}$$
2-ethyl-1-butene
(Named this way, even though there is a five-carbon chain present, because that chain does not include both carbons of the double bond.)

$$\overset{1}{C}H_2{=}\overset{2}{C}H{-}\overset{3}{C}H{=}\overset{4}{C}H_2$$
1,3-butadiene
(Note the *a* inserted in the name, to help in pronunciation.)

With cyclic hydrocarbons, we start numbering the ring with the carbons of the multiple bond.

cyclopentene
(No number is necessary, because there is only one possible structure.)

3-methylcyclopentene
(Start numbering at, and number through the double bond; 5-methylcyclopentene and 1-methyl-2-cyclopentene are incorrect names.)

1,3-cyclohexadiene

1,4-cyclohexadiene

PROBLEM 3.3 Name each of the following structures by the IUPAC system:

a. $CH_2=C(Cl)CH_3$ b. $(CH_3)_2C=C(CH_2CH_3)_2$ c. $FCH=CHCH_2CH_3$

d. 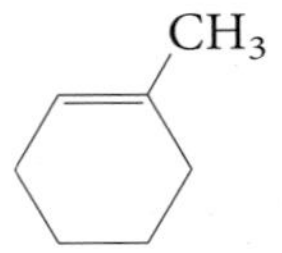 CH_3 e. $CH_2=C(Br)CH=CH_2$ f. $CH_3(CH_2)_3C\equiv CCH_3$

EXAMPLE 3.2

Write the structural formula for 3-methyl-2-pentene.

Solution To get the structural formula from the IUPAC name, first write the longest chain or ring, number it, and then locate the multiple bond. In this case, note that the chain has five carbons and that the double bond is located between carbon-2 and carbon-3:

$$\overset{1}{C}-\overset{2}{C}=\overset{3}{C}-\overset{4}{C}-\overset{5}{C}$$

Next, add the substituent:

$$\overset{1}{C}-\overset{2}{C}=\overset{3}{\underset{\underset{CH_3}{|}}{C}}-\overset{4}{C}-\overset{5}{C}$$

Finally, fill in the hydrogens:

$$CH_3-CH=\underset{\underset{CH_3}{|}}{C}-CH_2-CH_3$$

PROBLEM 3.4 Write structural formulas for the following:

a. 1,4-dichloro-2-pentene
b. 3-hexyne
c. 1,2-diethylcyclobutene
d. 2-bromo-1,3-pentadiene

In addition to the IUPAC rules, it is important to learn a few common names. For example, the simplest members of the alkene and alkyne series are frequently referred to by their older common names, ethylene, acetylene, and propylene.

$$CH_2=CH_2 \quad HC\equiv CH \quad CH_3CH=CH_2$$
ethylene   acetylene   propylene
(ethene)   (ethyne)   (propene)

Two important groups also have common names. They are the vinyl and allyl groups (their IUPAC names are in parentheses below), shown on the left. These groups are used in common names, illustrated in the examples on the right.

$$CH_2=CH- \qquad\qquad CH_2=CHCl$$
vinyl   vinyl chloride
(ethenyl)   (chloroethene)

$$CH_2=CH-CH_2- \qquad CH_2=CH-CH_2Cl$$
allyl   allyl chloride
(2-propenyl)   (3-chloropropene)

PROBLEM 3.5 Write the structural formula for

a. vinylcyclohexane
b. allylcyclobutane

3.3 / Some Facts about Double Bonds

Carbon–carbon double bonds have some special features that are different from those of single bonds. For example, each carbon atom of a double bond is connected to only *three* other atoms (instead of four atoms, as with sp^3 tetrahedral carbon). We speak of such a carbon as being **trigonal**. Furthermore, the two carbon atoms of a double bond and the four atoms that are attached to them lie in a single plane. This planarity is shown in Figure 3.1 for ethylene. The H—C—H and H—C═C angles in ethylene are approximately 120°. Although rotation occurs freely around single bonds, *rotation around double bonds is restricted.* Ethylene does not adopt any other conformation except the planar one. The doubly bonded carbons with two attached hydrogens do not rotate with respect to each other. Finally, carbon–carbon double bonds are shorter than carbon–carbon single bonds.

A **trigonal** carbon atom is bonded to only three other atoms.

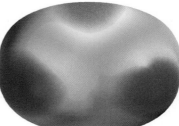

▰ **Figure 3.1**

Four models of ethylene: The dash-wedge, ball-and-stick, and space-filling models show that the four atoms attached to a carbon–carbon double bond lie in a single plane. The electrostatic potential map shows the electron density (red) above and below the plane that passes through the carbon and hydrogen nuclei.

These differences between single and double bonds are summarized in Table 3.1. Let us see how the orbital model for bonding can explain the structure and properties of double bonds.

TABLE 3.1 ▰ **Comparison of C—C and C═C Bonds**

Property	C—C	C═C
1. Number of atoms attached to a carbon	4 (tetrahedral)	3 (trigonal)
2. Rotation	relatively free	restricted
3. Geometry	many conformations are possible; staggered is preferred	planar
4. Bond angle	109.5°	120°
5. Bond length	1.54 Å	1.34 Å

The Orbital Model of a Double Bond; the Pi Bond

Figure 3.2 shows what must happen with the atomic orbitals of carbon to accommodate trigonal bonding, bonding to only three other atoms. The first part of this figure is exactly the same as Figure 1.6 (p. 24). But now we combine only *three* of the orbitals, to make *three equivalent sp^2-hybridized orbitals* (called sp^2 because they are formed by combining one s and two p orbitals). These orbitals lie in a plane and are directed to the corners of an equilateral triangle. The angle between them is 120°. This angle is preferred because repulsion between electrons in each orbital is minimized. Three valence electrons are placed in the three sp^2 orbitals. The fourth valence electron is placed in the remaining $2p$ orbital, whose axis is perpendicular to the plane formed by the three sp^2 hybrid orbitals (see Figure 3.3).

sp^2-Hybridized orbitals are one part s and two parts p in character and are directed toward the three vertices of an equilateral triangle. The angle between two sp^2 orbitals is 120°.

▪ **Figure 3.2**
Unhybridized vs. sp^2-hybridized orbitals on carbon.

▪ **Figure 3.3**
A trigonal carbon showing three sp^2 hybrid orbitals in a plane with a 120° angle between them. The remaining p orbital is perpendicular to the sp^2 orbitals. There is a small back lobe to each sp^2 orbital, which has been omitted for ease of representation.

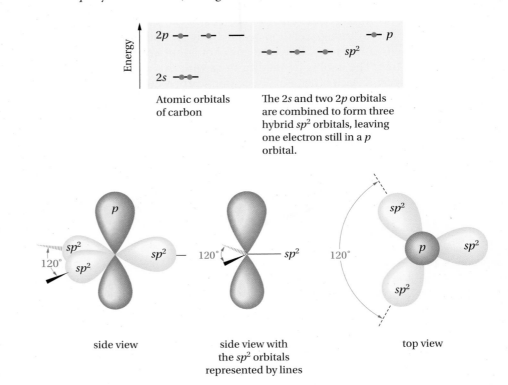

side view   side view with
                  the sp^2 orbitals
                  represented by lines

top view

Now let us see what happens when two sp^2-hybridized carbons are brought together to form a double bond. The process can be imagined as occurring stepwise (Figure 3.4). One of the two bonds, formed by *end-on* overlap of two sp^2 orbitals, is a **sigma (σ) bond** (p. 23). The second bond of the double bond is formed differently. If the two carbons are aligned with the p orbitals on each carbon parallel, lateral overlap can occur, as shown at the bottom of Figure 3.4. The bond formed by lateral p-orbital overlap is called a **pi (π) bond**. The bonding in ethylene is summarized in Figure 3.5.

A **sigma (σ) bond** is formed from the *end-on* overlap of two orbitals. A **pi (π) bond** is formed by lateral overlap of p orbitals on adjacent atoms.

The orbital model explains the facts about double bonds listed in Table 3.1. Rotation about a double bond is restricted because, for rotation to occur, we would have to "break" the pi bond, as seen in Figure 3.6. For ethylene, it takes about 62 kcal/mol (259 kJ/mol) to break the pi bond, much more thermal energy than is available at room temperature. With the pi bond intact, the sp^2 orbitals on each carbon lie in a single plane. The 120° angle between those orbitals minimizes repulsion between the electrons in them. Finally, the carbon–carbon double bond is shorter than the carbon–carbon single bond because the two shared electron pairs draw the nuclei closer together than a single pair does.

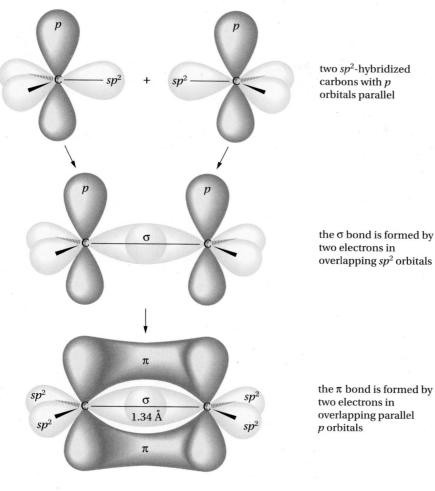

two sp^2-hybridized carbons with p orbitals parallel

the σ bond is formed by two electrons in overlapping sp^2 orbitals

the π bond is formed by two electrons in overlapping parallel p orbitals

Figure 3.4
Schematic formation of a carbon–carbon double bond. Two sp^2 carbons form a sigma (σ) bond (end-on overlap of two sp^2 orbitals) and a pi (π) bond (lateral overlap of two properly aligned p orbitals).

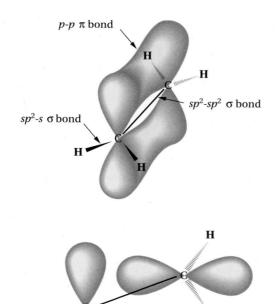

p-p π bond

sp^2-s σ bond

sp^2-sp^2 σ bond

Figure 3.5
The bonding in ethylene consists of one sp^2–sp^2 carbon–carbon σ bond, four sp^2–s carbon–hydrogen σ bonds, and one p–p π bond.

Figure 3.6
Rotation of one sp^2 carbon 90° with respect to another orients the p orbitals perpendicular to one another so that no overlap (and therefore no π bond) is possible.

A WORD ABOUT... The Chemistry of Vision

Andrew Ward/Life File/Photodisc/Getty Images

Carrots contain β-carotene.

Color in organic molecules is usually associated with extended conjugated systems of double bonds. A good example is **β-carotene**, a yellow-orange pigment found in carrots and many other plants. This $C_{40}H_{56}$ hydrocarbon has 11 carbon–carbon double bonds in conjugation. It is the biological precursor of the C_{20} unsaturated alcohol **vitamin A** (also called retinol), which in turn leads to the key substance involved in vision, **11-*cis*-retinal**. Notice in Figure 3.8 that the conversion of vitamin A to 11-*cis*-retinal involves not only oxidation of the alcohol group (—CH_2OH) to an aldehyde (—$CH=O$), but also *trans → cis* isomerism at the C_{11}—C_{12} double bond.

Cis–trans isomerism plays a key role in the process of vision. The rod cells in the retina of the eye contain a red, light-sensitive pigment called **rhodopsin**. This pigment consists of the protein **opsin** combined at its active site with 11-*cis*-retinal. When visible light with the appropriate energy is absorbed by rhodopsin, the complexed *cis*-retinal is isomerized to the *trans isomer.* This process is fantastically fast, occurring in only

picoseconds (10^{-12} seconds). As you can see from their structures, the shapes of the *cis* and *trans* isomers are very different.

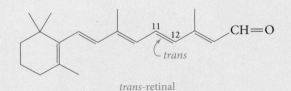

trans-retinal

The *trans*-retinal complex with opsin (called metarhodopsin-II) is less stable than the *cis*-retinal complex, and it dissociates into opsin and *trans*-retinal. This change in geometry triggers a response in the rod nerve cells, which is transmitted to the brain and perceived as vision.

If this were all that happened, we would be able to see for only a few moments, because all of the 11-*cis*-retinal present in the rod cells would be quickly consumed. Fortunately, the enzyme *retinal isomerase,* in the presence of light, converts the *trans*-retinal back to the 11-*cis* isomer so that the cycle can be repeated. Calcium ions in the cell and its membrane control how fast the visual system recovers after exposure to light. They also mediate the way in which cells adapt to various

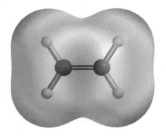

▬ Figure 3.7

Electrostatic potential map of ethylene showing accessibility of pi electrons (red) to attack by electron-seeking reagents.

To recap, according to the orbital model, the carbon–carbon double bond consists of one sigma bond and one pi bond. The two electrons in the sigma bond lie along the internuclear axis; the two electrons in the pi bond lie in a region of space above and below the plane formed by the two carbons and the four atoms attached to them. The π electrons are more exposed than the σ electrons and, as we will see, can be attacked by various electron-seeking reagents (see Figure 3.7).

But before we consider reactions at the double bond, let us examine an important result of the restricted rotation around double bonds.

3.5 *Cis–Trans* Isomerism in Alkenes

Because rotation at carbon–carbon double bonds is restricted, *cis–trans* isomerism (geometric isomerism) is possible in appropriately substituted alkenes. For example, 1,2-dichloroethene exists in two different forms:

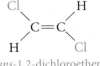

cis-1,2-dichloroethene   *trans*-1,2-dichloroethene
bp 60°C, mp −80°C   bp 47°C, mp −50°C

light levels. The following sequence summarizes the visual cycle:

This representation is simplified because there are actually several additional intermediates between rhodopsin and the fully dissociated *trans*-retinal and opsin.

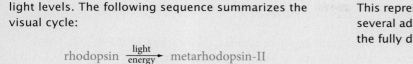

rhodopsin $\xrightarrow[\text{energy}]{\text{light}}$ metarhodopsin-II
(+ nerve impulse)

opsin + 11-*cis*-retinal $\xrightleftharpoons[\text{+ light}]{\substack{\text{retinal} \\ \text{isomerase}}}$ *trans*-retinal
+ opsin

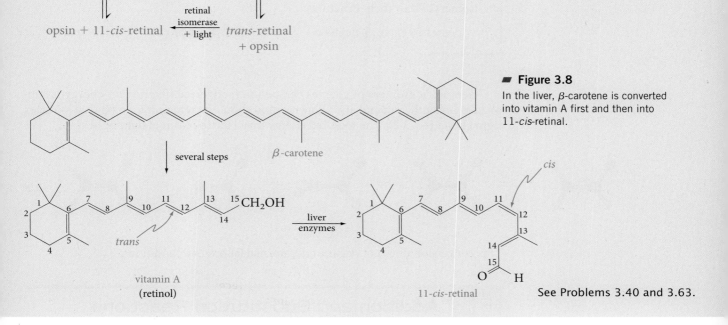

■ **Figure 3.8**
In the liver, β-carotene is converted into vitamin A first and then into 11-*cis*-retinal.

several steps

β-carotene

vitamin A
(retinol)

11-*cis*-retinal

See Problems 3.40 and 3.63.

These stereoisomers are *not* readily interconverted by rotation around the double bond at room temperature. Like *cis–trans* isomers of cycloalkanes, they are configurational stereoisomers and can be separated from one another by distillation, taking advantage of the difference in their boiling points.

EXAMPLE 3.3

Are *cis–trans* isomers possible for 1-butene and 2-butene?

Solution 2-Butene has *cis–trans* isomers, but 1-butene does not.

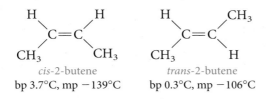

cis-2-butene
bp 3.7°C, mp −139°C

trans-2-butene
bp 0.3°C, mp −106°C

For 1-butene, carbon-1 has two identical hydrogen atoms attached to it; therefore, only one structure is possible.

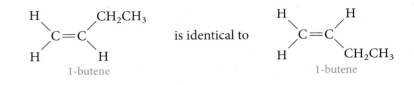
1-butene   is identical to   1-butene

For *cis–trans* isomerism to occur in alkenes, *each* carbon of the double bond must have two different atoms or groups attached to it.

PROBLEM 3.6 Which of the following compounds can exist as *cis–trans* isomers? Draw their structures.

a. pentene   b. 3-heptene   c. 2-methyl-2-pentene   d. 2-hexene

---

Geometric isomers of alkenes can be interconverted if sufficient energy is supplied to break the pi bond and allow rotation about the remaining, somewhat stronger, sigma bond (eq. 3.2). The required energy may take the form of light or heat.

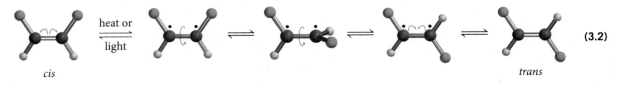

$$\text{(3.2)}$$

cis   *trans*

This conversion does not occur under normal laboratory conditions.

3.6 Addition and Substitution Reactions Compared

We saw in Chapter 2 that, aside from combustion, the most common reaction of alkanes is substitution (for example, halogenation, Sec. 2.12.b). This reaction type can be expressed by a general equation.

$$R—H + A—B \longrightarrow R—A + H—B \qquad \text{(3.3)}$$

where R—H stands for an alkane and A—B may stand for the halogen molecule.

With alkenes, on the other hand, the most common reaction is **addition**:

> The most common reaction of alkenes is **addition** of a reagent to the carbons of the double bond to give a product with a C—C single bond.

$$\underset{}{\overset{}{\text{C}=\text{C}}} + A—B \longrightarrow -\underset{A}{\overset{|}{\text{C}}}-\underset{B}{\overset{|}{\text{C}}}- \qquad \text{(3.4)}$$

In an addition reaction, group A of the reagent A—B becomes attached to one carbon atom of the double bond, group B becomes attached to the other carbon atom, and the product has only a single bond between the two carbon atoms.

What bond changes take place in an addition reaction? The pi bond of the alkene is broken, and the sigma bond of the reagent is also broken. Two new sigma bonds are formed. In other words, we break a pi and a sigma bond, and we make two sigma bonds. Because sigma bonds are usually stronger than pi bonds, the net reaction is favorable.

PROBLEM 3.7 Why, in general, is a sigma bond between two atoms stronger than a pi bond between the same two atoms?

3.7 Polar Addition Reactions

Several reagents add to double bonds by a two-step polar process. In this section, we will describe examples of this reaction type, after which we will consider details of the reaction mechanism.

3.7.a Addition of Halogens

Alkenes readily add chlorine or bromine.

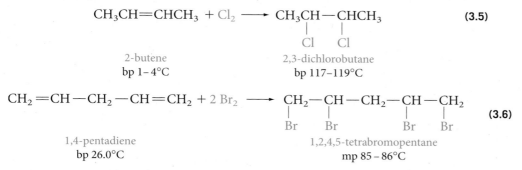

$$CH_3CH{=}CHCH_3 + Cl_2 \longrightarrow CH_3CH{-}CHCH_3 \qquad (3.5)$$

2-butene
bp 1–4°C

2,3-dichlorobutane
bp 117–119°C

$$CH_2{=}CH{-}CH_2{-}CH{=}CH_2 + 2\,Br_2 \longrightarrow CH_2{-}CH{-}CH_2{-}CH{-}CH_2 \qquad (3.6)$$

1,4-pentadiene
bp 26.0°C

1,2,4,5-tetrabromopentane
mp 85–86°C

Usually the halogen is dissolved in some inert solvent such as tri- or tetrachloromethane, and then this solution is added dropwise to the alkene. Reaction is nearly instantaneous, even at room temperature or below. No light or heat is required, as in the case of substitution reactions.

> **PROBLEM 3.8** Write an equation for the reaction of bromine at room temperature with
>
> a. propene   b. 4-methylcyclohexene

The addition of bromine can be used as a chemical test for the presence of unsaturation in an organic compound. Bromine solutions in tetrachloromethane are dark reddish-brown, and both the unsaturated compound and its bromine adduct are usually colorless. As the bromine solution is added to the unsaturated compound, the bromine color disappears. If the compound being tested is saturated, it will not react with bromine under these conditions, and the color will persist.

3.7.b Addition of Water (Hydration)

If an acid catalyst is present, water adds to alkenes. It adds as H—OH, and the products are alcohols.

$$CH_2{=}CH_2 + H{-}OH \xrightarrow{H^+} CH_2{-}CH_2 \quad (\text{or } CH_3CH_2OH) \qquad (3.7)$$

ethanol

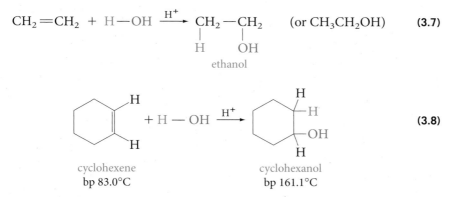

$$+ H{-}OH \xrightarrow{H^+} \qquad (3.8)$$

cyclohexene
bp 83.0°C

cyclohexanol
bp 161.1°C

Bromine solution (red-brown) is added to a saturated hydrocarbon (left) and an unsaturated hydrocarbon (right).

An acid catalyst is required in this case because the neutral water molecule is not acidic enough to provide protons to start the reaction. The stepwise mechanism for this reaction is given later in eq. 3.20. Hydration is used industrially and occasionally in the laboratory to synthesize alcohols from alkenes.

> **PROBLEM 3.9** Write an equation for the acid-catalyzed addition of water to
>
> a. 3-hexene   b. 2-butene   c. 4-methylcyclopentene

3.7.c Addition of Acids

A variety of acids add to the double bond of alkenes. The hydrogen ion (or proton) adds to one carbon of the double bond, and the remainder of the acid becomes connected to the other carbon.

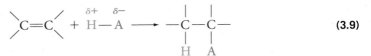

$$\begin{array}{c}\diagdown\\C=C\\\diagup\end{array}\diagup + \overset{\delta+}{H}-\overset{\delta-}{A} \longrightarrow -\overset{|}{\underset{H}{C}}-\overset{|}{\underset{A}{C}}- \tag{3.9}$$

Acids that add in this way are the hydrogen halides (H—F, H—Cl, H—Br, H—I) and sulfuric acid (H—OSO$_3$H). Here are two typical examples:

$$CH_2{=}CH_2 + H{-}Cl \longrightarrow \underset{\underset{H}{|}}{CH_2}{-}\underset{\underset{Cl}{|}}{CH_2} \quad (\text{or } CH_3CH_2Cl) \tag{3.10}$$

ethene   hydrogen chloride   chloroethane (ethyl chloride)

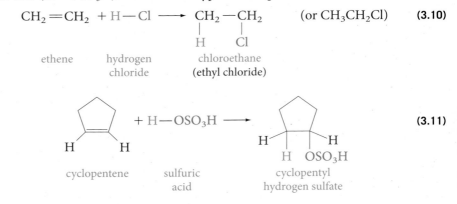

$$\text{(3.11)}$$

cyclopentene   sulfuric acid   cyclopentyl hydrogen sulfate

> **PROBLEM 3.10** Write an equation for each of the following reactions:
>
> a. 2-butene + HCl
> b. 3-hexene + HI
> c. 4-methylcyclopentene + HBr

Before we discuss the mechanism of these addition reactions, we must introduce a complication that we have carefully avoided in all of the examples given so far.

The products of addition of **unsymmetric reagents** to unsymmetric alkenes are called **regioisomers. Regiospecific** additions produce only one regioisomer. **Regioselective** additions produce mainly one regioisomer.

3.8 Addition of Unsymmetric Reagents to Unsymmetric Alkenes; Markovnikov's Rule

Reagents and alkenes can be classified as either **symmetric** or **unsymmetric** with respect to addition reactions. Table 3.2 illustrates what this means. If a reagent and/or an alkene is symmetric, only one addition product is possible. If you check

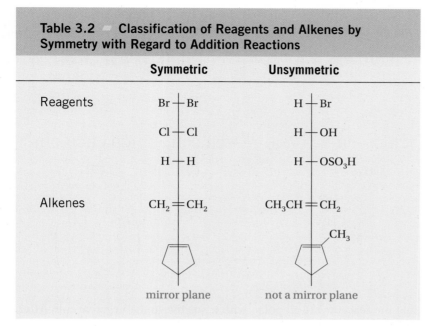

Table 3.2 ▪ **Classification of Reagents and Alkenes by Symmetry with Regard to Addition Reactions**

	Symmetric	Unsymmetric
Reagents	Br—Br	H—Br
	Cl—Cl	H—OH
	H—H	H—OSO$_3$H
Alkenes	CH$_2$=CH$_2$	CH$_3$CH=CH$_2$
		CH$_3$ (on ring)
	mirror plane	not a mirror plane

back through all of the equations and problems for addition reactions up to now, you will see that either the alkene or the reagent (or both) was symmetric. But if *both* the reagent *and* the alkene are *unsymmetric,* two products are, in principle, possible.

$$\underset{\substack{\text{unsymmetric} \\ \text{alkene}}}{\overset{R}{\underset{}{}}\overset{H}{}{C{=}C}} + \underset{\substack{\text{unsymmetric} \\ \text{reagent}}}{X{-}Y} \longrightarrow \overset{R\ H}{\underset{X\ Y}{-C-C-}} \quad \text{and/or} \quad \overset{R\ H}{\underset{Y\ X}{-C-C-}} \qquad \textbf{(3.12)}$$

The products of eq. 3.12 are sometimes called **regioisomers**. If a reaction of this type gives *only one* of the two possible regioisomers, it is said to be **regiospecific**. If it gives *mainly one* product, it is said to be **regioselective**.

Let us consider, as a specific example, the acid-catalyzed addition of water to propene. In principle, two products could be formed: 1-propanol or 2-propanol.

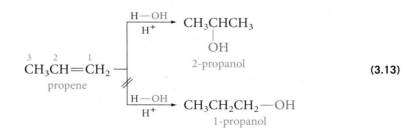

$$\underset{\text{propene}}{\overset{3\quad 2\quad 1}{CH_3CH{=}CH_2}}\ \begin{cases} \xrightarrow[H^+]{H-OH} & \underset{\underset{\text{2-propanol}}{OH}}{CH_3CHCH_3} \\[2em] \xrightarrow[H^+]{H-OH} & \underset{\text{1-propanol}}{CH_3CH_2CH_2-OH} \end{cases} \qquad \textbf{(3.13)}$$

That is, the hydrogen of the water could add to C-1 and the hydroxyl group to C-2 of propene, or vice versa. When the experiment is carried out, *only one product is observed. The addition is regiospecific, and the only product is 2-propanol.*

Most addition reactions of alkenes show a similar preference for the formation of only (or mainly) one of the two possible addition products. Here are some examples.

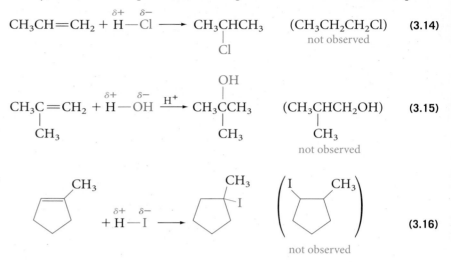

Notice that the reagents are all polar, with a positive and a negative end. After studying a number of such addition reactions, the Russian chemist Vladimir Markovnikov formulated the following rule more than 100 years ago: *When an unsymmetric reagent adds to an unsymmetric alkene, the electropositive part of the reagent bonds to the carbon of the double bond that has the greater number of hydrogen atoms attached to it.**

PROBLEM 3.11 Use Markovnikov's Rule to predict which regioisomer predominates in each of the following reactions:

a. 1-pentene + HBr
b. 2-methyl-2-hexene + H_2O (H^+ catalyst)

PROBLEM 3.12 What two products are *possible* from the addition of HCl to 2-octene? Would you expect the reaction to be regiospecific?

Let us now develop a rational explanation for Markovnikov's Rule in terms of modern chemical theory.

3.9   Mechanism of Electrophilic Addition to Alkenes

The pi electrons of a double bond are more exposed to an attacking reagent than are the sigma electrons. The pi bond is also weaker than the σ bond. It is the pi electrons, then, that are involved in additions to alkenes. The double bond can act as a supplier of pi electrons to an electron-seeking reagent (see Figure 3.7, p. 76).

Polar reactants can be classified as either **electrophiles** or **nucleophiles**. Electrophiles (literally, electron lovers) are electron-poor reagents; in reactions with some other molecule, they seek electrons. They are often positive ions (cations) or otherwise electron-deficient species. Nucleophiles (literally, nucleus lovers), on the other hand, are electron rich; they form bonds by donating electrons to an electrophile.

Electrophiles are electron-poor reactants; they seek electrons. **Nucleophiles** are electron-rich reactants; they form bonds by donating electrons to electrophiles.

---

*Actually, Markovnikov stated the rule a little differently. The form given here is easier to remember and apply. For an interesting historical article on what he actually said, when he said it, and how his name is spelled, see J. Tierney, *J. Chem. Educ.* **1988**, *65*, 1053–54.

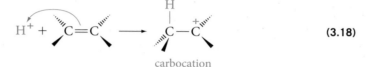

$$E^+ \quad + \quad :Nu^- \quad \longrightarrow \quad E:Nu \qquad (3.17)$$

electrophile   nucleophile

Let us now consider the mechanism of polar addition to a carbon–carbon double bond, specifically the addition of acids to alkenes. The carbon–carbon double bond, because of its pi electrons, is a nucleophile. The proton (H^+) is the attacking electrophile. As the proton approaches the pi bond, the two pi electrons are used to form a sigma bond between the proton and one of the two carbon atoms. Because this bond uses *both* pi electrons, the other carbon acquires a positive charge, producing a **carbocation**.

> A **carbocation** is a positively charged carbon atom bonded to three other atoms.

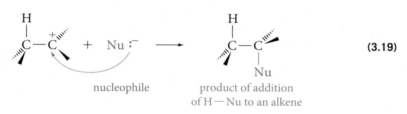

$$(3.18)$$

carbocation

The resulting carbocations are, however, extremely reactive because there are only six electrons (instead of the usual eight) around the positively charged carbon. The carbocation rapidly combines with some species that can supply it with two electrons, a nucleophile.

$$(3.19)$$

nucleophile   product of addition
of H—Nu to an alkene

Examples include the addition of H—Cl, H—OSO$_3$H, and H—OH to alkenes:

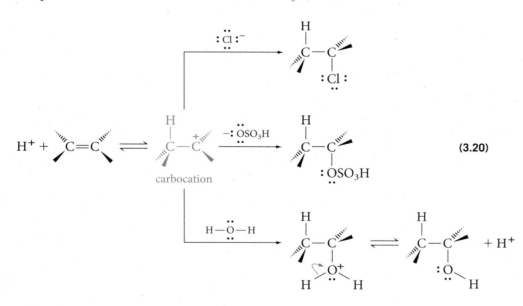

$$(3.20)$$

carbocation

In these reactions, the electrophile H^+ first adds to the alkene to give a carbocation. Then the carbocation combines with a nucleophile, in these examples, a chloride ion, a bisulfate ion, or a water molecule.

With most alkenes, the first step in this process—the formation of the carbocation—is the slower of the two steps. The resulting carbocation is usually so reactive that combination with the nucleophile is extremely rapid. *Since the first step in these additions is attack by the electrophile, the whole process is called an* **electrophilic addition reaction**.

> A reaction in which an electrophile is added to an alkene is called an **electrophilic addition reaction**.

Electrophilic addition of the halogens (Cl_2 and Br_2) to alkenes occurs in a similar manner. Although the mechanism is not identical to that for acids, the end results are the same. For example, when a molecule of Br_2 approaches the pi bond of an alkene, the Br—Br bond becomes polarized: $\overset{\delta+}{Br}\!-\!\overset{\delta-}{Br}$. The Br atom closer to the pi bond develops a partial positive charge and thus becomes an electrophile, while the other Br atom develops a partial negative charge and becomes the nucleophile. Although it is impossible to tell from the products, the addition occurs in Markovnikov fashion.*

EXAMPLE 3.4

Because carbocations are involved in the electrophilic addition reactions of alkenes, it is important to understand the bonding in these chemical intermediates. Describe the bonding in carbocations in orbital terms.

Solution The carbon atom is positively charged and therefore has only three valence electrons to use in bonding. Each of these electrons is in an sp^2 orbital. The three sp^2 orbitals lie in one plane with 120° angles between them, an arrangement that minimizes repulsion between the electrons in the three bonds. The remaining p orbital is perpendicular to that plane and is vacant.

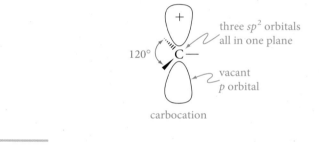

carbocation

3.10 / Markovnikov's Rule Explained

To explain Markovnikov's Rule, let us consider a specific example, the addition of H—Cl to propene. The first step is addition of a proton to the double bond. This can occur in two ways, to give either an isopropyl cation or a propyl cation.

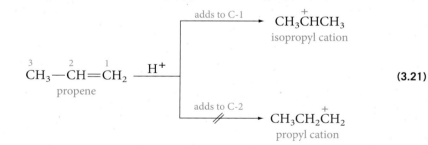

(3.21)

At this stage of the reaction, the structure of the product is already determined; when combining with chloride ion, the isopropyl cation can give only 2-chloropropane, and the propyl cation can give only 1-chloropropane. The only observed product is 2-chloropropane, so we must conclude that the *proton adds to C-1 to form only the isopropyl cation.* Why?

Carbocations can be classified as **tertiary**, **secondary**, or **primary**, depending on whether the positive carbon atom has attached to it three organic groups, two groups,

Carbocations are classified as **primary, secondary,** and **tertiary** when one, two, and three R groups, respectively, are attached to the positively charged carbon atom.

---

*Consult your instructor if you are curious about the detailed mechanism.

or only one group. From many studies, it has been established that the stability of carbocations decreases in the following order:

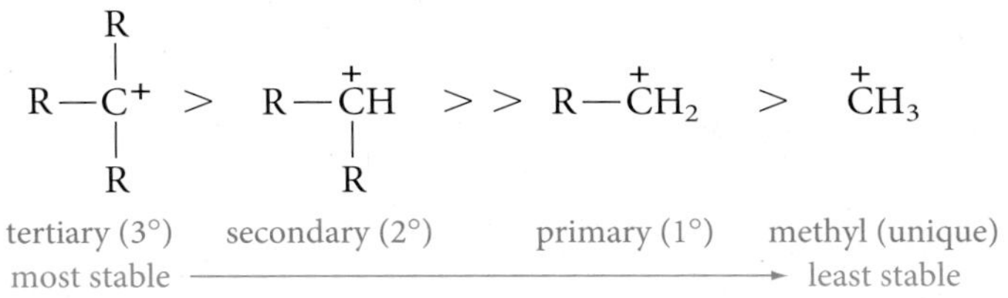

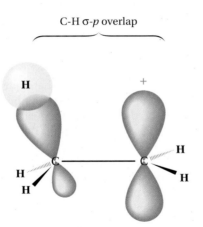

tertiary (3°)   secondary (2°)   primary (1°)   methyl (unique)

most stable ――――――――――――――――→ least stable

One reason for this order is the following: A carbocation will be more stable when the positive charge can be spread out, or delocalized, over several atoms in the ion, instead of being concentrated on a single carbon atom. In alkyl cations, this delocalization occurs by drift of electron density to the positive carbon from C—H and C—C sigma bonds that can align themselves with the empty *p* orbital on the positively charged carbon atom (Figure 3.9). If the positively charged carbon center is surrounded by other carbon atoms (alkyl groups), instead of by hydrogen atoms, more C—H and C—C bonds will be available to provide electrons to help delocalize the charge. This is the main reason for the observed stability order of carbocations.

C-H σ-*p* overlap

◼ Figure 3.9

Alkyl groups stabilize carbocations by donating electron density from C—H and C—C sigma bonds that can line up with the empty *p* orbital on the positively charged carbon atom.

Markovnikov's Rule can now be restated in modern and more generally useful terms: *The electrophilic addition of an unsymmetric reagent to an unsymmetric double bond proceeds in such a way as to involve the most stable carbocation.*

PROBLEM 3.13 Classify each of the following carbocations as primary, secondary, or tertiary:

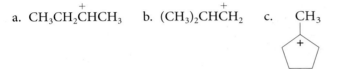

a. $CH_3CH_2\overset{+}{C}HCH_3$ b. $(CH_3)_2CH\overset{+}{C}H_2$ c.   CH₃

PROBLEM 3.14 Which carbocation in Problem 3.13 is most stable? Least stable?

PROBLEM 3.15 Write the steps in the electrophilic additions in eqs. 3.15 and 3.16, and in each case, show that reaction occurs via the more stable carbocation.

Discussion of Markovnikov's Rule raises two important general questions about chemical reactions: (1) Under what conditions is a reaction likely to proceed? (2) How rapidly will a reaction occur? We will consider these questions briefly in the next two sections before continuing our survey of the reactions of alkenes.

3.11 Reaction Equilibrium: What Makes a Reaction Go?

A chemical reaction can proceed in two directions. Reactant molecules can form product molecules, and product molecules can react to re-form the reactant molecules. For the reaction*

$$aA + bB \rightleftharpoons cC + dD \tag{3.22}$$

we describe the chemical equilibrium for the forward and backward reactions by the following equation:

$$K_{eq} = \frac{[C]^c[D]^d}{[A]^a[B]^b} \tag{3.23}$$

The **equilibrium constant**, K_{eq}, indicates the direction that is favored for a reaction.

In this equation, K_{eq}, the **equilibrium constant**, is equal to the product of the concentrations of the products divided by the product of the concentrations of the reactants. (The small letters a, b, c, and d are the numbers of molecules of reactants and products in the balanced reaction equation.)

The equilibrium constant tells us the direction that is favored for the reaction. If K_{eq} is greater than 1, the formation of products C and D will be favored over the formation of reactants A and B. The preferred direction for the reaction is from left to right. Conversely, if K_{eq} is less than 1, the preferred direction for the reaction is from right to left.

What determines whether a reaction will proceed to the right, toward products? A reaction will occur when the products are lower in energy (more stable) than the reactants. A reaction in which products are higher in energy than reactants will proceed to the left, toward reactants. When products are lower in energy than reactants, heat is given off in the course of the reaction. For example, heat is given off when an acid such as hydrogen bromide (HBr) is added to ethene (eq. 3.24). Such a reaction is **exothermic**.

$$
\begin{array}{c}
\text{H} \qquad\qquad \text{H} \\
\diagdown\qquad\quad\diagup \\
\text{C}\!=\!\text{C} \qquad + \text{ HBr} \rightleftharpoons \text{CH}_3\text{CH}_2\text{Br} \\
\diagup\qquad\quad\diagdown \\
\text{H} \qquad\qquad \text{H}
\end{array}
\tag{3.24}
$$

An **exothermic** reaction evolves heat energy; an **endothermic** reaction takes in heat energy. The chemists' term for heat energy is **enthalpy**, H.

On the other hand, heat must be added to ethane to produce two methyl radicals (eq. 1.3). This reaction is **endothermic** (takes in heat). The term used by chemists for heat energy is **enthalpy** and is designated by the symbol H. The difference in enthalpy between products and reactants is designated by the symbol ΔH (pronounced "delta H").

For the addition of HBr to ethene, the product (bromoethane) is more stable than the reactants (ethene and HBr), and the reaction proceeds to the right. For this reaction, ΔH is negative (heat is given off), and K_{eq} is much greater than 1 (Figure 3.10a). For the formation of two methyl radicals from ethane, ΔH is positive (heat is absorbed), and K_{eq} is much less than 1 (Figure 3.10b).**

---

*The double arrow indicates that this reaction goes both ways and reaches chemical equilibrium.

Actually, enthalpy is not the only factor that contributes to the energy difference between products and reactants. A factor called **entropy, S, also contributes to the total energy difference, which is known as the **Gibbs free-energy difference**, ΔG, according to the equation $\Delta G = \Delta H - T\Delta S$. For most organic reactions, however, the entropy contribution is very small compared to the enthalpy contribution.

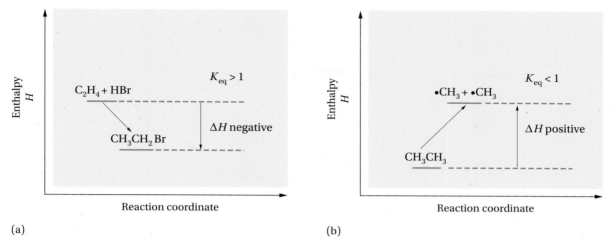

Figure 3.10
(a) The addition of HBr to ethene; the reaction equilibrium lies to the right. (b) The formation of methyl radicals from ethane; the reaction equilibrium lies to the left.

3.12 Reaction Rates: How Fast Does a Reaction Go?

The equilibrium constant for a reaction tells us whether or not products are more stable than reactants. However, *the equilibrium constant does not tell us anything about the rate of a reaction.* For example, the equilibrium constant for the reaction of gasoline with oxygen is very large, but gasoline can be safely handled in air because the reaction is very slow unless a spark is used to initiate it. The rate of addition of HBr to ethene is also very slow, although the reaction is exothermic.

In order to react, molecules must collide with each other with enough energy and with the right orientation so that the breaking and making of bonds can occur. The energy required for this process is a barrier to reaction, and the higher the energy barrier, the slower the reaction.

Chemists use **reaction energy diagrams** to show the changes in energy that occur in the course of a reaction. Figure 3.11 shows the reaction energy diagram for the polar addition of the acid HBr to ethene (eq. 3.24). This reaction occurs in two steps. In the first step, as a proton adds to the double bond, the π bond of the alkene is broken and a C—H σ bond is formed, giving a carbocation intermediate product. The reactants start with the energy shown at the left of the diagram. As the π bond begins to break and the new σ bond begins to form, the structure formed by the reactants reaches a maximum in energy. This structure with maximum energy is called the **transition state** for the first step. This structure cannot be isolated and continues to change until the carbocation product of the first step is fully formed.

The difference in energy between the transition state and the reactants is called the **activation energy**, E_a. It is this energy that determines the rate of the reaction. If E_a is large, the reaction will be slow. A small E_a means that the reaction will proceed rapidly.

In the second step of the reaction, a new carbon–bromine σ bond is formed. Again, the approach of the bromide ion to the positively charged carbon of the carbocation intermediate causes a rise in energy to a maximum. The structure at this energy maximum is the transition state for the second step. The difference in energy between the carbocation and this transition state is the activation energy E_a for this second step. This structure cannot be isolated and continues to change until the σ bond is fully formed, completing the formation of the product.

A **reaction energy diagram** shows the changes in energy that occur in the course of a reaction. A **transition state** is a structure with maximum energy for a particular reaction step. **Activation energy**, E_a, is the difference in energy between reactants and the transition state, and the activation energy determines the **reaction rate**.

▰ **Figure 3.11**

Reaction energy diagram for the
addition of HBr to an alkene.

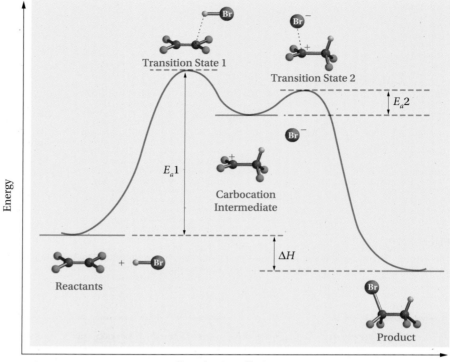

▰ **Figure 3.11**

Reaction energy diagram for the
addition of HBr to an alkene.

Notice in Figure 3.11 that although the final product of the reaction is lower in
energy (ΔH) than the reactants, the reactants must surmount two energy barriers
(E_a1 and E_a2), one for each step of the reaction. Between the two transition states, the
carbocation intermediate is at an energy minimum that is higher than reactants or
products. The first step of the reaction is *endothermic,* because the carbocation intermediate product is higher in energy than the reactants. The second step is exothermic because the product is lower in energy than the carbocation. The overall reaction
is *exothermic,* because the product is lower in energy than the reactants. However,
the rate of the reaction is determined by the highest energy barrier, E_a1. The second
activation energy, E_a2, is very low compared to the activation energy for the first step.

▰ **Figure 3.12**

Reaction energy diagram for
formation of the isopropyl and
propyl cations from propene
(eq. 3.21).

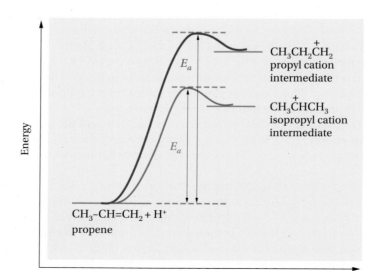

Therefore, as described in Section 3.9, the first step is the slower of the two steps, and the rate of the reaction is determined by the rate of this first step.

EXAMPLE 3.5

Sketch a reaction energy diagram for a one-step reaction that is very slow and slightly exothermic.

Solution A very slow reaction has a large E_a, and a slightly exothermic reaction has a small negative ΔH. Therefore, the diagram will look like this:

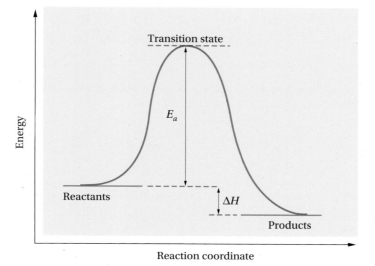

PROBLEM 3.16 Draw a reaction energy diagram for a one-step reaction that is very fast and very exothermic.

PROBLEM 3.17 Draw a reaction energy diagram for a one-step reaction that is very slow and slightly endothermic.

PROBLEM 3.18 Draw a reaction energy diagram for a two-step reaction that has an endothermic first step and an exothermic second step. Label the reactants, transition states, reaction intermediate, activation energies, and enthalpy differences.

Let us see how reaction rates are related to Markovnikov's Rule. In electrophilic addition reactions, more stable carbocations are formed more rapidly than less stable carbocations. This is because more stable carbocations are lower in energy than less stable carbocations, and it follows that the activation energy E_a for the formation of more stable carbocations is also lower. For example, both isopropyl and propyl cations could be formed from propene and H^+ (eq. 3.21), but the isopropyl cation is more stable (i.e., much lower in energy) than the propyl cation (Figure 3.12). Formation of the isopropyl cation, therefore, has a lower activation energy E_a and thus, the isopropyl carbocation is formed more rapidly than the propyl cation. Hence, the regioselectivity of electrophilic additions is the result of competing first steps, in which the more stable carbocation is formed at a faster rate.

Other factors that affect reaction rates are **temperature** and **catalysts**. Heating a reaction generally increases the rate at which the reaction occurs by providing the reactant

Increasing **temperature** or using a **catalyst** increases reaction rates.

molecules with more energy to surmount activation energy barriers. Catalysts speed up a reaction by providing an alternative pathway or mechanism for the reaction, one in which the activation energy is lower. Enzymes play this role in biochemical reactions.

In the next five sections, we will continue our survey of the reactions of alkenes.

3.13 Hydroboration of Alkenes

Hydroboration is the addition of H—B⟨ to an alkene.

Hydroboration was discovered by Professor Herbert C. Brown (1912–2004). This reaction is so useful in synthesis that Brown's work earned him a Nobel Prize in 1979. We will describe here only one practical example of hydroboration, a two-step alcohol synthesis from alkenes.

Hydroboration involves addition of a hydrogen–boron bond to an alkene. From the electronegativity values listed in Table 1.4, the H—B⟨ bond is polarized with the hydrogen $\delta-$ and the boron $\delta+$. Addition occurs so that the boron (the electrophile) adds to the less-substituted carbon.

$$R—CH=CH_2 + \overset{\delta-}{H}—\overset{\delta+}{B}⟨ \longrightarrow R—\underset{\underset{H}{|}}{CH}—CH_2—B⟨ \qquad \text{(3.25)}$$

Thus, it resembles a normal electrophilic addition to an alkene, following Markovnikov's Rule, even though the addition is concerted (that is, all bond-breaking and bond-making occur in one step).

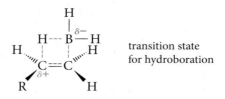

transition state for hydroboration

Because it has three B—H bonds, one molecule of borane, BH_3, can react with three molecules of an alkene. For example, propene gives tri-n-propylborane.

$$3\ CH_3CH=CH_2 + BH_3 \longrightarrow CH_3CH_2CH_2—B\overset{\displaystyle CH_2CH_2CH_3}{\underset{\displaystyle CH_2CH_2CH_3}{\Big\langle}} \qquad \text{(3.26)}$$

propene   borane   tri-n-propylborane

The trialkylboranes made in this way are usually not isolated but are treated with some other reagent to obtain the desired final product. For example, trialkylboranes can be oxidized by hydrogen peroxide and base to give alcohols.

$(CH_3CH_2CH_2)_3B + 3\ H_2O_2 + 3\ NaOH \longrightarrow$
tri-n-propylborane

$$3\ CH_3CH_2CH_2OH + Na_3BO_3 + 3\ H_2O \qquad \text{(3.27)}$$
n-propyl alcohol   sodium borate

One great advantage of this hydroboration–oxidation sequence is that it provides a route to alcohols that *cannot* be obtained by the acid-catalyzed hydration of alkenes (review eq. 3.13).

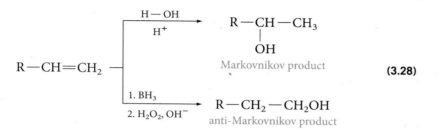

$$R—CH=CH_2 \quad (3.28)$$

- $\xrightarrow[\text{H}^+]{\text{H—OH}}$ R—CH—CH$_3$ | OH — Markovnikov product
- $\xrightarrow[\text{2. H}_2\text{O}_2,\ \text{OH}^-]{\text{1. BH}_3}$ R—CH$_2$—CH$_2$OH — anti-Markovnikov product

The overall result of the two-step hydroboration sequence *appears* to be the addition of water to the carbon–carbon double bond in the reverse of the usual Markovnikov sense.

EXAMPLE 3.6

What alcohol is obtained from this sequence?

$$CH_3—\underset{\underset{\displaystyle CH_3}{|}}{C}=CH_2 \xrightarrow{BH_3} \xrightarrow[\text{OH}^-]{H_2O_2}$$

Solution The boron adds to the less-substituted carbon; oxidation gives the corresponding alcohol. Compare this result with that of eq. 3.15.

$$3\ CH_3—\underset{\underset{\displaystyle CH_3}{|}}{C}=CH_2 \xrightarrow{BH_3} (CH_3—\underset{\underset{\displaystyle CH_3}{|}}{CH}—CH_2)_3B \xrightarrow[\text{OH}^-]{H_2O_2} 3\ CH_3—\underset{\underset{\displaystyle CH_3}{|}}{CH}—CH_2OH$$

PROBLEM 3.19 What alcohol is obtained by applying the hydroboration–oxidation sequence to 2-methyl-2-hexene?

PROBLEM 3.20 What alkene is needed to obtain 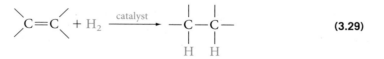 —CH$_2$CH$_2$OH

via the hydroboration–oxidation sequence? What product would this alkene give with acid-catalyzed hydration?

3.14 Addition of Hydrogen

Hydrogen adds to alkenes in the presence of an appropriate catalyst. The process is called **hydrogenation**.

> **Hydrogenation** is the addition of hydrogen to alkenes in the presence of a catalyst.

$$\underset{}{>}C=C\underset{}{<} + H_2 \xrightarrow{\text{catalyst}} —\underset{\underset{\displaystyle H}{|}}{C}—\underset{\underset{\displaystyle H}{|}}{C}— \quad (3.29)$$

The catalyst is usually a finely divided metal, such as nickel, platinum, or palladium. These metals adsorb hydrogen gas on their surfaces and activate the hydrogen–hydrogen bond. Both hydrogen atoms usually add from the catalyst surface to the same face of the double bond. For example, 1,2-dimethylcyclopentene gives mainly *cis*-1,2-dimethylcyclopentane.

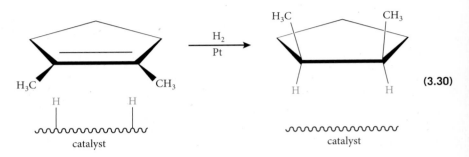

(3.30)

Catalytic hydrogenation of double bonds is used commercially to convert vegetable oils to margarine and other cooking fats (Sec. 15.2).

PROBLEM 3.21 Write an equation for the catalytic hydrogenation of

a. 2-methyl-2-pentene
b. 4-methylcyclopentene
c. 3-methylcyclohexene
d. vinylcyclobutane

3.15 Additions to Conjugated Systems

3.15.a Electrophilic Additions to Conjugated Dienes

Alternate double and single bonds of conjugated systems have special consequences for their addition reactions. When 1 mole of HBr adds to 1 mole of 1,3-butadiene, a rather surprising result is obtained. Two products are isolated.

$$\overset{1}{CH_2}{=}\overset{2}{CH}{-}\overset{3}{CH}{=}\overset{4}{CH_2} \xrightarrow{\text{HBr}}$$
1,3-butadiene

$$CH_2{-}CH{-}CH{=}CH_2 \quad \text{(1,2-addition)}$$
$${\vert}\phantom{{-}}\vert$$
$$H\phantom{{-}}Br$$
3-bromo-1-butene

$$CH_2{-}CH{=}CH{-}CH_2 \quad \text{(1,4-addition)}$$
$$\vert\phantom{{=}CH{-}CH}\vert$$
$$H\phantom{{=}CH{-}CH}Br$$
1-bromo-2-butene

(3.31)

In one of these products, HBr has added to one of the two double bonds, and the other double bond is still present in its original position. We call this the product of **1,2-addition**. The other product may at first seem unexpected. The hydrogen and bromine have added to carbon-1 and carbon-4 of the original diene, and a new double bond has appeared between carbon-2 and carbon-3. This process, known as **1,4-addition**, is quite general for electrophilic additions to conjugated systems. How can we explain it?

In **1,2-addition**, a reagent is added to the first and second carbons of a conjugated diene, whereas **1,4-addition** is addition to the first and fourth carbons.

In the first step, the proton adds to the terminal carbon atom, according to Markovnikov's Rule.

$$H^+ + CH_2{=}CH{-}CH{=}CH_2 \longrightarrow CH_3{-}\overset{+}{CH}{-}CH{=}CH_2$$

(3.32)

The resulting carbocation can be stabilized by resonance; in fact, it is a hybrid of two contributing resonance structures (see Sec. 1.12).

$$[CH_3-\overset{+}{C}H-CH=CH_2 \longleftrightarrow CH_3-CH=CH-\overset{+}{C}H_2]$$

The positive charge is delocalized over carbon-2 and carbon-4. When, in the next step, the carbocation reacts with bromide ion (the nucleophile), it can react either at carbon-2 to give the product of 1,2-addition or at carbon-4 to give the product of 1,4-addition.

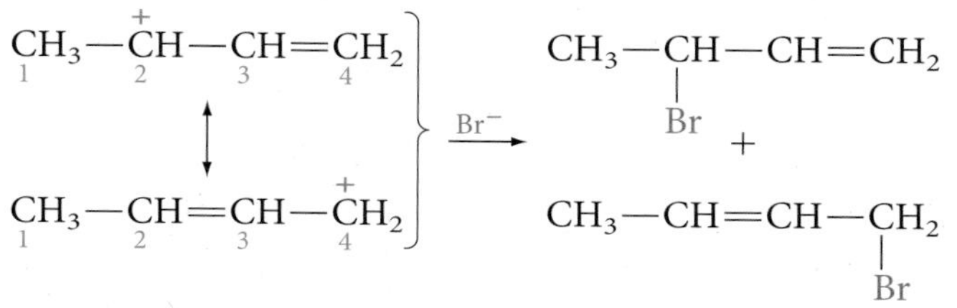

(3.33)

PROBLEM 3.22 Explain why, in the first step of this reaction, the proton adds to C-1 (eq. 3.32) and not to C-2.

The carbocation intermediate in these reactions is a single species, a resonance hybrid. This type of carbocation, with a carbon–carbon double bond adjacent to the positive carbon, is called an **allylic cation**. The parent allyl cation, shown below as a resonance hybrid, is a primary carbocation, but it is more stable than simple primary ions (such as propyl) because its positive charge is delocalized over the two end carbon atoms as shown in the electrostatic potential map accompanying eq. 3.34.

In an **allylic cation**, a carbon–carbon double bond is adjacent to the positively charged carbon atom.

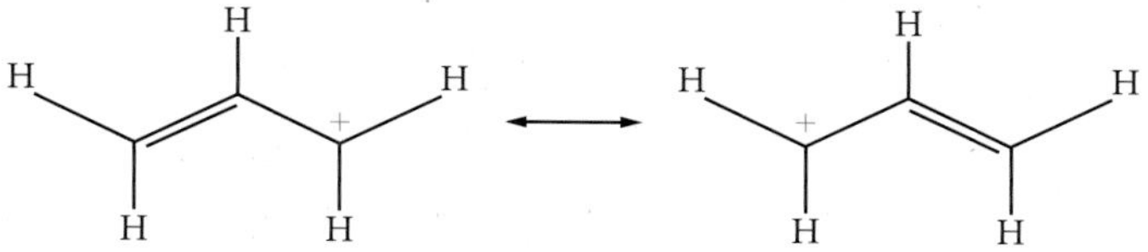

(3.34)

the allyl carbocation

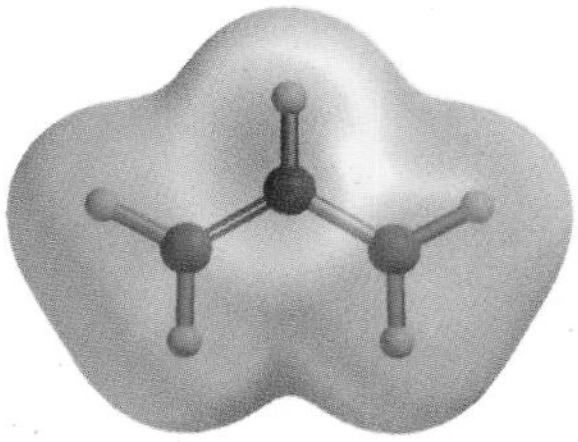

PROBLEM 3.23 Draw the contributors to the resonance hybrid structure of the 3-cyclopentenyl cation 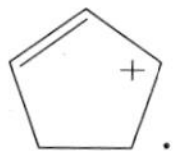.

PROBLEM 3.24 Write an equation for the expected products of 1,2-addition and 1,4-addition of bromine, Br_2, to 1,3-butadiene.

3.15.b Cycloaddition to Conjugated Dienes: The Diels–Alder Reaction

Conjugated dienes undergo another type of 1,4-addition when they react with alkenes (or alkynes). The simplest example is the addition of ethylene to 1,3-butadiene to give cyclohexene.

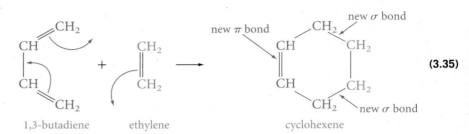

(3.35)

The Diels–Alder reaction is the **cycloaddition reaction** of a conjugated **diene** and a **dienophile** to give a cyclic product in which three π bonds are converted to two σ bonds and a new π bond.

This reaction is an example of a **cycloaddition reaction**, an addition that results in a cyclic product. This cycloaddition, which converts three π bonds to two σ bonds and one new π bond, is called the **Diels–Alder reaction**, after its discoverers, Otto Diels and Kurt Alder. It is so useful for making cyclic compounds that it earned the 1950 Nobel Prize in chemistry for its discoverers. As with hydroboration (Sec. 3.13), this reaction is *concerted*. All bond-breaking and bond-making occur at the same time.

The two reactants are a **diene** and a **dienophile** (diene lover). The simple example in eq. 3.35 is not typical of most Diels–Alder reactions because it proceeds only under pressure and not in good yield. However, this type of reaction gives excellent yields at moderate temperatures if the dienophile has *electron-withdrawing groups** attached, as in the following examples:

(3.36)

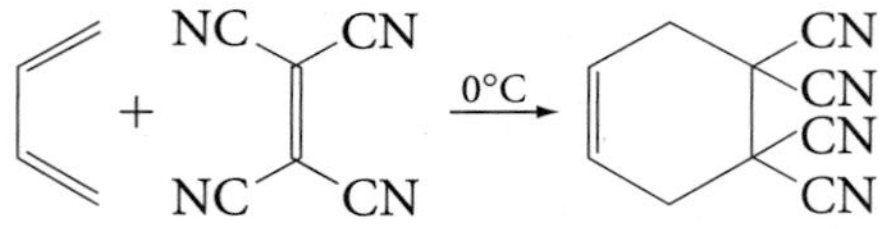

(3.37)

EXAMPLE 3.7

How could a Diels–Alder reaction be used to synthesize the following compound?

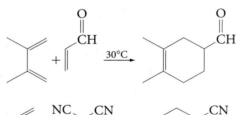

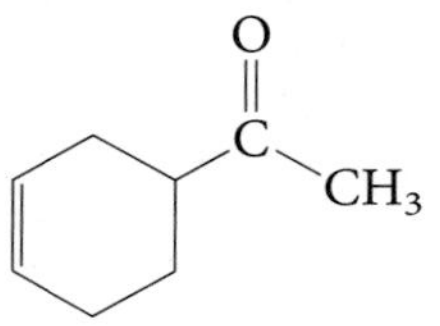

---

*Electron-withdrawing groups are groups of atoms that attract the electrons of the π bond, making the alkene electron poor and therefore more electrophilic toward the diene.

Solution Work backward. The double bond in the product was a single bond in the starting diene. Therefore,

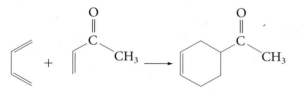

PROBLEM 3.25 Show how limonene (Figure 1.13) could be formed by a Diels–Alder reaction of isoprene (2-methyl-1,3-butadiene) with itself.

PROBLEM 3.26 Draw the structure of the product of each of the following cycloaddition reactions.

a. ![furan] $O + CH_2\!=\!CH\!-\!CN$

b. $CH_2\!=\!CH\!-\!CH\!=\!CH_2 + NC\!-\!C\!\equiv\!C\!-\!CN$

c. $CH_2\!=\!CH\!-\!CH\!=\!CH_2 + H_2C\!=\!CH\!-\!NO_2$

3.16 / Free-Radical Additions; Polyethylene

Some reagents add to alkenes by a free-radical mechanism instead of by an ionic mechanism. From a commercial standpoint, the most important of these free-radical additions are those that lead to polymers.

A **polymer** is a large molecule, usually with a high molecular weight, built up from small repeating units. The simple molecule from which these repeating units are derived is called a **monomer**, and the process of converting a monomer to a polymer is called **polymerization**.

The free-radical polymerization of ethylene gives **polyethylene**, a material that is produced on a very large scale (more than 150 billion pounds worldwide annually). The reaction is carried out by heating ethylene under pressure with a catalyst (eq. 3.38). How does this reaction occur?

A **polymer** is a large molecule containing a repeating unit derived from small molecules called **monomers**. The process of polymer formation is called **polymerization**.

$$CH_2\!=\!CH_2 \xrightarrow[\text{1000 atm, }>100°C]{\text{ROOR}} \ \ \ \ \text{(}CH_2\!-\!CH_2\text{)}_{\overline{n}} \qquad \textbf{(3.38)}$$

ethylene   polyethylene
(*n* = several thousand)

One common type of catalyst for polymerization is an organic peroxide. The O—O single bond is weak, and on heating, this bond breaks, with one electron going to each of the oxygens.

$$R\!-\!\overset{\frown}{O}\!-\!\overset{\frown}{O}\!-\!R \xrightarrow{\text{heat}} 2\,R\!-\!O\cdot \qquad \textbf{(3.39)}$$

organic peroxide   two radicals

A catalyst radical then adds to the carbon–carbon double bond:

$$RO\cdot \quad CH_2\!=\!CH_2 \longrightarrow RO\!-\!CH_2\!-\!\overset{\cdot}{C}H_2 \qquad \textbf{(3.40)}$$

catalyst   a carbon-centered
radical   free radical

The result of this addition is a carbon-centered free radical, which may add to another ethylene molecule, and another, and another, and so on.

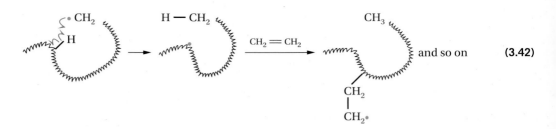

$$\text{ROCH}_2\dot{\text{C}}\text{H}_2 \xrightarrow{\text{CH}_2=\text{CH}_2} \text{ROCH}_2\text{CH}_2\text{CH}_2\dot{\text{C}}\text{H}_2 \xrightarrow{\text{CH}_2=\text{CH}_2}$$

$$\text{ROCH}_2\text{CH}_2\text{CH}_2\text{CH}_2\text{CH}_2\dot{\text{C}}\text{H}_2 \text{ and so on}$$

(3.41)

The carbon chain continues to grow in length until some chain-termination reaction occurs (perhaps a combination of two radicals).

We might think that only a single long chain of carbons will be formed in this way, but this is not always the case. A "growing" polymer chain may abstract a hydrogen atom from its back, so to speak, to cause chain branching.

(3.42)

A giant molecule with long and short branches is thus formed:

branched polyethylene

The degree of chain branching and other features of the polymer structure can often be controlled by the choice of catalyst and reaction conditions.

A polyethylene molecule is mainly saturated despite its name (polyethyl*ene*) and consists mostly of linked CH_2 groups, but with CH groups at the branch points and CH_3 groups at the ends of the branches. It also contains an OR group from the catalyst at one end, but since the molecular weight is very large, this OR group constitutes a minor and, as far as properties go, relatively insignificant fraction of the molecule.

Polyethylene made in this way is transparent and used in packaging and film (for example, for grocery bags as well as for freezer and sandwich bags).

In Chapter 14, we will describe many other polymers, some made by the process just described for polyethylene and some made by other methods.

Fish in polyethylene bag.

Mel Curtis/PhotoDisc, Inc.

3.17 / Oxidation of Alkenes

In general, alkenes are more easily oxidized than alkanes by chemical oxidizing agents. These reagents attack the pi electrons of the double bond. The reactions may be useful as chemical tests for the presence of a double bond or for synthesis.

3.17.a Oxidation with Permanganate; a Chemical Test

Alkenes react with alkaline potassium permanganate to form **glycols** (compounds with two adjacent hydroxyl groups).

Glycols are compounds with two hydroxyl groups on adjacent carbons.

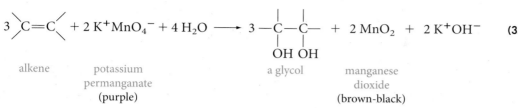

$$3 \, \text{C}=\text{C} + 2 \, \text{K}^+\text{MnO}_4{}^- + 4 \, \text{H}_2\text{O} \longrightarrow 3 \, \underset{\text{OH OH}}{-\text{C}-\text{C}-} + 2 \, \text{MnO}_2 + 2 \, \text{K}^+\text{OH}^- \qquad \textbf{(3.43)}$$

alkene   potassium   a glycol   manganese
              permanganate   dioxide
              (purple)   (brown-black)

As the reaction occurs, the purple color of the permanganate ion is replaced by the brown precipitate of manganese dioxide. Because of this color change, the reaction can be used as a chemical test to distinguish alkenes from alkanes, which normally do not react with potassium permanganate.

> **PROBLEM 3.27** Write an equation for the reaction of 2-hexene with potassium permanganate.

3.17.b Ozonolysis of Alkenes

Alkenes react rapidly and quantitatively with ozone, O_3. Ozone is produced naturally in lightning storms, but in the laboratory, ozone is generated by passing oxygen over a high-voltage electric discharge. The resulting gas stream is then bubbled at low temperature into a solution of the alkene in an inert solvent, such as dichloromethane. The first product, a molozonide, is formed by cycloaddition of the oxygen at each end of the ozone molecule to the carbon–carbon double bond. This product then rearranges rapidly to an ozonide. Since these products may be explosive if isolated, they are usually treated directly with a reducing agent, commonly zinc and aqueous acid, to give carbonyl compounds as the isolated products.

Hexane does not react with purple $KMnO_4$ (left); cyclohexene (right) reacts, producing a brown-black precipitate of MnO_2.

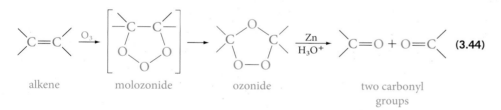

alkene   molozonide   ozonide   two carbonyl
                                                        groups

The net result of this reaction is to break the double bond of the alkene and to form two carbon–oxygen double bonds (carbonyl groups), one at each carbon of the original double bond. The overall process is called **ozonolysis**.

Ozonolysis can be used to locate the position of a double bond. For example, ozonolysis of 1-butene gives two different aldehydes, whereas 2-butene gives a single aldehyde.

Ozonolysis is the oxidation of alkenes with ozone to give carbonyl compounds.

$$\text{CH}_2=\text{CHCH}_2\text{CH}_3 \xrightarrow[\text{2. Zn, H}^+]{\text{1. O}_3} \underset{\text{formaldehyde}}{\text{CH}_2=\text{O}} \quad \underset{\text{propanal}}{\text{O}=\text{CHCH}_2\text{CH}_3} \qquad \textbf{(3.45)}$$

1-butene

$$\text{CH}_3\text{CH}=\text{CHCH}_3 \xrightarrow[\text{2. Zn, H}^+]{\text{1. O}_3} 2 \, \underset{\text{ethanal}}{\text{CH}_3\text{CH}=\text{O}} \qquad \textbf{(3.46)}$$

2-butene

Using ozonolysis, one can easily tell which butene isomer is which. By working backward from the structures of ozonolysis products, one can deduce the structure of an unknown alkene.

A WORD ABOUT...

Ethylene: Raw Material and Plant Hormone

Cranberry harvest.

Ethylene, the simplest alkene, ranks first among organic chemicals in industrial production. Worldwide, the current annual production of ethylene is over 200 billion pounds. Propene comes in second with about half that amount.

How is all this ethylene produced, and what is it used for? Most hydrocarbons can be "cracked" to give ethylene. (See "A Word About . . . Petroleum, Gasoline, and Octane Number" on pages 102–103.) In the United States, the major raw material for this purpose is ethane.

$$CH_3{-}CH_3 \xrightarrow{700{-}900°C} CH_2{=}CH_2 + H_2$$

A substantial fraction of industrial ethylene is, of course, converted to polyethylene, as described in Section 3.16; but ethylene is also a key raw material for the manufacture of other industrial organic chemicals, because of the reactivity of the carbon–carbon double bond. Shown in Figure 3.13 are 9 of the top 50 organic chemicals; each is produced from ethylene.

Ethylene is not only the most important industrial source of organic chemicals, but it also has some biochemical properties that are crucial to agriculture. Ethylene is a **plant hormone** that can cause seeds to sprout, flowers to bloom, fruit to ripen and fall, and leaves and petals to shrivel and turn brown. It is produced naturally by plants from the amino acid *methionine* via an unusual cyclic amino acid, *1-aminocyclopropane-1-carboxylic*

◾ **Figure 3.13**

Ethylene is central to the manufacture of many industrial organic chemicals. The numbers in parentheses give the recent U.S. production of these chemicals in *billions* of pounds.

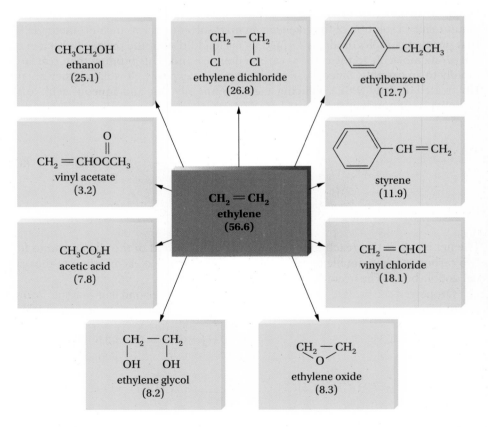

acid (ACC), which is then, in several steps, converted to ethylene.

$$CH_3—S—CH_2CH_2—CH—CO_2^- \xrightarrow{\text{several steps}}$$
$$|$$
$$NH_3$$
$$+$$

methionine

$$CH_2—C \begin{smallmatrix} CO_2^- \\ \\ \end{smallmatrix} \xrightarrow{\text{several steps}} CH_2{=}CH_2 + CO_2 + HCN$$
$$| \quad +$$
$$CH_2 \quad NH_3$$

ACC   ethylene

The mode by which ethylene functions biologically is still being studied.

Chemists have prepared synthetic compounds that can release ethylene in plants in a controlled manner.

One such example is 2-chloroethylphosphonic acid, $ClCH_2CH_2PO(OH)_2$. Sold by Dow Chemical under the trade name *ethrel*, it is water soluble and is taken up by plants, where it breaks down to ethylene, chloride, and phosphate. It has been used commercially to induce fruits, such as pineapples and tomatoes, to ripen uniformly so that an entire field can be harvested efficiently, as shown in the photo on the previous page. Ethylene has also been used to regulate the growth of other crops, such as wheat, apples, cherries, and cotton. Only a small amount need be used, since plants are very sensitive to ethylene and respond to concentrations lower than 0.1 part per million of the gas.

See Problem 3.60.

EXAMPLE 3.8

Ozonolysis of an alkene produces equal amounts of acetone and formaldehyde, $(CH_3)_2C{=}O$ and $CH_2{=}O$, respectively. Deduce the alkene structure.

Solution Connect to each other by a double bond the carbons that are bound to oxygen in the ozonolysis products. The alkene is $(CH_3)_2C{=}CH_2$.

PROBLEM 3.28 Which alkene will give only acetone, $(CH_3)_2C{=}O$, as the ozonolysis product?

3.17.c Other Alkene Oxidations

Various reagents can convert alkenes to epoxides (eq. 3.47).

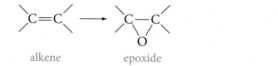

alkene   epoxide

$$(3.47)$$

This reaction and the chemistry of epoxides are detailed in Chapter 8.

Like alkanes (and all other hydrocarbons), alkenes can be used as fuels. Complete combustion gives carbon dioxide and water.

$$C_nH_{2n} + \tfrac{3n}{2} O_2 \longrightarrow nCO_2 + nH_2O \qquad (3.48)$$

3.18 / Some Facts About Triple Bonds

In the final sections of this chapter, we will describe some of the special features of triple bonds and alkynes.

A carbon atom that is part of a triple bond is directly attached to only *two* other atoms, and the bond angle is 180°. Thus, acetylene is linear, as shown in Figure 3.14. The carbon–carbon triple bond distance is about 1.21 Å, appreciably shorter than that of most double (1.34 Å) or single (1.54 Å) bonds. Apparently, three electron pairs between two carbons draw them even closer together than do two pairs. Because of the linear geometry, no *cis–trans* isomerism is possible for alkynes.

Now let us see how the orbital theory of bonding can be adapted to explain these facts.

▰ **Figure 3.14**

Models of acetylene, showing its linearity.

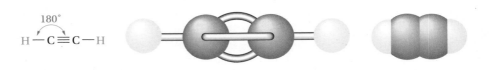

3.19 / The Orbital Model of a Triple Bond

The carbon atom of an acetylene is connected to only *two* other atoms. Therefore, we combine the 2s orbital with only one 2p orbital to make two **sp-hybrid orbitals** (Figure 3.15). These orbitals extend in opposite directions from the carbon atom. The angle between the two hybrid orbitals is 180° so as to minimize repulsion between any electrons placed in them. One valence electron is placed in each sp-hybrid orbital. The remaining two valence electrons occupy two different p orbitals that are perpendicular to each other and perpendicular to the hybrid sp orbitals.

*sp-*Hybrid orbitals are half *s* and half *p* in character. The angle between two *sp* orbitals is 180°.

The formulation of a triple bond from two *sp*-hybridized carbons is shown in Figure 3.16. End-on overlap of two *sp* orbitals forms a sigma bond between the two carbons, and lateral overlap of the properly aligned p orbitals forms two pi bonds (designated π_1 and π_2 in the figure). This model nicely explains the linearity of acetylenes.

▰ **Figure 3.15**

Unhybridized versus *sp*-hybridized orbitals on carbon.

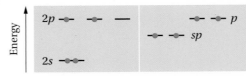

Atomic orbitals of carbon

The 2s and one 2p orbital are combined to form two hybrid *sp* orbitals, leaving one electron in each of two *p* orbitals.

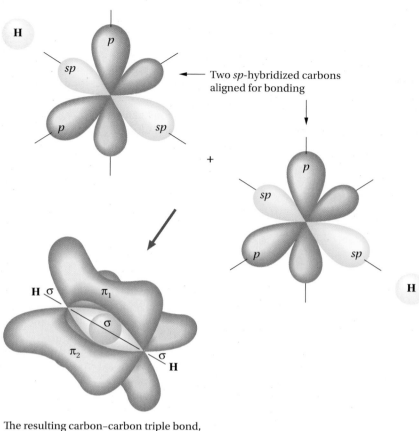

Two *sp*-hybridized carbons
aligned for bonding

The resulting carbon–carbon triple bond,
with a hydrogen atom attached to each
remaining *sp* bond. (The orbitals involved
in the C—H bonds are omitted for clarity.)

■ **Figure 3.16**
A triple bond consists of the end-on
overlap of two *sp*-hybrid orbitals
to form a σ bond and the lateral
overlap of two sets of parallel-
oriented *p* orbitals to form two
mutually perpendicular π bonds.

3.20 Addition Reactions of Alkynes

As in alkenes, the pi electrons of alkynes are exposed to electrophilic attack (see
Figure 3.17). Therefore, many addition reactions described for alkenes also occur,
though usually more slowly, with alkynes. For example, bromine adds as follows:

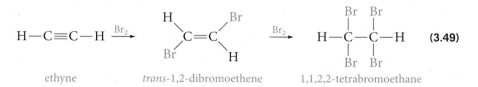

ethyne   *trans*-1,2-dibromoethene   1,1,2,2-tetrabromoethane

■ **Figure 3.17**
Electrostatic potential map of
acetylene, showing the exposure
of pi electrons (red) to attack by
electrophiles.

In the first step, the addition occurs mainly *trans*.

With an ordinary nickel or platinum catalyst, alkynes are hydrogenated all the way
to alkanes (eq. 3.1). However, a special palladium catalyst (called **Lindlar's catalyst**)
can control hydrogen addition so that only 1 mole of hydrogen adds. In this case, the

Lindlar's catalyst limits addition of
hydrogen to an alkyne to 1 mole
and produces a *cis* alkene.

A WORD ABOUT...   Petroleum, Gasoline, and Octane Number

Petroleum refinery, where crude oil is processed.

Petroleum is at present our most important fossil fuel. The need for petroleum to keep our industrial society going follows close behind our need for food, air, water, and shelter. What is black gold, as petroleum has been called, and how do we use it?

Petroleum is a complex mixture of hydrocarbons formed over eons of time through the gradual decay of buried animal and vegetable matter. **Crude oil** is a viscous black liquid that collects in vast underground pockets in sedimentary rock (the word *petroleum* literally means rock oil, from the Latin *petra*, rock, and *oleum*, oil). It must be brought to the surface via drilling and pumping. To be most useful, the crude oil must be refined.

The first step in petroleum refining is usually **distillation**. The crude oil is heated to about 400°C, and the vapors rise through a tall fractionating column. The lower boiling fractions rise faster and higher in the column before condensing to liquids; higher boiling fractions do not rise as high. By drawing off liquid at various column levels, technicians separate crude oil roughly into the fractions shown in Table 3.3.

The gasoline fraction comprises only about 25% of crude oil. It is the most valuable fraction, however, both as a fuel and as a source material for the petrochemical industry, the industry that furnishes our synthetic fibers,

plastics, and many other useful materials. For this reason, many processes have been developed for converting the other fractions into gasoline.

Higher boiling fractions can be "cracked" by heat and catalysts (mainly silica and alumina) to give products with shorter carbon chains and therefore lower boiling points. The carbon chain can break at many points.

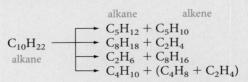

$$
C_{10}H_{22} \longrightarrow
\begin{cases}
\overset{\text{alkane}}{C_5H_{12}} + \overset{\text{alkene}}{C_5H_{10}} \\
C_8H_{18} + C_2H_4 \\
C_2H_6 + C_8H_{16} \\
C_4H_{10} + (C_4H_8 + C_2H_4)
\end{cases}
$$

To balance the number of hydrogens, any particular alkane must give at least one alkane and one alkene as products. Thus, catalytic cracking converts larger alkanes into a mixture of smaller alkanes and alkenes and increases the yield of gasoline from petroleum.

During cracking, large amounts of the lower gaseous hydrocarbons—ethene, propene, butanes, and butenes—are formed. Some of these, especially ethene, are used as petrochemical raw materials. To obtain more gasoline, scientists sought methods to convert these low-molecular-weight hydrocarbons to somewhat larger hydrocarbons that boil in the gasoline range. One such process is **alkylation**, the combination of an alkane with an alkene to form a higher-boiling alkane.

$$
C_2H_6 + C_4H_8 \xrightarrow{\text{catalyst}} C_6H_{14}
$$

$$
\underbrace{C_4H_{10} + C_4H_8}_{\text{gases}} \xrightarrow{\text{catalyst}} \underbrace{C_8H_{18}}_{\text{liquids}}
$$

Table 3.3 ▪ **Common Petroleum Fractions**

Boiling range, °C	Name	Range of carbon atoms per molecule	Use
<20	gases	C_1 to C_4	heating, cooking, petrochemical raw material
20–200	naphtha; straight-run gasoline	C_5 to C_{12}	fuel; lighter fractions (such as petroleum ether, bp 30°C–60°C) also used as laboratory solvents
200–300	kerosene	C_{12} to C_{15}	fuel
300–400	fuel oil	C_{15} to C_{18}	heating homes, diesel fuel
>400		over C_{18}	lubricating oil, greases, paraffin waxes, asphalt

These processes, which were developed in the 1930s, were important for producing aviation fuel during World War II and are still used to make high-octane gasoline, now for our much-improved automobile engines.

This brings us to **octane number** and why it is important. Some hydrocarbons, especially those with highly branched structures, burn smoothly in an automobile engine and drive the piston forward evenly. Other hydrocarbons, especially those with unbranched carbon chains, tend to explode in the cylinder and drive the piston forward violently. These undesirable explosions produce audible knocks. A scale was set up many years ago to evaluate this important knock property of gasolines. **Isooctane** (2,2,4-trimethylpentane), an excellent fuel with a highly branched structure, was arbitrarily given a rating of 100, and **heptane**, a very poor automotive fuel, was given a rating of 0. A "regular" gasoline with an octane number of 87 has the same "knock" properties as a mixture that is 87% isooctane and 13% heptane.

Small amounts of **tetraethyllead**, $(CH_3CH_2)_4Pb$, in gasoline improve its octane rating but are undesirable for environmental reasons, and most gasoline is now unleaded. However, unleaded gasoline must therefore contain hydrocarbons with a high octane rating. It became important to develop methods that convert straight-chain to branched-chain hydrocarbons, since these have higher octane ratings.

Certain catalysts can produce branched-chain alkanes from straight-chain alkanes. This process, called **isomerization**, is carried out on a large scale commercially.

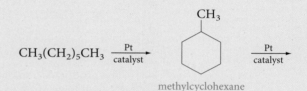

$$CH_3CH_2CH_2CH_3 \xrightarrow[\text{alumina}]{AlCl_3, \ HCl} CH_3CHCH_3$$

n-butane   isobutane

Aromatic hydrocarbons, such as benzene and toluene, also have a high octane rating. A platinum catalyst used in a process called **platforming** cyclizes and dehydrogenates alkanes to cycloalkanes and to aromatic hydrocarbons. Of course, large amounts of hydrogen gas are also formed during platforming. Millions of gallons of aromatic hydrocarbons are produced daily by such processes, not only to add to unleaded gasoline to improve its octane rating but also to supply raw materials for many other petrochemical-based products, as we will see in the next chapter.

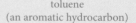

$$CH_3(CH_2)_5CH_3 \xrightarrow[\text{catalyst}]{Pt} \qquad \xrightarrow[\text{catalyst}]{Pt}$$

methylcyclohexane

toluene
(an aromatic hydrocarbon)

See Problem 3.65.

product is a *cis* alkene, because both hydrogens add to the same face of the triple bond from the catalyst surface.

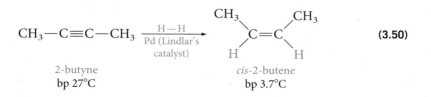

$$CH_3-C{\equiv}C-CH_3 \xrightarrow[\substack{\text{Pd (Lindlar's)} \\ \text{catalyst)}}]{H-H}$$ (3.50)

2-butyne
bp 27°C

cis-2-butene
bp 3.7°C

With unsymmetric triple bonds and unsymmetric reagents, Markovnikov's Rule is followed in each step, as shown in the following example:

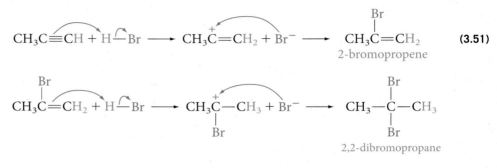

$$CH_3C{\equiv}CH + H{-}Br \longrightarrow CH_3\overset{+}{C}{=}CH_2 + Br^- \longrightarrow CH_3\underset{}{\overset{Br}{C}}{=}CH_2 \qquad (3.51)$$

2-bromopropene

$$CH_3\overset{Br}{C}{=}CH_2 + H{-}Br \longrightarrow CH_3\overset{+}{\underset{Br}{C}}{-}CH_3 + Br^- \longrightarrow CH_3{-}\underset{Br}{\overset{Br}{C}}{-}CH_3$$

2,2-dibromopropane

Addition of water to alkynes requires not only an acid catalyst but mercuric ion as well. The mercuric ion forms a complex with the triple bond and activates it for addition. Although the reaction is similar to that of alkenes, the initial product—a **vinyl alcohol** or **enol**—rearranges to a carbonyl compound.

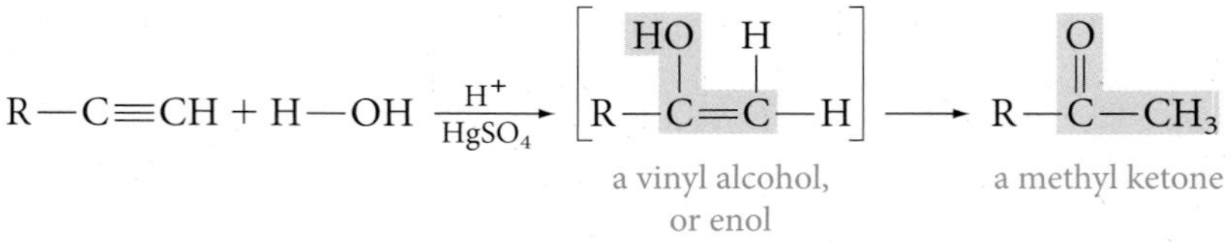

> A **vinyl alcohol** or **enol** is an alcohol with a carbon–carbon double bond on the carbon that bears the hydroxyl group.

$$R{-}C{\equiv}CH + H{-}OH \xrightarrow[HgSO_4]{H^+} \left[R{-}\overset{HO}{\underset{}{C}}{=}\overset{H}{\underset{}{C}}{-}H \right] \longrightarrow R{-}\overset{O}{\underset{}{C}}{-}CH_3 \qquad (3.52)$$

a vinyl alcohol, or enol   a methyl ketone

The product is a methyl ketone or, in the case of acetylene itself (R═H), acetaldehyde. We will have more to say about the chemistry of enols and the mechanism of the second step of eq. 3.52 in Chapter 9.

PROBLEM 3.29 Write equations for the following reactions:

a. $CH_3CH_2C{\equiv}CH + Br_2$ (1 mole)   c. 1-hexyne + HBr (1 and 2 moles)
b. $CH_3CH_2C{\equiv}CCH_3 + Cl_2$ (2 moles)   d. 1-butyne + H_2O (Hg^{2+}, H^+)

3.21 Acidity of Alkynes

A hydrogen atom on a triply bonded carbon is weakly acidic and can be removed by a very strong base. Sodium amide, for example, converts acetylenes to acetylides.

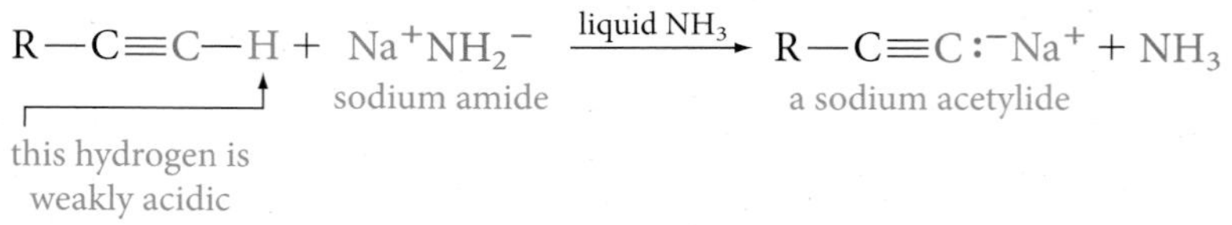

$$R{-}C{\equiv}C{-}H + Na^+NH_2^- \xrightarrow{\text{liquid } NH_3} R{-}C{\equiv}C{:}^-Na^+ + NH_3 \qquad (3.53)$$

this hydrogen is weakly acidic   sodium amide   a sodium acetylide

This type of reaction occurs easily with a hydrogen attached to a carbon-carbon triple bond (i.e., RC≡C—H), but less so when the hydrogen is adjacent to a double or single bond. Why? Consider the hybridization of the carbon atom in each type of C—H bond:

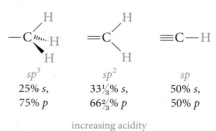

sp^3 sp^2 sp
25% s,   33⅓% s,   50% s,
75% p   66⅔% p   50% p

increasing acidity →

A CLOSER LOOK AT... Petroleum

Conduct research on the Internet to find more information on petroleum and to answer the following questions.

Petroleum Consumption and Extraction

1. How much oil does the world use in a year? What percentage of U.S. energy needs is supplied through oil?

2. What are some of the earliest known examples of oil use by humans? When did the modern oil industry come into being?

3. What are some of the techniques used to extract petroleum (crude oil) from rock? Describe some

of the new technologies being developed to extract oil.

Chemical Processing

1. What is cracking? What is the difference between thermal and catalytic cracking?

2. *Unification* and *alteration* are other methods of chemical processing. Define these processes and explain why they are used.

As the hybridization at carbon becomes more s-like and less p-like, the acidity of the attached hydrogen increases. Recall that s orbitals are closer to the nucleus than are p orbitals. Consequently, the bonding electrons are closest to the carbon nucleus in the ≡C—H bond, making it easiest for a base to remove that type of proton. Sodium amide is a sufficiently strong base for this purpose.*

PROBLEM 3.30 Write an equation for the reaction of 1-hexyne with sodium amide in liquid ammonia.

Though acidic, 1-alkynes are much less so than water. Acetylides can therefore be hydrolyzed to alkynes by water. Internal alkynes have no exceptionally acidic hydrogens.

PROBLEM 3.31 Write an equation for the reaction of a sodium acetylide with water.

PROBLEM 3.32 Will 2-hexyne react with sodium amide? Explain.

---

*See Table C in the Appendix for the relative acidities of organic functional groups.

REACTION SUMMARY

1. Reactions of Alkenes

a. Addition of Halogens (Sec. 3.7a)

$$\text{C}=\text{C} + X_2 \longrightarrow -\overset{|}{\underset{X}{\text{C}}}-\overset{|}{\underset{X}{\text{C}}}- \quad (X = \text{Cl, Br})$$

b. Addition of Polar Reagents (Sec. 3.7b and Sec. 3.7c)

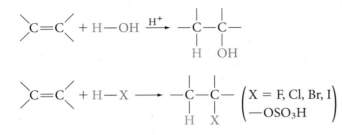

$$\text{C}=\text{C} + \text{H}-\text{OH} \xrightarrow{\text{H}^+} -\overset{|}{\underset{\text{H}}{\text{C}}}-\overset{|}{\underset{\text{OH}}{\text{C}}}-$$

$$\text{C}=\text{C} + \text{H}-\text{X} \longrightarrow -\overset{|}{\underset{\text{H}}{\text{C}}}-\overset{|}{\underset{\text{X}}{\text{C}}}- \left(\begin{array}{l} X = \text{F, Cl, Br, I} \\ -\text{OSO}_3\text{H} \end{array}\right)$$

c. Hydroboration–Oxidation (Sec. 3.13)

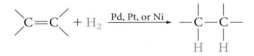

$$3\ \text{RCH}=\text{CH}_2 \xrightarrow{\text{BH}_3} (\text{RCH}_2\text{CH}_2)_3\text{B} \xrightarrow[\text{HO}^-]{\text{H}_2\text{O}_2} 3\ \text{RCH}_2\text{CH}_2\text{OH}$$

d. Addition of Hydrogen (Sec. 3.14)

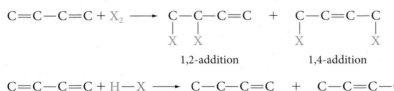

$$\text{C}=\text{C} + \text{H}_2 \xrightarrow{\text{Pd, Pt, or Ni}} -\overset{|}{\underset{\text{H}}{\text{C}}}-\overset{|}{\underset{\text{H}}{\text{C}}}-$$

e. Addition of X₂ and HX to Conjugated Dienes (Sec. 3.15a)

$$\text{C}=\text{C}-\text{C}=\text{C} + X_2 \longrightarrow \underset{\underset{\text{1,2-addition}}{\text{X}\quad\text{X}}}{\text{C}-\text{C}-\text{C}=\text{C}} \quad + \quad \underset{\underset{\text{1,4-addition}}{\text{X}\qquad\text{X}}}{\text{C}-\text{C}=\text{C}-\text{C}}$$

$$\text{C}=\text{C}-\text{C}=\text{C} + \text{H}-\text{X} \longrightarrow \underset{\underset{\text{1,2-addition}}{\text{H}\quad\text{X}}}{\text{C}-\text{C}-\text{C}=\text{C}} \quad + \quad \underset{\underset{\text{1,4-addition}}{\text{H}\qquad\text{X}}}{\text{C}-\text{C}=\text{C}-\text{C}}$$

(X = Cl, Br)

f. Cycloaddition to Conjugated Dienes (Sec. 3.15b)

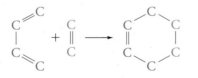

g. **Polymerization of Ethylene (Sec. 3.16)**

$$n\text{H}_2\text{C}=\text{CH}_2 \xrightarrow{\text{catalyst}} \text{-}(\text{CH}_2-\text{CH}_2)_n$$

h. **Oxidation to Diols or Carbonyl-Containing Compounds (Sec. 3.17)**

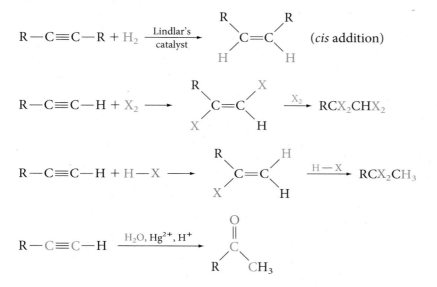

2. **Reactions of Alkynes**

a. **Additions to the Triple Bond (Sec. 3.20)**

b. **Formation of Acetylide Anions (Sec. 3.21)**

$$\text{R}-\text{C}\equiv\text{C}-\text{H} + \text{Na}^+\text{NH}_2^- \xrightarrow{\text{NH}_3} \text{R}-\text{C}\equiv\text{C}:^- \text{Na}^+ + \text{NH}_3$$

MECHANISM SUMMARY

1. **Electrophilic Addition (E^+ = electrophile and $\text{Nu}:^-$ = nucleophile; Sec. 3.9)**

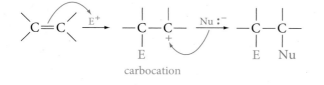

2. 1,2-Addition and 1,4-Addition (Sec. 3.15a)

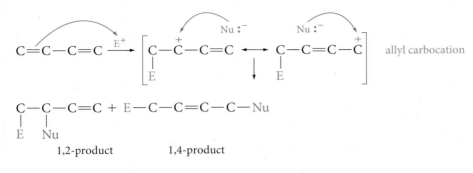

$$C-C-C=C + E-C-C=C-C-Nu$$

$$\underset{E \quad Nu}{|\quad|}$$

1,2-product   1,4-product

3. Cycloaddition (Sec. 3.15b)

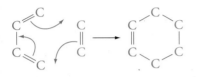

4. Free-Radical Polymerization of Ethylene (Sec. 3.16)

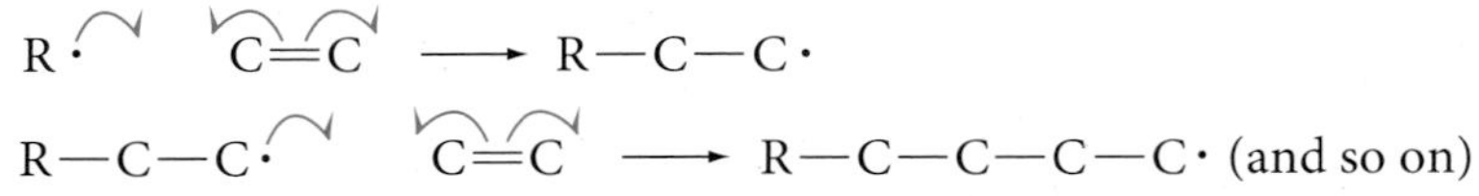

$$R\cdot \quad C=C \longrightarrow R-C-C\cdot$$

$$R-C-C\cdot \quad C=C \longrightarrow R-C-C-C-C\cdot \text{ (and so on)}$$

ADDITIONAL PROBLEMS

ꙮWL Interactive versions of these problems are assignable in OWL.

Alkenes and Alkynes: Nomenclature and Structure

3.33 For the following compounds, write structural formulas and IUPAC names for all possible isomers having the indicated number of multiple bonds:

    a. C_4H_6 (one triple bond)   **b.** C_5H_{10} (one double bond)   **c.** C_5H_8 (two double bonds)

3.34 Name the following compounds by the IUPAC system:

    a. $CH_3CH=C(CH_2CH_2CH_3)_2$ **b.** $(CH_3)_2CHCH=CHCH_3$ **c.**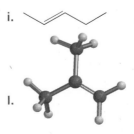

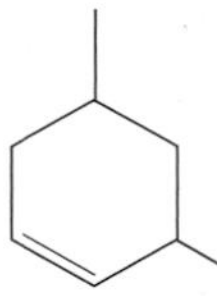

    d. $CH_3C\equiv CCH(Cl)CH_2CH_3$ **e.** $CH_3-C\equiv C-CH_2-CH=CHCH_3$ **f.** $CH_2=CH-C(Br)=CH_2$

    g. $CH_3-C\equiv C-CH=CH_2$ **h.**

    i.

    j. 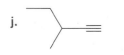   **k.**    **l.**

3.35 Write a structural formula for each of the following compounds:

a. 1-bromo-3-heptene
b. 3-methylcyclopentene
c. vinyl bromide
d. vinylcyclohexane
e. 1,3-difluoro-2-butene
f. 4,5-dimethyl-2-heptyne
g. 3-ethyl-1,4-cyclohexadiene
h. 1,3-dimethylcyclopentene
i. vinylcyclopentane
j. allyl chloride
k. 2,3-dichloro-1,3-cyclopentadiene

3.36 Explain why the following names are incorrect and give a correct name in each case:

a. 5-octyne
b. 3-pentene
c. 3-buten-1-yne
d. 1-methyl-2-pentene
e. 2-methylcyclopentene
f. 2-propyl-1-propene
g. 3-pentyne-1-ene
h. 3-ethyl-1,3-butadiene

3.37 a. What are the usual lengths for the single (sp^3–sp^3), double (sp^2–sp^2), and triple (sp–sp) carbon–carbon bonds?
   b. The *single* bond in each of the following compounds has the length shown. Suggest a possible explanation for the observed shortening.

$$CH_2{=}CH{-}CH{=}CH_2 \qquad CH_2{=}CH{-}C{\equiv}CH \qquad HC{\equiv}C{-}C{\equiv}CH$$

$$\uparrow \qquad\qquad\qquad \uparrow \qquad\qquad\qquad \uparrow$$

$$1.47\ \text{Å} \qquad\qquad 1.43\ \text{Å} \qquad\qquad 1.37\ \text{Å}$$

3.38 Which of the following compounds can exist as *cis–trans* isomers? If such isomerism is possible, draw the structures in a way that clearly illustrates the geometry.

a. 3-octene
b. 3-chloropropene
c. 1-hexene
d. 1-bromopropene
e. 4-methylcyclohexene
f. 1,3,5,7-octatetraene
g. 2,3-difluoro-2-butene

3.39 The mold metabolite and antibiotic *mycomycin* has the formula:

$$HC{\equiv}C{-}C{\equiv}C{-}CH{=}C{=}CH{-}CH{=}CH{-}CH{=}CH{-}CH_2{-}\overset{\displaystyle O}{\overset{\displaystyle \|}{C}}{-}OH$$

Number the carbon chain, starting with the carbonyl carbon.

a. Which multiple bonds are conjugated?
b. Which multiple bonds are cumulated?
c. Which multiple bonds are isolated?

3.40 Certain tropical plants create extra protection from hungry arthropods, such as caterpillars, by secreting volatile terpenoids, such as nerolidol and 4,8-dimethyl-1,3,7-nonatriene, in order to attract the herbivore's natural enemies:

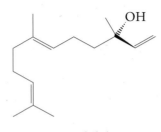

nerolidol

Which double bond(s) in nerolidol and 4,8-dimethyl-1,3,7-nonatriene can exist as *cis–trans* isomers?

Electrophilic Addition to Alkenes

3.41 Write the structural formula and name of the product when each of the following reacts with one mole of bromine.

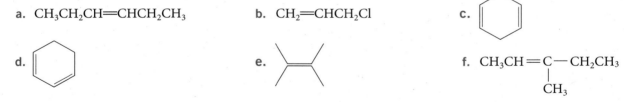

a. $CH_3CH_2CH{=}CHCH_2CH_3$

b. $CH_2{=}CHCH_2Cl$

c.

d.

e.

f. $CH_3CH{=}\underset{\underset{\displaystyle CH_3}{|}}{C}{-}CH_2CH_3$

3.42 What reagent will react by addition to what unsaturated hydrocarbon to form each of the following compounds?

a. $CH_3CHBrCHBrCH_3$

b. $(CH_3)_2CHOSO_3H$

c. $(CH_3)_3COH$

d. 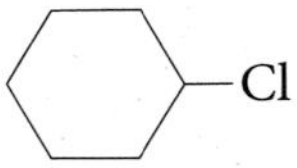 ⬡—Cl

e. $CH_3CH{=}CHCH_2Cl$

f. $CH_3CH_2CCl_2CCl_2CH_3$

g. 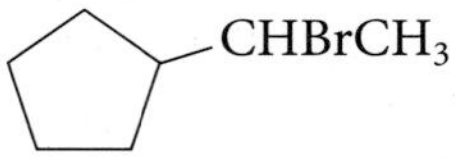 ⬠—CHBrCH_3

h.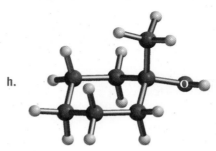

3.43 Which of the following reagents are electrophiles? Which are nucleophiles?

a. H_3O^+
e. H_2SO_4

b. HCl
f. $AlBr_3$

c. Br^-
g. HO^-

d. $FeCl_3$

3.44 The acid-catalyzed hydration of 1-methylcyclohexene gives 1-methylcyclohexanol.

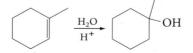

Write every step in the mechanism of this reaction.

3.45 When 2-methylpropene reacts with water and an acid catalyst, only one product alcohol is observed: *tert*-butyl alcohol (2-methyl-2-propanol).

a. Draw the structures of the two intermediate carbocations that could form from the protonation of 2-methyl-propene. Which is more stable (has lower energy)? (*Hint:* See eq. 3.21.)

b. Draw a reaction energy diagram for the formation of the two intermediate carbocations in 3.45a from protonation of 2-methylpropene. Use your diagram to explain why only one alcohol is formed (see Figure 3.11).

3.46 *Caryophyllene* is an unsaturated hydrocarbon mainly responsible for the odor of oil of cloves. It has the molecular formula $C_{15}H_{24}$. Hydrogenation of caryophyllene gives a saturated hydrocarbon $C_{15}H_{28}$. Does caryophyllene contain any rings? How many? What else can be learned about the structure of caryophyllene from its hydrogenation?

3.47 Water can act as an electrophile or as a nucleophile. Explain.

3.48 Predict the structures of the two possible monohydration products of limonene (Figure 1.13). These alcohols are called *terpineols*. Predict the structure of the diol (dialcohol) obtained by hydrating both double bonds in limonene. These alcohols are used in the cough medicine "elixir of terpin hydrate."

Reactions of Conjugated Dienes

3.49 Draw the resonance contributors to the carbocation

$$(CH_3)_2CHCHCH{=\!=}CHCH(CH_3)_2$$

with the $+$ charge on the central CH.

Does the ion have a symmetric structure?

3.50 Adding 1 mole of hydrogen chloride (HCl) to 1,3-octadiene gives two products. Give their structures, and write all of the steps in a reaction mechanism that explains how each product is formed.

3.51 Predict the product of each of the following Diels–Alder reactions for the diene (left) and dienophile (right) as shown below.

a.

b.

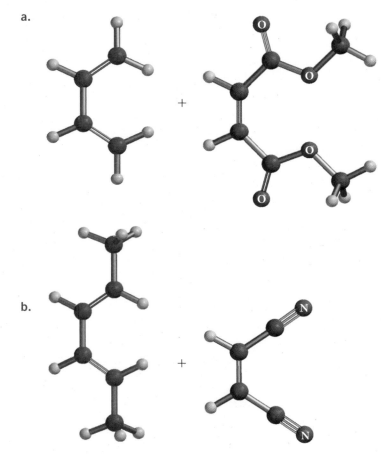

3.52 From what diene and dienophile could each of the following be made?

a.

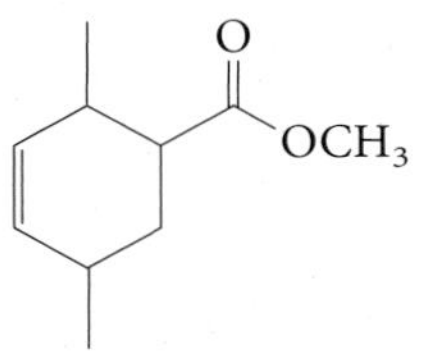

O

OCH₃

b.

CN

CN

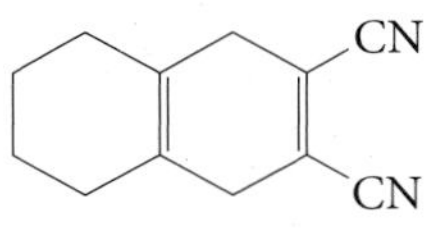

Other Reactions of Alkenes

3.53 Write an equation that clearly shows the structure of the alcohol obtained from the sequential hydroboration and H_2O_2/OH^- oxidation of

a. 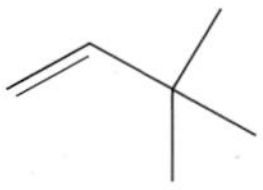

b. 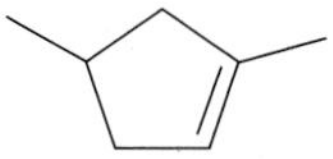

c. 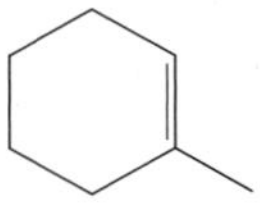

3.54 Write equations to show how 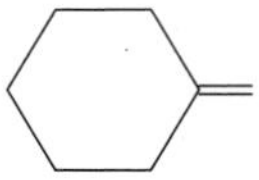 CH_2 could be converted to:

a. 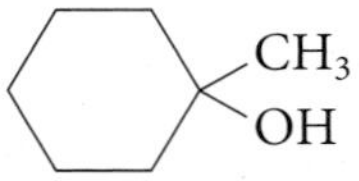

b. 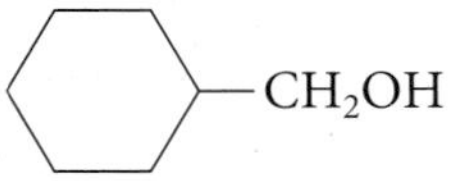

3.55 Describe two simple chemical tests that could be used to distinguish methylcyclohexane from methylcyclohexene. (*Hint:* Both tests produce color changes when alkenes are present.)

3.56 Give the structural formulas of the alkenes that, on ozonolysis, give:

a. $(CH_3)_2C{=}O$ and $CH_2{=}O$
b. only $(CH_3CH_2)_2C{=}O$
c. $CH_3CH{=}O$ and $CH_3CH_2CH{=}O$
d. $O{=}CHCH_2CH_2CH_2CH{=}O$

3.57 Given the information that free-radical stability follows the same order as carbocation stability (3° > 2° > 1°), predict the structure of polypropylene produced by the free-radical polymerization of propene. It should help to write out each step in the mechanism, as in eqs. 3.40 and 3.41.

Reactions of Alkynes

3.58 Write equations for the following reactions:

a. 2-octyne + H_2 (1 mole, Lindlar's catalyst)
b. 3-hexyne + Br_2 (2 moles)
c. 1-hexyne + sodium amide in liquid ammonia
d. 1-butyne + H_2O (H^+, Hg^{2+} catalyst)

3.59 Determine what alkyne and what reagent will give

a. 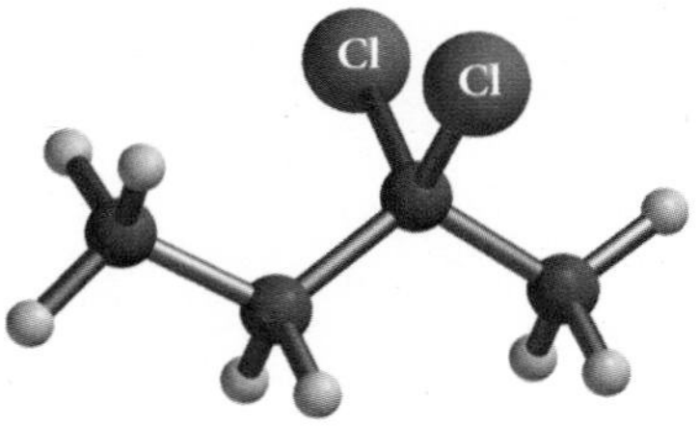

b. 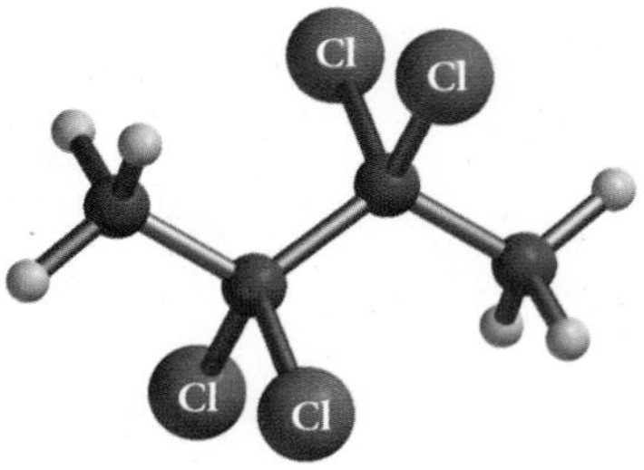

Summary Problems

3.60 As discussed in "A Word About . . . Ethylene" on pp. 98–99, 2-chloroethylphosphonic acid, $ClCH_2CH_2PO(OH)_2$, is a commercially synthesized compound that is used for inducing the ripening of fruit.

a. Write a balanced equation for the conversion of $ClCH_2CH_2PO(OH)_2$ with water to form ethylene, chloride, and phosphate.
b. Which functional group in 2-chloroethylphosphonic acid is responsible for its water solubility?

3.61 Write an equation for the reaction of $CH_2{=}CHCH_2CH_3$ with each of the following reagents:

a. hydrogen chloride
b. bromine
c. hydrogen (Pt catalyst)
d. H_2O, H^+
e. ozone, followed by H^+
f. $KMnO_4$, OH^-
g. BH_3 followed by H_2O_2, OH^-
h. oxygen (combustion)

3.62 Write a complete reaction mechanism for the addition of HCl to 1-butyne (Problem 3.59a).

3.63 For the structures of nerolidol and 4,8-dimethyl-1,3,7-nonatriene in Problem 3.40, provide the products for each compound after:

a. hydrogenation (3 moles H_2, Pt catalyst)   b. addition of 1 mole of Br_2 c. ozonolysis

3.64 When 1-butyne is treated with $[(CH_3)_2CHCH]_2BH$ followed by H_2O_2 and OH^-, the product isolated is the aldehyde
$$\underset{CH_3}{|}$$

butanal: $CH_3CH_2CH_2-\overset{\overset{O}{\|}}{C}-H$.

a. What reaction of alkenes is similar to this reaction?

b. Compare the product with the product of Problem 3.58d. Write the structure of an intermediate product (not isolated) that rearranges to form butanal. (*Hint:* See eq. 3.52.)

3.65 As discussed in "A Word About . . . Petroleum, Gasoline, and Octane Number" on p. 103, isomerization is often used to convert one alkane to a more substituted alkane. Suggest the highly branched product obtained from the isomerization of pentane using a mixture of $AlCl_3$ and HCl over an alumina catalyst. Provide the correct IUPAC name for the product.

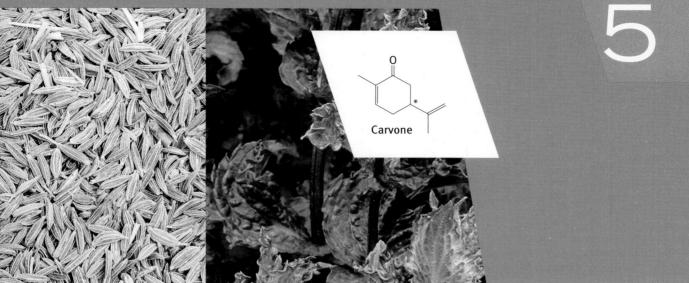

The odors of caraway seeds (left) and mint leaves (right) arise from the enantiomers of carvone, which differ in arrangement of the atoms attached to the indicated (*) carbon.

Carvone

© PhotoDisc, Inc.   Okapia/Photo Researchers

Stereoisomerism

Stereoisomers have the same order of attachment of the atoms, but different arrangements of the atoms in space. The differences between stereoisomers are more subtle than those between structural isomers. Yet stereoisomerism is responsible for significant differences in chemical properties of molecules. The effectiveness of a drug often depends on which stereoisomer is used, as does the presence or absence of side effects (see "A Word About . . . Enantiomers and Biological Activity," pp. 172–173). The chemistry of life itself is affected by the natural predominance of particular stereoisomers in biological molecules such as carbohydrates (Chapter 16), amino acids (Chapter 17), and nucleic acids (Chapter 18).

We have already seen that stereoisomers can be characterized according to the ease with which they can be interconverted (see Sec. 2.11 and Figure 2.8). That is, they may be **conformers**, which can be interconverted by rotation about a single bond, or they may be **configurational isomers**, which can be interconverted only by breaking and remaking covalent bonds. Here we will consider other useful ways to categorize stereoisomers, ways that are particularly helpful in describing their properties.

OWL

Online homework for this chapter can be assigned in OWL, an online homework assessment tool.

Stereoisomers have the same order of attachment of atoms but different spatial arrangements of atoms. **Conformers** and **configurational isomers** are two classes of stereoisomers (Sec. 2.11).

Chiral molecules possess the property of handedness, whereas **achiral** molecules do not.

5.1 Chirality and Enantiomers

Consider the difference between a pair of gloves and a pair of socks. A sock, like its partner, can be worn on either the left or the right foot. But a left-hand glove, unlike its partner, cannot be worn on the right hand. Like a pair of gloves, certain molecules possess this property of "handedness," which affects their chemical behavior. Let us examine the idea of molecular handedness.

A molecule (or object) is either **chiral** or **achiral**. The word *chiral*, pronounced "kairal" to rhyme with spiral, comes from the Greek χειρ (*cheir,* hand). A chiral molecule (or object) is one that exhibits the property of handedness. An achiral molecule does not have this property.

What test can we apply to tell whether a molecule (or object) is chiral or achiral? We examine the molecule (or object) *and its mirror image. The mirror image of a chiral molecule cannot be superimposed on the molecule itself. The mirror image of an achiral molecule, however, is identical to or superimposable on the molecule itself.*

Let us apply this test to some specific examples. Figure 5.1 shows one of the more obvious examples. The mirror image of a left hand is not another left hand, but a right hand. A hand and its mirror image are *not* superimposable. A hand is chiral. But the mirror image of a ball (sphere) is also a ball (sphere), so a ball (sphere) is achiral.

PROBLEM 5.1 Which of the following objects are chiral and which are achiral?

a. golf club   b. teacup   c. football   d. corkscrew
e. tennis racket f. shoe   g. portrait   h. pencil

▰ **Figure 5.1**
The mirror-image relationships of chiral and achiral objects.

The mirror image of a left hand is not a left hand, but a right hand.

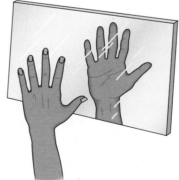
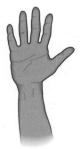

Chiral object

The mirror image of a ball is identical with the object itself.

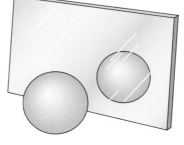

Achiral object

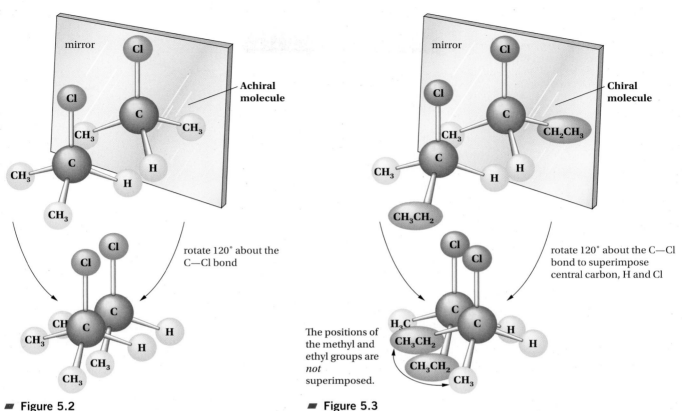

■ Figure 5.2

Model of 2-chloropropane and its mirror image. The mirror image is superimposable on the original molecule.

■ Figure 5.3

Model of 2-chlorobutane and its mirror image. The mirror image is *not* superimposable on the original molecule. The two forms of 2-chlorobutane are enantiomers.

Now let us look at two molecules, 2-chloropropane and 2-chlorobutane, and their mirror images.* Figure 5.2 shows that 2-chloropropane is achiral. Its mirror image is superimposable on the molecule itself. Therefore 2-chloropropane has only one possible structure.

On the other hand, as Figure 5.3 shows, 2-chlorobutane has two possible structures, related to one another as nonsuperimposable mirror images. We call a pair of molecules that are related as nonsuperimposable mirror images **enantiomers**. Every molecule, of course, has a mirror image. Only those that are *nonsuperimposable* are called enantiomers.

Enantiomers are a pair of molecules related as nonsuperimposable mirror images.

5.2 | Stereogenic Centers; the Stereogenic Carbon Atom

What is it about their structures that leads to chirality in 2-chlorobutane but not in 2-chloropropane? Notice that, in 2-chlorobutane, carbon atom 2, the one marked with an asterisk, has four different groups attached to it (Cl, H, CH_3, and CH_2CH_3). A carbon atom with four different groups attached to it is called a **stereogenic carbon atom**. This type of carbon is also called a **stereogenic center** because it gives rise to stereoisomers.

A **stereogenic carbon atom** or **stereogenic center** is a carbon atom with four different groups attached to it.

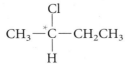

---

*Build 3D models of these molecules to visualize them better. In general, using 3D models while reading this chapter will help you understand the concepts.

▰ **Figure 5.4**

The chirality of enantiomers. Looking down the C—A bond, we have to read clockwise to spell BED for the model on the left, but we must read counterclockwise for its mirror image.

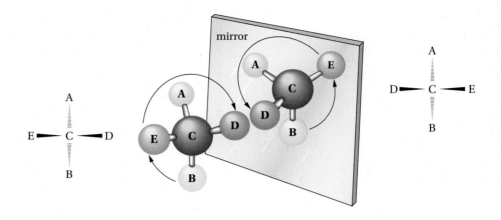

Let us examine the more general case of a carbon atom with any four different groups attached; let us call the groups A, B, D, and E. Figure 5.4 shows such a molecule and its mirror image. That the molecules on each side of the mirror in Figure 5.4 are non-superimposable mirror images (enantiomers) becomes clear by examining Figure 5.5. (We strongly urge you to use molecular models when studying this chapter. It is sometimes difficult to visualize three-dimensional structures when they are drawn on a two-dimensional surface [this page or a blackboard], though with experience, your ability to do so will improve.) The handedness of these molecules is also illustrated in Figure 5.4, where the clockwise or counterclockwise arrangement of the groups (we might call them right- or left-handed arrangements) is apparent.

What happens when all four of the groups attached to the central carbon atom are *not* different from one another? Suppose two of the groups are identical—say, A, A, B, and D. Figure 5.6 describes this situation. The molecule and its mirror image are now *identical,* and the molecule is achiral. This is exactly the situation with 2-chloropropane, where two of the four groups attached to carbon-2 are identical (CH_3, CH_3, H, and Cl).

▰ **Figure 5.5**

When the four different groups attached to a stereogenic carbon atom are arranged to form mirror images, the molecules are not superimposable. The models may be twisted or turned in any direction, but as long as no bonds are broken, only two of the four attached groups can be made to coincide.

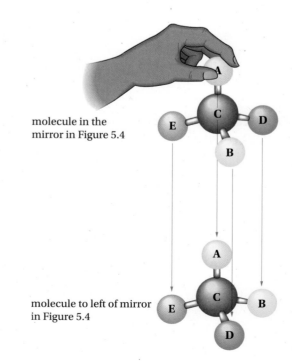

molecule in the mirror in Figure 5.4

molecule to left of mirror in Figure 5.4

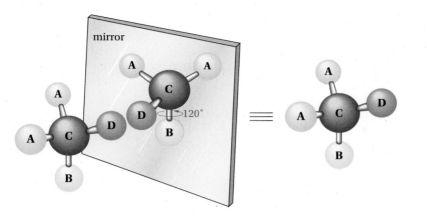

■ **Figure 5.6**
The tetrahedral model at the left has two corners occupied by identical groups (A). It has a plane of symmetry that passes through atoms B, C, and D and bisects angle ACA. Its mirror image is identical to itself, seen by a 120° rotation of the mirror image about the C—B bond. Hence the model is achiral.

Notice that the molecule in Figure 5.6 has a plane of symmetry. This plane passes through atoms B, C, and D and bisects the ACA angle. On the other hand, the molecule in Figure 5.4 does *not* have a symmetry plane.

A **plane of symmetry** (sometimes called a mirror plane) is a plane that passes through a molecule (or object) in such a way that what is on one side of the plane is the exact reflection of what is on the other side. *Any molecule with a plane of symmetry is achiral. Chiral molecules do not have a plane of symmetry.* Seeking a plane of symmetry is usually one quick way to tell whether a molecule is chiral or achiral.

What is on one side of a **plane of symmetry**, or mirror plane, is the exact reflection of what is on the other side.

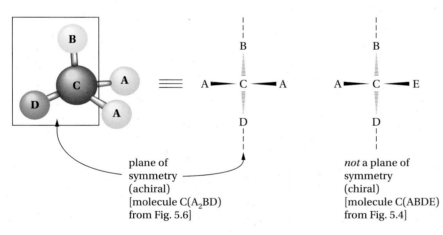

plane of symmetry (achiral) [molecule C(A₂BD) from Fig. 5.6]

not a plane of symmetry (chiral) [molecule C(ABDE) from Fig. 5.4]

To summarize, a molecule with a stereogenic center (in our examples, the stereogenic center is a carbon atom with four different groups attached to it) can exist in two stereoisomeric forms, that is, as a pair of enantiomers. Such a molecule does not have a symmetry plane. Compounds with a symmetry plane are achiral.

EXAMPLE 5.1

Locate the stereogenic center in 3-methylhexane.

Solution Draw the structure, and look for a carbon atom with four different groups attached.

$$\overset{1}{C}H_3\overset{2}{C}H_2\overset{3}{C}H\overset{4}{C}H_2\overset{5}{C}H_2\overset{6}{C}H_3$$
$$\underset{\displaystyle CH_3}{|}$$

All of the carbons except carbon-3 have at least two hydrogens (two identical groups) and therefore cannot be stereogenic centers. But carbon-3 has four different groups attached (H, CH_3—, CH_3CH_2—, and $CH_3CH_2CH_2$—) and is therefore a stereogenic center. By convention, we sometimes mark such centers with an asterisk.

$$CH_3CH_2\overset{*}{C}HCH_2CH_2CH_3$$
$$|$$
$$CH_3$$

EXAMPLE 5.2

Draw the two enantiomers of 3-methylhexane.

Solution There are many ways to do this. Here are two of them. First draw carbon-3 with four tetrahedral bonds.

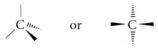

Then attach the four different groups, in any order.

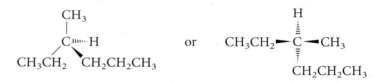

Now draw the mirror image, or interchange the positions of any two groups.

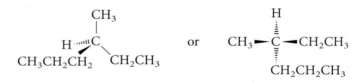

To convince yourself that the *interchange of any two groups at a stereogenic center produces the enantiomer,* work with molecular models.

PROBLEM 5.2 Find the stereogenic centers in

a. $CH_3CH_2CHBrCH_2CH_2CH_2CH_3$ b. 3-methylcyclohexene
c. ClFCHCH$_3$ d. 2,3-dibromobutane

PROBLEM 5.3 Which of the following compounds is chiral?

a. 1-bromo-1-phenylethane   b. 1-bromo-2-phenylethane

PROBLEM 5.4 Draw three-dimensional structures for the two enantiomers of the chiral compound in Problem 5.3.

PROBLEM 5.5 Locate the planes of symmetry in the eclipsed conformation of ethane. In this conformation, is ethane chiral or achiral?

PROBLEM 5.6 Does the staggered conformation of ethane have planes of symmetry? In this conformation, is ethane chiral or achiral? *(Careful!)*

PROBLEM 5.7 Locate the planes of symmetry in *cis*- and *trans*-1,2-dichloroethene. Are these molecules chiral or achiral? *(Careful!)*

Enantiomers differ in the arrangement of the groups attached to the stereogenic center. This arrangement of groups is called the **configuration** of the stereogenic center. *Enantiomers are another type of configurational isomer; they are said to have opposite configurations.*

The arrangement of four groups attached to a stereogenic center is called the **configuration** of that center.

When referring to a particular enantiomer, we would like to be able to specify which configuration we mean without having to draw the structure. A convention for doing this is known as the *R-S* or Cahn–Ingold–Prelog* system. Here is how it works.

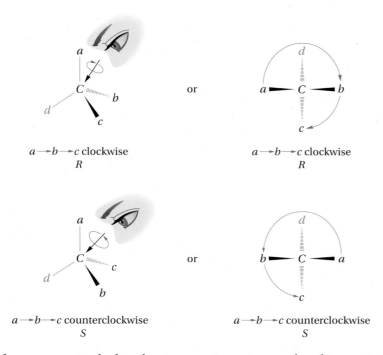

The four groups attached to the stereogenic center are placed in a priority order (by a system we will describe next), $a \rightarrow b \rightarrow c \rightarrow d$. The stereogenic center is then observed *from the side opposite the lowest priority group, d.* If the remaining three groups ($a \rightarrow b \rightarrow c$) form a clockwise array, the configuration is designated *R* (from the Latin *rectus,* right).** If they form a *counterclockwise* array, the configuration is designated as *S* (from the Latin *sinister,* left).

The priority order of the four groups is set in the following way:

Rule 1

The atoms directly attached to the stereogenic center are ranked according to *atomic number:* the higher the atomic number, the higher the priority.

$$Cl > O > C > H$$
high priority — low priority

---

*Named after R. S. Cahn and C. K. Ingold, both British organic chemists, and V. Prelog, a Swiss chemist and Nobel Prize winner.

**More precisely, *rectus* means "right" in the sense of "correct, or proper," and not in the sense of direction (which is *dexter* = right, opposite to left). It may not be entirely coincidental that the initials of one of the inventors of this system are *R. S.*

If one of the four groups is H, it always has the lowest priority, and one views the stereogenic center looking down the C—H bond from C to H.

Rule 2

If a decision cannot be reached with rule 1 (that is, if two or more of the directly attached atoms are the same), work outward from the stereogenic center until a decision is reached. For example, the ethyl group has a higher priority than the methyl group, because at the first point of difference, working outward from the stereogenic center, we come to a *carbon* (higher priority) in the ethyl group and a *hydrogen* (lower priority) in the methyl group.

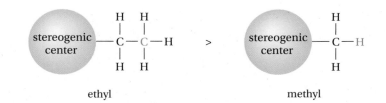

ethyl   methyl

EXAMPLE 5.3

Assign a priority order to the following groups: —H, —Br, —CH$_2$CH$_3$, and —CH$_2$OCH$_3$.

Solution —Br > —CH$_2$OCH$_3$ > —CH$_2$CH$_3$ > —H

The atomic numbers of the directly attached atoms are ordered Br > C > H. To prioritize the two carbon groups, we must continue along the chain until a point of difference is reached.

$$—CH_2OCH_3 > —CH_2CH_3 \qquad (O > C)$$

PROBLEM 5.8 Assign a priority order to each of the following sets of groups:

a. —CH(CH$_3$)$_2$, —CH$_3$, —H, —NH$_2$
b. —OH, —Br, —CH$_3$, —CH$_2$OH
c. —OCH$_3$, —NH(CH$_3$)$_2$, —CH$_2$NH$_2$, —OH
d. —CH$_2$CH$_2$CH$_3$, —CH$_2$CH$_3$, —C(CH$_3$)$_3$, —CH(CH$_3$)$_2$

For stereogenic centers in cyclic compounds, the same rule for assigning priorities is followed. For example, in 1,1,3-trimethylcyclohexane, the four groups attached to carbon-3 in order of priority are —CH$_2$C(CH$_3$)$_2$CH$_2$ > —CH$_2$CH$_2$ > —CH$_3$ > —H.

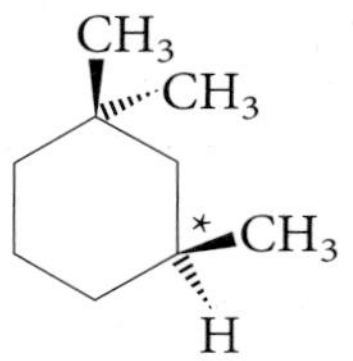

1,1,3-trimethylcyclohexane

A third, somewhat more complicated, rule is required to handle double or triple bonds and aromatic rings (which are written in the Kekulé fashion).

Rule 3

Multiple bonds are treated as if they were an equal number of single bonds. For example, the vinyl group —CH=CH$_2$ is counted as

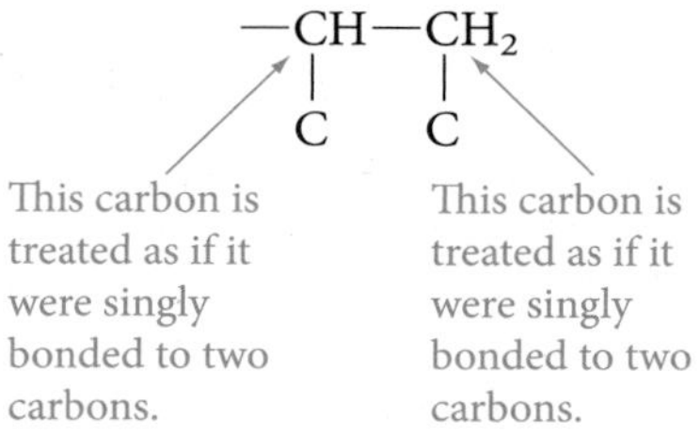

$$—CH—CH_2$$
$$\diagup \mid \quad \mid \diagdown$$
$$C \quad C$$

This carbon is treated as if it were singly bonded to two carbons.

This carbon is treated as if it were singly bonded to two carbons.

Similarly,

$$—C{\equiv}CH \quad \text{is treated as} \quad \begin{array}{cc} C & C \\ \mid & \mid \\ —C—C—H \\ \mid & \mid \\ C & C \end{array}$$

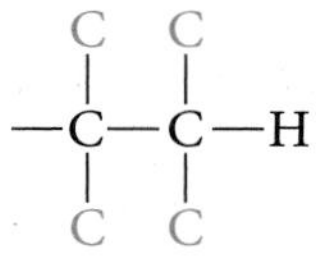

and

$$—CH{=}O \quad \text{is treated as} \quad \begin{array}{c} H \\ \mid \\ —C—O \\ \mid \quad \mid \\ O \quad C \end{array}$$

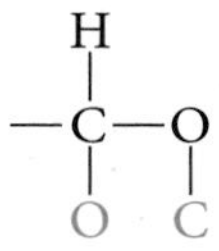

EXAMPLE 5.4

Which group has the higher priority, isopropyl or vinyl?

Solution The vinyl group has the higher priority. We continue along the chain until we reach a difference, shown in color.

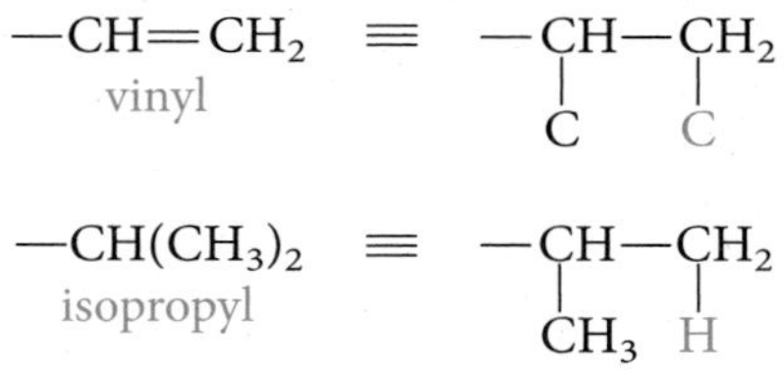

$$—CH{=}CH_2 \quad \equiv \quad \begin{array}{cc} —CH—CH_2 \\ \mid \quad \mid \\ C \quad C \end{array}$$
vinyl

$$—CH(CH_3)_2 \quad \equiv \quad \begin{array}{cc} —CH—CH_2 \\ \mid \quad \mid \\ CH_3 \quad H \end{array}$$
isopropyl

PROBLEM 5.9 Assign a priority order to

a. —C≡CH and —CH=CH$_2$ b. —CH=CH$_2$ and ⬡

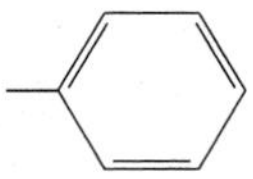

c. —CH=O, —CH=CH$_2$, —CH$_2$CH$_3$, and —CH$_2$OH

Now let us see how these rules are applied.

EXAMPLE 5.5

Assign the configuration (*R* or *S*) to the following enantiomer of 3-methyl-hexane (see Example 5.2).

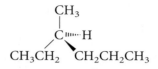

Solution First assign the priority order to the four different groups attached to the stereogenic center.

$$-CH_2CH_2CH_3 > -CH_2CH_3 > -CH_3 > -H$$

Now view the molecule *from the side opposite the lowest-priority group* (—H) and determine whether the remaining three groups, from high to low priority, form a clockwise (*R*) or counterclockwise (*S*) array.

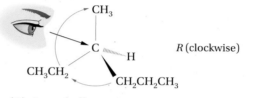

We write the name (*R*)-3-methylhexane.

If we view the other representation of this molecule shown in Example 5.2, we come to the same conclusion.

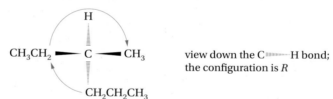

PROBLEM 5.10 Determine the configuration (*R* or *S*) at the stereogenic center in

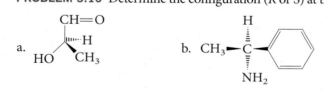

EXAMPLE 5.6

Draw the structure of (*R*)-2-bromobutane.

Solution First, write out the structure and prioritize the groups attached to the stereogenic center.

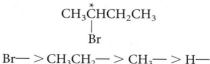

$$Br- > CH_3CH_2- > CH_3- > H-$$

Now make the drawing with the H (lowest priority group) "away" from you, and place the three remaining groups (Br → CH$_3$CH$_2$ → CH$_3$) in a clockwise (*R*) array.

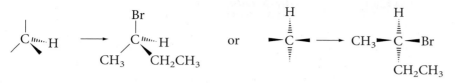

Of course, we could have started with the top-priority group at either of the other two bonds to give the following structures, which are equivalent to the previous structures:

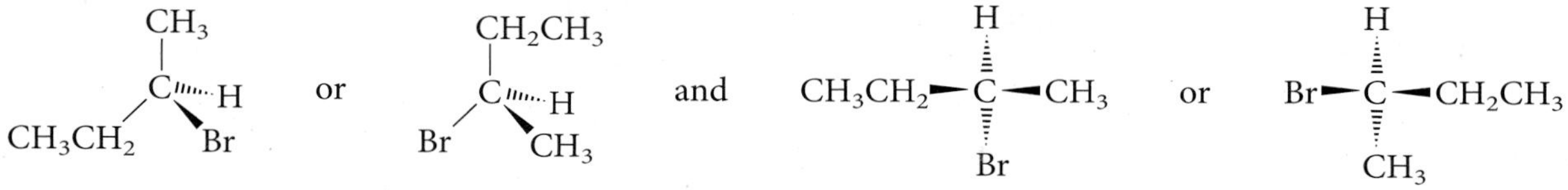

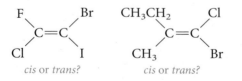

PROBLEM 5.11 Draw the structure of

a. (*S*)-3-phenylheptane
b. (*S*)-3-methylcyclopentene
c. (*R*)-4-methyl-2-hexene

5.4 The *E-Z* Convention for *Cis–Trans* Isomers

Before we continue with other aspects of chirality, let us digress briefly to describe a useful extension of the Cahn–Ingold–Prelog system of nomenclature to *cis–trans* isomers. Although we can easily use *cis–trans* nomenclature for 1,2-dichloroethene or 2-butene (see Sec. 3.5), that system is sometimes ambiguous, as in the following examples:

$$
\underset{Cl}{\overset{F}{\diagdown}}C=C\underset{I}{\overset{Br}{\diagup}}
\qquad
\underset{CH_3}{\overset{CH_3CH_2}{\diagdown}}C=C\underset{Br}{\overset{Cl}{\diagup}}
$$

cis or trans? cis or trans?

The system we have just discussed for stereogenic centers has been extended to double-bond isomers. We use exactly the same priority rules. *The two groups attached to each carbon of the double bond are assigned priorities.* If the two higher-priority groups are on *opposite* sides of the double bond, the prefix *E* (from the German *entgegen,* opposite) is used. If the two higher-priority groups are on the *same* side of the double bond, the prefix is *Z* (from the German *zusammen,* together). The higher-priority groups for the previous examples are shown here in color, and the correct names are given below the structures.

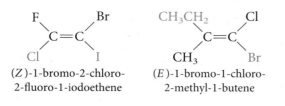

(*Z*)-1-bromo-2-chloro-   (*E*)-1-bromo-1-chloro-
2-fluoro-1-iodoethene   2-methyl-1-butene

PROBLEM 5.12 Name each compound by the *E-Z* system.

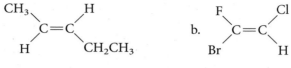

a.

b.

PROBLEM 5.13 Write the structure for

a. (*E*)-1,3-hexadiene

b. (*Z*)-2-butene

5.5 Polarized Light and Optical Activity

The concept of molecular chirality follows logically from the tetrahedral geometry of carbon, as developed in Sections 5.1 and 5.2. Historically, however, these concepts were developed in the reverse order; how this happened is one of the most elegant and logically beautiful stories in the history of science. The story began in the early eighteenth century with the discovery of polarized light and with studies on how molecules placed in the path of such a light beam affect it.

An ordinary light beam consists of waves that vibrate in all possible planes perpendicular to its path. However, if this light beam is passed through certain types of substances, the waves of the transmitted beam will all vibrate in parallel planes. Such a light beam, said to be **plane polarized**, is illustrated in Figure 5.7. One convenient way to polarize light is to pass it through a device composed of Iceland spar (crystalline calcium carbonate) called a Nicol prism (invented in 1828 by the British physicist William Nicol). A more recently developed polarizing material is Polaroid, invented by the American E. H. Land. It contains a crystalline organic compound properly oriented and embedded in a transparent plastic. Sunglasses, for example, are often made from Polaroid.

Plane-polarized light is a light beam consisting of waves that vibrate in parallel planes.

◢ **Figure 5.7**
A beam of light, AB, initially vibrating in all directions, passes through a polarizing substance that "strains" the light so that only the vertical component emerges.

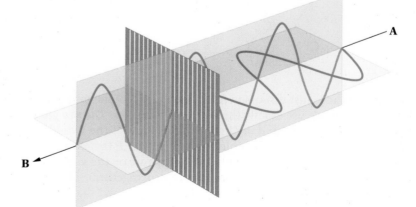

A light beam will pass through *two* samples of polarizing material only if their polarizing axes are aligned. If the axes are perpendicular, no light will pass through. This result, illustrated in Figure 5.8, is the basis of an instrument used to study the effect of various substances on plane-polarized light.

■ **Figure 5.8**

The two sheets of polarizing material shown have their axes aligned perpendicularly. Although each disk alone is almost transparent, the area where they overlap is opaque. You can duplicate this effect using two pairs of Polaroid sunglasses. Try it! (Courtesy of the Polaroid Corporation.)

A **polarimeter** is shown schematically in Figure 5.9. Here is how it works. With the light on and the sample tube empty, the analyzer prism is rotated so that the light beam that has been polarized by the polarizing prism is completely blocked and the field of view is dark. At this point, the prism axes of the polarizer prism and the analyzer prism are perpendicular to one another. Now the sample is placed in the sample tube. If the substance is **optically inactive**, nothing changes. The field of view remains dark. But if an **optically active** substance is placed in the tube, it rotates the plane of polarization, and some light passes through the analyzer to the observer. By turning the analyzer prism clockwise or counterclockwise, the observer can again block the light beam and restore the dark field.

A polarimeter, or spectropolarimeter, is an instrument used to detect optical activity. An **optically active** substance rotates plane-polarized light, whereas an **optically inactive** substance does not.

The angle through which the analyzer prism must be rotated in this experiment is called α, the **observed rotation**. It is equal to the number of degrees that the optically active substance rotated the beam of plane-polarized light. If the analyzer must be rotated to the *right* (clockwise), the optically active substance is said to be **dextrorotatory** ($+$); if rotated to the *left* (counterclockwise), the substance is **levorotatory** ($-$).*

The observed rotation, α, of a sample of an optically active substance depends on its molecular structure and also on the number of molecules in the sample tube, the

An optically active substance that is **dextrorotatory** would rotate plane-polarized light to the right (clockwise), while a **levorotatory** compound would rotate plane-polarized light to the left (counterclockwise).

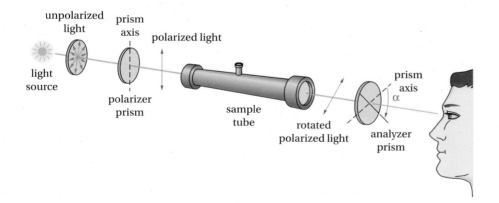

■ **Figure 5.9**

Diagram of a polarimeter.

---

*It is not possible to tell from a single measurement whether a rotation is $+$ or $-$. For example, is a reading $+10°$ or $-350°$? We can distinguish between these alternatives by, for example, increasing the sample concentration by 10%. Then a $+10°$ reading would change to $+11°$, and a $-350°$ reading would change to $-385°$ (that is, $-25°$).

A WORD ABOUT...

Pasteur's Experiments and the van't Hoff–LeBel Explanation

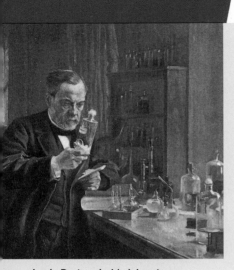

Louis Pasteur in his laboratory.
Louis Pasteur (1822–95) in his Laboratory, 1885 (oil on canvas), Edelfelt, Albert Gustaf Aristides (1854–1905)/Musee d'Orsay, Paris, France/Giraudon/The Bridgeman Art Library

The great French scientist Louis Pasteur (1822–1895) was the first to recognize that optical activity is related to what we now call chirality. He realized that similar molecules that rotate plane-polarized light through equal angles but in opposite directions must be related to one another as an object and its non-superimposable mirror image (that is, as a pair of enantiomers). Here is how he came to that conclusion.

Working in the mid-nineteenth century in a country famous for its wine industry, Pasteur was aware of two *isomeric* acids that deposit in wine casks during fermentation. One of these, called **tartaric acid**, was optically active and dextrorotatory. The other, at the time called **racemic acid**, was optically inactive.

Pasteur prepared various salts of these acids. He noticed that *crystals* of the sodium ammonium salt of *tartaric acid* were *not* symmetric (that is, they were not identical to their mirror images). In other words, they exhibited the property of handedness (chirality). Let us say that the crystals were all left-handed.

When Pasteur next examined crystals of the same salt of *racemic acid,* he found that they, too, were chiral but that some of the crystals were left-handed and others were right-handed. The crystals were related to one another as an object and its nonsuperimposable mirror image, and they were present in equal amounts. With a magnifying lens and a pair of tweezers, Pasteur carefully separated these crystals into two piles: the left-handed ones and the right-handed ones.

Then Pasteur made a crucial observation. When he *dissolved* the two types of crystals *separately* in water and placed the solutions in a polarimeter, he found that each solution was optically active (remember, he obtained these crystals from racemic acid, which was optically inactive). One solution had a specific rotation identical to that of the sodium ammonium salt of tartaric acid! The other had an equal but *opposite* specific rotation. This meant that it must be the mirror image, or levorotatory tartaric acid. Pasteur correctly concluded that racemic acid was not really a single substance, but a 50:50 mixture of (+) and (−)-tartaric acids. Racemic acid was optically inactive because it contained equal amounts of two enantiomers. We now define a **racemic mixture** as a 50:50 mixture of enantiomers, and of course, such a mixture is optically inactive because the rotations of the two enantiomers cancel out.

Pasteur recognized that optical activity must be due to some property of tartaric acid molecules themselves,

---

*The **specific rotation** of an optically active substance (a standardized version of its **observed rotation**) is a characteristic physical property of the substance.*

length of the tube, the wavelength of the polarized light, and the temperature. All of these have to be standardized if we want to compare the optical activity of different substances. This is done using the **specific rotation** [α], defined as follows:

$$\text{Specific rotation} = [\alpha]_\lambda^t = \frac{\alpha}{l \times c}\,(\text{solvent})$$

where *l* is the length of the sample tube in *decimeters, c* is the concentration in *grams per milliliter, t* is the temperature of the solution, and λ is the wavelength of light. The solvent used is indicated in parentheses. Measurements are usually made at room temperature, and the most common light source is the D-line of a sodium vapor lamp ($\lambda = 589.3$ nm), although modern instruments called **spectropolarimeters** allow the light wavelength to be varied at will. The specific rotation of an optically active substance at a particular wavelength is as definite a property of the substance as its melting point, boiling point, or density.

not to some property of the crystals, because the crystalline shape was lost when the crystals were dissolved in water in order to measure the specific rotation. However, the precise explanation in terms of molecular structure eluded Pasteur and was not to come for another 25 years.

Pasteur's experiments were performed at about the same time that Kekulé in Germany was developing his theories about organic structures. Kekulé recognized that carbon is tetravalent, and there is even a hint in some of his writings (about 1867) and also in the writings of the Russian chemist A. M. Butlerov (1862) and the Italian E. Paterno (1869) that carbon might be tetrahedral. But it was not until 1874 that the Dutch physical chemist J. H. van't Hoff (1852–1911) and the Frenchman J. A. LeBel (1847–1930) simultaneously, but quite independently, made a bold hypothesis about carbon that would explain the optical activity of some organic molecules and the optical inactivity of others.

These scientists knew their solid geometry. They knew that four different objects can be arranged in two different ways at the corners of a tetrahedron, and that these two ways are related to one another as an object and its nonsuperimposable mirror image. They also knew that this arrangement resulted in right- and left-handedness, as shown in the drawing at the top of the next column.

They made the bold hypothesis that the four valences of carbon were directed toward the corners of a tetrahedron, and that optically active molecules would contain at least one carbon atom with four different groups attached to it. This idea would explain

why Pasteur's (+) and (−)-tartaric acids rotated plane-polarized light to equalextents but in opposite (right- and left-handed) directions. Optically inactive organic substances would either contain no asymmetric carbon atom (stereogenic carbon) or be a 50:50 mixture of enantiomers.

This, then, is how the tetrahedral geometry of carbon was first recognized.* The boldness and brilliance of this proposal is remarkable when one realizes that neither the electron nor the nucleus of an atom had yet been discovered and that almost nothing was then known about the physical nature of chemical bonds. At the time they made their proposal, van't Hoff and LeBel were relatively unknown chemists. Their hypothesis was ridiculed by at least one establishment chemist at the time, but it was soon generally accepted, has survived many tests, and can now be regarded as fact. In 1901, van't Hoff received the first Nobel Prize in chemistry.

See Problem 5.60.

---

*Actually, LeBel developed his ideas based on symmetry considerations, whereas van't Hoff based his (at least at first) on the idea of an asymmetric carbon atom. For a stimulating article on these differences, see R. B. Grossman, *J. Chem. Educ.* **1989**, *66*, 30–33.

PROBLEM 5.14 Camphor is optically active. A camphor sample (1.5 g) dissolved in ethanol (optically inactive) to a total volume of 50 mL, placed in a 5-cm polarimeter sample tube, gives an observed rotation of +0.66° at 20°C (using the sodium D-line). Calculate and express the specific rotation of camphor.

In the early nineteenth century, the French physicist Jean Baptiste Biot (1774–1862) studied the behavior of a great many substances in a polarimeter. Some, such as turpentine, lemon oil, solutions of camphor in alcohol, and solutions of cane sugar in water, were optically active. Others, such as water, alcohol, and solutions of salt in water, were optically inactive. Later, many natural products (carbohydrates, proteins, and steroids, to name just a few) were added to the list of optically active compounds. What is it about the structure of molecules that causes some to be optically active and others inactive?

When plane-polarized light passes through a single molecule, the light and the electrons in the molecule interact. This interaction causes the plane of polarization to rotate slightly.* But when we place a substance in a polarimeter, *we do not place a single molecule there; we place a large collection of molecules there* (recall that even as little as one-thousandth of a mole contains 6×10^{20} molecules).

Now, if the substance is achiral, then for every single molecule in one conformation that rotates the plane of polarization in one direction, there will be another molecule with the mirror-image conformation that will rotate the plane of polarization an equal amount in the opposite direction. Every conceivable conformation will be present in a large sample of achiral molecules, and the effects of these conformers will cancel one another out. The result is that the light beam passes through a sample of achiral molecules without any net change in the plane of polarization. *Achiral molecules are optically inactive.*

But for chiral molecules, the situation is different. A 50:50 mixture of a pair of enantiomers will not rotate the plane of polarization for the same reason that achiral molecules do not rotate it. Consider, however, a sample of *one enantiomer* (say, *R*) of a chiral molecule. For any molecule with a given configuration in the sample, *there can be no mirror-image configuration* (because the mirror image gives a different molecule, the *S* enantiomer). Therefore, the rotation in the polarization plane caused by one molecule is *not* canceled by any other molecule, and the light beam passes through the sample with a net change in the plane of polarization. *Single enantiomers of chiral molecules are optically active.***

5.6 Properties of Enantiomers

In what properties do enantiomers differ from one another? Enantiomers differ only with respect to chirality. In all other respects, they are identical. For this reason, they differ from one another *only in properties that are also chiral.* Let us illustrate this idea first with familiar objects.

A left-handed baseball player (chiral) can use the same ball or bat (achiral) as can a right-handed player. But, of course, a left-handed player (chiral) can use only a left-handed baseball glove (chiral). A bolt with a right-handed thread (chiral) can use the same washer (achiral) as a bolt with a left-handed thread, but it can only fit into a nut (chiral) with a right-handed thread. To generalize, *the chirality of an object is most significant when the object interacts with another chiral object.*

Enantiomers have identical achiral properties, such as melting point, boiling point, density, and various types of spectra. Their solubilities in an ordinary, achiral solvent are also identical. However, *enantiomers have different chiral properties,* one of which is the *direction* in which they rotate plane-polarized light (clockwise or counterclockwise). Although enantiomers rotate plane-polarized light in opposite directions, they have specific rotations of the same magnitude (but with opposite signs), because the *number of degrees* is not a chiral property. Only the *direction* of rotation is a chiral property. Here is a specific example.

Lactic acid is an optically active hydroxyacid that is important in several biological processes. It has one stereogenic center. Its structure and some of its properties are shown in Figure 5.10. Note that both enantiomers have identical melting points and, *except for sign,* identical specific rotations.

---

*This is because the electric and magnetic fields that result from electronic motions in the molecule affect the electric and magnetic fields of the light. Even achiral molecules have this effect, because they can have chiral conformations (for example, the enantiomeric gauche conformations of 1,2-dichloroethane).

**Mixtures of enantiomers that contain more of one enantiomer than the other are also optically active.

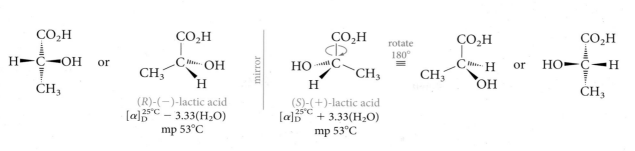

(R)-(−)-lactic acid
$[\alpha]_D^{25°C} - 3.33(H_2O)$
mp 53°C

(S)-(+)-lactic acid
$[\alpha]_D^{25°C} + 3.33(H_2O)$
mp 53°C

■ **Figure 5.10**
The structures and properties of the lactic acid enantiomers.

There is no obvious relationship between configuration (*R* or *S*) and sign of rotation (+ or −). For example, (*R*)-lactic acid is levorotatory. When (*R*)-lactic acid is converted to its methyl ester (eq. 5.1), the configuration is unchanged because none of the bonds to the stereogenic carbon is involved in the reaction. Yet the sign of rotation of the product, a physical property, changes from − to +.

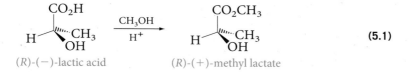

(R)-(−)-lactic acid   (R)-(+)-methyl lactate   **(5.1)**

Enantiomers often behave differently in a biological setting because these properties usually involve a reaction with another chiral molecule. For example, the enzyme *lactic acid dehydrogenase* will oxidize (+)-lactic acid to pyruvic acid, but it will *not* oxidize (−)-lactic acid (eq. 5.2).

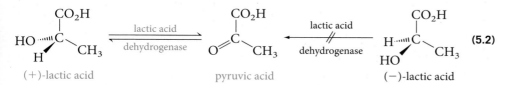

(+)-lactic acid   pyruvic acid   (−)-lactic acid   **(5.2)**

Why? The enzyme itself is chiral and can distinguish between right- and left-handed lactic acid molecules, just as a right hand distinguishes between left-handed and right-handed gloves.

Enantiomers differ in many types of biological activity. One enantiomer may be a drug, whereas its enantiomer may be ineffective. For example, only (−)-adrenaline is a cardiac stimulant; (+)-adrenaline is ineffective. One enantiomer may be toxic, another harmless. One may be an antibiotic, the other useless. One may be an insect sex attractant, the other without effect or perhaps a repellant. Chirality is of paramount importance in the biological world.

5.7 Fischer Projection Formulas

Instead of using dashed and solid wedges to show the three-dimensional arrangements of groups in a chiral molecule, it is sometimes convenient to have a two-dimensional way of doing so. A useful way to do this was devised many years ago by Emil Fischer*; the formulas are called **Fischer projections**.

A **Fischer projection** is a type of two-dimensional formula of a molecule used to represent the three-dimensional configurations of stereogenic centers.

---

*Emil Fischer (1852–1919), who devised these formulas, was one of the early giants in the field of organic chemistry. He did much to elucidate the structures of carbohydrates, proteins, and other natural products and received the 1902 Nobel Prize in chemistry.

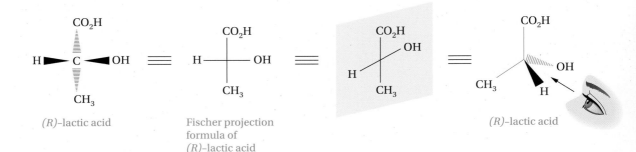

(R)-lactic acid   Fischer projection   *(R)*-lactic acid
                          formula of
                          (R)-lactic acid

◾ **Figure 5.11**

Projecting the model at the right
onto a plane gives the Fischer
projection formula.

Consider the formula for *(R)*-lactic acid, to the left of the mirror in Figure 5.10. If
we project that three-dimensional formula onto a plane, as illustrated in Figure 5.11,
we obtain the flattened Fischer projection formula.

There are two important things to notice about Fischer projection formulas. First,
the C for the stereogenic carbon atom is omitted and is represented simply as the
crossing point of the horizontal and vertical lines. Second, horizontal lines connect
the stereogenic center to groups that project *above* the plane of the page, *toward* the
viewer; vertical lines lead to groups that project *below* the plane of the page, *away* from
the viewer. As with other stereorepresentations, interchange of any two groups always
gives the enantiomer.

PROBLEM 5.15 Draw a Fischer projection formula for *(S)*-lactic acid.

The following example demonstrates how the absolute configuration of a stereocenter is determined from its Fischer projection.

EXAMPLE 5.7

Determine the absolute (*R* or *S*) configuration of the stereoisomer of
2-chlorobutane shown in the following Fischer projection.

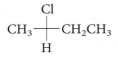

Solution First prioritize the four groups attached to the central carbon
according to the Cahn–Ingold–Prelog rules:

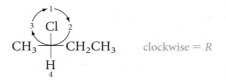

Because atoms attached to vertical arms project away from the viewer, you
can now determine whether the sequence 1→2→3 is clockwise or counterclockwise. In this case, it is clockwise, so the absolute configuration of this
enantiomer of 2-chlorobutane is *R*.

Note that if the lowest-priority group is on a horizontal arm, you can still determine the absolute configuration of the stereocenter. This can be done by *rotating three* of the four groups so that the lowest-priority group is located on a vertical arm and then proceeding as above:

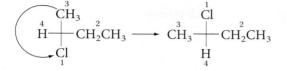

It can also be done by remembering that a substituent on a horizontal arm is pointing out at the viewer. If the sequence of the three priority groups 1→2→3 is counterclockwise, as in this case, the absolute configuration is *R*. (If the direction were clockwise, the absolute configuration would be *S*.)

PROBLEM 5.16 Determine the absolute configuration of the following enantiomer of 2-butanol from its Fischer projection:

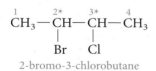

Fischer projections are used extensively in biochemistry and in carbohydrate chemistry, where compounds frequently contain more than one stereocenter. In the next section, you will see how useful Fischer projections are in dealing with compounds containing more than one stereogenic center.

5.8 Compounds with More Than One Stereogenic Center; Diastereomers

Compounds may have more than one stereogenic center, so it is important to be able to determine how many isomers exist in such cases and how they are related to one another. Consider the molecule 2-bromo-3-chlorobutane.

$$\overset{1}{CH_3}-\overset{2*}{CH}-\overset{3*}{CH}-\overset{4}{CH_3}$$
$$\qquad\quad | \qquad |$$
$$\qquad\quad Br \quad\; Cl$$

2-bromo-3-chlorobutane

As indicated by the asterisks, the molecule has two stereogenic centers. Each of these could have the configuration *R* or *S*. Thus, four isomers in all are possible: (2*R*,3*R*), (2*S*,3*S*), (2*R*,3*S*), and (2*S*,3*R*). We can draw these four isomers as shown in Figure 5.12. Note that there are two pairs of enantiomers. The (2*R*,3*R*) and (2*S*,3*S*) forms are nonsuperimposable mirror images, and the (2*R*,3*S*) and (2*S*,3*R*) forms are another such pair.

Let us see how to use Fischer projection formulas for these molecules. Consider the (2*R*,3*R*) isomer, the one at the left in Figure 5.12. The solid-dashed wedge drawing has horizontal groups projecting out of the plane of the paper toward us and vertical

■ **Figure 5.12**

The four stereoisomers of 2-bromo-3-chlorobutane, a compound with two stereogenic centers.

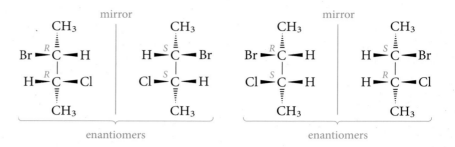

groups going away from us, behind the paper. These facts are expressed in the equivalent Fischer projection formula as shown.*

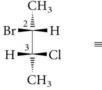

solid-dashed wedge formula   Fischer projection formula

PROBLEM 5.17 Draw the Fischer projection formulas for the remaining stereoisomers of 2-bromo-3-chlorobutane shown in Figure 5.12.

Now we come to an extremely important new idea. Consider the relationship between, for example, the (2*R*,3*R*) and (2*R*,3*S*) forms of the isomers in Figure 5.12. These forms are *not* mirror images because they have the *same* configuration at carbon-2, though they have opposite configurations at carbon-3. They are certainly stereoisomers, but they are not enantiomers. For such pairs of stereoisomers, we use the term **diastereomers**. Diastereomers are stereoisomers that are not mirror images of one another.

Diastereomers are stereoisomers that are not mirror images of each other.

*Make 3D models of the molecules in Figure 5.12 to help you visualize them. Notice that these structures are derived from an eclipsed conformation of the molecule, viewed from above so that horizontal groups project toward the viewer. The actual molecule is an equilibrium mixture of several staggered conformations, one of which is shown below. Fischer formulas are used to represent the correct *configurations*, but not necessarily the lowest energy *conformations* of a molecule.

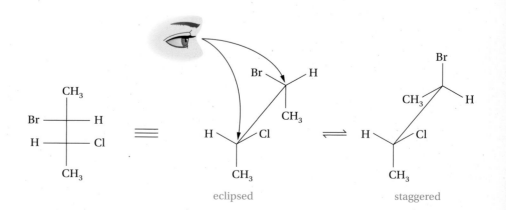

eclipsed   staggered

There is an important, fundamental difference between enantiomers and diastereomers. Because they are mirror images, enantiomers differ *only* in mirror-image (chiral) properties. They have the same achiral properties, such as melting point, boiling point, and solubility in ordinary solvents. Enantiomers cannot be separated from one another by methods that depend on achiral properties, such as recrystallization or distillation. On the other hand, diastereomers are *not* mirror images. They may differ in *all* properties, whether chiral or achiral. As a consequence, diastereomers may differ in melting point, boiling point, and solubility, not only in direction but also in the number of degrees that they rotate plane-polarized light—in short, they behave as two different chemical substances.

PROBLEM 5.18 How do you expect the specific rotations of the (2R,3R) and (2S,3S) forms of 2-bromo-3-chlorobutane to be related? Answer the same question for the (2R,3R) and (2S,3R) forms.

Can we generalize about the number of stereoisomers possible when a larger number of stereogenic centers is present? Suppose, for example, that we add a third stereogenic center to the compounds shown in Figure 5.12 (say, 2-bromo-3-chloro-4-iodopentane). The new stereogenic center added to each of the four structures can once again have either an R or an S configuration, so that with three different stereogenic centers, eight stereoisomers are possible. The situation is summed up in a single rule: If a molecule has n different stereogenic centers, it may exist in a maximum of 2^n stereoisomeric forms. There will be a maximum of $2^n/2$ pairs of enantiomers.

PROBLEM 5.19 The Fischer projection formula for glucose (blood sugar, Sec. 16.4, p. 466) is

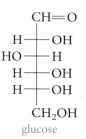

glucose

Altogether, how many stereoisomers of this sugar are possible?

Polarized light micrograph of glucose crystals.

Actually, the number of isomers predicted by this rule is the *maximum* number possible. Sometimes, certain structural features reduce the actual number of isomers. In the next section, we examine a case of this type.

5.9 Meso Compounds; the Stereoisomers of Tartaric Acid

Consider the stereoisomers of 2,3-dichlorobutane. There are two stereogenic centers.

$$\overset{1}{CH_3}-\overset{2*}{CH}-\overset{3*}{CH}-\overset{4}{CH_3}$$
$$\quad\quad | \quad\quad |$$
$$\quad\quad Cl \quad\quad Cl$$

2,3-dichlorobutane

■ **Figure 5.13**

Fischer projections of
the stereoisomers of
2,3-dichlorobutane.

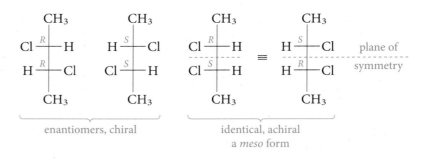

enantiomers, chiral   identical, achiral
                              a *meso* form

We can write out the stereoisomers just as we did in Figure 5.12; they are shown in Figure 5.13. Once again, the (R,R) and (S,S) isomers constitute a pair of nonsuperimposable mirror images, or enantiomers. *However, the other "two" structures, (R,S) and (S,R), in fact, now represent a single compound.*

Look more closely at the structures to the right in Figure 5.13. Notice that they have a plane of symmetry that is perpendicular to the plane of the paper and bisects the central C—C bond. The reason is that each stereogenic center has the *same* four groups attached. The structures are identical, superimposable mirror images and therefore *achiral*. We call such a structure a **meso compound**. A *meso* compound is an achiral diastereomer of a compound with stereogenic centers. Its stereogenic centers have opposite configurations. Being achiral, *meso* compounds are optically inactive.*

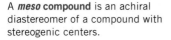

A **meso** compound is an achiral diastereomer of a compound with stereogenic centers.

Now let us take a look at tartaric acid, the compound whose optical activity was so carefully studied by Louis Pasteur (see "A Word About . . . Pasteur's Experiments" on pages 160–161). It has two identical stereogenic centers.

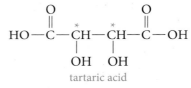

tartaric acid

The structures of these three stereoisomers and two of their properties are shown in Figure 5.14. Note that the enantiomers have identical properties except for the *sign* of the specific rotation, whereas the *meso* form, being a diastereomer of each enantiomer, differs from them in both properties.

For about 100 years after Pasteur's research, it was still not possible to determine the configuration associated with a particular enantiomer of tartaric acid. For example, it was not known whether (+)-tartaric acid had the (R,R) or the (S,S)

■ **Figure 5.14**

The stereoisomers of tartaric acid.

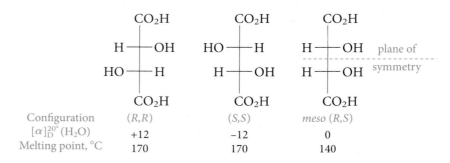

	(R,R)	(S,S)	meso (R,S)
Configuration	(R,R)	(S,S)	meso (R,S)
$[\alpha]_D^{20°}$ (H$_2$O)	+12	−12	0
Melting point, °C	170	170	140

---

*Fischer projections may be turned 180° in the plane of the paper without changing configuration. You can see that such an operation on the enantiomeric pair in Figure 5.13 does *not* interconvert them, but when performed on the *meso* form, it does.

configuration. It was known that (+)-tartaric acid had to have one of these two configurations and that (−)-tartaric acid had to have the opposite configuration, but which isomer had which?

In 1951, the Dutch scientist J. M. Bijvoet developed a special x-ray technique that solved the problem. Using this technique on crystals of the sodium rubidium salt of (+)-tartaric acid, Bijvoet showed that it had the (R,R) configuration. So this was the tartaric acid studied by Pasteur, and racemic acid was a 50:50 mixture of the (R,R) and (S,S) isomers. The *meso* form was not studied until later.

Since tartaric acid had been converted chemically into other chiral compounds and these in turn into still others, it became possible as a result of Bijvoet's work to assign **absolute configurations** (that is, the correct R or S configuration for each stereocenter) to many pairs of enantiomers.

The correctly assigned (R or S) configuration of a stereocenter in a molecule is called the **absolute configuration** of the stereocenter.

PROBLEM 5.20 Show that *trans*-1,2-dimethylcyclopentane can exist in chiral, enantiomeric forms.

PROBLEM 5.21 Is *cis*-1,2-dimethylcyclopentane chiral or achiral? What stereochemical term can we give to it?

5.10 Stereochemistry: A Recap of Definitions

We have seen here and in Section 2.11 that *stereoisomers* can be classified in three different ways. They may be either *conformers* or *configurational isomers*; they may be *chiral* or *achiral*; and they may be *enantiomers* or *diastereomers*.

A
- *Conformers:* interconvertible by rotation about single bonds
- *Configurational Isomers:* not interconvertible by rotation, only by breaking and making bonds

B
- *Chiral:* mirror image not superimposable on itself
- *Achiral:* molecule and mirror image are identical

C
- *Enantiomers:* mirror images; have opposite configurations at all stereogenic centers
- *Diastereomers:* stereoisomers but not mirror images; have same configuration at one or more centers, but differ at the remaining stereogenic centers

Various combinations of these three sets of terms can be applied to any pair of stereoisomers. Here are a few examples:

1. *Cis*- and *trans*-2-butene (*Z*- and *E*-2-butene).

These isomers are *configurational* (not interconverted by rotation about single bonds), *achiral* (the mirror image of each is superimposable on the original), and *diastereomers* (although they are stereoisomers, they are *not* mirror images of one another; hence they must be diastereomers).

2. Staggered and eclipsed ethane.

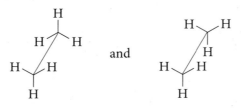

and

These are *achiral conformers*. They are *diastereomeric conformers* (but without stereogenic centers) because they are not mirror images.

3. (*R*)- and (*S*)-lactic acid.

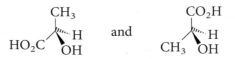

and

These isomers are *configurational,* each is *chiral,* and they constitute a pair of *enantiomers*.

4. *Meso-* and (*R*,*R*)-tartaric acids.

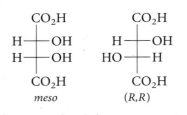

These isomers are *configurational* and *diastereomers*. One is *achiral,* and the other is *chiral*.

Enantiomers, such as (*R*)- and (*S*)-lactic acid, differ only in chiral properties and therefore cannot be separated by ordinary achiral methods such as distillation or recrystallization. Diastereomers differ in all properties, chiral or achiral. *If* they are also configurational isomers [such as *cis-* and *trans-*2-butene, or *meso-* and (*R*,*R*)-tartaric acid], they can be separated by ordinary achiral methods, such as distillation or recrystallization. *If,* on the other hand, they are conformers (such as staggered and eclipsed ethane], they may interconvert so readily by bond rotation as to not be separable.

> **PROBLEM 5.22** Draw the two stereoisomers of 1,3-dimethylcyclobutane, and classify the pair according to the categories listed in A, B, and C above.

5.11 Stereochemistry and Chemical Reactions

How important is stereochemistry in chemical reactions? The answer depends on the nature of the reactants. First, consider the formation of a chiral product from achiral reactants; for example, the addition of hydrogen bromide to 1-butene to give 2-bromobutane in accord with Markovnikov's Rule.

$$CH_3CH_2CH{=}CH_2 + HBr \longrightarrow CH_3CH_2\overset{*}{C}HCH_3 \quad\quad (5.3)$$
$$\underset{\text{1-butene}}{} \quad\quad\quad\quad \underset{\text{2-bromobutane}}{\overset{|}{Br}}$$

The product has one stereogenic center, marked with an asterisk, but both enantiomers are formed in exactly equal amounts. The product is a **racemic mixture**. Why? Although this result will be obtained *regardless* of the reaction mechanism, let us consider the generally accepted mechanism.

A **racemic mixture** is a 50:50 mixture of a pair of enantiomers.

$$CH_3CH_2CH{=}CH_2 + H^+ \longrightarrow CH_3CH_2\overset{+}{C}HCH_3 \xrightarrow{Br^-} CH_3CH_2CHCH_3 \quad (5.4)$$
$$\underset{\text{2-butyl cation}}{} \quad\quad\quad\quad\quad \underset{Br}{\overset{|}{}}$$

The intermediate 2-butyl cation obtained by adding a proton to the end carbon is planar, and bromide ion can combine with it from the "top" or "bottom" side with exactly equal probability.

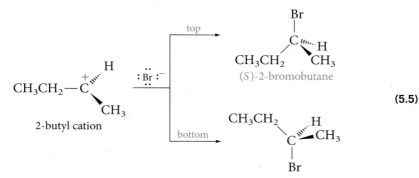

(5.5)

Therefore, the product is a racemic mixture, an optically inactive 50:50 mixture of the two enantiomers.

We can generalize this result. *When chiral products are obtained from achiral reactants, both enantiomers are formed at the same rates, in equal amounts.*

PROBLEM 5.23 Show that, if the mechanism of addition of HBr to 1-butene involved *no* intermediates, but *simultaneous one-step* addition (in the Markovnikov sense), the product would still be racemic 2-bromobutane.

PROBLEM 5.24 Show that the chlorination of butane at carbon-2 will give a 50:50 mixture of enantiomers.

Now consider a different situation, the reaction of a *chiral* molecule with an achiral reagent to create a second stereogenic center. Consider, for example, the addition of HBr to 3-chloro-1-butene.

$$CH_3\overset{*}{C}HCH{=}CH_2 + HBr \longrightarrow CH_3\overset{*}{C}H{-}\overset{*}{C}HCH_3 \quad\quad (5.6)$$
$$\underset{Cl}{\overset{|}{}} \quad\quad\quad\quad\quad\quad \underset{Cl}{\overset{|}{}} \;\; \underset{Br}{\overset{|}{}}$$
$$\underset{\text{3-chloro-1-butene}}{} \quad\quad\quad\quad \underset{\text{2-bromo-3-chlorobutane}}{}$$

A WORD ABOUT... Enantiomers and Biological Activity

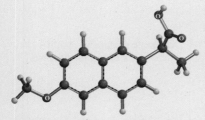

Ball-and-stick structure of (S)-naproxen.

Enantiomers of chiral molecules can elicit vastly different biological responses when ingested by living organisms. The tastes, odors, medicinal properties, toxicity, bactericidal, fungicidal, insecticidal, and other properties of enantiomers often differ widely. Here are some examples: The amino acid (R)-asparagine tastes sweet, while (S)-asparagine tastes bitter; (R)-carvone has the odor of spearmint, whereas (S)-carvone is responsible for the smell of caraway; (S)-naproxen is an important anti-inflammatory drug, while its enantiomer is a liver toxin; (R,R)-chloramphenicol is a useful antibiotic but its enantiomer is harmless to bacteria; (R,R)-paclobutrazol is a fungicide, while its enantiomer is a plant growth regulator; and (R)-thalidomide is a sedative and hypnotic, while its enantiomer is a potent teratogen.

How can it be that two molecules as similar in structure as enantiomers have such different biological activities? The reason is that biological activity is initiated by binding of the small molecule to a receptor molecule in the living organism to form a small molecule–receptor complex. The receptors are usually chiral, nonracemic molecules such as proteins, complex carbohydrates, or nucleic acids that bind well to only one of a pair of enantiomers. Because of their different three-dimensional shapes, (R)-asparagine binds to a receptor in humans that triggers a sensation of sweetness, whereas (S)-asparagine does not bind to that receptor. Instead, it binds to a differently shaped receptor that results in a bitter sensation.

A useful analogy for this selective binding is the manner in which your left shoe (receptor) interacts with your left and right feet (a pair of enantiomers). The left foot fits (binds) into the shoe comfortably (one response) whereas the right foot does not, or only uncomfortably (a different response).

There are now a number of examples where one enantiomer of a chiral molecule elicits a desirable biological response, while the other enantiomer results in a detrimental response (naproxen, for example). Therefore, it has become increasingly important for chiral pharmaceutical and agrochemical compounds to be marketed as single enantiomers rather than as racemic mixtures. This has recently stimulated the development of new synthetic

---

Suppose we start with one pure enantiomer of 3-chloro-1-butene, say, the *R* isomer. What can we say about the stereochemistry of the products? One way to see the answer quickly is to draw Fischer projections.

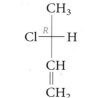

$$(R)\text{-3-chloro-1-butene} \xrightarrow{\text{HBr}} (2R,3R)\text{-2-bromo-3-chlorobutane} + (2S,3R)\text{-2-bromo-3-chlorobutane}$$

(5.7)

The configuration where the chloro substituent is located remains *R* and unchanged, but the new stereogenic center can be either *R* or *S*. Therefore, the products are *diastereomers*. Are they formed in equal amounts? No. Looking at the starting material in eq. 5.7, we can see that it has no plane of symmetry. Approach of the bromine to the double bond from the H side or from the Cl side of the stereogenic center should not occur with equal ease.

We can generalize this result. *Reaction of a chiral reagent with an achiral reagent, when it creates a new stereogenic center, leads to diastereomeric products at different rates and in unequal amounts.*

methods that provide only a single enantiomer of a chiral molecule, a process called *asymmetric synthesis*. In fact, the 2001 Nobel Prize in chemistry was awarded to William S. Knowles (Monsanto), K. Barry Sharpless (Scripps Institute), and Ryoji Noyori (Nagoya University) for their seminal and practical contributions to this field of research.

The need for enantiomerically pure compounds has also led to the development of new methods for separating racemic mixtures into their enantiomeric components, a process called resolution.

See Problem 5.57.

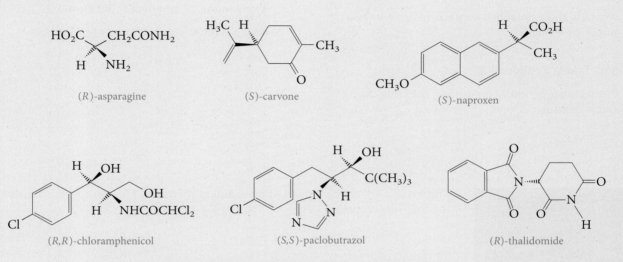

(*R*)-asparagine

(*S*)-carvone

(*S*)-naproxen

(*R,R*)-chloramphenicol

(*S,S*)-paclobutrazol

(*R*)-thalidomide

Enantiomers of Some Biologically Active Compounds

PROBLEM 5.25 Let us say that the (2*R*,3*R*) and (2*S*,3*R*) products in eq. 5.7 are formed in a 60:40 ratio. What products would be formed and in what ratio by adding HBr to pure (*S*)-3-chloro-1-butene? By adding HBr to a racemic mixture of (*R*)- and (*S*)-3-chloro-1-butene?

5.12   Resolution of a Racemic Mixture

We have just seen (eq. 5.5) that, when reaction between two achiral reagents leads to a chiral product, it always gives a racemic (50:50) mixture of enantiomers. Suppose we want to obtain each enantiomer pure and free of the other. The process of separating a racemic mixture into its enantiomers is called **resolution**. Since enantiomers have identical achiral properties, how can we resolve a racemic mixture into its components? The answer is to convert them to diastereomers, separate the *diastereomers,* and then reconvert the now-separated diastereomers back to enantiomers.

To separate two enantiomers, we first let them react with a chiral reagent. The product will be a pair of *diastereomers.* These, as we have seen earlier, differ in all types of

The process of separating the two enantiomers of a racemic (50:50) mixture is called **resolution**.

A CLOSER LOOK AT... Thalidomide

Conduct research on the Internet to find more information on thalidomide and to answer the following questions.

The History of Thalidomide

1. When and where was the drug thalidomide first used?

2. For what purpose was it used?

3. What are the unintended consequences of its use by pregnant women?

Patients Taking Thalidomide

1. During what period of pregnancy does this drug cause damage?

2. In addition to its teratogenic effects, thalidomide also can give rise to other side effects. What are some of these side effects?

Why We Still Use Thalidomide

1. What are some diseases for which thalidomide is proving to be an effective medication?

2. What are other potential uses of this drug?

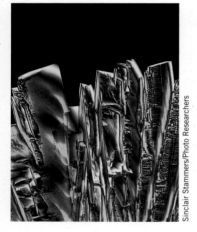

Tartaric acid crystals under polarized light.

properties and can be separated by ordinary methods. This principle is illustrated in the following equation:

$$\begin{Bmatrix} R \\ S \end{Bmatrix} + R \longrightarrow \begin{Bmatrix} R\!-\!R \\ S\!-\!R \end{Bmatrix} \qquad \textbf{(5.8)}$$

pair of enantiomers (not separable)   chiral reagent   diastereomeric products (separable)

After the diastereomers are separated, we then carry out reactions that regenerate the chiral reagent and the separated enantiomers.

$$R\!-\!R \longrightarrow R + R$$

and

$$S\!-\!R \longrightarrow S + R \qquad \textbf{(5.9)}$$

Louis Pasteur was the first to resolve a racemic mixture when he separated the sodium ammonium salts of (+)- and (−)-tartaric acid. In a sense, he was the chiral reagent, since he could distinguish between the right- and left-handed crystals. In Chapter 11, we will see a specific example of how this is done chemically.

The principle behind the resolution of racemic mixtures is the same as the principle involved in the specificity of many biological reactions. That is, a chiral reagent (in a cell, usually an enzyme) can discriminate between enantiomers.

Sinclair Stammers/Photo Researchers

A WORD ABOUT...   Green Chemistry: L-DOPA

Enantiomers often have very different properties when interacting with biological enzymes that are chiral. As we just discussed, sometimes we use a resolution to convert an enantiomeric mixture to a set of diastereomers in order to separate them. This technique of resolving one enantiomer from another is a practical approach, but it is not necessarily good for the environment. Additional steps are needed to prepare and to separate the diastereomers, and then the enantiomers need to be regenerated as discussed in Section 5.12. Each of these steps would need solvents and, of course, would generate some waste. A greener approach is to prepare the desired enantiomer in its pure form and without formation of the undesired enantiomer.

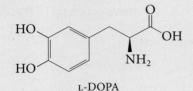

L-DOPA

L-DOPA is an amino acid that is found in some foods and herbs. L-DOPA is the precursor to a number of neurotransmitters, including dopamine and adrenaline (page 163). In 2000, Arvid Carlsson won a Nobel Prize

amino acids, but only the L-enantiomer is biologically useful. Many researchers have investigated the chemistry and biochemistry of L-DOPA. In 2001, the Nobel Prize in chemistry was awarded to work related to L-DOPA; one-fourth of the prize went to William Knowles for his work at the Monsanto company on the synthesis of this compound by an asymmetric hydrogenation reaction.

Why was a Nobel Prize awarded for the synthesis of L-DOPA? In an attempt to avoid many steps in resolution, Knowles and his coworkers prepared L-DOPA in an enantiomerically pure manner by using a chiral hydrogenation reaction to synthesize L-DOPA in 95% enantiomerically pure form. In this rhodium-catalyzed hydrogenation, they used a chiral and enantiomerically pure (R,R)-DiPAMP phosphine ligand. Since the phosphine ligand that surrounded the Rh metal was chiral, the formation of each of the two products occurred through a different transition state (an analogous situation to Figure 3.12).

Therefore, there was a lower activation barrier that created a kinetic preference for one enantiomer to be made over the other. The preferred enantiomeric product from that reaction could then be converted to the desired L-DOPA with a simple aqueous hydrolysis step with acid.

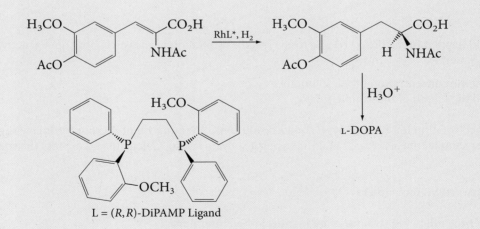

L = (R,R)-DiPAMP Ligand

in physiology or medicine for his work with L-DOPA that showed its ability to increase dopamine concentrations in the brains of Parkinson's patients.

L-DOPA has a stereogenic center and is chiral. Biochemically, it can be synthesized from other essential

This synthetic process avoided a number of purification steps and is an excellent example of environmentally efficient green chemistry.

See Problem 5.59.

ADDITIONAL PROBLEMS

ⵙWL Interactive versions of these problems are assignable in OWL.

Stereochemistry: Definitions and Stereogenic Centers

5.26 Define or describe the following terms.

a. diastereomers	**b.** plane of symmetry	**c.** stereogenic center
d. *meso* form	**e.** racemic mixture	**f.** plane-polarized light
g. specific rotation	**h.** chiral molecule	**i.** enantiomers
j. resolution		

5.27 Which of the following substances contain stereogenic centers? (*Hint:* Drawing the structures will help you answer this question.)

a. 2,2-dibromobutane	**b.** 3-methylcyclopentene	**c.** 1,2-difluoropropane
d. 2,3-dimethylheptane	**e.** methylcyclobutane	**f.** 1-deuteriopropanol (CH_3CH_2CHDOH)

5.28 Locate with an asterisk the stereogenic centers (if any) in the following structures.

a. $HOCH_2CH(OH)CH(OH)CHO$ **b.** $C_6H_5CH_2CH(OH)CO_2H$ **c.** $CH_3CHBrCF_3$

d. 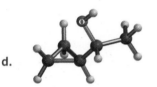   **e.** 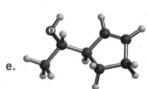   **f.**

Optical Activity

5.29 What would happen to the observed and to the *specific* rotation if, in measuring the optical activity of a solution of sugar in water, we

a. doubled the concentration of the solution?
b. doubled the length of the sample tube?

5.30 The observed rotation for 100 mL of an aqueous solution containing 1 g of sucrose (ordinary sugar), placed in a 2-decimeter sample tube, is +1.33° at 25°C (using a sodium lamp). Calculate and express the specific rotation of sucrose.

Relationships Between Stereoisomers

5.31 Tell whether the following structures are identical or enantiomers:

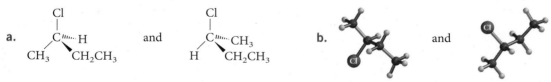

5.32 Draw a structural formula for an optically active compound with the molecular formula

a. C_6H_{14}	**b.** $C_5H_{11}Br$
c. $C_4H_{10}O$	**d.** $C_4H_8Cl_2$

5.33 Draw the formula of an unsaturated bromide, C_5H_9Br, that can show

    a. neither *cis–trans* isomerism nor optical activity
    b. *cis–trans* isomerism but no optical activity
    c. no *cis–trans* isomerism but optical activity
    d. *cis–trans* isomerism and optical activity

The *R-S* and *E-Z* Conventions

5.34 Place the members of the following groups in order of decreasing priority according to the *R-S* convention:

    a. CH_3—, H—, C_6H_5—, CH_3CH_2— (see page 120 for structure of C_6H_5— group)
    b. CH_3CH_2—, $CH_3CH_2CH_2$—, CH_2=CH—, O=CH—
    c. CH_3CH_2—, HS—, H—, Br—
    d. CH_3—, HS—, $BrCH_2$—, $HOCH_2$—

5.35 Assume that the four groups in each part of Problem 5.34 are attached to one carbon atom.

    a. Draw a three-dimensional formula for the *R* configuration of the molecule in 5.34a and 5.34b.
    b. Draw a three-dimensional formula for the *S* configuration of the molecule in 5.34c and 5.34d.

5.36 Tell whether the stereogenic centers marked with an asterisk in the following structures have the *R* or the *S* configuration:

a.

(−)-menthone
(found in peppermint)

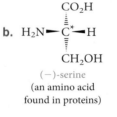

b. H_2N—$\overset{*}{C}$—H

(−)-serine
(an amino acid
found in proteins)

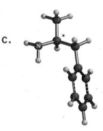

c.

(+)-amphetamine
(central nervous
system stimulant)

5.37 Determine the configuration, *R* or *S*, of (+)-carvone (page 147), the compound responsible for the odor of caraway seeds.

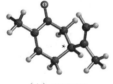

(+)-carvone

5.38 In a recent collaboration, French and American chemists found that (−)-bromochlorofluoromethane (CHBrClF), one of the simplest chiral molecules, has the *R* configuration. Draw a three-dimensional structural formula for (*R*)-(−)-bromochlorofluoromethane.

5.39 Name the following compounds, using *E-Z* notation:

a.   **b.**   **c.**   **d.**

5.40 Two possible isomers of 1,2-bromoethene are:

and

Classify them fully, according to the discussion in Section 5.10.

5.41 4-Chloro-2-pentene has a double bond that can have either the *E* or the *Z* configuration and a stereogenic center that can have either the *R* or the *S* configuration. How many stereoisomers are possible altogether? Draw the structure of each, and group the pairs of enantiomers.

5.42 How many stereoisomers are possible for each of the following structures? Draw them, and name each by the *R-S* and *E-Z* conventions. (See Problem 5.41.)

    a. 2,5-dichloro-3-hexene   **b.** 2-chloro-5-fluoro-3-hexene
    c. 3-methyl-1,4-pentadiene   **d.** 3-methyl-1,4-heptadiene

Fischer and Newman Projections

5.43 Which of the following Fischer projection formulas have the same configuration as **A**, and which are the enantiomer of **A?**

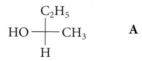

    a.   **b.** 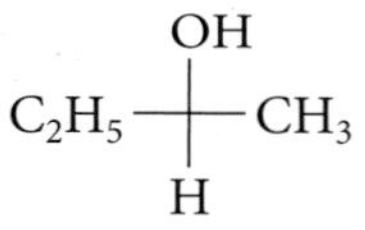   **c.**

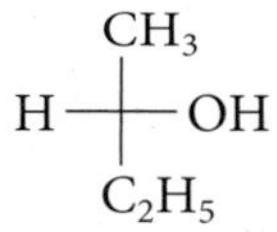

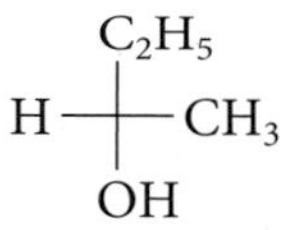

5.44 Following are Newman projections for the three tartaric acids (*R,R*), (*S,S*), and *meso*. Which is which?

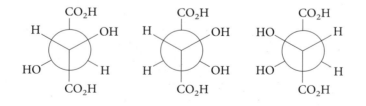

5.45 Convert the following sawhorse formula for one isomer of tartaric acid to a Fischer projection formula. Which isomer of tartaric acid is it?

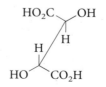

5.46 Two possible isomeric structures of 1,2-dichloroethane are

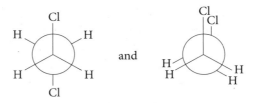

and

Classify them fully, according to the discussion in Section 5.10.

5.47 Two possible configurations for a molecule with three different stereogenic centers are (R,R,R) and its mirror image (S,S,S). What are all of the remaining possibilities? Repeat for a compound with four different stereogenic centers.

Stereochemistry: Natural and Synthetic Applications

5.48 The formula for muscarine, a toxic constituent of poisonous mushrooms, is

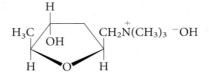

Is it chiral? How many stereoisomers of this structure are possible? An interesting murder mystery, which you might enjoy reading and which depends for its solution on the distinction between optically active and racemic forms of this poison, is Dorothy L. Sayers's *The Documents in the Case,* published in paperback by Avon Books. (See an article by H. Hart, "Accident, Suicide, or Murder? A Question of Stereochemistry," *J. Chem. Educ.,* **1975,** *52,* 444.)

5.49 Chloramphenicol is an antibiotic that is particularly effective against typhoid fever. Its structure is

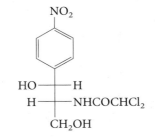

What is the configuration (R,S) at each stereogenic center?

5.50 Methoprene (marketed as Precor), an insect juvenile hormone mimic used in flea control products for pets, works by preventing the development of flea eggs and larvae. The effective form of methoprene, shown here, is optically active. Locate the stereogenic center and determine its configuration (R,S).

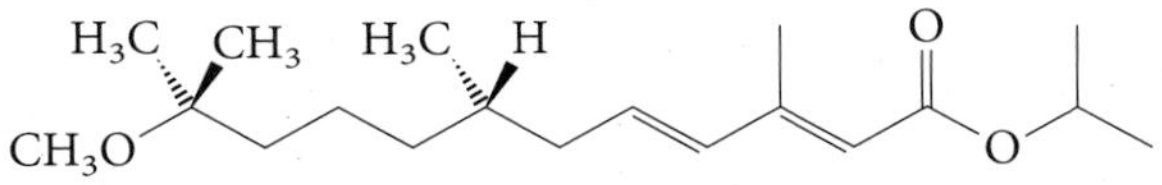

methoprene

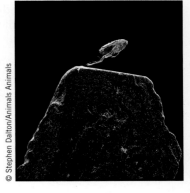

Adult cat flea jumping.

5.51 A South Korean research group has isolated and synthesized "daumone," the pheromone that induces hibernation in *Caenorhabditis elegans* worms when food becomes scarce, thus extending their life span (*Nature*, **2005**, *433*, 541). Following is a ball-and-stick representation of daumone.

Caenorhabditis elegans worms.

a. What is the absolute configuration, *R* or *S*, of the stereogenic carbon marked with an asterisk?

b. There are four additional stereogenic carbons in daumone. Locate these carbons and determine their absolute configurations.

c. Draw a representation of the enantiomer of daumone.

d. Do you think the enantiomer of daumone would induce hibernation in *Caenorhabditis elegans* worms? Why or why not?

5.52 Mature crocodiles secrete from their skin glands the compound with the following structure. This compound is thought to be a communication pheromone for nesting or mating.

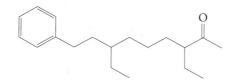

Adult crocodiles.

a. How many stereogenic centers are there in this compound? Mark them with an asterisk.

b. Two stereoisomers of this compound have been isolated from crocodile skin gland secretions. How many possible stereoisomers of this compound are there?

5.53 The structure of nerolidol is shown in Problem 3.40. What is the absolute configuration, *R* or *S*, of the stereogenic carbon in nerolidol?

5.54 Extract of *Ephedra sinica*, a Chinese herbal treatment for asthma, contains the compound ephedrine, which dilates the air passages of the lungs. The naturally occurring stereoisomer is levorotatory and has the structure shown here. (a) What is the configuration (*R,S*) at each stereogenic center? (b) How many stereoisomers of ephedrine are possible altogether? (c) Compare the structure of (−)-ephedrine to that of (−)-epinephrine. How are they similar and how do they differ?

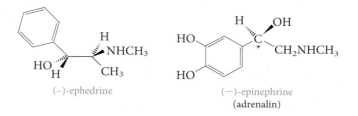

(−)-ephedrine   (−)-epinephrine
                                        (adrenalin)

5.55 The structure of kavain, a natural relaxant popular in the South Pacific, is shown here. Draw a three-dimensional structure for the *R* configuration of the molecule.

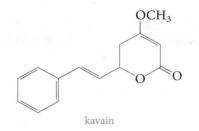

kavain

Stereochemistry and Chemical Reactions

5.56 When (*R*)-2-chlorobutane is chlorinated, we obtain some 2,3-dichlorobutane. It consists of 71% *meso* isomer and 29% racemic isomers. Explain why the mixture need not be 50:50 *meso* and (2*R*,3*R*)-2,3-dichlorobutane.

5.57 (+)- and (−)-Carvone [see Problem 5.37 for the structure of (+)-carvone] are enantiomers that have very different odors and are responsible for the odors of caraway seeds and spearmint, respectively. Suggest a possible explanation.

5.58 What can you say about the stereochemistry of the products in the following reactions? (See Sec. 5.11 and eq. 3.28.)

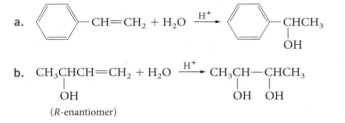

5.59 As discussed in the "A Word About . . . Green Chemistry: L-DOPA" on page 175, the (*R*,*R*)-DiPAMP phosphine ligand was used to prepare the precursor to L-DOPA. What is the absolute configuration, *R* or *S*, of the stereogenic carbon in L-DOPA? What do you expect to be the product of the analogous hydrogenation reaction if (*S*,*S*)-DiPAMP was used as the phosphine ligand?

5.60 As discussed in the "A Word About . . . Pasteur's Experiments and the van't Hoff-LeBel Explanation" on pages 160–161, a critical experiment and observation made by Pasteur was that when he dissolved pure forms of the left- and right-handed crystals, he found that each solution was optically active, even though each set of crystals was obtained from crystallization of the racemic acid. The optical rotations of (*R*,*R*)- and (*S*,*S*)-tartaric acid are provided in Figure 5.14. Predict the specific rotation of a solution that contains 75% (*R*,*R*) and 25% (*S*,*S*) crystals of tartaric acid.

6

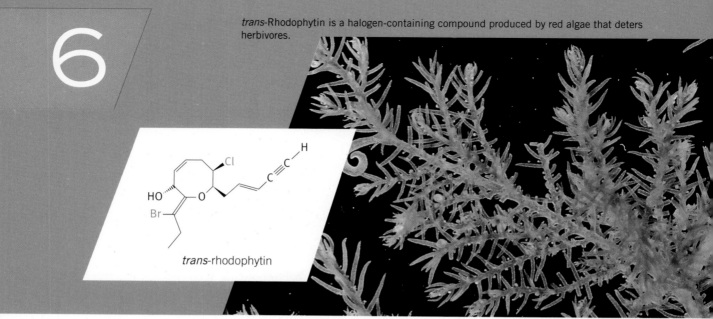

trans-Rhodophytin is a halogen-containing compound produced by red algae that deters herbivores.

trans-rhodophytin

Dr. D. P. Wilson/Photo Researchers

Organic Halogen Compounds; Substitution and Elimination Reactions

Chlorine- and bromine-containing natural products have been isolated from various species that live in the sea—sponges, mollusks, and other ocean creatures that adapted to their environment by metabolizing inorganic chlorides and bromides that are prevalent there. With these exceptions, most organic halogen compounds are creatures of the laboratory.

Halogen compounds are important for several reasons. Simple alkyl and aryl halides, especially chlorides and bromides, are versatile reagents in syntheses. Through *substitution reactions*, which we will discuss in this chapter, halogens can be replaced by many other functional groups. Organic halides can be converted to unsaturated compounds through dehydrohalogenation. Also, some halogen compounds, especially those that contain two or more halogen atoms per molecule, have practical uses; for example, as solvents, insecticides, herbicides, fire retardants, cleaning fluids, and refrigerants, and in polymers such as Teflon. In this chapter, we will discuss all of the aspects of halogen compounds described.

OWL

Online homework for this chapter can be assigned in OWL, an online homework assessment tool.

6.1 Nucleophilic Substitution

Let us look at a typical **nucleophilic substitution reaction**. Ethyl bromide (bromoethane) reacts with hydroxide ion to give ethyl alcohol and bromide ion.*

$$HO^- + \underset{\text{ethyl bromide}}{CH_3CH_2-Br} \xrightarrow{H_2O} \underset{\text{ethanol}}{CH_3CH_2-OH} + Br^- \qquad \textbf{(6.1)}$$

Alkyl halides undergo **nucleophilic substitution reactions**, in which a nucleophile displaces the halide **leaving group** from the alkyl halide substrate.

Hydroxide ion is the *nucleophile* (Sec. 3.9). It reacts with the **substrate** (ethyl bromide) and displaces bromide ion. The bromide ion is called the **leaving group**.

In reactions of this type, one covalent bond is broken, and a new covalent bond is formed. In this example, the carbon–bromine bond is broken and the carbon–oxygen bond is formed. The leaving group (bromide) takes with it *both* of the electrons from the carbon–bromine bond, and the nucleophile (hydroxide ion) supplies *both* electrons for the new carbon–oxygen bond.

These ideas are generalized in the following equations for a nucleophilic substitution reaction:

$$\underset{\substack{\text{nucleophile}\\(\text{neutral})}}{Nu:} + \underset{\text{substrate}}{R:L} \longrightarrow \underset{\text{product}}{R:\overset{+}{Nu}} + \underset{\substack{\text{leaving}\\\text{group}}}{:L^-} \qquad \textbf{(6.2)}$$

$$\underset{\substack{\text{nucleophile}\\(\text{anion})}}{Nu:^-} + \underset{\text{substrate}}{R:L} \longrightarrow \underset{\text{product}}{R:Nu} + \underset{\substack{\text{leaving}\\\text{group}}}{:L^-} \qquad \textbf{(6.3)}$$

If the nucleophile and substrate are neutral (eq. 6.2), the product will be positively charged. If the nucleophile is a negative ion and the substrate is neutral (eq. 6.3), the product will be neutral. In either case, an unshared electron pair on the nucleophile supplies the electrons for the new covalent bond.

In principle, of course, these reactions may be reversible because the leaving group also has an unshared electron pair that can be used to form a covalent bond. However, we can use various methods to force the reactions to go in the forward direction. For example, we can choose the nucleophile so that it is a *stronger* nucleophile than the leaving group. Or we can shift the equilibrium by using a large excess of one reagent or by removing one of the products as it is formed. Nucleophilic substitution is a versatile reaction, widely used in organic synthesis.

6.2 Examples of Nucleophilic Substitutions

Nucleophiles can be classified according to the kind of atom that forms a new covalent bond. For example, the hydroxide ion in eq. 6.1 is an *oxygen* nucleophile. In the product, a new carbon–*oxygen* bond is formed. *The most common nucleophiles are oxygen, nitrogen, sulfur, halogen, and carbon nucleophiles.* Table 6.1 shows some examples of nucleophiles and the products that they form when they react with an alkyl halide.

Let us consider a few specific examples of these reactions, to see how they may be used in synthesis.

---

*The nomenclature of alkyl halides was discussed in Section 2.4.

Table 6.1 ▬ **Reactions of Common Nucleophiles with Alkyl Halides (Eqs. 6.2 and 6.3)**

Nu		R—Nu		
Formula	**Name**	**Formula**	**Name**	**Comments**
Oxygen nucleophiles				
1. $HO:^-$	hydroxide	$R-OH$	alcohol	
2. $RO:^-$	alkoxide	$R-OR$	ether	
3. HOH	water	$R-\overset{+}{O}\overset{H}{\underset{H}{}}$	alkyloxonium ion	These ions lose a proton and the products are alcohols and ethers. $\xrightarrow{-H^+}$ ROH (alcohol)
4. ROH	alcohol	$R-\overset{+}{O}\overset{R}{\underset{H}{}}$	dialkyloxonium ion	$\xrightarrow{-H^+}$ ROR (ether)
5. $R-C\overset{O}{\underset{O:^-}{}}$	carboxylate	$R-O\overset{O}{\overset{\|}{C}}-R$	ester	
Nitrogen nucleophiles				
6. NH_3	ammonia	$R-\overset{+}{N}H_3$	alkylammonium ion	With a base, these ions readily lose a proton to give amines. $\xrightarrow{-H^+}$ RNH_2
7. RNH_2	primary amine	$R-\overset{+}{N}H_2R$	dialkylammonium ion	$\xrightarrow{-H^+}$ R_2NH
8. R_2NH	secondary amine	$R-\overset{+}{N}HR_2$	trialkylammonium ion	$\xrightarrow{-H^+}$ $R_3N:$
9. R_3N	tertiary amine	$R-\overset{+}{N}R_3$	tetraalkylammonium ion	
Sulfur nucleophiles				
10. $HS:^-$	hydrosulfide	$R-SH$	thiol	
11. $RS:^-$	mercaptide	$R-SR$	thioether (sulfide)	
12. $R_2S:$	thioether	$R-\overset{+}{S}R_2$	trialkylsulfonium ion	
Halogen nucleophiles				
13. $:I:^-$	iodide	$R-I:$	alkyl iodide	The usual solvent is acetone. Sodium iodide is soluble in acetone, but sodium bromide and sodium chloride are not.
Carbon nucleophiles				
14. $^-:C\equiv N:$	cyanide	$R-C\equiv N:$	alkyl cyanide (nitrile)	Sometimes the isonitrile, $R-\overset{+}{N}\equiv\overset{-}{C}:$, is formed.
15. $^-:C\equiv CR$	acetylide	$R-C\equiv CR$	alkyne	

EXAMPLE 6.1

Use Table 6.1 to write an equation for the reaction of sodium ethoxide with bromoethane.

Solution

$$CH_3CH_2\overset{..}{\underset{..}{O}}:^- Na^+ + CH_3CH_2Br \longrightarrow CH_3CH_2\overset{..}{\underset{..}{O}}CH_2CH_3 + Na^+Br^-$$

$\quad\quad$ sodium ethoxide $\quad\quad$ bromoethane $\quad\quad\quad\quad$ diethyl ether

Ethoxide is the nucleophile (entry 2 in Table 6.1), bromoethane is the substrate, and bromide ion is the leaving group. The product is diethyl ether, which is used as an anesthetic. Notice that the counterion of the nucleophile, Na^+, is merely a spectator during the reaction. It is present at the beginning and end of the reaction.

EXAMPLE 6.2

Devise a synthesis for propyl cyanide in which a nucleophilic substitution reaction is used.

Solution First, write the structure of the desired product.

$$CH_3CH_2CH_2\!\!-\!\!C\!\equiv\!N:$$
$\quad\quad\quad\quad\quad$ propyl cyanide

If we use cyanide ion as the nucleophile (entry 14 in Table 6.1), the alkyl halide must have the halogen (Cl, Br, or I) attached to a propyl group. The equation is

$$^-:C\!\equiv\!N: + CH_3CH_2CH_2Br \longrightarrow CH_3CH_2CH_2C\!\equiv\!N: + Br^-$$

Sodium cyanide or potassium cyanide can be used to supply the nucleophile.

EXAMPLE 6.3

Show how 1-butyne could be converted to 3-hexyne using a nucleophilic substitution reaction.

Solution Compare the starting material with the product.

$$CH_3CH_2C\!\equiv\!CH \quad\quad CH_3CH_2C\!\equiv\!CCH_2CH_3$$
$\quad\quad$ 1-butyne $\quad\quad\quad\quad\quad$ 3-hexyne

From Table 6.1, entry 15, we see that acetylides react with alkyl halides to give acetylenes. We therefore need to convert 1-butyne to an acetylide (review eq. 3.53), then treat it with a 2-carbon alkyl halide.

$$CH_3CH_2C\!\equiv\!CH + NaNH_2 \xrightarrow{NH_3} CH_3CH_2C\!\equiv\!C:^- Na^+$$

$$CH_3CH_2C\!\equiv\!C:^- Na^+ + CH_3CH_2Br \longrightarrow CH_3CH_2C\!\equiv\!CCH_2CH_3 + Na^+Br^-$$

EXAMPLE 6.4

Complete the following equation:

$$:NH_3 + CH_3CH_2CH_2Br \longrightarrow$$

Solution Ammonia is a nitrogen nucleophile (Table 6.1, entry 6). Since both reactants are neutral, the product has a positive charge (the formal +1 charge is on the nitrogen—check it out!).

$$:NH_3 + CH_3CH_2CH_2Br \longrightarrow CH_3CH_2CH_2 \overset{+}{-} NH_3 + Br^-$$

PROBLEM 6.1 Using Table 6.1, write complete equations for the following nucleophilic substitution reactions:

a. $Na^+ {}^-OH + CH_3CH_2CH_2Br$

b. $(CH_3CH_2)_3N: + CH_3CH_2Br$

c. $Na^+ {}^-SH +$ 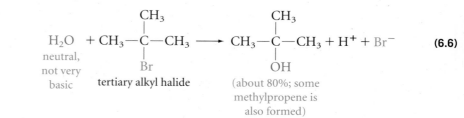 $-CH_2Br$

PROBLEM 6.2 Write an equation for the preparation of each of the following compounds, using a nucleophilic substitution reaction. In each case, label the nucleophile, the substrate, and the leaving group.

a. $(CH_3CH_2)_3N$

b. $CH_3CH_2CH_2OH$

c. $(CH_3)_2CHCH_2C \equiv N$

d. $CH_3CH_2CH_2CH_2OCH_3$

e. $(CH_3CH_2)_3 S^+Br^-$

f. $CH_2 \equiv CHCH_2I$

The substitution reactions in Table 6.1 have some limitations with respect to the structure of the *R* group in the alkyl halide. For example, these are reactions of *alkyl* halides (halogen bonded to sp^3-hybridized carbon). *Aryl* halides and *vinyl* halides, in which the halogen is bonded to sp^2-hybridized carbon, do not undergo this type of nucleophilic substitution reaction. Another important limitation often occurs when the nucleophile is an anion or a base or both. For example,

$$\underset{\text{anion}}{^-CN} + \underset{\text{primary alkyl halide}^*}{CH_3CH_2CH_2CH_2Br} \longrightarrow CH_3CH_2CH_2CH_2CN + Br^- \tag{6.4}$$

but

$$\underset{\text{anion}}{^-CN} + \underset{\substack{\text{tertiary alkyl halide}}}{CH_3 - \overset{\overset{\displaystyle CH_3}{|}}{\underset{\underset{\displaystyle Br}{|}}{C}} - CH_3} \longrightarrow \underset{\text{methylpropene}}{CH_3 - \overset{\overset{\displaystyle CH_2}{||}}{C} - CH_3} + HCN + Br^- \tag{6.5}$$

Another example is

$$\underset{\substack{\text{neutral,} \\ \text{not very} \\ \text{basic}}}{H_2O} + \underset{\text{tertiary alkyl halide}}{CH_3 - \overset{\overset{\displaystyle CH_3}{|}}{\underset{\underset{\displaystyle Br}{|}}{C}} - CH_3} \longrightarrow \underset{\substack{\text{(about 80\%; some} \\ \text{methylpropene is} \\ \text{also formed)}}}{CH_3 - \overset{\overset{\displaystyle CH_3}{|}}{\underset{\underset{\displaystyle OH}{|}}{C}} - CH_3} + H^+ + Br^- \tag{6.6}$$

*For the definition of primary, secondary, and tertiary alkyl groups, review Section 3.10.

but

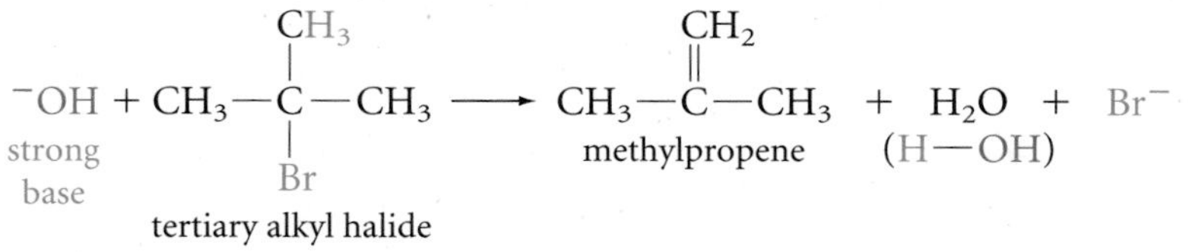

$$^-OH + CH_3-\underset{\underset{Br}{|}}{\overset{\overset{CH_3}{|}}{C}}-CH_3 \longrightarrow CH_3-\underset{}{\overset{\overset{CH_2}{\|}}{C}}-CH_3 + H_2O + Br^- \quad \textbf{(6.7)}$$

strong base   tertiary alkyl halide   methylpropene   (H—OH)

To understand these differences, we must consider the mechanisms by which the substitutions in Table 6.1 take place.

6.3 Nucleophilic Substitution Mechanisms

As a result of experiments that began more than 70 years ago, we now understand the mechanisms of nucleophilic substitution reactions rather well. We use the plural because such *nucleophilic substitutions occur by more than one mechanism*. The mechanism observed in a particular case depends on the structures of the nucleophile and the alkyl halide, the solvent, the reaction temperature, and other factors.

There are two main nucleophilic substitution mechanisms. These are described by the symbols S_N2 and S_N1, respectively. The S_N part of each symbol stands for "substitution, nucleophilic." The meaning of the numbers 2 and 1 will become clear as we discuss each mechanism.

6.4 The S_N2 Mechanism

The **S_N2 mechanism** is a one-step process, represented by the following equation:

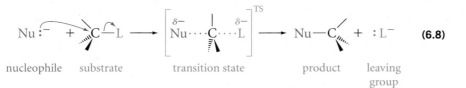

nucleophile   substrate   transition state   product   leaving group

> The **S_N2 mechanism** is a one-step process in which the bond to the leaving group begins to break as the bond to the nucleophile begins to form.

The nucleophile attacks from the *back*side of the C—L bond (remember, there is a small "back" lobe to an sp^3 hybrid bond orbital; see Figure 1.7). At some stage (the transition state), the nucleophile *and* the leaving group are *both* partly bonded to the carbon at which substitution occurs. As the leaving group departs *with its electron pair*, the nucleophile supplies another electron pair to the carbon atom.

The number 2 is used in describing this mechanism because the reaction is *bi*molecular. That is, two molecules—the nucleophile and the substrate—are involved in the key step (the *only* step) in the reaction mechanism. The reaction shown in eq. 6.1 occurs by an S_N2 mechanism. A reaction energy diagram is shown in Figure 6.1.

PROBLEM 6.3 Draw a reaction energy diagram for the reaction between $CH_3CH_2CH_2Br$ and sodium cyanide (NaCN). Label the energy of activation (E_a) and ΔH for the reaction. (Refer to Sec. 3.12 if you need help.)

How can we recognize when a particular nucleophile and substrate react by the S_N2 mechanism? There are several telltale signs.

▰ **Figure 6.1**
Reaction energy diagram for an
S$_N$2 reaction.

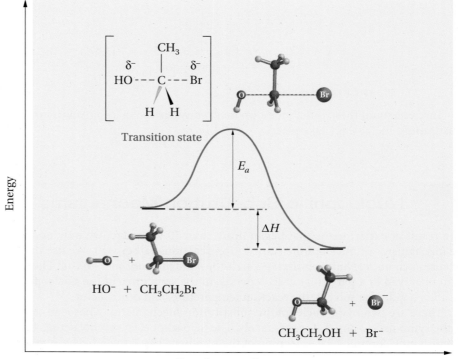

Reaction coordinate

1. *The rate of the reaction depends on both the nucleophile and the substrate concentrations.* The reaction of hydroxide ion with ethyl bromide (eq. 6.1) is an example of an S$_N$2 reaction. If we double the nucleophile concentration (HO$^-$), the reaction goes twice as fast. The same thing happens if we double the ethyl bromide concentration. We will see shortly that this rate behavior is *not* observed in the S$_N$1 mechanism.

2. *Every S$_N$2 displacement occurs with inversion of configuration.* For example, if we treat (*R*)-2-bromobutane with sodium hydroxide, we obtain (*S*)-2-butanol.

$$\text{HO}^- \ + \ \underset{\substack{\text{H} \\ \text{CH}_2\text{CH}_3}}{\overset{\text{CH}_3}{\text{C}}}\!\!-\!\!\text{Br} \ \longrightarrow \ \text{HO}-\underset{\substack{\\ \text{CH}_2\text{CH}_3}}{\overset{\text{CH}_3}{\text{C}}}\!\!\cdots\!\!\text{H} \ + \ \text{Br}^- \qquad \textbf{(6.9)}$$

(*R*)-2-bromobutane   (*S*)-2-butanol

This experimental result, which at first came as a surprise to chemists, meant that the OH group did *not* take the exact position occupied by the Br. If it had, the configuration would have been retained; (*R*)-bromide would have given (*R*)-alcohol. What is the only reasonable explanation? The hydroxide ion must attack the C—Br bond from the rear. As substitution occurs, the three groups attached to the *sp*^{3} carbon *invert,* somewhat like an umbrella caught in a strong wind.*

3. The reaction is fastest when the alkyl group of the substrate is methyl or primary and slowest when it is tertiary. Secondary alkyl halides react at an intermediate rate. The reason for this reactivity order is fairly obvious if we think about the S$_N$2 mechanism. The rear side of the carbon, where displacement occurs, is more crowded if more alkyl groups are attached to it, thus slowing down the reaction rate.**

---

*Because HO$^-$ is both an anion and a base, a competing reaction is the formation of alkenes (see eqs. 6.5 and 6.7). We will see this again in Section 6.7.
**In eqs. 6.10 and 6.11, the leaving group L (see eq. 6.8) is a halide, which is given the general symbol X. We will see later (Chapter 7) that groups other than halides can behave as leaving groups.

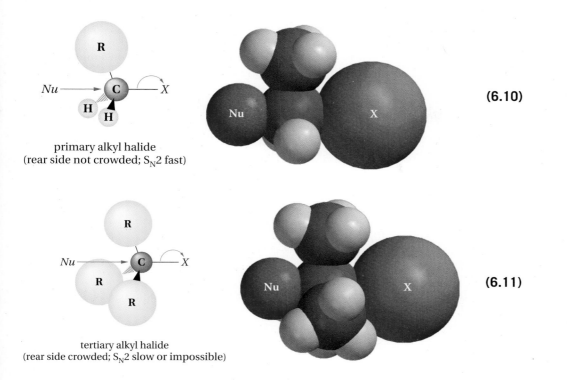

primary alkyl halide
(rear side not crowded; S_N2 fast)

(6.10)

tertiary alkyl halide
(rear side crowded; S_N2 slow or impossible)

(6.11)

EXAMPLE 6.5

Predict the product from the S_N2 reaction of *cis*-4-methylcyclohexyl bromide with cyanide ion.

Solution

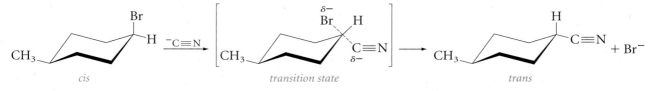

Cyanide ion attacks the C—Br bond from the rear and therefore the cyano group ends up *trans* to the methyl group.

PROBLEM 6.4 Predict the product from the S_N2 reaction of

a. *trans*-4-methylcyclohexyl bromide with cyanide ion.
b. (*S*)-2-bromopentane with cyanide ion.
c. (*R*)-2-chlorobutane with NaSH.

PROBLEM 6.5 Arrange the following compounds in order of *decreasing* S_N2 reactivity toward sodium ethoxide:

$$\underset{CH_3CH_2CHBr}{\overset{CH_3}{|}} \qquad \underset{CH_3CHCH_2Br}{\overset{CH_3}{|}} \qquad CH_3CH_2CH_2CH_2Br$$

To summarize, the S_N2 mechanism is a one-step process favored for methyl and primary halides. It occurs more slowly with secondary halides and usually not at all with tertiary halides. An S_N2 reaction occurs with inversion of configuration, and its rate depends on the concentration of *both* the nucleophile and the substrate (the alkyl halide).

Now let us see how these features differ for the S_N1 mechanism.

6.5 | The S_N1 Mechanism

The **S_N1 mechanism** is a two-step process. In the first step, which is slow, the bond between the carbon and the leaving group breaks as the substrate dissociates (ionizes).

The S_N1 mechanism is a two-step process: the bond between the carbon and the leaving group breaks first and then the resulting carbocation combines with the nucleophile.

(6.12)

The electrons of the C—L bond go with the leaving group, and a carbocation is formed.

In the second step, which is fast, the carbocation combines with the nucleophile to give the product.

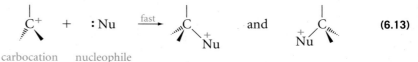

(6.13)

When the nucleophile is a neutral molecule, such as water or an alcohol, loss of a proton from the nucleophilic oxygen, in a third step, gives the final product.

Figure 6.2

Reaction energy diagram for an S_N1 reaction.

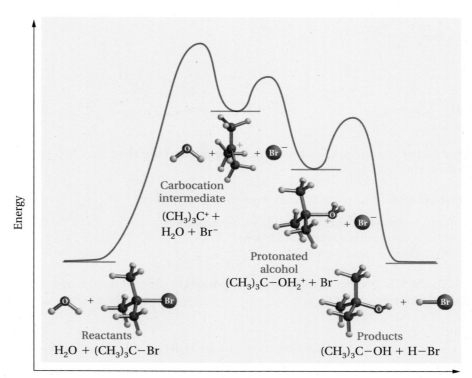

Carbocation intermediate
$(CH_3)_3C^+ +$
$H_2O + Br^-$

Protonated alcohol
$(CH_3)_3C-OH_2^+ + Br^-$

Reactants
$H_2O + (CH_3)_3C-Br$

Products
$(CH_3)_3C-OH + H-Br$

Energy

Reaction coordinate

The number 1 is used to designate this mechanism because the slow, or rate-determining, step involves *only one* of the two reactants: the substrate (eq. 6.12). It does *not* involve the nucleophile at all. That is, the first step is *uni*molecular. The reaction shown in eq. 6.6 occurs by an S$_N$1 mechanism, and a reaction energy diagram for that reaction is shown in Figure 6.2. Notice that the energy diagram for this reaction, and all S$_N$1 reactions, resembles that of an electrophilic addition to an alkene (Figure 3.11), another reaction that has a carbocation intermediate. Also notice that the energy of activation for the first step (the rate-determining step) is much greater than for subsequent steps. This first step forms the highest energy (most unstable) species in the reaction energy diagram.

> **PROBLEM 6.6** What are the products expected from the reaction of (CH$_3$)$_3$C—Cl with CH$_3$—OH? Draw a reaction energy diagram for the reaction.

How can we recognize when a particular nucleophile and substrate react by the S$_N$1 mechanism? Here are the signs:

1. *The rate of the reaction does not depend on the concentration of the nucleophile.* The first step is rate-determining, and the nucleophile is not involved in this step. Therefore, the bottleneck in the reaction rate is the rate of formation of the carbocation, not the rate of its reaction with the nucleophile, which is nearly instantaneous.

2. If the carbon bearing the leaving group is stereogenic, the reaction occurs mainly with loss of optical activity (that is, with racemization). In carbocations, only three groups are attached to the positively charged carbon. Therefore, the positively charged carbon is *sp²*-hybridized and planar. As shown in eq. 6.13, the nucleophile can react at either "face" of the carbocation to give a 50:50 mixture of two enantiomers, a racemic mixture. For example, the reaction of (*R*)-3-bromo-3-methylhexane with water gives the racemic alcohol.

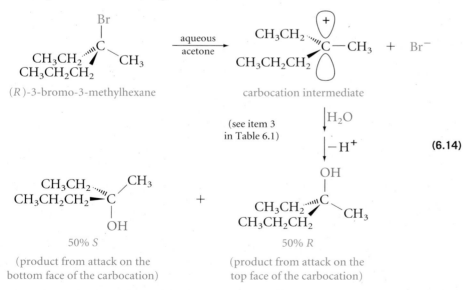

The intermediate carbocation is planar and achiral. Combination with H$_2$O from the "top" or "bottom" of the carbocation intermediate is equally probable, giving the *R* and *S* alcohols, respectively, in equal amounts.

3. The reaction is fastest when the alkyl group of the substrate is tertiary and slowest when it is primary. The reason is that S$_N$1 reactions proceed via carbocations, so the reactivity order corresponds to that of carbocation stability (3° > 2° > 1°).

That is, the easier it is to form the carbocation, the faster the reaction will proceed. For this reason, S_N1 reactivity is also favored for resonance-stabilized carbocations, such as allylic carbocations (see Sec. 3.15). Likewise, S_N1 reactivity is disfavored for aryl and vinyl halides because aryl and vinyl carbocations are unstable and not easily formed.

PROBLEM 6.7 Which of the following bromides will react faster with methanol (via an S_N1 reaction)? What are the reaction products in each case?

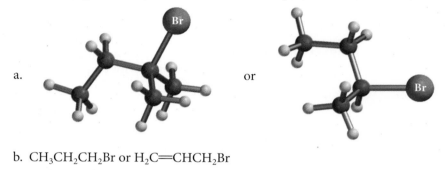

a.   or

b. $CH_3CH_2CH_2Br$ or $H_2C{=}CHCH_2Br$

To summarize, the S_N1 mechanism is a two-step process and is favored when the alkyl halide is tertiary. Primary halides normally do not react by this mechanism. The S_N1 process occurs with racemization, and its rate is independent of the nucleophile's concentration.

6.6 The S_N1 and S_N2 Mechanisms Compared

How can we tell whether a particular nucleophilic substitution reaction will proceed by an S_N2 or an S_N1 mechanism? And why do we care? Well, we care for several reasons. When we perform a reaction in the laboratory, we want to be sure that the reaction will proceed at a rate fast enough to obtain the product in a reasonable time. If the reaction has stereochemical consequences, we want to know in advance what that outcome will be: inversion or racemization.

Table 6.2 should be helpful. It summarizes what we have said so far about the two substitution mechanisms, and it compares them with respect to two other variables, solvent and nucleophile structure, which we will discuss here.

Primary halides almost always react by the S_N2 mechanism, whereas tertiary halides react by the S_N1 mechanism. Only with secondary halides are we likely to encounter both possibilities.

One experimental variable that we can use to help control the mechanism is the solvent polarity. Water and alcohols are **polar protic solvents** (protic because of the proton-donating ability of the hydroxyl groups). How will such solvents affect S_N1 and S_N2 reactions?

The first step of the S_N1 mechanism involves the formation of ions. Since polar solvents can solvate ions, the rate of S_N1 processes is enhanced by polar solvents. On the other hand, solvation of nucleophiles ties up their unshared electron pairs. Therefore, S_N2 reactions, whose rates depend on nucleophile effectiveness, are usually retarded by polar protic solvents. Polar but *aprotic* solvents [examples are acetone, dimethyl sulfoxide, $(CH_3)_2S{=}O$, or dimethylformamide, $(CH_3)_2NCHO$] solvate cations preferentially. These solvents *accelerate* S_N2 reactions because, by solvating the cation (say, K^+ in $K^{+-}CN$), they leave the anion more "naked" or unsolvated, thus improving its nucleophilicity.

Polar protic solvents are solvents such as water or alcohols that can donate protons.

Table 6.2 ■ **Comparison of S$_N$2 and S$_N$1 Substitutions**

Variables	S$_N$2	S$_N$1
Halide structure		
Primary or CH$_3$	Common	Rarely*
Secondary	Sometimes	Sometimes
Tertiary	Rarely	Common
Stereochemistry	Inversion	Racemization
Solvent	Rate is retarded by polar protic solvents and increased by polar aprotic solvents	Because the intermediates are ions, the rate is increased by polar solvents
Nucleophile	Rate depends on nucleophile concentration; mechanism is favored when the nucleophile is an anion	Rate is independent of nucleophile concentration; mechanism is more likely with neutral nucleophiles

*Allyl and benzyl substrates are the common exceptions (see Problem 6.7b).

A WORD ABOUT... ▸ S$_N$2 Reactions in Nature: Biological Methylations

Substitution and elimination reactions are so useful that it is not surprising that they occur in nature. Alkyl halides, however, are not compatible with cytoplasm because they are hydrocarbon-like and therefore insoluble in water. In the cell, alkyl phosphates play the role that alkyl halides do in the laboratory. **Adenosine triphosphate** (ATP) is an example of a biologically important alkyl phosphate. We will abbreviate its structure here as follows (the full structure is given in Sec. 18.12).

$$Ad-O-\underset{\underset{OH}{|}}{\overset{\overset{O}{\|}}{P}}-O-\underset{\underset{OH}{|}}{\overset{\overset{O}{\|}}{P}}-O-\underset{\underset{OH}{|}}{\overset{\overset{O}{\|}}{P}}-OH \quad or \quad Ad-OPPP$$

Ad = adenosyl (p. 546)

Many compounds in nature have a methyl group attached to an oxygen (RO—CH$_3$) or nitrogen atom (R$_2$N—CH$_3$).

Examples include mescaline, an hallucinogen derived from the peyote cactus, and morphine (p. 405), the pain-relieving drug derived from opium. How do the methyl groups get there? Two steps are involved, both of them nucleophilic substitutions.

The methyl carrier in most biochemical methylations is a sulfur-containing amino acid called **methionine**. In the first step, methionine is alkylated by ATP to form **S-adenosylmethionine**. This reaction is a biological example of reaction 12 in Table 6.1. The methionine acts as a sulfur nucleophile in an S$_N$2 reaction and displaces the triphosphate ion. In the second step, the oxygen or nitrogen atom to be methylated acts as a nucleophile. The S-adenosylmethionine acts just like a methyl halide. Indeed, it has been shown that these methylation reactions take place with inversion of configuration.

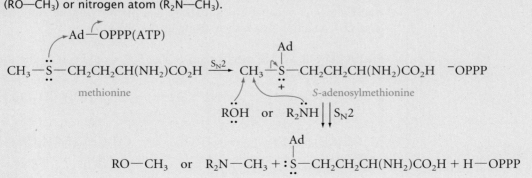

See Problem 6.19.

Now let us consider the other variable in Table 6.2—the nucleophile. As we have seen, the rate of an S_N2 reaction (but *not* an S_N1 reaction) depends on the nucleophile. If the nucleophile is *strong*, the S_N2 mechanism will be favored. How can we tell whether a nucleophile is strong or weak, or whether one nucleophile is stronger than another? Here are a few useful generalizations.

1. *Negative ions are more nucleophilic, or better electron suppliers, than the corresponding neutral molecules.* Thus,

$$HO^- > HOH \qquad RS^- > RSH \qquad RO^- > ROH$$

2. *Elements low in the periodic table tend to be more nucleophilic than elements above them in the same column.* Thus,

$$HS^- > HO^- \qquad I^- > Br^- > Cl^- > F^- \qquad \text{(in protic solvents)}$$

3. *Across a row in the periodic table, more electronegative elements (that is, the more tightly an element holds electrons to itself) tend to be less nucleophilic.* Thus,

$$\underset{\underset{R}{|}}{\overset{\overset{R}{|}}{R-C^-}} > \underset{\underset{R}{|}}{\overset{\overset{R}{|}}{N^-}} > R-O^- > F^- \qquad \text{and} \qquad H_3N\colon > H_2\ddot{O}\colon > H\ddot{F}\colon$$

Can we juggle all of these factors to make some predictions about particular substitution reactions? Here are some examples.

EXAMPLE 6.6

Which mechanism, S_N1 or S_N2, would you predict for this reaction?

$$(CH_3)_3CBr + CH_3OH \longrightarrow (CH_3)_3COCH_3 + HBr$$

Solution S_N1, because the substrate is a tertiary alkyl halide. Also, methanol is a weak, neutral nucleophile and, if used as the reaction solvent, rather polar. Thus, it favors ionization.

EXAMPLE 6.7

Which mechanism, S_N1 or S_N2, would you predict for this reaction?

$$CH_3CH_2-I + NaOCH_3 \longrightarrow CH_3CH_2-OCH_3 + NaI$$

Solution S_N2, because the substrate is a primary halide, and methoxide (CH_3O^-), an anion, is a rather strong nucleophile.

PROBLEM 6.8 Which mechanism, S_N1 or S_N2, would you predict for each of the following reactions?

a. $\underset{\underset{Br}{|}}{CH_3CHCH_2CH_2CH_3} + Na^{+\,-}SH \longrightarrow \underset{\underset{SH}{|}}{CH_3CHCH_2CH_2CH_3} + NaBr$

b. $\underset{\underset{Br}{|}}{CH_3CHCH_2CH_2CH_3} + CH_3OH \longrightarrow \underset{\underset{OCH_3}{|}}{CH_3CHCH_2CH_2CH_3} + HBr$

6.7 Dehydrohalogenation, an Elimination Reaction; the E2 and E1 Mechanisms

We have seen several examples of reactions in which two reactants give not a single product but mixtures. Examples include halogenation of alkanes (eq. 2.13), addition to double bonds (eq. 3.31), and electrophilic aromatic substitutions (Sec. 4.11), where more than one isomer may be formed from the same two reactants. Even in nucleophilic substitution, more than one substitution product may form. For example, hydrolysis of a single alkyl bromide gives a mixture of two alcohols in eq. 6.14. But sometimes we find two entirely different reaction types occurring at the same time between the same two reactants, to give two (or more) entirely different types of products. Let us consider one example.

When an alkyl halide with a hydrogen attached to the carbon *adjacent* to the halogen-bearing carbon reacts with a nucleophile, two competing reaction paths are possible: substitution or **elimination**.

In **elimination** (or **dehydrohalogenation**) reactions of alkyl halides, a hydrogen atom and a halogen atom from adjacent carbons are eliminated and a carbon–carbon double bond is formed.

$$\text{substitution (S)} \qquad (6.15)$$
$$\text{elimination (E)} \qquad (6.16)$$

In the substitution reaction, the nucleophile replaces the halogen X. In the elimination reaction, the nucleophile acts as a base and removes a proton from carbon-2, the carbon next to the one that bears the halogen X. The halogen X and the hydrogen from the *adjacent* carbon atom are *eliminated,* and a new bond (a pi bond) is formed between carbons-1 and -2.* The symbol E is used to designate an elimination process. Since in this case a hydrogen halide is eliminated, the reaction is called **dehydrohalogenation**. Elimination reactions provide a useful way to prepare compounds with double or triple bonds.

Often substitution and elimination reactions occur simultaneously with the same set of reactants—a nucleophile and a substrate. One reaction type or the other may predominate, depending on the structure of the nucleophile, the structure of the substrate, and other reaction conditions. As with substitution reactions, *there are two main mechanisms for elimination reactions, designated E2 and E1.* To learn how to control these reactions, we must first understand each mechanism.

Like the S_N2 mechanism, the **E2 mechanism** is a one-step process. The nucleophile, acting as a base, removes the proton (hydrogen) on a carbon atom adjacent to the one that bears the leaving group. At the same time, the leaving group departs and a double bond is formed. The bond breaking and bond making that occurs during an E2 reaction is shown by the curved arrows:

The **E2 mechanism** is a process in which HX is eliminated and a C=C bond is formed in the same step.

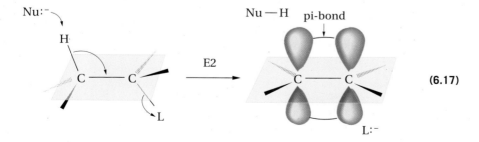

$$(6.17)$$

---

*For a discussion of pi bonds and bonding in alkenes, review Section 3.4.

The preferred conformation for the substrate in an E2 reaction is also shown in eq. 6.17. The H—C—C—L atoms lie in a single plane, with H and L in an *anti*-arrangement. The reason for this preference is that the C—H and C—L bonds are parallel in this conformation. This alignment is needed to form the new pi bond as the C—H and C—L bonds break.

The **E1 mechanism** is a two-step process and has the same first step as the S_N1 mechanism, the slow and rate-determining ionization of the substrate to give a carbocation (compare with eq. 6.12).

> The **E1 mechanism** is a two-step process with the same first step as an S_N1 reaction.

$$\text{(6.18)}$$

Two reactions are then possible for the carbocation. It may combine with a nucleophile (the S_N1 process), or it may lose a proton from a carbon atom adjacent to the positive carbon, as shown by the curved arrow, to give an alkene (the E1 process).

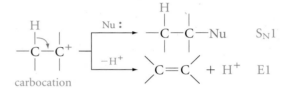

$$\text{(6.19)}$$

6.8 Substitution and Elimination in Competition

Now we can consider how substitution and elimination reactions compete with one another. Let us consider the options for each class of alkyl halide.

6.8.a Tertiary Halides

Substitution can only occur by the S_N1 mechanism, but elimination can occur by either the E1 or the E2 mechanism. With weak nucleophiles and polar solvents, the S_N1 and E1 mechanisms compete with each other. For example,

$$
(CH_3)_3CBr \underset{}{\overset{H_2O}{\rightleftharpoons}} (CH_3)_3C^+ + Br^-
\begin{cases}
\xrightarrow{H_2O,\,S_N1} (CH_3)_3COH \quad \text{(about 80\%)} \\
\xrightarrow{E1} (CH_3)_2C=CH_2 + H^+ \quad \text{(about 20\%)}
\end{cases}
$$

$$\text{(6.20)}$$

t-butyl bromide

If we use a strong nucleophile (which can act as a base) instead of a weak one, and if we use a less polar solvent, we favor elimination by the E2 mechanism. Thus, with OH^- or CN^- as nucleophiles, only elimination occurs (eqs. 6.5 and 6.7), and the exclusive product is the alkene.

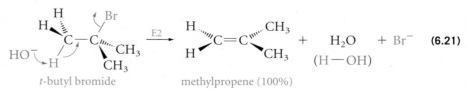

$$\text{(6.21)}$$

Because the tertiary carbon is too hindered sterically for S_N2 attack (eq. 6.11), substitution does not compete with elimination.

6.8.b Primary Halides

Only the S_N2 and E2 mechanisms are possible, because ionization to a primary carbocation, the first step required for the S_N1 or E1 mechanisms, does not occur.

With most nucleophiles, primary halides give mainly substitution products (S_N2). Only with very bulky, strongly basic nucleophiles do we see that the E2 process is favored. For example,

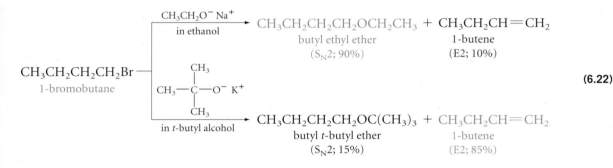

$$\text{CH}_3\text{CH}_2\text{CH}_2\text{CH}_2\text{OCH}_2\text{CH}_3 \ + \ \text{CH}_3\text{CH}_2\text{CH}{=}\text{CH}_2$$

butyl ethyl ether   1-butene
(S_N2; 90%)   (E2; 10%)

$$\text{CH}_3\text{CH}_2\text{CH}_2\text{CH}_2\text{OC(CH}_3)_3 \ + \ \text{CH}_3\text{CH}_2\text{CH}{=}\text{CH}_2$$

butyl *t*-butyl ether   1-butene
(S_N2; 15%)   (E2; 85%)

(6.22)

Potassium *t*-butoxide is a bulky base (Figure 6.3). Hence substitution is retarded, and the main reaction is elimination.

(a)

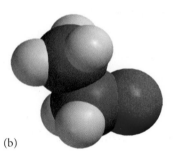

(b)

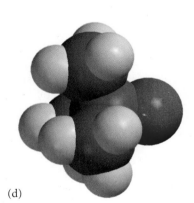

(c)   (d)

▪ **Figure 6.3**

Ball-and-stick (a) and space-filling (b) structure for ethoxide ($\text{CH}_3\text{CH}_2\text{O}^-$) and for *t*-butoxide [$(\text{CH}_3)_3\text{CO}^-$] as ball-and-stick (c) and space-filling (d) models.

6.8.c Secondary Halides

All four mechanisms, S_N2 and E2 as well as S_N1 and E1, are possible. The product composition is sensitive to the nucleophile (its strength as a nucleophile and as a base) and to the reaction conditions (solvent, temperature). In general, substitution is favored with stronger nucleophiles that are not strong bases (S_N2) or by weaker nucleophiles in polar solvents (S_N1), but elimination is favored by strong bases (E2).

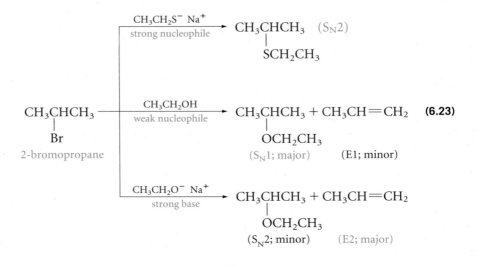

$$CH_3CHCH_3 \quad (S_N2)$$
$$| \atop SCH_2CH_3$$

$$CH_3CHCH_3 + CH_3CH{=}CH_2 \quad \textbf{(6.23)}$$
$$| \atop OCH_2CH_3$$
(S_N1; major)   (E1; minor)

$$CH_3CHCH_3 + CH_3CH{=}CH_2$$
$$| \atop OCH_2CH_3$$
(S_N2; minor)   (E2; major)

EXAMPLE 6.8

Predict the product of the reaction of 1-bromo-1-methylcyclohexane with

a. sodium ethoxide in ethanol.
b. refluxing ethanol.

Solution The alkyl bromide is tertiary

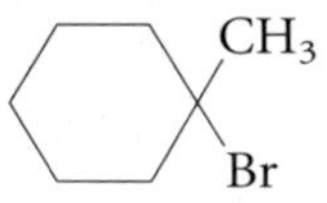

a. The first set of conditions favors the E2 process, because sodium ethoxide is a strong base. Two elimination products are possible, depending on whether the base attacks a hydrogen on an adjacent CH_2 or CH_3 group.

b. This set of conditions favors ionization, because the ethanol is neutral (hence a weak nucleophile) and, as a solvent, fairly polar. The S_N1 process predominates, and the main product is the ether.

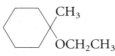

Some of the above alkenes will also be formed by the E1 mechanism.

PROBLEM 6.9 Draw structures for *all* possible elimination products obtainable from 2-chloro-2-methylpentane.

PROBLEM 6.10 Treatment of the alkyl halide in Problem 6.9 with KOH in methanol gives mainly a mixture of the alkenes whose structures you drew. But treatment with only methanol gives a different product. What is it, and by what mechanism is it formed?

6.9 Polyhalogenated Aliphatic Compounds

Because of their useful properties, many polyhalogenated compounds are produced commercially. As industrial chemicals, they are usually given common names.

Chlorinated methanes* are made by the chlorination of methane (eqs. 2.10 and 2.12). Carbon tetrachloride (CCl_4, bp 77°C), chloroform ($CHCl_3$, bp 62°C), and methylene chloride (CH_2Cl_2, bp 40°C) are all *insoluble* in water, but they are effective solvents for organic compounds. Also important for this purpose are trichloroethylenes and tetrachloroethylenes, used in dry cleaning and as degreasing agents in metal and textile processing.

$$Cl_2C\!=\!CHCl \qquad\qquad Cl_2C\!=\!CCl_2$$
trichloroethylene   tetrachloroethylene
bp 87°C   bp 121°C

Because some of these chlorinated compounds are suspected carcinogens, adequate ventilation is essential when they are used as solvents.

Tetrafluoroethylene is the raw material for **Teflon**, a polymer related to polyethylene (Sec. 3.16) but with all of the hydrogens replaced by fluorine atoms.

$$n\ CF_2\!=\!CF_2 \xrightarrow[\text{catalyst}]{\text{peroxide}} \left(\!CF_2CF_2\!\right)_n \qquad\qquad \textbf{(6.24)}$$
Teflon

Teflon has exceptional properties. It is resistant to almost all chemicals and is widely used as a nonstick coating for pots, pans, and other cooking utensils. Another use of Teflon is in Gore-Tex-like fabrics, materials with as many as nine billion pores per square inch. These pores are the right size to transmit water vapor, but not liquid water. Thus, perspiration vapor can pass through the fabric, but wind, rain, and snow cannot. Gore-Tex has revolutionized cold- and wet-weather gear for both military and civilian uses. It is used in skiwear, boots, sleeping bags, tents, and other rugged outdoor gear.

Nonpolymeric perfluorochemicals (hydrocarbons, ethers, or amines in which all of the hydrogens are replaced by fluorine atoms) also have fascinating and useful properties. For example, perfluorochemicals such as perfluorotributylamine, $(CF_3CF_2CF_2CF_2)_3N$, can dissolve as much as 60% oxygen by volume. By contrast, whole blood dissolves only about 20%, and blood plasma about 0.3%. Because of this property, these perfluorochemicals are important components of artificial blood.

Other polyhalogenated compounds that contain two or three different halogens per molecule are commercially important. The best known are the **chlorofluorocarbons** (**CFCs**, formerly known as **Freons**). The two that have been produced on the largest scale are CFC-11 and CFC-12, made by fluorination of carbon tetrachloride.

Chlorofluorocarbons (CFCs, also known as **Freons**) are polyhalogenated compounds containing chlorine and fluorine. Bromine-containing compounds of this type are called **Halons**.

$$CCl_4 \xrightarrow[\text{SbF}_5]{\text{HF}} CCl_3F \xrightarrow[\text{SbF}_5]{\text{HF}} CCl_2F_2 \qquad\qquad \textbf{(6.25)}$$
(bp 77°C)   trichlorofluoromethane   dichlorodifluoromethane
                  (CFC-11)   (CFC-12)
                  bp 24°C   bp −30°C

They are used as refrigerants, as blowing agents in the manufacture of foams, as cleaning fluids, and as aerosol propellants. They are exceptionally stable. Because of this stability, they accumulate in the upper stratosphere, where they damage the earth's ozone layer. Consequently, their use for nonessential propellant purposes is now banned in most countries, and the search is on for replacements (see "A Word About... CFCs, the Ozone Layer, and Trade-Offs.")

---

*The analogous F, Br, and I compounds are also known, but are more expensive and not commercially important.

A WORD ABOUT...   CFCs, the Ozone Layer, and Trade-Offs

The story of chlorofluorocarbons (CFCs) has many lessons for us. Fluorine's reputation as one of the most reactive of the elements was widespread. It was quite remarkable and unexpected, therefore, that fluorocarbons and CFCs should be so extremely *unreactive*. (Indeed, Thomas Midgley, the American who discovered CFCs, used to demonstrate their nontoxicity, nonflammability, and noncorrosiveness by inhaling them and then puffing out a candle.)

Because of these and other properties, at least *four* major commercial uses of CFCs were developed. Their low boiling points (bp's) and other heat properties make them excellent *refrigerants*, far superior to ammonia, sulfur dioxide, and other rather difficult-to-handle refrigerants. Thus CFCs became widely used in freezers, refrigerators, and air conditioners. CFCs make excellent *blowing agents* for rigid foams (such as those used for ice chests, fast-food take-out boxes, and other packaging materials) and for flexible foams (like those used to make pillows and furniture cushions). Their low surface tension and low viscosity give them excellent wetting properties, which led to their use as *cleaning fluids* for printed computer circuits, artificial limbs, and other products. Finally, they were used as *propellants* in aerosol sprays. CFCs were manufactured on such a scale that they constituted a multibillion-dollar industry.

But their extreme stability led to a major world problem. CFCs are so stable that, when they are released into the atmosphere, they do not decompose in the lower atmosphere, as do most other industrial chemicals. Instead, they eventually rise to the stratosphere where, through ultraviolet radiation, the C—Cl bonds are broken and chlorine atoms are released. These chlorine atoms initiate a chain of reactions that damages the ozone layer, which is needed to protect life on earth from harmful ultraviolet rays.*

How do we solve the problem? Ban all use of CFCs? To do so could bring about a major crisis for civilization. How, without refrigeration, could we ensure safe and adequate food supplies to urban areas, or delivery of heat-sensitive medical supplies? A return to old-fashioned refrigerants would also be fraught with environmental hazards. So the solution is not simple.

What has been done is to cut back or ban some less essential uses gradually. For example, in the United States (but *not* worldwide), all nonessential aerosol use of CFCs is banned. In 1987, 24 countries signed the Montreal Protocol, an agreement that called for cutting CFC use to half of the 1986 level by 1998. This was later expanded to a complete ban on CFC production and use by 1996.

Chemists and other scientists have been seeking replacements to fill the gap left by elimination of CFC production and use. The properties of polyhalogenated compounds are so uniquely useful that for the moment the best chance to find CFC substitutes is among this type of compound. For example, it was found that introducing one or more hydrogen atoms into the molecule substantially increases its decomposition rate in the lower atmosphere, where no damage to the ozone layer is possible. Hydrochlorofluorocarbon (HCFC) and hydrofluorocarbon (HFC) compounds such as CF_3CHCl_2 (HCFC-123, bp 28°C) and CF_3CH_2F (HFC-134a, bp −26°C) are now being used as replacements for CFC-11 and CFC-12, respectively.

The Montreal Protocol has brought results. Worldwide production of CFCs has declined from more than 1 million metric tons per year in 1986 to about 150,000 metric tons in 1997. But significant problems remain. CFC production is still legal in some countries and a black market trade in CFCs has developed because of the cost associated with replacing CFC equipment, such as chillers and air conditioners, with HCFC and HFC equipment. Nonetheless, the market for CFC replacements is rapidly growing, and this conversion should have positive environmental consequences.

CFCs are just one of many examples of the trade-offs between beneficial and possible harmful effects of a new research product. During World War II, the use of CFCs as propellants for the insecticide DDT saved the lives of many troops in the Pacific zone who were suffering more casualties from malaria than from enemy action. But later, indiscriminate use of CFCs as propellants for all sorts of trivial purposes led to problems with their environmental accumulation. Chemicals (in this case, CFCs) are neither good nor evil, but we must exercise good judgment in how we use them.

---

*For an account of the discovery and development of the CFC–ozone problem by F. Sherwood Rowland and Mario J. Molina, chemists who initiated ozone depletion research, see *Chemical and Engineering News*, **1994**, *77* (33), 8–13. Rowland, Molina, and Paul Crutzen shared the 1995 Nobel Prize in chemistry for their contributions to atmospheric chemistry. For one overview of the situation, see *Chemical and Engineering News*, **1997**, *75* (37), 24.

See Problem 6.30.

Bromine-containing aliphatic compounds are now widely used to extinguish fires. Called **Halons**, the best known are

CBrClF$_2$ CBrF$_3$

bromochloro-   bromotrifluoro-
difluoromethane   methane
(Halon-1211)   (Halon-1301)

Halons are much more effective than carbon tetrachloride. They are very important in air safety because of their ability to douse fires within seconds, a particularly important feature on airplanes. However, compared to chlorine- and fluorine-containing CFCs, bromine-containing compounds are even more effective at ozone depletion in the stratosphere. While chemists search for replacements of bromine-containing halons, many of these compounds are still in use for fire suppression applications.

© Tom Pantages

Halon fire extinguisher.

A WORD ABOUT... Halogenated Organic Compounds from the Sea

Terrestrial plants and animals have long served as a source of substances for treatment of various maladies. For example, extracts of willow bark, now known to contain salicylic acid—the active component in aspirin—were used more than three millennia ago to treat pain. Marine organisms have also been used as a source of folk medicines, but only recently have chemists begun to determine the structures of biologically active compounds from the sea. It turns out that many of these substances are halogenated organic compounds, perhaps not surprising given the abundance of bromide and chloride ions in seawater. A few examples are shown in Figure 6.4.

Halomon, a polyhalogenated terpene produced by red algae, kills a variety of tumor cells and is being investigated as a lead compound for the development of new anticancer agents.* Moloka'iamine, a halogenated aromatic compound that inhibits the growth of

barnacles, has been isolated from a marine sponge. Such compounds might be of interest as antifouling agents to the boating industry. It is possible that the two bromines in moloka'iamine are introduced by an electrophilic aromatic substitution reaction in which bromide ion is oxidized to provide an electrophilic source of bromine. 3,4,5-Tribromopyrrole-2-carboxylic acid has been isolated from sponges and structurally related hexahalogenated bipyrroles (HHBPs) have been isolated from seabird eggs, leading to speculation that halogenated organic compounds produced by marine organisms might accumulate in terrestrial animals that live by the sea. These are but a few examples of the many fascinating halogenated compounds that come from the sea.

*See Section 15.9 for the definition of *terpene*.

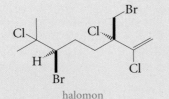

halomon

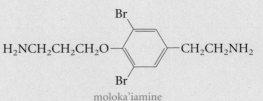

moloka'iamine

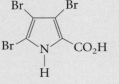

3,4,5-tribromopyrrole-2-carboxylic acid

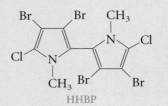

HHBP

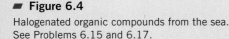 **Figure 6.4**

Halogenated organic compounds from the sea.
See Problems 6.15 and 6.17.

REACTION SUMMARY

1. Nucleophilic Substitutions (S_N1 and S_N2)

Alkyl halides react with a variety of nucleophiles to give alcohols, ethers, alkyl halides, alkynes, and other families of compounds. Examples are shown in Table 6.1 and Section 6.2.

$$Nu: + R-X \longrightarrow R-Nu^+ + X^- \qquad Nu:^- + R-X \longrightarrow R-Nu + X^-$$

2. Elimination Reactions (E1 and E2)

Alkyl halides react with bases to give alkenes (Sec. 6.7).

$$H-\overset{|}{\underset{|}{C}}-\overset{|}{\underset{|}{C}}-X \xrightarrow{B:^-} \underset{/}{\overset{\backslash}{C}}=\underset{\backslash}{\overset{/}{C}} + BH + X^-$$

MECHANISM SUMMARY

1. S_N2: Bimolecular Nucleophilic Substitution (Sec. 6.4)

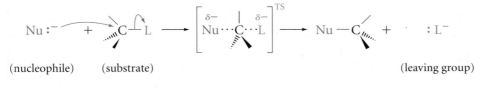

(nucleophile)   (substrate)   (leaving group)

2. S_N1: Unimolecular Nucleophilic Substitution (Sec. 6.5)

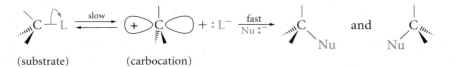

(substrate)   (carbocation)

3. E2: Bimolecular Elimination (Sec. 6.7)

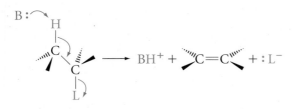

4. E1: Unimolecular Elimination (Sec. 6.7)

$$-\overset{H}{\underset{|}{\overset{|}{C}}}-\overset{|}{\underset{|}{C}}-L \rightleftharpoons -\overset{H}{\underset{|}{\overset{|}{C}}}-\overset{|}{\underset{|}{C}}{}^+ \longrightarrow \underset{/}{\overset{\backslash}{C}}=\underset{\backslash}{\overset{/}{C}} + H^+$$

$$+$$
$$:L^-$$

ADDITIONAL PROBLEMS

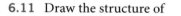

◔WL Interactive versions of these problems are assignable in OWL.

Alkyl Halide Structure

6.11 Draw the structure of

    a. a primary alkyl chloride, C_4H_9Cl.   **b.** a tertiary alkyl bromide, $C_5H_{11}Br$.
    c. a secondary alkyl iodide, $C_6H_{11}I$.

Nucleophilic Substitution Reactions of Alkyl Halides

6.12 Using Table 6.1, write an equation for each of the following substitution reactions:

    a. *p*-methylbenzyl chloride + sodium acetylide   **b.** *n*-propyl bromide + sodium cyanide
    c. 2-iodopropane + sodium hydrosulfide   **d.** 1-bromopentane + sodium iodide
    e. 2-chlorobutane + sodium ethoxide   **f.** *t*-butyl bromide + ethanol
    g. 1,6-dibromohexane + sodium cyanide (excess)   **h.** allyl chloride + ammonia (2 equivalents)
    i. 1-methyl-1-chlorocyclohexane + water

6.13 Select an alkyl halide and a nucleophile that will give each of the following products:

    a. $CH_3OCH_2CH_2CH_2CH_3$ **b.** $HC{\equiv}CCH_2CH_2CH_3$
    c. $CH_3CH_2CH_2NH_2$ **d.** $CH_3CH_2CH_2SCH_2CH_2CH_3$
    e.   **f.**

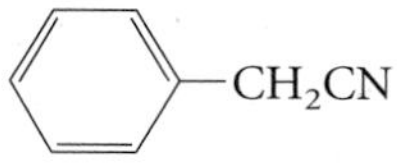

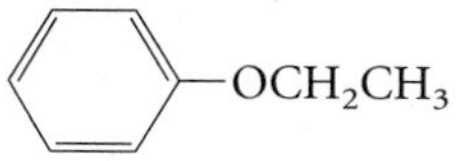

Stereochemistry of Nucleophilic Substitution Reactions

6.14 Draw each of the following equations in a way that shows clearly the stereochemistry of the reactants and products.

    a. (*R*)-2-bromobutane + sodium methoxide (in methanol) $\xrightarrow{S_N2}$ 2-methoxybutane
    b. (*S*)-3-bromo-3-methylhexane + methanol $\xrightarrow{S_N1}$ 3-methoxy-3-methylhexane
    c. *cis*-1-bromo-4-methylcyclohexane + NaSH $\longrightarrow$ 4-methylcyclohexanethiol

6.15 The (+) enantiomer of the inhalation anesthetic desflurane ($CF_3CHFOCHF_2$) has the *S* configuration. Draw a three-dimensional representation of (*S*)-(+)-desflurane.

6.16 When treated with sodium iodide, a solution of (*R*)-2-iodooctane in acetone gradually loses all of its optical activity. Explain.

6.17 In Figure 6.4 and in the "A Word About...Halogenated Organic Compounds from the Sea," halomon, a polyhalogenated terpene produced by red algae, is shown.

    a. Assign *R* or *S* configuration to the different stereogenic centers in halomon.
    b. Of the two carbon centers bonded to Br, which one would be more reactive with a nucleophile like cyanide ion? Explain.

6.18 Draw a Fischer projection formula for the product of this S_N2 reaction:

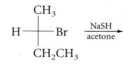

6.19 Predict the product of the reaction if $CH_3-S-CH_2CH_2CH_2CH_2-Br$ is heated in a polar organic solvent, such as methanol. Similarly, what would be the product for hexyl bromide in methanol? (In hexyl bromide, note that the S has been replaced by a CH_2 group.) Explain why the reaction of $CH_3-S-CH_2CH_2CH_2CH_2-Br$ is much faster. (*Hint*: see the "A Word About...S_N2 Reactions in Nature: Biological Methylations" on page 193.)

Nucleophilic Substitution and Elimination Reaction Mechanisms

6.20 Equation 6.20 shows that hydrolysis of *t*-butyl bromide gives about 80% $(CH_3)_3COH$ and 20% $(CH_3)_2C=CH_2$. The same ratio of alcohol to alkene is obtained whether the starting halide is *t*-butyl chloride or *t*-butyl iodide. Explain.

6.21 Determine the order of reactivity for $(CH_3)_2CHCH_2Br$, $(CH_3)_3CBr$, and $CH_3CHCH_2CH_3$ in substitution reactions with

    a. sodium cyanide.   **b.** 50% aqueous acetone. $|$
                                                                                             Br

6.22 Tell what product you expect, and by what mechanism it is formed, for each of the following reactions:

    a. 1-chloro-1-methylcyclohexane + ethanol
    b. 1-chloro-1-methylcyclohexane + sodium ethoxide (in ethanol)

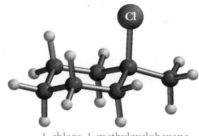

1-chloro-1-methylcyclohexane

6.23 Give the structures of all possible products when 2-chloro-2-methylhexane reacts by the E1 mechanism.

6.24 Explain the different products of the following two reactions by considering the mechanism by which each reaction proceeds. As part of your explanation, use the curved arrow formalism to draw a mechanism for each reaction.

$$CH_2=CH-\underset{\underset{Br}{|}}{CH}-CH_3 + Na^{+-}OCH_3 \xrightarrow{CH_3OH} CH_2=CH-\underset{\underset{OCH_3}{|}}{CH}-CH_3$$

$$CH_2=CH-\underset{\underset{Br}{|}}{CH}-CH_3 + CH_3OH \longrightarrow CH_2=CH-\underset{\underset{OCH_3}{|}}{CH}-CH_3 + CH_2CH=CHCH_3$$
$$\underset{\underset{OCH_3}{|}}{}$$

Nucleophilic Substitution and Elimination Reactions in Organic Synthesis

6.25 Provide equations for the synthesis of the following compounds from 1-bromo-1-phenylethane.

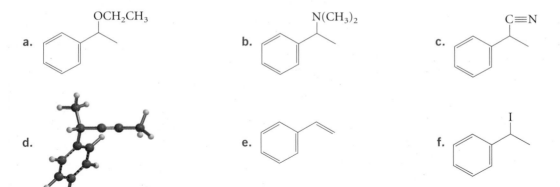

    a.   **b.**   **c.**

    d.   **e.**   **f.**

6.26 Devise a synthesis of

   a. $CH_3OCH_2CH_2CH_3$ from an alkoxide and an alkyl halide.
   b. $CH_3OC(CH_3)_3$ from an alcohol and an alkyl halide.

6.27 Provide an equation for the preparation of the following alkene from an alkyl halide. Do you anticipate problems with formation of other elimination or substitution reactions? Explain.

6.28 Combine the reaction in eq. 3.53 with a nucleophilic substitution to devise

   a. a two-step synthesis of $CH_3C \equiv C - CH_2 -$ ⟨ ⟩ from ⟨ ⟩ $- CH_2Br$.

   b. a four-step synthesis of $CH_3C \equiv CCH_2CH_3$ from acetylene and appropriate alkyl halides.

6.29 Combine a nucleophilic substitution with a catalytic hydrogenation to synthesize

   a. *cis*-3-heptene from butyne and bromopropane.
   b. $CH_3CH_2CH_2OH$ from $CH_2 = CHCH_2Br$.

6.30 HCFC-123 (CF_3CHCl_2) and HFC-134a (CF_3CH_2F) are replacements for chlorofluorocarbons (CFCs), which are known to deplete the stratospheric ozone layer, as described in the "A Word About…CFCs, the Ozone Layer, and Trade-Offs" on page 200. Predict the products from the base-induced elimination reactions of HCFC-123 and HFC-134a.

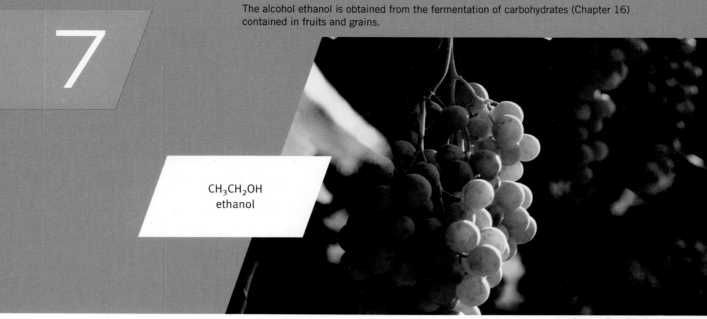

7

The alcohol ethanol is obtained from the fermentation of carbohydrates (Chapter 16) contained in fruits and grains.

CH₃CH₂OH
ethanol

Izzy Schwartz/PhotoDisc/Getty Images

Alcohols, Phenols, and Thiols

The word *alcohol* immediately brings to mind ethanol, the intoxicating compound in wine and beer. But ethanol is just one member of a family of organic compounds called alcohols that abound in nature. Naturally occurring alcohols include 2-phenylethanol, the compound responsible for the intoxicating smell of a rose; cholesterol, a tasty alcohol with which many of us have developed a love–hate relationship; sucrose, a sugar we use to satisfy our sweet tooth; and many others. In this chapter, we will discuss the structural and physical properties as well as the main chemical reactions of alcohols and their structural relatives, phenols and thiols.

water   an alcohol   a phenol

a thiol   a thiophenol

⏻WL

Online homework for this chapter can be assigned in OWL, an online homework assessment tool.

Alcohols have the general formula R—OH and are characterized by the presence of a **hydroxyl group,** —**OH.** They are structurally similar to water, but with one of the hydrogens replaced by an alkyl group. **Phenols** have a hydroxyl group attached directly to an aromatic ring. **Thiols** and thiophenols are similar to alcohols and phenols, except the oxygen is replaced by sulfur.

Alcohols contain the **hydroxyl** (—**OH**) **group.** In **phenols,** the hydroxyl group is attached to an aromatic ring, and in **thiols,** oxygen is replaced by sulfur.

7.1 Nomenclature of Alcohols

In the IUPAC system, the hydroxyl group in alcohols is indicated by the ending **-ol.** In common names, the separate word *alcohol* is placed after the name of the alkyl group. The following examples illustrate the use of IUPAC rules, with common names given in parentheses.

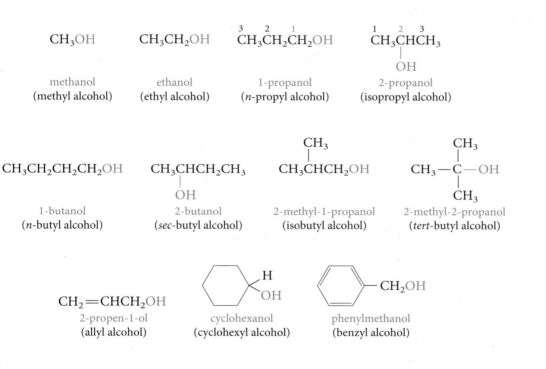

With unsaturated alcohols, two endings are needed: one for the double or triple bond and one for the hydroxyl group (see the IUPAC name for allyl alcohol). In these cases, the *-ol* suffix comes last and takes precedence in numbering.

EXAMPLE 7.1

Name the following alcohols by the IUPAC system:

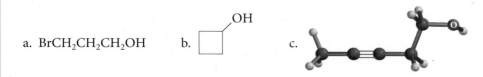

a. $BrCH_2CH_2CH_2OH$ b.   c.

Solution

a. 3-bromopropanol (number from the hydroxyl-bearing carbon)
b. cyclobutanol
c. 3-pentyne-1-ol (*not* 2-pentyne-5-ol)

PROBLEM 7.1 Name these alcohols by the IUPAC system:

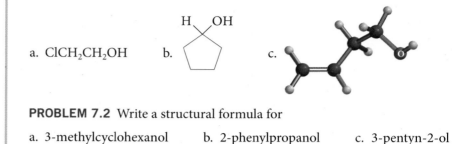

a. $ClCH_2CH_2OH$ b.   c.

PROBLEM 7.2 Write a structural formula for

a. 3-methylcyclohexanol   b. 2-phenylpropanol   c. 3-pentyn-2-ol

---

A WORD ABOUT... Industrial Alcohols

The lower alcohols (those with up to four carbon atoms) are manufactured on a large scale. They are used as raw materials for other valuable chemicals and also have important uses in their own right.

Methanol was at one time produced from wood by distillation and is still sometimes called wood alcohol. At present, however, methanol is manufactured from carbon monoxide and hydrogen.

$$CO + 2H_2 \xrightarrow[400°C,\ 150\ atm]{ZnO-Cr_2O_3} CH_3OH$$

The U.S. production of methanol is 1.4 billion gallons per year. Most of it is used to produce formaldehyde and other chemicals, but some is used as a solvent and as an anti-freeze. Methanol is highly toxic and can cause permanent blindness because when taken internally, it is oxidized to formaldehyde ($CH_2{=}O$), which binds to opsin, preventing formation of rhodopsin, the light-sensitive pigment needed for vision (see "A Word About . . . The Chemistry of Vision," pages 76–77).

Ethanol is prepared from multiple sources, and the total U.S. production of ethanol is 9.0 billion gallons per year. Ethanol is prepared by the fermentation of black-strap molasses, the residue that results from the purification of cane sugar.

$$\underset{\text{cane sugar}}{C_{12}H_{22}O_{11}} + H_2O \xrightarrow{\text{yeast}} 4\ CH_3CH_2OH + 4\ CO_2$$
$$\text{ethanol}$$

The starch in corn, sugar beets, grain, potatoes, and rice can be fermented similarly to produce ethanol, sometimes called grain alcohol.

Besides fermentation, ethanol is also manufactured by the acid-catalyzed hydration of ethylene (eq. 3.7). This method, using sulfuric acid or other acid catalysts, results in an annual U.S. production of 170 million gallons.

Commercial alcohol is a constant-boiling mixture containing 95% ethanol and 5% water and cannot be further purified by distillation. To remove the remaining water to obtain **absolute alcohol**, one adds quicklime (CaO), which reacts with water to form calcium hydroxide but does not react with ethanol.

Since earlier times, ethanol has been known as an ingredient in fermented beverages (beer, wine, and whiskey). The term *proof*, as used in the United States in reference to alcoholic beverages, is approximately twice the volume percentage of alcohol present. For example 100-proof whiskey contains 50% ethanol.

Ethanol is used as a solvent, as a topical antiseptic (for example, when drawing blood), and as a starting material for the manufacture of ethers (Chapter 8) and ethyl esters (Chapter 10). It also can be used as a fuel, often as a blend with gasoline (e.g., E85: 85% ethanol, 15% gasoline). In many states, ethanol is added to gasoline to provide an EPA-mandated oxygen content, in order to improve air quality in the troposphere.

2-Propanol (isopropyl alcohol) is manufactured commercially by the acid-catalyzed hydration of propene (eq. 3.13). It is the main component of rubbing alcohol and is used in many household and personal care products.

See Problem 7.45.

7.2 / Classification of Alcohols

Alcohols are classified as primary (1°), secondary (2°), or tertiary (3°), depending on whether one, two, or three organic groups are connected to the hydroxyl-bearing carbon atom.

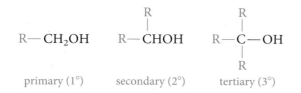

R—CH$_2$OH　　R—CHOH　　R—C—OH

primary (1°)　　secondary (2°)　　tertiary (3°)

Methyl alcohol, which is not strictly covered by this classification, is usually grouped with the primary alcohols. This classification is similar to that for carbocations (Sec. 3.10). We will see that the chemistry of an alcohol sometimes depends on its class.

PROBLEM 7.3 Classify as 1°, 2°, or 3° the eleven alcohols listed in Section 7.1.

7.3 / Nomenclature of Phenols

Phenols are usually named as derivatives of the parent compounds.

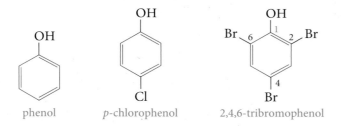

phenol　　　*p*-chlorophenol　　　2,4,6-tribromophenol

The hydroxyl group is named as a substituent when it occurs in the same molecule with carboxylic acid, aldehyde, or ketone functionalities, which have priority in naming. Examples are

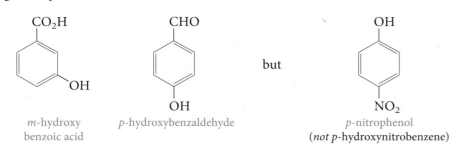

m-hydroxy
benzoic acid　　　*p*-hydroxybenzaldehyde　　　　*p*-nitrophenol
(*not p*-hydroxynitrobenzene)

PROBLEM 7.4 Write the structure for

a. pentachlorophenol (an insecticide for termite control, and a fungicide)
b. *m*-isopropylphenol
c. *o*-hydroxyacetophenone (for the structure of acetophenone, see Sec. 4.6)
d. 3-hydroxy-5-nitrobenzaldehyde

7.4 | Hydrogen Bonding in Alcohols and Phenols

The boiling points (bp's) of alcohols are much higher than those of ethers or hydrocarbons with similar molecular weights.

	CH_3CH_2OH	CH_3OCH_3	$CH_3CH_2CH_3$
mol wt	46	46	44
bp	+78.5°C	−24°C	−42°C

Why? Because alcohols form *hydrogen bonds* with one another (see Sec. 2.7). The O—H bond is polarized by the high electronegativity of the oxygen atom. This polarization places a partial positive charge on the hydrogen atom and a partial negative charge on the oxygen atom (Figure 7.1). Because of its small size and partial positive charge, the hydrogen atom can link two electronegative atoms such as oxygen.

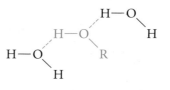

$$\underset{\text{two separate alcohol molecules}}{\underset{\delta-\;\delta+}{\overset{R}{O}-H} + \underset{\delta-\;\delta+}{\overset{R}{O}-H}} \;\rightleftharpoons\; \underset{\text{a hydrogen bond}}{\underset{\delta-\;\delta+}{\overset{R}{O}-H}---\underset{\delta-\;\delta+}{\overset{R}{O}-H}} \qquad (7.1)$$

Two or more alcohol molecules thus become loosely bonded to one another through hydrogen bonds.

Hydrogen bonds are weaker than ordinary covalent bonds.* Nevertheless, their strength is significant, about 5 to 10 kcal/mol (20 to 40 kJ/mol). Consequently, alcohols and phenols have relatively high boiling points because we must not only supply enough heat (energy) to vaporize each molecule but must also supply enough heat to break the hydrogen bonds before each molecule can be vaporized.

Water, of course, is also a hydrogen-bonded liquid (see Figure 2.2). The lower-molecular-weight alcohols can readily replace water molecules in the hydrogen-bonded network.

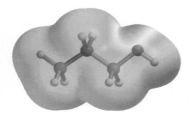

Figure 7.1

Electrostatic potential map for 1-propanol, revealing the electron-rich (red) nature of the oxygen and the electron-poor (blue) nature of the attached proton.

This accounts for the complete miscibility of the lower alcohols with water. However, as the organic chain lengthens and the alcohol becomes relatively more hydrocarbon-like, its water solubility decreases. Table 7.1 illustrates these properties.

Table 7.1   ■   Boiling Point and Water Solubility of Some Alcohols

Name	Formula	bp, °C	Solubility in H_2O g/100 g at 20°C
methanol	CH_3OH	65	completely miscible
ethanol	CH_3CH_2OH	78.5	completely miscible
1-propanol	$CH_3CH_2CH_2OH$	97	completely miscible
1-butanol	$CH_3CH_2CH_2CH_2OH$	117.7	7.9
1-pentanol	$CH_3CH_2CH_2CH_2CH_2OH$	137.9	2.7
1-hexanol	$CH_3CH_2CH_2CH_2CH_2CH_2OH$	155.8	0.59

*Covalent O—H bond strengths are about 120 kcal/mol (480 kJ/mol).

7.5 Acidity and Basicity Reviewed

The acid–base behavior of organic compounds often helps to explain their chemistry; this is certainly true of alcohols. It is a good idea, therefore, to review the fundamental concepts of acidity and basicity.

Acids and **bases** are defined in two ways. According to the **Brønsted–Lowry definition**, an acid is a proton donor, and a base is a proton acceptor. For example, in eq. 7.2, which represents what occurs when hydrogen chloride dissolves in water, the water accepts a proton from the hydrogen chloride.

A **Brønsted–Lowry acid** is a proton donor, whereas a **Brønsted–Lowry base** is a proton acceptor.

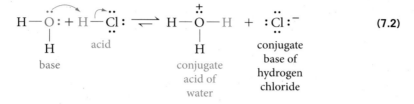

$$\text{(7.2)}$$

Here water acts as a base or proton acceptor, and hydrogen chloride acts as an acid or proton donor. The products of this proton exchange are called the *conjugate acid* and the *conjugate base*.

The strength of an acid (in water) is measured quantitatively by its **acidity constant**, or **ionization constant**, K_a. For example, any acid dissolved in water is in equilibrium with hydronium ions and its conjugate base A^-:

The **acidity** (or **ionization**) **constant**, K_a, of an acid is a quantitative measure of its strength in water.

$$HA + H_2O \rightleftharpoons H_3O^+ + A^- \qquad \text{(7.3)}$$

K_a is related to the equilibrium constant (see page 86) for this reaction and is defined as follows*:

$$K_a = \frac{[H_3O^+][A^-]}{[HA]} \qquad \text{(7.4)}$$

The stronger the acid, the more this equilibrium is shifted to the right, thus increasing the concentration of H_3O^+ and the value of K_a.

For water, these expressions are

$$H_2O + H_2O \rightleftharpoons H_3O^+ + HO^- \qquad \text{(7.5)}$$

and

$$K_a = \frac{[H_3O^+][HO^-]}{[H_2O]} = 1.8 \times 10^{-16} \qquad \text{(7.6)}$$

PROBLEM 7.5 Verify from eq. 7.6 and from the molarity of water (55.5 M) that the concentrations of both H_3O^+ and HO^- in water are 10^{-7} moles per liter.

---

*The square brackets used in the expression for K_a indicate concentration, at equilibrium, of the enclosed species in moles per liter. The acidity constant K_a is related to the equilibrium constant for the reaction shown in eq. 7.3; only the concentration of water [H_2O] is omitted from the denominator of the expression since it remains nearly constant at 55.5 M, very large compared to the concentrations of the other three species. For a discussion of reaction equilibria and equilibrium constants, see Section 3.11.

The **pK_a** of an acid is the negative logarithm of the acidity constant.

To avoid using numbers with negative exponents, such as those we have just seen for the acidity constant K_a for water, we often express acidity as **pK_a**, the negative logarithm of the acidity constant.

$$pK_a = -\log K_a \tag{7.7}$$

The pK_a of water is

$$-\log(1.8 \times 10^{-16}) = -\log 1.8 - \log 10^{-16} = -0.26 + 16 = +15.74$$

The mathematical relationship between the values for K_a and pK_a means that *the smaller K_a or the larger pK_a, the weaker the acid.*

It is useful to keep in mind that there is an inverse relationship between the strength of an acid and the strength of its conjugate base. In eq. 7.2, for example, hydrogen chloride is a *strong* acid since the equilibrium is shifted largely to the right. It follows that the chloride ion must be a *weak* base, since it has relatively little affinity for a proton. Similarly, since water is a *weak* acid, its conjugate base, hydroxide ion, must be a *strong* base.

A **Lewis acid** is an electron pair acceptor; a **Lewis base** is an electron pair donor.

Another way to define acids and bases was first proposed by G. N. Lewis. A **Lewis acid** is a substance that can accept an electron pair, and a **Lewis base** is a substance that can donate an electron pair. According to this definition, a proton is considered to be a Lewis acid because it can accept an electron pair from a donor (a Lewis base) to fill its 1s shell.

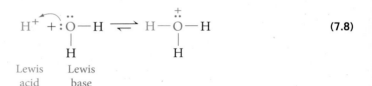

$$\tag{7.8}$$

Any atom with an unshared electron pair can act as a Lewis base.

Compounds with an element whose valence shell is incomplete also act as Lewis acids. For example,

$$\tag{7.9}$$

Similarly, when FeCl₃ or AlCl₃ acts as a catalyst for electrophilic aromatic chlorination (eqs. 4.13 and 4.14) or the Friedel–Crafts reaction (eqs. 4.20 and 4.22), they are acting as Lewis acids; the metal atom accepts an electron pair from chlorine or from an alkyl or acyl chloride to complete its valence shell of electrons.

Finally, some substances can act as either an acid or a base, depending on the other reactant. For example, in eq. 7.2, water acts as a base (a proton acceptor). However, in its reaction with ammonia, water acts as an acid (a proton donor).

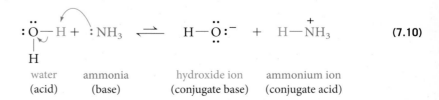

$$\tag{7.10}$$

An **amphoteric** substance can act as an acid or as a base.

Water acts as a base toward acids that are stronger than itself (HCl) and as an acid toward bases that are stronger than itself (NH₃). Substances that can act as either an acid or a base are said to be **amphoteric**.

PROBLEM 7.6 The K_a for ethanol is 1.0×10^{-16}. What is its pK_a?

PROBLEM 7.7 The pK_a's of hydrogen cyanide and acetic acid are 9.2 and 4.7, respectively. Which is the stronger acid?

PROBLEM 7.8 Which of the following are Lewis acids and which are Lewis bases?

a. Mg^{2+} b. $(CH_3)_3C:^-$ c. CH_3NH_2
d. Zn^{2+} e. $CH_3CH_2OCH_2CH_3$ f. $(CH_3)_3C^+$
g. $(CH_3)_3B$ h. $(CH_3)_3N$ i. $H:^-$

PROBLEM 7.9 In eq. 3.53, is the amide ion, NH_2^-, functioning as an acid or as a base?

7.6 The Acidity of Alcohols and Phenols

Like water, alcohols and phenols are weak acids. The hydroxyl group can act as a proton donor, and dissociation occurs in a manner similar to that for water:

$$\ddot{R\ddot{O}} - H \;\rightleftharpoons\; R\ddot{O}:^- + H^+ \tag{7.11}$$

alcohol   alkoxide
ion

The conjugate base of an alcohol is an **alkoxide ion** (for example, *meth*oxide ion from *meth*anol, *eth*oxide ion from *eth*anol, and so on).

Table 7.2 lists pK_a values for selected alcohols and phenols.* Methanol and ethanol have nearly the same acid strength as water; bulky alcohols such as *t*-butyl alcohol are somewhat weaker because their bulk makes it difficult to solvate the corresponding alkoxide ion (see Figure 6.3).

Phenol is a much stronger acid than ethanol. How can we explain this acidity difference between alcohols and phenols, since in both types of compounds, the proton donor is a hydroxyl group?

Phenols are stronger acids than alcohols mainly because the corresponding phenoxide ions are stabilized by resonance. The negative charge of an alkoxide ion is concentrated on the oxygen atom, but the negative charge on a phenoxide ion can be delocalized to the *ortho* and *para* ring positions through resonance.

> The conjugate base of an alcohol is an **alkoxide ion.**

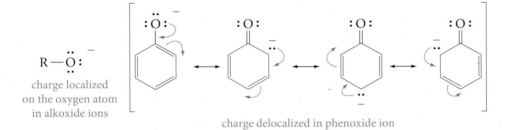

charge localized
on the oxygen atom
in alkoxide ions

charge delocalized in phenoxide ion

Because phenoxide ions are stabilized in this way, the equilibrium for their formation is more favorable than that for alkoxide ions. Thus, phenols are stronger acids than alcohols.

---

*To compare the acidity of alcohols and phenols with that of other organic compounds, see Table C in the Appendix.

Table 7.2 ▪ pK_a's of Selected Alcohols and Phenols in Aqueous Aolution		
Name	**Formula**	**pK_a**
water	HO—H	15.7
methanol	CH_3O—H	15.5
ethanol	CH_3CH_2O—H	15.9
t-butyl alcohol	$(CH_3)_3CO$—H	18
2,2,2-trifluoroethanol	CF_3CH_2O—H	12.4
phenol	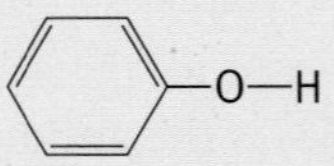 ⬡—O—H	10.0
p-nitrophenol	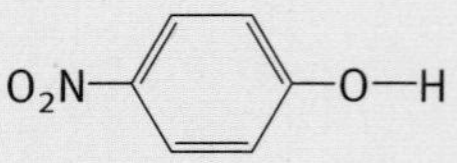 O_2N—⬡—O—H	7.2
picric acid	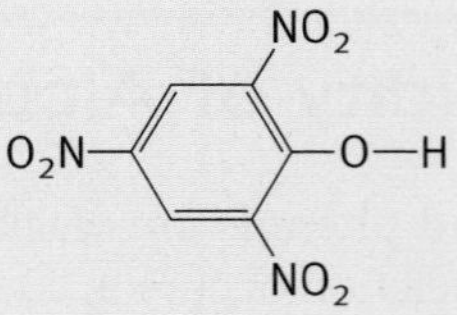 O_2N—⬡—O—H (with NO_2, NO_2)	0.25

We see in Table 7.2 that 2,2,2-trifluoroethanol is a much stronger acid than ethanol. How can we explain this effect of fluorine substitution? Again, think about the stabilities of the respective anions. Fluorine is a strongly electronegative element, so each C—F bond is polarized, with the fluorine partially negative and the carbon partially positive.

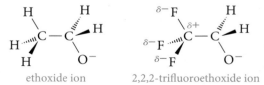

ethoxide ion   2,2,2-trifluoroethoxide ion

The positive charge on the carbon is located near the negative charge on the nearby oxygen atom, where it can partially neutralize and hence stabilize it. This **inductive effect**, as it is called, is absent in ethoxide ion.

The acidity-increasing effect of fluorine seen here is not a special case, but a general phenomenon. *All electron-withdrawing groups increase acidity* by stabilizing the conjugate base. *Electron-donating groups decrease acidity* because they destabilize the conjugate base.

Here is another example. p-Nitrophenol (Table 7.2) is a much stronger acid than phenol. In this case, the nitro group acts in two ways to stabilize the p-nitrophenoxide ion.

*Polar bonds that place a partial positive charge near the negative charge on an alkoxide ion stabilize the ion by an **inductive effect**.*

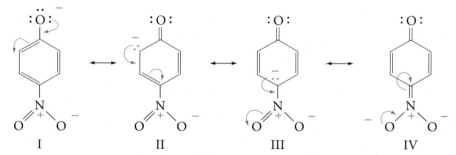

p-nitrophenoxide ion resonance contributors

First, the nitrogen atom has a formal positive charge and is therefore strongly electron withdrawing. Thus, it increases the acidity of p-nitrophenol through an inductive effect. Second, the negative charge on the oxygen of the phenoxide can be delocalized through resonance, not only to the *ortho* and *para* ring carbons, as in phenoxide itself, but to the oxygen atoms of the nitro group as well (structure IV). Both the inductive and the resonance effects of the nitro group are acid strengthening.

Additional nitro groups on the benzene ring further increase phenolic acidity. Picric acid (2,4,6-trinitrophenol) is an even stronger acid than p-nitrophenol.

PROBLEM 7.10 Draw the resonance contributors for the 2,4,6-trinitrophenoxide (picrate) ion, and show that the negative charge can be delocalized to every oxygen atom.

PROBLEM 7.11 Rank the following five compounds in order of increasing acid strength: 2-chloroethanol, p-chlorophenol, p-methylphenol, ethanol, and phenol.

Alkoxides, the conjugate bases of alcohols, are strong bases just like hydroxide ion. They are ionic compounds and are frequently used as strong bases in organic chemistry. They can be prepared by the reaction of an alcohol with sodium or potassium metal (eq. 7.12) or with a metal hydride (eq. 7.13). These reactions proceed irreversibly to give the metal alkoxides that can frequently be isolated as white solids.

$$2\ \overset{..}{\underset{..}{R\ddot{O}}}-H + 2\ K \longrightarrow 2\ \overset{..}{\underset{..}{R\ddot{O}}}:^{-}\ K^{+} + H_2 \qquad (7.12)$$

alcohol   potassium alkoxide

$$\overset{..}{\underset{..}{R\ddot{O}}}-H + NaH \longrightarrow \overset{..}{\underset{..}{R\ddot{O}}}:^{-}\ Na^{+} + H-H \qquad (7.13)$$

sodium hydride   sodium alkoxide

PROBLEM 7.12 Write the equation for the reaction of t-butyl alcohol with potassium metal. Name the product.

Ordinarily, treatment of alcohols with sodium hydroxide does not convert them to their alkoxides. This is because alkoxides are stronger bases than hydroxide ion, so the reaction goes in the reverse direction. Phenols, however, can be converted to phenoxide ions in this way.

$$ROH + Na^{+}HO^{-} \xrightleftharpoons{\ \ \cancel{\ \ }\ \ } RO^{-}Na^{+} + H_2O \qquad (7.14)$$

$$\text{phenol} \quad \langle\!\!\!\bigcirc\!\!\!\rangle-OH + Na^{+}HO^{-} \longrightarrow \langle\!\!\!\bigcirc\!\!\!\rangle-O^{-}Na^{+} + HOH \qquad (7.15)$$

phenol   sodium phenoxide

PROBLEM 7.13 Write an equation for the reaction, if any, between

a. p-nitrophenol and aqueous potassium hydroxide
b. cyclohexanol and aqueous potassium hydroxide

7.7 The Basicity of Alcohols and Phenols

Alcohols (and phenols) function not only as weak acids but also as weak bases. They have unshared electron pairs on the oxygen and are therefore Lewis bases. They can be protonated by strong acids. The product, analogous to the oxonium ion, H_3O^+, is an alkyloxonium ion.

$$R-\overset{..}{\underset{..}{O}}-H \ + \ H^+ \ \rightleftharpoons \ R-\overset{\overset{\textstyle H}{|}}{\underset{\underset{\textstyle +}{..}}{O}}-H \tag{7.16}$$

alcohol acting
as a base   alkyloxonium ion

This protonation is the first step in two important reactions of alcohols that are discussed in the following two sections: their dehydration to alkenes and their conversion to alkyl halides.

7.8 Dehydration of Alcohols to Alkenes

Alcohols can be dehydrated by heating them with a strong acid. For example, when ethanol is heated at 180°C with a small amount of concentrated sulfuric acid, a good yield of ethylene is obtained.

$$H-CH_2CH_2-OH \ \xrightarrow{H^+,\ 180°C} \ CH_2{=}CH_2 \ + \ H-OH \tag{7.17}$$

ethanol   ethylene

This type of reaction, which can be used to prepare alkenes, is the reverse of hydration (Sec. 3.7.b). It is an *elimination reaction* and can occur by either an E1 or an E2 mechanism, depending on the class of the alcohol.

Tertiary alcohols dehydrate by the E1 mechanism. *t*-Butyl alcohol is a typical example. The first step involves rapid and reversible protonation of the hydroxyl group.

$$(CH_3)_3C-\overset{..}{\underset{..}{O}}H \ + \ H^+ \ \rightleftharpoons \ (CH_3)_3C-\overset{\overset{\textstyle +}{..}}{\underset{\underset{\textstyle H}{|}}{O}}-H \tag{7.18}$$

Ionization (the rate-determining step), with water as the leaving group, occurs readily because the resulting carbocation is tertiary.

$$(CH_3)_3C-\overset{\overset{\textstyle +}{..}}{\underset{\underset{\textstyle H}{|}}{O}}-H \ \rightleftharpoons \ (CH_3)_3C^+ \ + \ H_2O \tag{7.19}$$

t-butyl cation

Proton loss from a carbon atom adjacent to the positive carbon completes the reaction.

$$\underset{\underset{\textstyle CH_3}{|}}{\overset{\overset{\textstyle H \quad CH_3}{| \quad\ \ |}}{CH_2-C^+}} \ \longrightarrow \ CH_2{=}C\underset{\diagdown CH_3}{\overset{\diagup CH_3}{}} \ + \ H^+ \tag{7.20}$$

The overall dehydration reaction is the sum of all three steps.

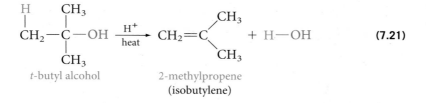

$$t\text{-butyl alcohol} \qquad \text{2-methylpropene (isobutylene)}$$

With a primary alcohol, a primary carbocation intermediate is avoided by combining the last two steps of the mechanism. The loss of water and an adjacent proton occurs simultaneously in an E2 mechanism.

$$CH_3CH_2\overset{..}{\underset{..}{O}}H + H^+ \rightleftharpoons CH_3CH_2 - \overset{+}{\overset{..}{O}} - H \qquad \textbf{(7.22)}$$
$$\qquad\qquad\qquad\qquad\qquad\qquad\qquad | \\ \qquad\qquad\qquad\qquad\qquad\qquad\qquad H$$

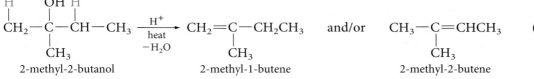

$$\qquad\qquad CH_2 = CH_2 + H^+ + H_2O \qquad \textbf{(7.23)}$$

The important things to remember about alcohol dehydrations are that (1) they all begin by protonation of the hydroxyl group (that is, the alcohol acts as a base) and (2) the ease of alcohol dehydration is 3° > 2° > 1° (the same as the order of carbocation stability).

Sometimes a single alcohol gives two or more alkenes because the proton lost during dehydration can come from any carbon atom that is directly attached to the hydroxyl-bearing carbon. For example, 2-methyl-2-butanol can give two alkenes.

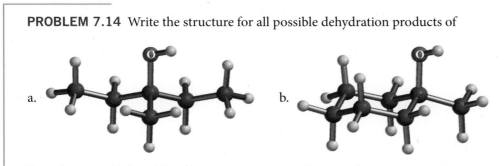

2-methyl-2-butanol   2-methyl-1-butene   2-methyl-2-butene

In these cases, *the alkene with the most substituted double bond usually predominates.* By "most substituted," we mean the alkene with the greatest number of alkyl groups on the doubly bonded carbons. Thus, in the example shown, the major product is 2-methyl-2-butene.

PROBLEM 7.14 Write the structure for all possible dehydration products of

a.   b.

In each case, which product do you expect to predominate?

7.9 The Reaction of Alcohols with Hydrogen Halides

Alcohols react with hydrogen halides (HCl, HBr, and HI) to give alkyl halides (chlorides, bromides, and iodides).

$$\underset{\text{alcohol}}{R\text{—}OH} + H\text{—}X \longrightarrow \underset{\text{alkyl halide}}{R\text{—}X} + H\text{—}OH \tag{7.25}$$

This substitution reaction provides a useful general route to alkyl halides. Because halide ions are good nucleophiles, we obtain mainly substitution products instead of dehydration. Once again, the reaction rate and mechanism depend on the class of alcohol (tertiary, secondary, or primary).

Tertiary alcohols react the fastest. For example, we can convert t-butyl alcohol to t-butyl chloride simply by shaking it for a few minutes at room temperature (rt) with concentrated hydrochloric acid.

$$\underset{t\text{-butyl alcohol}}{(CH_3)_3COH} + H\text{—}Cl \xrightarrow[\text{15 min}]{\text{rt}} \underset{t\text{-butyl chloride}}{(CH_3)_3C\text{—}Cl} + H\text{—}OH \tag{7.26}$$

The reaction occurs by an S_N1 mechanism and involves a carbocation intermediate. The first two steps in the mechanism are identical to those shown in eqs. 7.18 and 7.19. The final step involves capture of the t-butyl carbocation by chloride ion.

$$(CH_3)_3C^+ + Cl^- \xrightarrow{\text{fast}} (CH_3)_3CCl \tag{7.27}$$

On the other hand, 1-butanol, a primary alcohol, reacts slowly and must be heated for several hours with a mixture of concentrated hydrochloric acid and a Lewis acid catalyst such as zinc chloride to accomplish the same type of reaction.

$$\underset{\text{1-butanol}}{CH_3CH_2CH_2CH_2OH} + H\text{—}Cl \xrightarrow[\text{several hours}]{\text{heat, ZnCl}_2} \underset{\text{1-chlorobutane}}{CH_3CH_2CH_2CH_2\text{—}Cl} + H\text{—}OH \tag{7.28}$$

The reaction occurs by an S_N2 mechanism. In the first step, the alcohol is protonated by the acid.

$$CH_3CH_2CH_2CH_2\text{—}\overset{..}{\underset{..}{O}}H + H^+ \rightleftharpoons CH_3CH_2CH_2CH_2\text{—}\overset{+}{\underset{|}{O}}\text{—}H \tag{7.29}$$
$$\phantom{CH_3CH_2CH_2CH_2\text{—}\overset{+}{\underset{|}{O}}\text{—}}H$$

In the second step, chloride ion displaces water in a typical S_N2 process. The zinc chloride is a good Lewis acid and can serve the same role as a proton in sharing an electron pair of the hydroxyl oxygen. It also increases the chloride ion concentration, thus speeding up the S_N2 displacement.

$$Cl^- \overset{\displaystyle CH_3CH_2CH_2}{\underset{\underset{H}{\overset{\text{\tiny''''}}{\diagup}}}{\diagdown}}\overset{+}{\underset{|}{\overset{..}{O}}}\text{—}H \longrightarrow CH_3CH_2CH_2CH_2Cl + H_2O \tag{7.30}$$

Secondary alcohols react at intermediate rates by both S_N1 and S_N2 mechanisms.

EXAMPLE 7.2

Explain why *t*-butyl alcohol reacts at equal rates with HCl, HBr, and HI (to form, in each case, the corresponding *t*-butyl halide).

Solution *t*-Butyl alcohol is a tertiary alcohol; thus it reacts by an S_N1 mechanism. As in all S_N1 reactions, the rate-determining step involves formation of a carbocation; in this case, the *t*-butyl carbocation. The rate of this step does not depend on which acid is used, so all of the reactions proceed at equal rates.

$$(CH_3)_3COH + H^+ \rightleftharpoons (CH_3)_3C-\overset{..}{\underset{\underset{H}{|+}}{O}}-H \xrightarrow[\text{slow step}]{S_N1} (CH_3)_3C^+ + H_2O$$
$$\text{\textit{t}-butyl cation}$$

The reaction of the carbocation with Cl^-, Br^-, or I^- is then fast.

PROBLEM 7.15 Explain why 1-butanol reacts with hydrogen halides in the rate order HI > HBr > HCl (to form, in each case, the corresponding butyl halide).

PROBLEM 7.16 Write equations for reactions of the following alcohols with concentrated HBr.

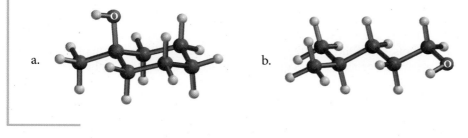

a.   b.

7.10 Other Ways to Prepare Alkyl Halides from Alcohols

Since alkyl halides are extremely useful in synthesis, it is not surprising that chemists have devised several ways to prepare them from alcohols. For example, thionyl chloride (eq. 7.31) reacts with alcohols to give alkyl chlorides. The alcohol is first converted to a chlorosulfite ester intermediate, a step that converts the hydroxyl group into a good leaving group. This is followed by a nucleophilic substitution whose mechanism (S_N1 or S_N2) depends on whether the alcohol is primary, secondary, or tertiary.

$$R-OH + \underset{\text{thionyl chloride}}{Cl-\overset{\overset{O}{\|}}{S}-Cl} \xrightarrow{\text{heat}} \underset{\substack{\text{chlorosulfite ester} \\ \text{intermediate}}}{\left[R-O-\overset{\overset{O}{\|}}{S}-Cl \right]}^{Cl^- \; H^+} \longrightarrow R-Cl + \overset{\overset{O}{\|}}{\underset{\|}{\underset{O}{S}}}\uparrow + HCl\uparrow \qquad (7.31)$$

One advantage of this method is that two of the reaction products, hydrogen chloride and sulfur dioxide, are gases and evolve from the reaction mixture (indicated by the upward pointing arrows), leaving behind only the desired alkyl chloride. The method is not effective, however, for preparing low-boiling alkyl chlorides (in which R has only a few carbon atoms), because they easily boil out of the reaction mixture with the gaseous products.

Phosphorus halides (eq. 7.32) also convert alcohols to alkyl halides.

$$3\ ROH\ +\ \underset{\substack{\text{phosphorus} \\ \text{halide}}}{PX_3}\ \longrightarrow\ 3\ RX\ +\ H_3PO_3\ (X\ =\ Cl\ or\ Br) \qquad \textbf{(7.32)}$$

In this case, the other reaction product, phosphorous acid, has a rather high boiling point. Thus, the alkyl halide is usually the lowest boiling component of the reaction mixture and can be isolated by distillation.

Both of these methods are used mainly with primary and secondary alcohols, whose reaction with hydrogen halides is slow.

PROBLEM 7.17 Write balanced equations for the preparation of the following alkyl halides from the corresponding alcohol and $SOCl_2$, PCl_3, or PBr_3.

a. ⬡—CH_2Br b. ⬡—Cl

7.11 A Comparison of Alcohols and Phenols

Because they have the same functional group, alcohols and phenols have many similar properties. But whereas it is relatively easy, with acid catalysis, to break the C—OH bond of alcohols, this bond is difficult to break in phenols. Protonation of the phenolic hydroxyl group can occur, but loss of a water molecule would give a phenyl cation.

a phenyl cation

$$\qquad\qquad\qquad\qquad\qquad\qquad\qquad\qquad\qquad\qquad\qquad\qquad\qquad \textbf{(7.33)}$$

With only two attached groups, the positive carbon in a phenyl cation should be sp-hybridized and linear. But this geometry is prevented by the structure of the benzene ring, so *phenyl cations are energetically unstable and are exceedingly difficult to form.* Consequently, phenols cannot undergo replacement of the hydroxyl group by an S_N1 mechanism. Neither can phenols undergo displacement by the S_N2 mechanism. (The geometry of the ring makes the usual inversion mechanism impossible.) Therefore, hydrogen halides, phosphorus halides, or thionyl halides cannot readily cause replacement of the hydroxyl group by halogens in phenols.

PROBLEM 7.18 Compare the reactions of cyclohexanol and phenol with

a. HBr   b. H_2SO_4, heat

7.12 Oxidation of Alcohols to Aldehydes, Ketones, and Carboxylic Acids

Alcohols with at least one hydrogen attached to the hydroxyl-bearing carbon can be oxidized to carbonyl compounds. Primary alcohols give aldehydes, which may be further oxidized to carboxylic acids. Secondary alcohols give ketones. Notice that as an alcohol is oxidized to an aldehyde or ketone and then to a carboxylic acid, the number of bonds between the reactive carbon atom and oxygen atoms increases from one to two to three. In other words, we say that the oxidation state of that carbon increases as we go from an alcohol to an aldehyde or from a ketone to a carboxylic acid.

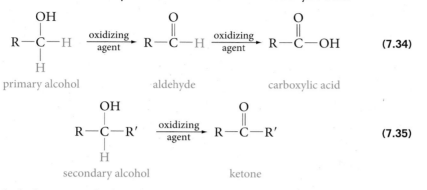

$$
\begin{array}{ccc}
\text{primary alcohol} & \text{aldehyde} & \text{carboxylic acid}
\end{array}
\qquad \text{(7.34)}
$$

$$
\begin{array}{cc}
\text{secondary alcohol} & \text{ketone}
\end{array}
\qquad \text{(7.35)}
$$

Tertiary alcohols, having no hydrogen atom on the hydroxyl-bearing carbon, do not undergo this type of oxidation.

A common laboratory oxidizing agent for alcohols is chromic anhydride, CrO_3, dissolved in aqueous sulfuric acid (**Jones' reagent**). Acetone is used as a solvent in such oxidations. Typical examples are

Jones' reagent is an oxidizing agent composed of CrO_3 dissolved in aqueous H_2SO_4.

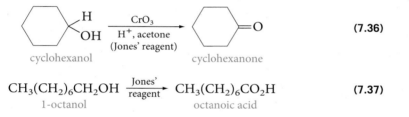

$$
\begin{array}{cc}
\text{cyclohexanol} & \text{cyclohexanone}
\end{array}
\qquad \text{(7.36)}
$$

$$
CH_3(CH_2)_6CH_2OH \xrightarrow[\text{reagent}]{\text{Jones'}} CH_3(CH_2)_6CO_2H \qquad \text{(7.37)}
$$

$$
\begin{array}{cc}
\text{1-octanol} & \text{octanoic acid}
\end{array}
$$

With primary alcohols, oxidation can be stopped at the aldehyde stage by special reagents, such as pyridinium chlorochromate (PCC), shown in eq. 7.38.*

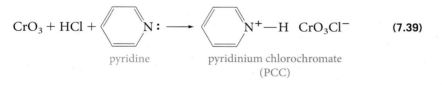

$$
CH_3(CH_2)_6CH_2OH \xrightarrow[\text{CH}_2\text{Cl}_2,\ 25°C]{\text{PCC}} CH_3(CH_2)_6\overset{\displaystyle O}{\overset{\|}{C}}-H \qquad \text{(7.38)}
$$

$$
\begin{array}{cc}
\text{1-octanol} & \text{octanal}
\end{array}
$$

PCC is prepared by dissolving CrO_3 in hydrochloric acid and then adding pyridine:

$$
CrO_3 + HCl + \underset{\text{pyridine}}{\bigcirc\!\!\!N:} \longrightarrow \underset{\substack{\text{pyridinium chlorochromate} \\ \text{(PCC)}}}{\bigcirc\!\!\!N^+\!\!-H\ \ CrO_3Cl^-} \qquad \text{(7.39)}
$$

PROBLEM 7.19 Write an equation for the oxidation of

a. 4-methyl-1-octanol with Jones' reagent
b. 4-methyl-1-octanol with PCC
c. 4-phenyl-2-butanol with Jones' reagent
d. 4-phenyl-2-butanol with PCC

---

*In the oxidation reactions shown in eqs. 7.36–7.38, the chromium is reduced from Cr^{6+} to Cr^{3+}. Aqueous solutions of Cr^{6+} are orange, whereas aqueous solutions of Cr^{3+} are green. This color change has been used as the basis for detecting ethanol in Breathalyzer tests.

A WORD ABOUT... Biologically Important Alcohols and Phenols

The hydroxyl group appears in many biologically important molecules.

Four metabolically important unsaturated primary alcohols are 3-methyl-2-buten-1-ol, 3-methyl-3-buten-1-ol, geraniol, and farnesol.

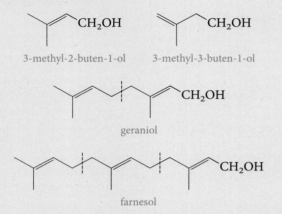

3-methyl-2-buten-1-ol   3-methyl-3-buten-1-ol

geraniol

farnesol

The two smaller alcohols contain a five-carbon unit, called an **isoprene unit**, that is present in many natural products (see page 452). This unit consists of a four-carbon chain with a one-carbon branch at carbon-2. These five-carbon alcohols can combine to give geraniol (10 carbons), which then can add yet another five-carbon unit to give farnesol (15 carbons). Note the isoprene units, marked off by dotted lines, in the structures of geraniol and farnesol.

Compounds of this type are called **terpenes**. Terpenes occur in many plants and flowers. They have 10, 15, 20, or more carbon atoms and are formed by linking isoprene units in various ways.

Geraniol, as its name implies, occurs in oil of geranium but also constitutes about 50% of rose oil, the extract of rose petals. **Farnesol**, which occurs in the essential oils of rose and cyclamen, has a pleasing lily-of-the-valley odor. Both geraniol and farnesol are used in making perfumes.

Combination of two farnesol units leads to **squalene**, a 30-carbon hydrocarbon present in small amounts in the livers of most higher animals. Squalene is the biological precursor of steroids.

Cholesterol, a typical steroidal alcohol, has the following structure:

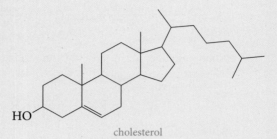

cholesterol

Although it has 27 carbon atoms (instead of 30) and is therefore not strictly a terpene, cholesterol is synthesized in the body from the terpene squalene through a complex process that, in its final stages, involves the loss of three carbon atoms.

Phenols are less involved than alcohols in fundamental metabolic processes. Three phenolic alcohols do, however, form the basic building blocks of **lignins**, complex polymeric substances that, together with cellulose, form the woody parts of trees and shrubs. They have very similar structures.

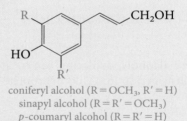

coniferyl alcohol (R=OCH₃, R′=H)
sinapyl alcohol (R=R′=OCH₃)
p-coumaryl alcohol (R=R′=H)

Some phenolic natural products to be avoided are **urushiols**, the active allergenic ingredients in poison ivy and poison oak.

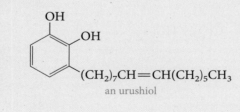

an urushiol

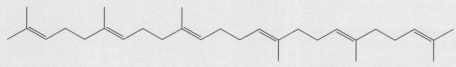

squalene

See Problems 7.30, 7.44, and 7.52.

In the body, similar oxidations are accomplished by enzymes, together with a rather complex coenzyme called nicotinamide adenine dinucleotide, NAD^+ (for its structure, see page 547). Oxidation occurs in the liver and is a key step in the body's attempt to rid itself of imbibed alcohol.

$$CH_3CH_2OH + NAD^+ \underset{\text{dehydrogenase}}{\overset{\text{alcohol}}{\rightleftharpoons}} CH_3\overset{\overset{\textstyle O}{\|}}{C}-H + NADH \qquad \textbf{(7.40)}$$

ethanol   acetaldehyde

The resulting acetaldehyde—also toxic—is further oxidized in the body to acetic acid and eventually to carbon dioxide and water.

7.13 Alcohols with More Than One Hydroxyl Group

Compounds with two adjacent alcohol groups are called *glycols* (page 97). The most important example is **ethylene glycol.*** Compounds with more than two hydroxyl groups are also known, and several, such as **glycerol** and **sorbitol**, are important commercial chemicals.

Some important polyols are **ethylene glycol, glycerol,** and **sorbitol.**

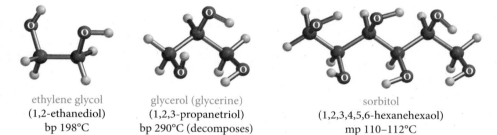

ethylene glycol	glycerol (glycerine)	sorbitol
(1,2-ethanediol)	(1,2,3-propanetriol)	(1,2,3,4,5,6-hexanehexaol)
bp 198°C	bp 290°C (decomposes)	mp 110–112°C

Ethylene glycol is used as the "permanent" antifreeze in automobile radiators and as a raw material in the manufacture of Dacron. Ethylene glycol is completely miscible with water. Because of its increased capacity for hydrogen bonding, ethylene glycol has an exceptionally high boiling point for its molecular weight—much higher than that of ethanol.

Glycerol is a syrupy, colorless, water-soluble, high-boiling liquid with a distinctly sweet taste. Its soothing qualities make it useful in shaving and toilet soaps and in cough drops and syrups. Triesters of glycerol are fats and oils, whose chemistry is discussed in Chapter 15.

Nitration of glycerol gives glyceryl trinitrate (nitroglycerine), a powerful and shock-sensitive explosive. Alfred Nobel, who invented dynamite in 1866, found that glyceryl trinitrate could be controlled by absorbing it on an inert porous material. Dynamite contains about 15% glyceryl (and glycol) nitrate along with other explosive materials. Dynamite is used mainly in mining and construction.

$$\begin{array}{l} CH_2OH \\ | \\ CHOH \\ | \\ CH_2OH \end{array} + 3\ HONO_2 \xrightarrow{H_2SO_4} \begin{array}{l} CH_2ONO_2 \\ | \\ CHONO_2 \\ | \\ CH_2ONO_2 \end{array} + 3\ H_2O \qquad \textbf{(7.41)}$$

glycerol   nitric   glyceryl trinitrate
                acid   (nitroglycerine)

Nitroglycerine is also used in medicine as a vasodilator, to prevent heart attacks in patients who suffer with angina.

---

*Notice that despite the *-ene* ending in the common name of ethylene glycol, there is *no double bond* between the carbons.

Sorbitol, with its many hydroxyl groups, is water soluble. It is almost as sweet as cane sugar and is used in candy making and as a sugar substitute for diabetics. In Chapter 16, we will see that carbohydrates, for example, sucrose (table sugar), starch, and cellulose, have many hydroxyl groups.

7.14 Aromatic Substitution in Phenols

Now we will examine some reactions that occur with phenols, but not with alcohols. Phenols undergo electrophilic aromatic substitution under very mild conditions because the hydroxyl group is strongly ring activating. For example, phenol can be nitrated with *dilute aqueous* nitric acid.

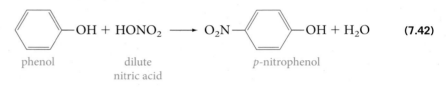

$$\text{(7.42)}$$

An unshared electron pair on the oxygen atom helps to delocalize the positive charge.

Phenol is also brominated rapidly with *bromine* in water, to produce 2,4,6-tribromophenol.

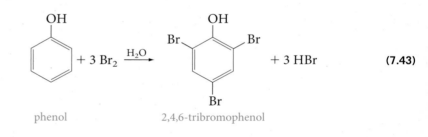

$$\text{(7.43)}$$

EXAMPLE 7.3

Draw the intermediate in electrophilic aromatic substitution *para* to a hydroxyl group, and show how the intermediate benzenonium ion is stabilized by the hydroxyl group.

Solution

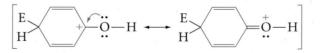

An unshared electron pair on the oxygen atom helps to delocalize the positive charge.

PROBLEM 7.20 Explain why phenoxide ion undergoes electrophilic aromatic substitution even more easily than does phenol.

PROBLEM 7.21 Write an equation for the reaction of

a. *p*-methylphenol + $HONO_2$ (1 mole)
b. *o*-chlorophenol + Br_2 (1 mole)

A WORD ABOUT... Quinones and the Bombardier Beetle

Bombardier beetle spraying.

The bombardier beetle has a curious way of defending itself from attack by a predator. It sprays the attacker with a hot mixture of noxious chemicals. These are discharged with remarkable accuracy and an audible pop from a pair of glands at the tip of its abdomen. The components of the spray are 1,4-benzoquinone, 2-methyl-1,4-benzoquinone, and hot water. The propellant is oxygen. This surprising and unpleasant event deters predators and provides the beetle with a chance to retreat to cover. How does the bombardier beetle accomplish this feat?

Each abdominal gland of the bombardier beetle consists of two connected chambers. The inner chamber contains a solution of 1,4-hydroquinone, 2-methyl-1,4-hydroquinone, and hydrogen peroxide dissolved in water. This is connected by a tube to an outer chamber. A one-way valve in the tube prevents the contents of the two chambers from mixing when closed, and allows flow only from the inner chamber to the outer chamber when opened. The outer chamber contains a water solution of enzymes called **peroxidases** and **catalases**. The peroxidase promotes a reaction between the hydrogen peroxide and hydroquinones to produce **quinones**, while the catalase converts hydrogen peroxide to water and oxygen. These reactions are exothermic enough to rapidly bring water to its boiling point. When under attack, the bombardier beetle opens the valve, and the contents of the inner compartment flow into the outer compartment. The aforementioned chemical reactions occur and the quinones and hot water are, by pressure produced by the oxygen, ejected as a pulsating spray through a vent in the outer chamber, accompanied by the audible pop.

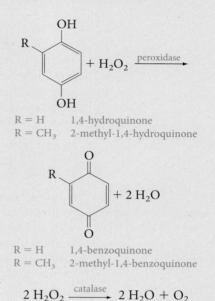

R = H   1,4-hydroquinone
R = CH₃   2-methyl-1,4-hydroquinone

R = H   1,4-benzoquinone
R = CH₃   2-methyl-1,4-benzoquinone

$$2\ H_2O_2 \xrightarrow{\text{catalase}} 2\ H_2O + O_2$$

Although the delivery system used by the bombardier beetle is particularly impressive, quinones are also used by other beetles, and certain earwigs, cockroaches, and spiders, as components of defensive secretions. Furthermore, two-chambered glands related to that of the bombardier beetle are used by other organisms to deliver defensive substances (Sec. 9.10). For some fascinating reading, see W. Agosta, *Bombardier Beetles and Fever Trees: A Close-Up Look at Chemical Warfare and Signals in Animals and Plants*, Addison-Wesley (1996). Also see T. Eisner and J. Meinwald, *Science*, **1966**, *153*, 1341.
See Problem 7.56.

7.15 / Oxidation of Phenols

As indicated in the "A Word About . . . Quinones and the Bombardier Beetle" box on this page 225, phenols are easily oxidized. Samples that stand exposed to air for some time often become highly colored due to the formation of oxidation products. With hydroquinone (1,4-dihydroxybenzene), the reaction is easily controlled to give 1,4-benzoquinone (commonly called *quinone*).

$$(7.44)$$

hydroquinone
colorless, mp 171°C

1,4-benzoquinone
yellow, mp 116°C

Hydroquinone and related compounds are used in photographic developers. They reduce silver ion that has not been exposed to light to metallic silver (and, in turn, they are oxidized to quinones). The oxidation of hydroquinones to quinones is reversible; this interconversion plays an important role in several biological oxidation–reduction reactions.

7.16 / Phenols as Antioxidants

Phenols are **antioxidants,** preventing oxidation of substances sensitive to air oxidation.

Substances that are sensitive to air oxidation, such as foods and lubricating oils, can be protected by phenolic additives. Phenols function as **antioxidants**. They react with and destroy peroxy (ROO·) and hydroxy (HO·) radicals, which otherwise react with the alkenes present in foods and oils to cause their degradation. The peroxy and hydroxy radicals abstract the phenolic hydrogen atom to produce more stable phenoxy radicals that cause less damage to the alkenes (eq. 7.45).

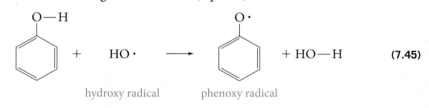

$$(7.45)$$

hydroxy radical   phenoxy radical

> **PROBLEM 7.22** Write resonance structures that indicate how the unpaired electron in the phenoxy radical can be delocalized to the *ortho* and *para* positions (reason by analogy with the resonance structures for the phenoxide anion on page 215).

Two commercial phenolic antioxidants are BHA (butylated hydroxyanisole) and BHT (butylated hydroxytoluene). BHA is used as an antioxidant in foods, especially meat products. BHT is used not only in foods, animal feeds, and vegetable oils, but also in lubricating oils, synthetic rubber, and various plastics.

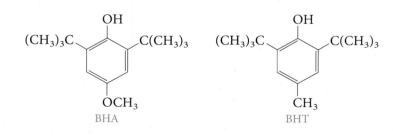

BHA   BHT

> **PROBLEM 7.23** Write an equation for the reaction of BHT with hydroxy radical.

Human beings and other animals also use antioxidants for protection against biological sources of peroxy and hydroxy radicals. **Vitamin E** (α-tocopherol) is a natural phenolic antioxidant that protects the body against free radicals; see also "A Word About . . . Vitamin E: Tocopherols and Tocotrienols," page 128. Vitamin E is obtained largely through dietary sources such as leafy vegetables, egg yolks, wheat germ, vegetable oil, and legumes. Deficiencies of vitamin E can cause eye problems in premature infants and nerve damage in older children. Resveratrol is another phenolic natural product that is a common constituent of the human diet. It is found in a number of foods, including peanuts and grapes. Resveratrol is also an antioxidant and has been studied as a possible cancer chemopreventive agent.

> **Vitamin E** is a natural phenolic antioxidant that protects the body against free radicals.

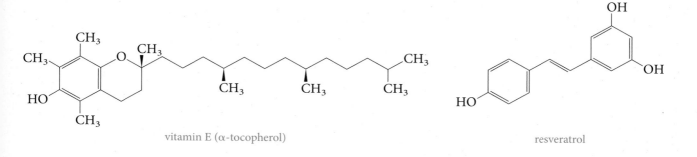

vitamin E (α-tocopherol)   resveratrol

7.17 Thiols, the Sulfur Analogs of Alcohols and Phenols

Sulfur is immediately beneath oxygen in the periodic table and can often take its place in organic structures. The —**SH** group, called the **sulfhydryl group**, is the functional group of thiols (page 207). Thiols are named as follows:

> The **sulfhydryl group**, —**SH**, is the functional group of thiols.

$$CH_3SH \qquad CH_3CH_2CH_2CH_2SH \qquad$$ $$-SH$$

methanethiol   1-butanethiol   thiophenol
(methyl mercaptan)   (*n*-butyl mercaptan)   (phenyl mercaptan)

Thiols are sometimes called **mercaptans**, a name that refers to their reaction with mercuric ion to form mercury salts, called **mercaptides**.

> Thiols are also called **mercaptans**; their mercury salts are called **mercaptides**.

$$2\ RSH + HgCl_2 \longrightarrow (RS)_2Hg + 2\ HCl \qquad \textbf{(7.46)}$$
a mercaptide

PROBLEM 7.24 Draw the structure for

a. cyclohexyl mercaptan   b. 2-hexanethiol   c. isobutyl mercaptan

---

Alkyl thiols can be made from alkyl halides by nucleophilic displacement with sulfhydryl ion (Table 6.1, entry 10).

$$R—X + {}^-SH \longrightarrow R—SH + X^- \qquad \textbf{(7.47)}$$

Perhaps the most distinctive feature of thiols is their intense and disagreeable odor. The thiols $CH_3CH{=}CHCH_2SH$ and $(CH_3)_2CHCH_2CH_2SH$, for example, are responsible for the odor of a skunk. The structurally related thiol $(CH_3)_2C{=}CHCH_2SH$ has recently been shown to be responsible for the skunky odor and taste of beer that has been exposed to light.

A WORD ABOUT...   Hair—Curly or Straight

Hair consists of a fibrous protein called **keratin**, which, as proteins go, contains an unusually large percentage of the sulfur-containing amino acid **cystine**. Horse hair, for example, contains about 8% cystine:

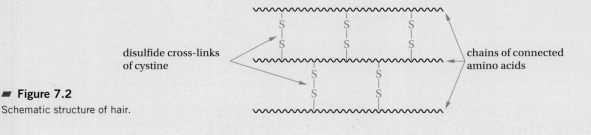

cystine (CyS—SCy)

The disulfide link in cystine serves to cross-link the chains of amino acids that make up the protein (Figure 7.2).

The chemistry used in waving or straightening hair involves the oxidation–reduction chemistry of the disulfide bond (eq. 7.49). First, the hair is treated with a reducing agent, which breaks the S—S bonds, converting each sulfur to an —SH group. This breaks the cross-links between the long protein chains. The reduced hair can now be shaped as desired, either waved or straightened. Finally, the reduced and rearranged hair is treated with an oxidizing agent to reform the disulfide cross-links. The new disulfide bonds, no longer in their original positions, hold the hair in its new shape.

disulfide cross-links of cystine   chains of connected amino acids

■ **Figure 7.2**
Schematic structure of hair.

The striped skunk (*Mephitis mephitis*) sprays a foul mixture of thiols at its enemies.

Disulfides are compounds containing an S—S bond.

Thiols are more acidic than alcohols. The pK_a of ethanethiol, for example, is 10.6 whereas that of ethanol is 15.9. Hence, thiols react with aqueous base to give thiolates.

$$RSH + Na^+OH^- \longrightarrow RS^-Na^+ + HOH \qquad \textbf{(7.48)}$$

a sodium thiolate

PROBLEM 7.25 Write an equation for the reaction of propanethiol ($CH_3CH_2CH_2SH$) with

a. NaH
b. $CH_3CH_2O^-Na^+$
c. KOH
d. $HgCl_2$

Thiols are easily oxidized to **disulfides,** compounds containing an S—S bond, by mild oxidizing agents such as hydrogen peroxide or iodine. A naturally occurring disulfide whose smell you are probably familiar with is diallyl disulfide ($CH_2=CHCH_2S—SCH_2CH=CH_2$), which is responsible for the odor of fresh garlic.*

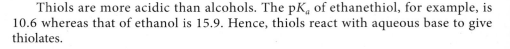

$$2\,RS{-}H \underset{\text{reduction}}{\overset{\text{oxidation}}{\rightleftharpoons}} RS{-}SR \qquad \textbf{(7.49)}$$

thiol   disulfide

The reaction shown in eq. 7.49 can be reversed with a variety of reducing agents. Since proteins contain disulfide links, these reversible oxidation–reduction reactions can be used to manipulate the three-dimensional shapes of proteins.

_____

*Garlic belongs to the plant family *Allium,* from which the *allyl* group gets its name.

REACTION SUMMARY

1. Alcohols

a. Conversion to Alkoxides (Sec. 7.6)

$$2 \text{ RO—H} + 2 \text{ Na} \longrightarrow 2 \text{ RO}^- \text{Na}^+ + \text{H}_2$$

$$\text{RO—H} + \text{NaH} \longrightarrow \text{RO}^- \text{Na}^+ + \text{H}_2$$

b. Dehydration to Alkenes (Sec. 7.8)

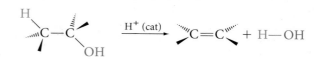

c. Conversion to Alkyl Halides (Secs. 7.9–7.10)

$$\text{R—OH} + \text{HX} \longrightarrow \text{R—X} + \text{H}_2\text{O} \ (\text{X}=\text{Cl, Br, I})$$

$$\text{R—OH} + \text{SOCl}_2 \longrightarrow \text{R—Cl} + \text{HCl} + \text{SO}_2$$

$$3 \text{ R—OH} + \text{PX}_3 \longrightarrow 3 \text{ R—X} + \text{H}_3\text{PO}_3 \ (\text{X}=\text{Cl, Br})$$

d. Oxidation (Sec. 7.12)

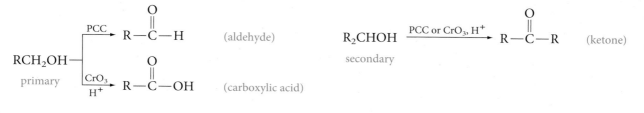

2. Phenols

a. Preparation of Phenoxides (Sec. 7.6)

$$\text{ArO—H} + \text{NaOH} \longrightarrow \text{ArO}^- \text{Na}^+ + \text{H}_2\text{O}$$

b. Electrophilic Aromatic Substitution (Sec. 7.14)

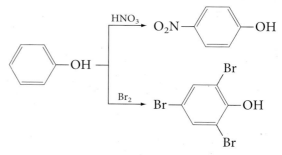

c. Oxidation to Quinones (Sec. 7.15)

quinone

3. Thiols

a. Conversion to Thiolates (Sec. 7.17)

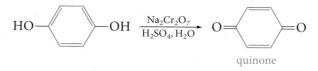

$$\underset{\text{thiol}}{\text{RS—H}} + \text{NaOH} \longrightarrow \underset{\text{thiolate}}{\text{RS}^- \text{Na}^+} + \text{H}_2\text{O}$$

b. Oxidation to Disulfides (Sec. 7.17)

$$2 \underset{\text{thiol}}{\text{RSH}} \xrightarrow{\text{oxidation}} \underset{\text{disulfide}}{\text{RS—SR}}$$

ADDITIONAL PROBLEMS

OWL Interactive versions of these problems are assignable in OWL.

Nomenclature and Structure of Alcohols

7.26 Write a structural formula for each of the following compounds:

a. 1-methylcyclohexanol
b. *p*-bromophenol
c. 2,3-butanediol
d. 2,2-dimethyl-1-butanol
e. sodium ethoxide
f. *cis*-2-methylcyclopentanol
g. (*S*)-2-butanethiol
h. 2-phenylpropanol
i. 2-methyl-2-propen-1-ol
j. 2-cyclohexenol

7.27 Name each of the following alcohols:

a. $CH_3CH(Cl)CH(OH)CH_2CH_3$
b. $CH_3CH(OH)CH_2CH_3$
c. $(CH_3)_2C(Cl)CH(OH)CH_2CH_3$
d. $CH_3CH(Cl)CH_2CH(OH)CH_3$

7.28 Name each of the following compounds:

a. $HOCH_2CH(OH)CH(OH)CH_2OH$
b. $(CH_3)_3CO^-K^+$

c.

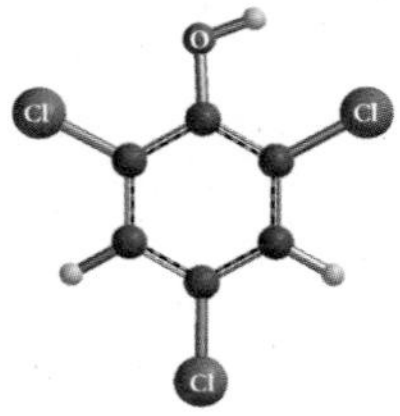

d.

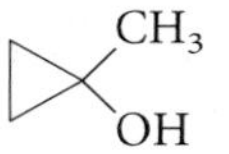

    CH_3
    △$<$
       OH

e.

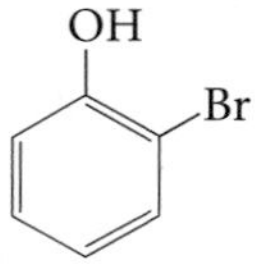

  OH
      Br

f.

      OH
  ☐
      CH₃

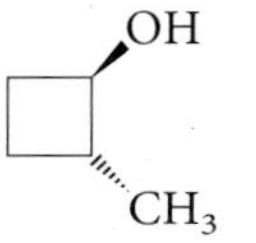

g. $CH_3CH{=}CHCH_2OH$

h.

i. $CH_3CH_2CH(OH)CH_3$

j. $CH_3CHBrC(CH_3)_2OH$

7.29 Explain why each of the following names is unsatisfactory, and give a correct name:

a. 2-ethyl-1-propanol
b. 2,2-dimethyl-3-butanol
c. 1-propene-3-ol
d. 2-chloro-4-pentanol
e. 3,6-dibromophenol

7.30 Members of the fungus-like genus *Phytophthora* are responsible for many crop diseases that threaten plants around the world. Sexual reproduction for this genus is modulated by a mating hormone, shown below:

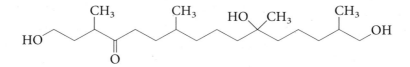

a. How many stereogenic centers are present in this compound?
b. Draw structures for the unique stereoisomers of this hormone and provide the name of each structure.

7.31 The odor of a human's armpit is due to a number of molecules, including some sulfur-containing compounds. Indeed, the major component in the odor of sweat is (S)-3-methyl-3-mercapto-1-hexanol. Draw the structure of this thiol.

7.32 Thymol is an antibacterial oil obtained from thyme (*Thymus vulgaris*). The IUPAC name of this compound is 2-isopropyl-5-methylphenol. Draw the structure of thymol.

Thyme (*Thymus vulgaris*), source of the antibacterial oil thymol.

Properties of Alcohols

7.33 Classify the alcohols in parts a, d, f, h, i, and j of Problem 7.26 as primary, secondary, or tertiary.

7.34 Arrange the compounds in each of the following groups in order of increasing solubility in water, and briefly explain your answers:

a. 1-octanol; ethanol; ethyl chloride
b. $HOCH_2(CHOH)_3CH_2OH$; 1,5-pentanediol; 1-pentanol

Acid–Base Reactions of Alcohols and Thiols

7.35 The following classes of organic compounds are Lewis bases. Write an equation that shows how each class might react with H^+.

a. amine, R_3N:
b. ether, $R\ddot{O}R$
c. ketone, $R_2C{=}\ddot{O}$

7.36 Arrange the following compounds in order of increasing acidity, and explain the reasons for your choice of order: cyclopentanol, phenol, *p*-nitrophenol, and 2-chlorocyclopentanol.

7.37 Which is the stronger base, potassium *t*-butoxide or potassium ethoxide? (*Hint:* Use the data in Table 7.2.)

7.38 Complete each of the following equations:

a. $CH_3CH(OH)CH_2CH_3 + K \longrightarrow$

b. $(CH_3)_2CHOH + NaH \longrightarrow$

c.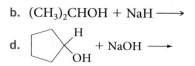

d. a cyclopentane ring with H and OH substituents $+ NaOH \longrightarrow$

e. $CH_3CH{=}CHCH_2SH + NaOH \longrightarrow$

7.39 Explain why your answers to parts c, d, and e of Problem 7.38 are consistent with the pK_a's of the starting acids and product acids (see eqs. 7.14, 7.15, and 7.48).

Acid-Catalyzed Dehydration of Alcohols

7.40 Show the structures of all possible acid-catalyzed dehydration products of the following. If more than one alkene is possible, predict which one will be formed in the largest amount.

a. 3-methylcyclopentanol
b. 1-methylcyclopentanol
c. 2-phenylethanol
d. 2-hexanol

7.41 Explain why the reaction shown in eq. 7.19 occurs much more easily than the reaction $(CH_3)_3C{-}OH \rightleftharpoons (CH_3)_3C^+ + HO^-$. (That is, why is it necessary to protonate the alcohol before ionization can occur?)

7.42 Draw a reaction energy diagram for the dehydration of *tert*-butyl alcohol (eq. 7.21). Include the steps shown in eqs. 7.18–7.20 in your diagram.

7.43 Write out all of the steps in the mechanism for eq. 7.24, showing how each product is formed.

7.44 The sesquiterpene, (3S)-(E)-nerolidol (structure shown in Problem 3.40), is derived from multiple isoprene units as are some of the biologically important alcohols discussed on page 222. What products would result from the acid-catalyzed dehydration of (3S)-(E)-nerolidol?

7.45 2-Propanol is prepared commercially from the acid-catalyzed hydration of propene (see "A Word About . . . Industrial Alcohols" on page 208). Write out all of the steps in this acid-catalyzed mechanism.

Alkyl Halides from Alcohols

7.46 Although the reaction shown in eq. 7.26 occurs faster than that shown in eq. 7.28, the yield of product is lower. The yield of t-butyl chloride is only 80%, whereas the yield of n-butyl chloride is nearly 100%. What by-product is formed in eq. 7.26, and by what mechanism is it formed? Why is a similar by-product *not* formed in eq. 7.28?

7.47 Treatment of 3-buten-2-ol with concentrated hydrochloric acid gives a mixture of two products, 3-chloro-1-butene and 1-chloro-2-butene. Write a reaction mechanism that explains how both products are formed.

Synthesis and Reactions of Alcohols

7.48 Write an equation for each of the following reactions:

a. 2-methyl-2-butanol + HCl
b. 3-pentanol + Na
c. cyclohexanol + PBr_3
d. 2-phenylethanol + $SOCl_2$
e. 1-methylcyclopentanol + H_2SO_4, heat
f. ethylene glycol + $HONO_2$
g. 1-octanol + HBr + $ZnBr_2$
h. 1-pentanol + aqueous NaOH
i. 1-pentanol + CrO_3, H^+
j. 2-cyclohexylethanol + PCC

7.49 Write an equation for each of the following two-step syntheses:

a. cyclohexene to cyclohexanone
b. 1-chlorobutane to butanal
c. 1-butanol to 1-butanethiol

Oxidation Reactions of Alcohols, Phenols, and Thiols

7.50 The alcohol citronellol is a terpene found in rose oil. The product formed when citronellol is oxidized with pyridinium chlorochromate (PCC) is a constituent of lemon oil. Draw the structure of the product when citronellol is oxidized with PCC.

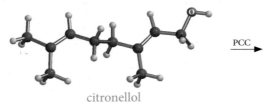

$$\xrightarrow{\text{PCC}}$$

citronellol

7.51 What product do you expect from the oxidation of cholesterol with CrO_3 and H^+? (See page 222 for the formula of cholesterol.)

7.52 Linoleic acid (Table 15.1) is an unsaturated vegetable oil found in soybean, sunflower, and corn oils. Often these unsaturated vegetable oils are considered to be good for one's heart since unsaturated vegetable oils do not contribute to levels of bad cholesterol (see "A Word About . . . Biologically Important Alcohols and Phenols," page 222). However, it has been reported that heating linoleic acid at frying temperatures, such as 365°F for 30 minutes or longer, leads to the formation of a toxic aldehyde, (2E)-4-hydroxy-2-nonenal. What is the structure of (2E)-4-hydroxy-2-nonenal? If (2E)-4-hydroxy-2-nonenal was oxidized by PCC, what would be the expected product? If (2E)-4-hydroxy-2-nonenal was oxidized by Jones' reagent, what would be the expected product?

7.53 Draw the structure of the quinone expected from the oxidation of

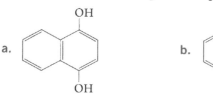

a.

b.

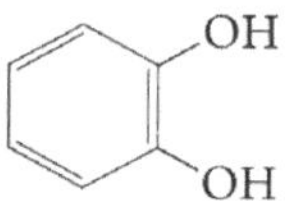

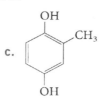

c.

7.54 Dimethyl disulfide, $CH_3S—SCH_3$, found in the vaginal secretions of female hamsters, acts as a sexual attractant for the male hamster. Write an equation for its synthesis from methanethiol.

7.55 The disulfide shown below is a component of the odorous secretion of mink. Describe a synthesis of this disulfide, starting with 3-methyl-1-butanol.

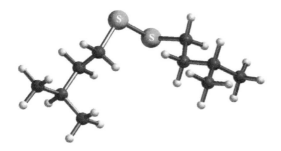

7.56 2,3,6-Trimethyl-1,4-naphthoquinone (TMNQ) is a quinone that was recently isolated from tobacco leaves and was shown to slow the metabolism of dopamine, a neurotransmitter whose depletion can lead to Parkinson's disease. What is the structure of the hydroquinone whose oxidation gives TMNQ?

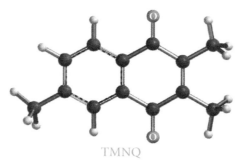

TMNQ

The civet cat (*Viverra civetta*) is the original source of civetone, a sweet and pungent ketone, now produced synthetically and used as a fixative in perfumery.

civetone

9

Aldehydes and Ketones

Aldehydes and ketones are a large family of organic compounds that permeate our everyday lives. They are responsible for the fragrant odors of many fruits and fine perfumes. For example, cinnamaldehyde (an aldehyde) provides the smell we associate with cinnamon, and civetone (a ketone) is used to provide the musky odor of many perfumes. Formaldehyde is a component of many building materials we use to construct our houses. The ketones testosterone and estrone are known to many as hormones responsible for our sexual characteristics. And the chemistry of aldehydes and ketones plays a role in how we digest food and even in how we can see the words on this page (see "A Word About... The Chemistry of Vision" on pages 76–77). So what are aldehydes and ketones?

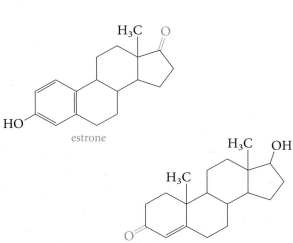

cinnamaldehyde

formaldehyde

estrone

testosterone

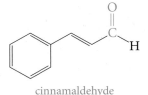

OWL

Online homework for this chapter can be assigned in OWL, an online homework assessment tool.

© Nigel J. Dennis / Photo Researchers

The **carbonyl group** is a C=O unit. **Aldehydes** have at least one hydrogen atom attached to the carbonyl carbon atom. In **ketones**, the carbonyl carbon atom is connected to two other carbon atoms.

Aldehydes and ketones are characterized by the presence of the **carbonyl group**, perhaps the most important functional group in organic chemistry. Aldehydes have at least one hydrogen atom attached to the carbonyl carbon atom. The remaining group may be another hydrogen atom or any aliphatic or aromatic organic group. The —CH=O group characteristic of aldehydes is often called a **formyl group**. In ketones, the carbonyl carbon atom is connected to two other carbon atoms.

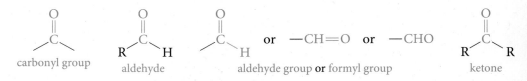

We will see that the carbonyl group appears in many other organic compounds, including carboxylic acids and their derivatives (Chapter 10). This chapter, however, will focus only on aldehydes and ketones.

9.1   Nomenclature of Aldehydes and Ketones

In the IUPAC system, the characteristic ending for aldehydes is -*al* (from the first syllable of *aldehyde*). The following examples illustrate the system:

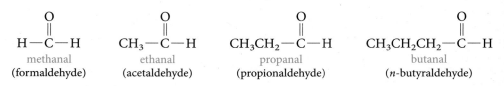

The common names shown below the IUPAC names are frequently used, so you should learn them.

For substituted aldehydes, we number the chain starting with the aldehyde carbon, as the following examples illustrate:

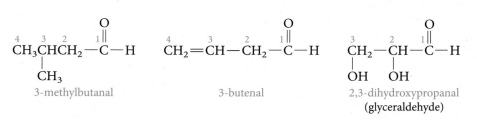

Notice from the last two examples that an aldehyde group has priority over a double bond or a hydroxyl group, not only in numbering but also as the suffix. For cyclic aldehydes, the suffix -*carbaldehyde* is used. Aromatic aldehydes often have common names:

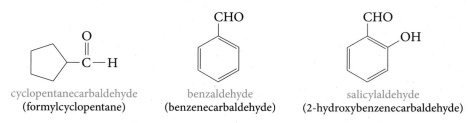

In the IUPAC system, the ending for ketones is -*one* (from the last syllable of *ketone*). The chain is numbered so that the carbonyl carbon has the lowest possible number. Common names of ketones are formed by adding the word *ketone* to the names of the alkyl or aryl groups attached to the carbonyl carbon. In still other cases, traditional names are used. The following examples illustrate these methods:

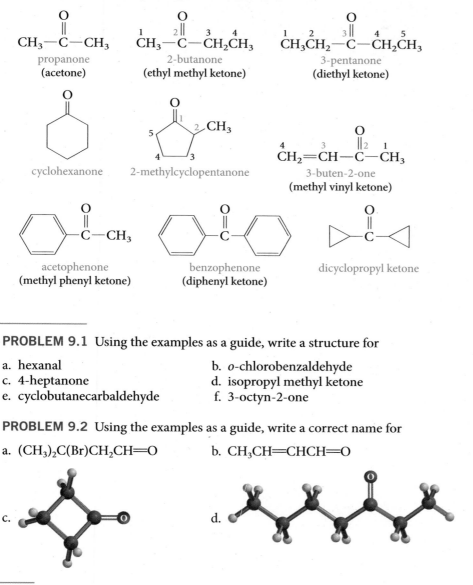

PROBLEM 9.1 Using the examples as a guide, write a structure for

a. hexanal
b. *o*-chlorobenzaldehyde
c. 4-heptanone
d. isopropyl methyl ketone
e. cyclobutanecarbaldehyde
f. 3-octyn-2-one

PROBLEM 9.2 Using the examples as a guide, write a correct name for

a. $(CH_3)_2C(Br)CH_2CH{=}O$
b. $CH_3CH{=}CHCH{=}O$

c.

d.

9.2 Some Common Aldehydes and Ketones

Formaldehyde ($HCH{=}O$), the simplest aldehyde, is manufactured on a very large scale by the oxidation of methanol.

$$CH_3OH \xrightarrow[\text{600–700°C}]{\text{Ag catalyst}} CH_2{=}O \ + \ H_2 \qquad (9.1)$$

formaldehyde

Annual world production is more than 46 billion pounds. Formaldehyde is a gas (bp −21°C), but it cannot be stored in a free state because it polymerizes readily.*

---

*The polymer derived from formaldehyde is a long chain of alternating CH_2 and oxygen units, which can be described by the structure $(CH_2O)_n$. See Chapter 14 for a discussion of polymers.

Normally it is supplied as a 37% aqueous solution called formalin. In this form, it is used as a disinfectant and preservative, but formaldehyde is mostly used in the manufacture of plastics, building insulation, particleboard, and plywood.

Acetaldehyde ($CH_3CH{=}O$) boils close to room temperature (bp 20°C). It is manufactured mainly by the oxidation of ethylene over a palladium–copper catalyst, and about 1 billion pounds are produced worldwide each year.

$$2\ CH_2{=}CH_2 + O_2 \xrightarrow[100-300°C]{Pd-Cu} 2\ CH_3CH{=}O \qquad \textbf{(9.2)}$$

About half of the acetaldehyde produced annually is oxidized to acetic acid. The rest is used for the production of 1-butanol and other commercial chemicals.

Acetone (($CH_3)_2C{=}O$), the simplest ketone, is also produced on a large scale— about 4 billion pounds annually. The most common methods for its commercial synthesis are the oxidation of propene (analogous to eq. 9.2), the oxidation of isopropyl alcohol (eq. 7.35, R = R′ = CH_3), and the oxidation of isopropylbenzene (eq. 9.3).

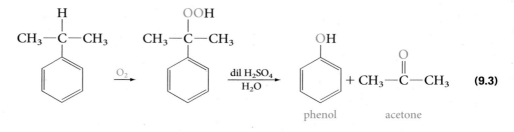

phenol   acetone

About 30% of the acetone is used directly, because it is not only completely miscible with water but is also an excellent solvent for many organic substances (resins, paints, dyes, and nail polish). The rest is used to manufacture other commercial chemicals, including bisphenol-A for epoxy resins (Sec. 14.9).

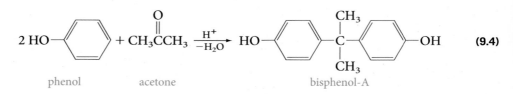

phenol   acetone   bisphenol-A

Quinones constitute a unique class of carbonyl compounds. They are cyclic conjugated diketones. The simplest example is 1,4-benzoquinone (eq. 7.44). All quinones are colored, and many are naturally occurring pigments that are used as dyes. Alizarin is an orange–red quinone that was used to dye the red coats of the British army during the American Revolution. Vitamin K is a quinone that is required for the normal clotting of blood.

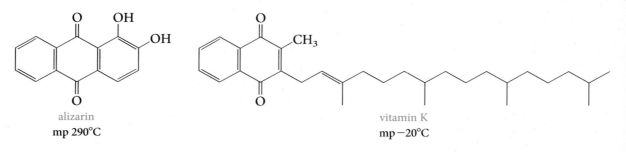

alizarin
mp 290°C

vitamin K
mp −20°C

9.3 Synthesis of Aldehydes and Ketones

We have already seen, in previous chapters, several ways to prepare aldehydes and ketones. One of the most useful is the oxidation of alcohols.

$$\underset{OH}{\overset{H}{\underset{\Big|}{C}}} \xrightarrow[\text{agent}]{\text{oxidizing}} \quad C{=}O \qquad\qquad (9.5)$$

Oxidation of a primary alcohol gives an aldehyde, and oxidation of a secondary alcohol gives a ketone. Chromium reagents, such as pyridinium chlorochromate (PCC), are commonly used in the laboratory for this purpose (review Sec. 7.12).

PROBLEM 9.3 Give the product expected from treatment of

a. cyclohexanol with Jones' reagent (see Sec. 7.12)
b. 3-methylcyclopentanol with pyridinium chlorochromate
c. 5-methyl-1-heptanol with Jones' reagent
d. 5-methyl-1-heptanol with pyridinium chlorochromate

EXAMPLE 9.1

Write an equation for the oxidation of an appropriate alcohol to $(CH_3)_2CHCH_2CHO$ (3-methylbutanal).

Solution Aldehydes are prepared by oxidation of 1° alcohols (RCH_2OH) with PCC. First, find the carbonyl carbon in 3-methylbutanal (marked with an asterisk). Convert this carbon to a primary alcohol. A proper equation is:

$$(CH_3)_2CHCH_2{-}CH_2{-}OH \xrightarrow{\text{PCC}} (CH_3)_2CHCH_2{-}\overset{\overset{\displaystyle O}{\|}}{\underset{*}{C}}{-}H$$

PROBLEM 9.4 Write an equation for the oxidation of an appropriate alcohol to

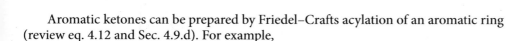

a. 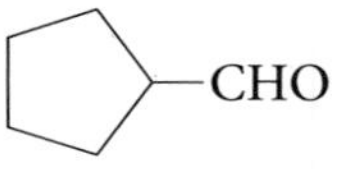 ⬠—CHO   b. 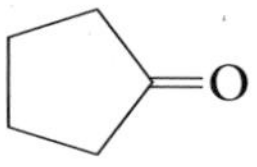 ⬠=O

Aromatic ketones can be prepared by Friedel–Crafts acylation of an aromatic ring (review eq. 4.12 and Sec. 4.9.d). For example,

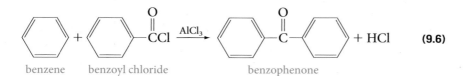

$$\text{benzene} + \text{benzoyl chloride} \xrightarrow{\text{AlCl}_3} \text{benzophenone} + HCl \qquad (9.6)$$

© Kristen Brockmann/Fundamental Photographs, NYC

Cloves, source of 2-heptanone.

PROBLEM 9.5 Complete the following equation and name the product:

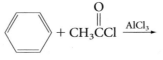

Methyl ketones can be prepared by hydration of terminal alkynes, catalyzed by acid and mercuric ion (review eq. 3.52). For example,

$$CH_3(CH_2)_5C{\equiv}CH \xrightarrow[Hg^{2+}]{H^+, H_2O} CH_3(CH_2)_5\overset{O}{\overset{\|}{C}}CH_3 \qquad (9.7)$$

1-octyne   2-octanone

PROBLEM 9.6 What alkyne would be useful for the synthesis of 2-heptanone (oil of cloves)?

© Patti Murray/Animals Animals

Vanilla beans, source of vanillin.

9.4 Aldehydes and Ketones in Nature

Aldehydes and ketones occur very widely in nature. Figures 1.12 and 1.13 show three examples, and Figure 9.1 gives several more. Many aldehydes and ketones have pleasant odors and flavors and are used for these properties in perfumes and other consumer products (soaps, bleaches, and air fresheners, for example). However, the gathering and extraction of these fragrant substances from flowers, plants, and animal glands are extremely expensive. Chanel No. 5, introduced to the perfume market in 1921, was the first fine fragrance to use *synthetic* organic chemicals. Today most fragrances do.

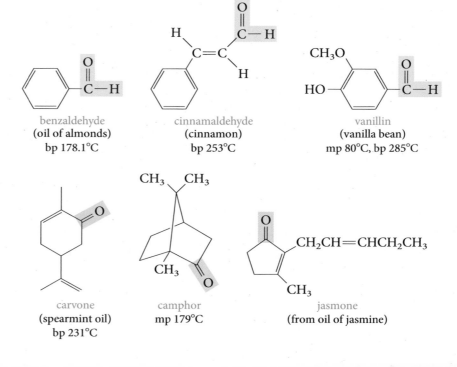

benzaldehyde
(oil of almonds)
bp 178.1°C

cinnamaldehyde
(cinnamon)
bp 253°C

vanillin
(vanilla bean)
mp 80°C, bp 285°C

carvone
(spearmint oil)
bp 231°C

camphor
mp 179°C

jasmone
(from oil of jasmine)

■ **Figure 9.1**
Some naturally occurring aldehydes and ketones.

9.5 The Carbonyl Group

To best understand the reactions of aldehydes, ketones, and other carbonyl compounds, we must first appreciate the structure and properties of the carbonyl group.

The carbon–oxygen double bond consists of a sigma bond and a pi bond (Figure 9.2). The carbon atom is sp^2-hybridized. *The three atoms attached to the carbonyl carbon lie in a plane with bond angles of 120°.* The pi bond is formed by overlap of a *p* orbital on carbon with an oxygen *p* orbital. There are also two unshared electron pairs on the oxygen atom. The C=O bond distance is 1.24 Å, shorter than the C—O distance in alcohols and ethers (1.43 Å).

Oxygen is much more electronegative than carbon. Therefore, the electrons in the C=O bond are attracted to the oxygen, producing a highly polarized bond. This effect is especially pronounced for the pi electrons and can be expressed in the following ways:

resonance contributors
to the carbonyl group

polarization of the
carbonyl group

As a consequence of this polarization, *most carbonyl reactions involve* nucleophilic attack *at the carbonyl carbon,* often accompanied by addition of a proton to the oxygen, consistent with the electrostatic potential map (Figure 9.2c) showing that the oxygen is electron rich (red).

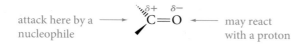

attack here by a → nucleophile

may react ← with a proton

C=O bonds are quite different, then, from C=C bonds, which are not polarized and where attack at carbon is usually by an electrophile (Sec. 3.9).

In addition to its effect on reactivity, polarization of the C=O bond influences the physical properties of carbonyl compounds. For example, carbonyl compounds boil at higher temperatures than hydrocarbons, but at lower temperatures than alcohols of comparable molecular weight.

$$CH_3(CH_2)_4CH_3 \qquad CH_3(CH_2)_3CH{=}O \qquad CH_3(CH_2)_3CH_2OH$$
hexane (bp 69°C)   pentanal (bp 102°C)   pentanol (bp 118°C)

Why is this so? Unlike hydrocarbon molecules, which can be temporarily polarized, molecules of carbonyl compounds have *permanently polar C=O bonds* and thus have a stronger tendency to associate. *The positive part of one molecule is attracted to the negative part of another molecule.* These intermolecular forces of attraction, called **dipole–dipole interactions**, are generally stronger than van der Waals attractions (Sec. 2.7) but not as strong as hydrogen bonds (Sec. 7.4). Carbonyl compounds such

Dipole–dipole interactions are opposite pole attractions between polar molecules.

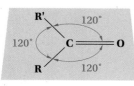

(a)

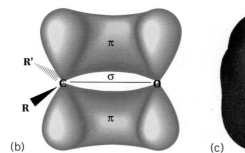

(b)

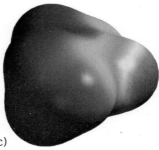

(c)

■ **Figure 9.2**

Bonding in the carbonyl group: (a) carbonyl carbon is sp^2-hybridized, (b) C=O group consists of sigma and pi bonds, (c) electrostatic potential map illustrates the electron-poor nature (blue) of the carbonyl carbon and the electron-rich nature (red) of the oxygen.

as aldehydes and ketones that have a C=O bond, but no O—H bond, cannot form hydrogen bonds with one another, as can alcohols. Consequently, carbonyl compounds require more energy (heat) than hydrocarbons of comparable molecular weight to overcome intermolecular attractive forces when converted from liquid to vapor, but less than alcohols.

The polarity of the carbonyl group also affects the solubility properties of aldehydes and ketones. For example, carbonyl compounds with low molecular weights are soluble in water. Although they cannot form hydrogen bonds with themselves, they can form hydrogen bonds with O—H or N—H compounds.

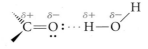

PROBLEM 9.7 Arrange benzaldehyde (mol. wt. 106), benzyl alcohol (mol. wt. 108), and *p*-xylene (mol. wt. 106) in order of

a. increasing boiling point　　　　b. increasing water solubility

9.6　Nucleophilic Addition to Carbonyl Groups: An Overview

Nucleophiles attack the carbon atom of a carbon–oxygen double bond because that carbon has a partial positive charge. The pi electrons of the C=O bond move to the oxygen atom, which, because of its electronegativity, can easily accommodate the negative charge that it acquires. When these reactions are carried out in a hydroxylic solvent such as alcohol or water, the reaction is usually completed by addition of a proton to the negative oxygen. The overall reaction involves addition of a nucleophile and a proton across the pi bond of the carbonyl group.

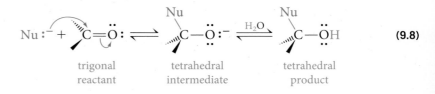

(9.8)

The carbonyl carbon, which is trigonal and sp^2-hybridized in the starting aldehyde or ketone, becomes tetrahedral and sp^3-hybridized in the reaction product.

Because of the unshared electron pairs on the oxygen atom (Figure 9.2c), carbonyl compounds are weak Lewis bases and can be protonated. *Acids can catalyze the addition of weak nucleophiles to carbonyl compounds* by protonating the carbonyl oxygen atom.

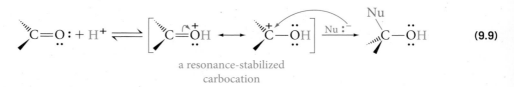

(9.9)

This converts the carbonyl carbon to a carbocation and enhances its susceptibility to attack by nucleophiles.

Nucleophiles can be classified as those that add reversibly to the carbonyl carbon and those that add irreversibly. Nucleophiles that add reversibly are also good leaving groups. In other words, they are the conjugate bases of relatively strong acids. Nucleophiles that add irreversibly are poor leaving groups, the conjugate bases of weak acids. This classification will be useful when we consider the mechanism of carbonyl additions.

In general, *ketones are somewhat less reactive than aldehydes toward nucleophiles.* There are two main reasons for this reactivity difference. The first reason is *steric*. The carbonyl carbon atom is more crowded in ketones (two organic groups) than in aldehydes (one organic group and one hydrogen atom). In nucleophilic addition, we bring these attached groups closer together because the hybridization changes from sp^2 to sp^3 and the bond angles decrease from 120° to 109.5° (eq. 9.8). Less strain is involved in additions to aldehydes than in additions to ketones because one of the groups (H) is small. The second reason is *electronic*. As we have already seen in connection with carbocation stability, alkyl groups are usually electron-donating compared to hydrogen (Sec. 3.10). Therefore, they tend to neutralize the partial positive charge on the carbonyl carbon, decreasing its reactivity toward nucleophiles. Ketones have two such alkyl groups; aldehydes have only one. If, however, the attached groups are strongly electron-withdrawing (contain halogens, for example), they can have the opposite effect and increase carbonyl reactivity toward nucleophiles.

In the following discussion, we will classify nucleophilic additions to aldehydes and ketones according to the type of new bond formed to the carbonyl carbon. We will consider oxygen, carbon, and nitrogen nucleophiles, in that sequence.

9.7 Addition of Alcohols: Formation of Hemiacetals and Acetals

The reactions discussed in this section are extremely important because they are crucial to understanding the chemistry of carbohydrates, which we will discuss in Chapter 16.

Alcohols are oxygen nucleophiles. They add to the C=O bond, the OR group becoming attached to the carbon and the proton becoming attached to the oxygen:

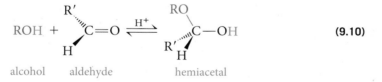

(9.10)

alcohol   aldehyde   hemiacetal

Because alcohols are *weak* nucleophiles, an acid catalyst is required.* The product is a **hemiacetal**; it contains both alcohol and ether functional groups on the same carbon atom. The addition is reversible.

The mechanism of hemiacetal formation involves three steps. First, the carbonyl oxygen is protonated by the acid catalyst. The alcohol oxygen then attacks the carbonyl carbon, and a proton is lost from the resulting positive oxygen. *Each step is reversible.* In terms of acid–base reactions, the starting acid in each step is converted to a product acid of similar strength (Sec. 7.5).

> A **hemiacetal** contains both alcohol and ether functional groups on the same carbon atom.

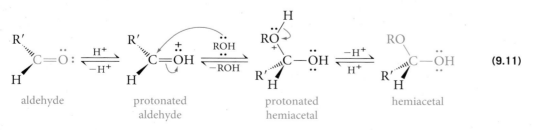

(9.11)

aldehyde   protonated   protonated   hemiacetal
                  aldehyde   hemiacetal

---

*Many acid catalysts can be used. Sulfuric acid and *p*-toluenesulfonic acid are commonly used in the laboratory.

PROBLEM 9.8 Write an equation for the formation of a hemiacetal from propanal (CH_3CH_2CHO), methanol (CH_3OH), and H^+. Show each step in the reaction mechanism.

An **acetal** has two ether functional groups on the same carbon atom.

In the presence of *excess alcohol*, hemiacetals react further to form **acetals**.

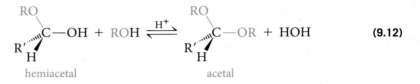

       hemiacetal   acetal   **(9.12)**

The hydroxyl group of the hemiacetal is replaced by an alkoxyl group. Acetals have two ether functions at the same carbon atom.

The mechanism of acetal formation involves the following steps.

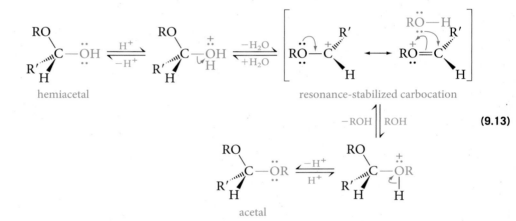

    hemiacetal   resonance-stabilized carbocation

                                                                (9.13)

                       acetal

Either oxygen of the hemiacetal can be protonated. When the hydroxyl oxygen is protonated, loss of water leads to a resonance-stabilized carbocation. Reaction of this carbocation with the alcohol, which is usually the solvent and is present in large excess, gives (after proton loss) the acetal. The mechanism is like an S_N1 reaction. *Each step is reversible.*

PROBLEM 9.9 Write an equation for the reaction of the hemiacetal

$$\overset{\displaystyle OH}{\underset{\displaystyle |}{CH_3CHOCH_2CH_3}}$$

with excess ethanol and H^+. Show each step in the mechanism.

In a **cyclic hemiacetal**, the ether functional group is cyclic.

Aldehydes that have an appropriately located hydroxyl group *in the same molecule* may exist in equilibrium with a **cyclic hemiacetal**, formed by *intramolecular* nucleophilic addition. For example, 5-hydroxypentanal exists mainly in the cyclic hemiacetal form:

                                                           (9.14)

         5-hydroxypentanal   hemiacetal form
                                 of 5-hydroxypentanal

The hydroxyl group is favorably located to act as a nucleophile toward the carbonyl carbon, and cyclization occurs by the following mechanism:

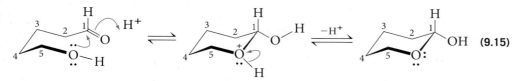

$$(9.15)$$

Compounds with a hydroxyl group that is four or five carbons away from the aldehyde group tend to form cyclic hemiacetals and acetals because the ring size (five- or six-membered) is relatively strain free. As we will see in Chapter 16, these structures are crucial to the chemistry of carbohydrates. For example, glucose is an important carbohydrate that exists as a cyclic hemiacetal.

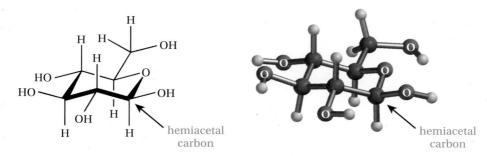

hemiacetal
carbon

hemiacetal
carbon

Ketones also form acetals. If, as in the following example, a glycol is used as the alcohol, the product will be cyclic.

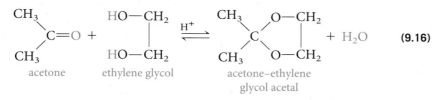

$$(9.16)$$

acetone   ethylene glycol   acetone–ethylene
glycol acetal

To summarize, aldehydes and ketones react with alcohols to form, first, hemiacetals and then, if excess alcohol is present, acetals.

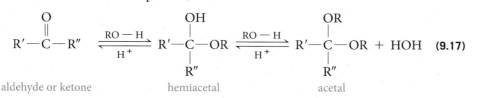

$$(9.17)$$

aldehyde or ketone   hemiacetal   acetal

Write an equation for the reaction of benzaldehyde with excess methanol and an acid catalyst.

Solution

$$(9.18)$$

PROBLEM 9.10 Show the steps in the mechanism for eq. 9.18.

PROBLEM 9.11 Write an equation for the acid catalyzed reactions between cyclohexanone and

a. excess ethanol   b. excess ethylene glycol ($HOCH_2CH_2OH$)

Acetal hydrolysis is the reverse of acetal formation.

Notice that acetal formation is a reversible process that involves a series of equilibria (eq. 9.17). How can these reactions be driven in the forward direction? One way is to use a large excess of alcohol. Another way is to remove water, a product of the forward reaction, as it is formed.* The reverse of acetal formation, called **acetal hydrolysis**, cannot proceed without water. On the other hand, an acetal can be hydrolyzed to its aldehyde or ketone and alcohol components by treatment with *excess water* in the presence of an acid catalyst. The hemiacetal intermediate in both the forward and reverse processes usually cannot be isolated when R′ and R″ are simple alkyl or aryl groups.

EXAMPLE 9.3

Write an equation for the reaction of benzaldehyde dimethylacetal with aqueous acid.

Solution

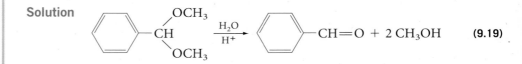

$$ \qquad \xrightarrow[\text{H}^+]{\text{H}_2\text{O}} \qquad CH{=}O + 2\ CH_3OH \qquad \textbf{(9.19)} $$

PROBLEM 9.12 Show the steps in the mechanism for eq. 9.19.

The acid-catalyzed cleavage of acetals occurs much more readily than the acid-catalyzed cleavage of simple ethers (Sec. 8.6) because the intermediate carbocation is resonance stabilized. However, acetals, like ordinary ethers, are stable toward bases.

9.8 Addition of Water; Hydration of Aldehydes and Ketones

Water, like alcohols, is an oxygen nucleophile and can add reversibly to aldehydes and ketones. For example, formaldehyde in aqueous solution exists mainly as its hydrate.

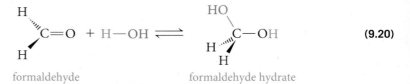

$$ \textbf{(9.20)} $$

formaldehyde   formaldehyde hydrate

With most other aldehydes or ketones, however, the hydrates cannot be isolated because they readily lose water to reform the carbonyl compound; that is, the equilibrium constant (Sec. 3.11) is less than 1. An exception is trichloroacetaldehyde (chloral), which forms a stable crystalline hydrate, $CCl_3CH(OH)_2$. Chloral hydrate is used in medicine as a sedative and in veterinary medicine as a narcotic and anesthetic** for horses, cattle, swine, and poultry. The potent drink known as a Mickey Finn is a combination of alcohol and chloral hydrate.

PROBLEM 9.13 Hydrolysis of $CH_3CBr_2CH_3$ with sodium hydroxide does *not* give $CH_3C(OH)_2CH_3$. Instead, it gives acetone. Explain.

---

*In the laboratory, this can be accomplished in several ways. One method involves distilling the water from the reaction mixture. Another method involves trapping the water with molecular sieves, inorganic materials with cavities of the size and shape required to absorb water molecules.

**See also "A Word about Ether and Anesthesia" in Chapter 8, page 243.

9.9 Addition of Grignard Reagents and Acetylides

Grignard reagents act as carbon nucleophiles toward carbonyl compounds. The R group of the Grignard reagent adds irreversibly to the carbonyl carbon, forming a new carbon–carbon bond. In terms of acid–base reactions, the addition is favorable because the product (an alkoxide) is a much weaker base than the starting carbanion (Grignard reagent). The alkoxide can be protonated to give an alcohol.

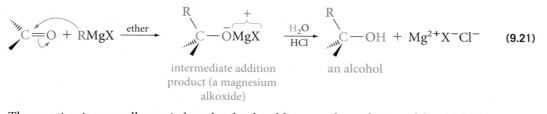

$$\text{C}{=}\text{O} + \text{RMgX} \xrightarrow{\text{ether}} \underset{\substack{\text{intermediate addition} \\ \text{product (a magnesium} \\ \text{alkoxide)}}}{\text{C}{-}\overset{+}{\bar{\text{O}}}\text{MgX}} \xrightarrow[\text{HCl}]{\text{H}_2\text{O}} \underset{\text{an alcohol}}{\text{C}{-}\text{OH}} + \text{Mg}^{2+}\text{X}^-\text{Cl}^- \qquad (9.21)$$

The reaction is normally carried out by slowly adding an ether solution of the aldehyde or ketone to an ether solution of the Grignard reagent. After all of the carbonyl compound is added and the reaction is complete, the resulting magnesium alkoxide is hydrolyzed with aqueous acid.

The reaction of a Grignard reagent with a carbonyl compound provides a useful route to alcohols. The type of carbonyl compound chosen determines the class of alcohol produced. *Formaldehyde gives primary alcohols.*

$$\text{R}{-}\text{MgX} + \underset{\text{formaldehyde}}{\text{H}{-}\overset{\overset{\text{O}}{\|}}{\text{C}}{-}\text{H}} \longrightarrow \text{R}{-}\overset{\overset{\text{H}}{|}}{\underset{\underset{\text{H}}{|}}{\text{C}}}{-}\text{OMgX} \xrightarrow[\text{H}^+]{\text{H}_2\text{O}} \underset{\text{a primary alcohol}}{\text{R}{-}\overset{\overset{\text{H}}{|}}{\underset{\underset{\text{H}}{|}}{\text{C}}}{-}\text{OH}} \qquad (9.22)$$

Other aldehydes give secondary alcohols.

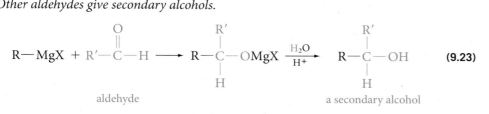

$$\text{R}{-}\text{MgX} + \underset{\text{aldehyde}}{\text{R}'{-}\overset{\overset{\text{O}}{\|}}{\text{C}}{-}\text{H}} \longrightarrow \text{R}{-}\overset{\overset{\text{R}'}{|}}{\underset{\underset{\text{H}}{|}}{\text{C}}}{-}\text{OMgX} \xrightarrow[\text{H}^+]{\text{H}_2\text{O}} \underset{\text{a secondary alcohol}}{\text{R}{-}\overset{\overset{\text{R}'}{|}}{\underset{\underset{\text{H}}{|}}{\text{C}}}{-}\text{OH}} \qquad (9.23)$$

Ketones give tertiary alcohols.

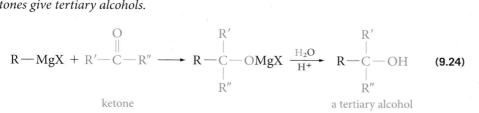

$$\text{R}{-}\text{MgX} + \underset{\text{ketone}}{\text{R}'{-}\overset{\overset{\text{O}}{\|}}{\text{C}}{-}\text{R}''} \longrightarrow \text{R}{-}\overset{\overset{\text{R}'}{|}}{\underset{\underset{\text{R}''}{|}}{\text{C}}}{-}\text{OMgX} \xrightarrow[\text{H}^+]{\text{H}_2\text{O}} \underset{\text{a tertiary alcohol}}{\text{R}{-}\overset{\overset{\text{R}'}{|}}{\underset{\underset{\text{R}''}{|}}{\text{C}}}{-}\text{OH}} \qquad (9.24)$$

Note that only *one* of the R groups (shown in black) attached to the hydroxyl-bearing carbon of the alcohol comes from the Grignard reagent. The rest of the alcohol's carbon skeleton comes from the carbonyl compound.

EXAMPLE 9.4

What is the product expected from the reaction between ethylmagnesium bromide and 3-pentanone followed by hydrolysis?

Solution 3-Pentanone is a ketone. Following eq. 9.24 as an example, the product is 3-ethyl-3-pentanol.

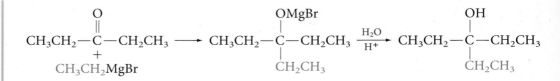

PROBLEM 9.14 Provide the products expected from the reaction of

a. formaldehyde with benzylmagnesium bromide followed by hydrolysis
b. pentanal with phenylmagnesium bromide followed by hydrolysis
c. benzaldehyde with ethylmagnesium bromide followed by hydrolysis
d. cyclohexanone with methylmagnesium bromide followed by hydrolysis

---

EXAMPLE 9.5

Show how the following alcohol can be synthesized from a Grignard reagent and a carbonyl compound:

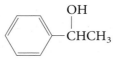

Solution The alcohol is secondary, so the carbonyl compound must be an aldehyde. We can use either a methyl or a phenyl Grignard reagent.

The equations are

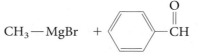

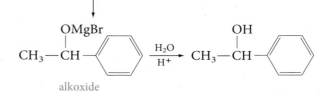   **(9.25)**

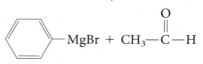

The choice between the possible sets of reactants may be made by availability or cost of reactants, or for chemical reasons (for example, the more reactive aldehyde or ketone might be selected).

PROBLEM 9.15 Show how each of the following alcohols can be made from a Grignard reagent and a carbonyl compound:

a.

b.

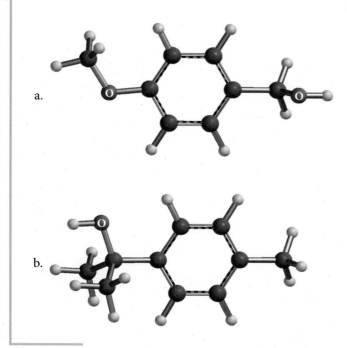

Other organometallic reagents, such as organolithium compounds and acetylides, react with carbonyl compounds in a similar fashion to Grignard reagents. For example,

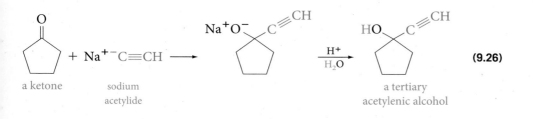

a ketone   sodium   a tertiary
               acetylide   acetylenic alcohol

PROBLEM 9.16 Write the structural formula of the product expected from the reaction of $CH_3C\equiv C^-Na^+$ with 3-pentanone followed by H_3O^+.

9.10 Addition of Hydrogen Cyanide; Cyanohydrins

Cyanohydrins are compounds with a hydroxyl and a cyano group attached to the same carbon.

Hydrogen cyanide adds reversibly to the carbonyl group of aldehydes and ketones to form **cyanohydrins**, compounds with a hydroxyl and a cyano group attached to the same carbon. A basic catalyst is required.

$$\text{C}{=}\text{O} + \text{HCN} \xrightarrow{\text{KOH}} \begin{array}{c} \text{NC} \\ | \\ \text{C}{-}\text{OH} \end{array} \qquad (9.27)$$

a cyanohydrin

Acetone, for example, reacts as follows:

$$\begin{array}{c} \text{O} \\ \| \\ \text{CH}_3{-}\text{C}{-}\text{CH}_3 \end{array} + \text{HCN} \xrightarrow{\text{KOH}} \begin{array}{c} \text{OH} \\ | \\ \text{CH}_3{-}\text{C}{-}\text{CH}_3 \\ | \\ \text{CN} \end{array} \qquad (9.28)$$

acetone   acetone cyanohydrin

Hydrogen cyanide has no unshared electron pair on its carbon, so it cannot function as a carbon nucleophile. The base converts some of the hydrogen cyanide to cyanide ion (NC^-), however, which then acts as a carbon nucleophile.

$$\text{C}{=}\ddot{\text{O}}\colon + {}^-\colon\text{C}{\equiv}\text{N}\colon \rightleftharpoons \begin{array}{c} \text{NC} \\ | \\ \text{C}{-}\ddot{\text{O}}\colon^- \end{array} \xrightarrow{\text{HCN}} \begin{array}{c} \text{NC} \\ | \\ \text{C}{-}\ddot{\text{O}}\text{H} \end{array} + {}^-\text{CN} \qquad (9.29)$$

cyanohydrin

PROBLEM 9.17 Write an equation for the addition of HCN to

a. propanal   b. cyclopentanecarbaldehyde   c. benzophenone (Sec. 9.1)

Cyanohydrin chemistry plays a central role in the defense system of *Apheloria corrugata*. This millipede uses a two-chamber gland much like that used by the bombardier beetle (see "A Word About . . . Quinones and the Bombardier Beetle" in Chapter 7) to deliver a secretion that contains hydrogen cyanide. *Apheloria* stores benzaldehyde cyanohydrin and, when threatened, converts it to a mixture of benzaldehyde and hydrogen cyanide, which is then secreted. The hydrogen cyanide gas that emanates from the secretion is an effective deterrent of predators.

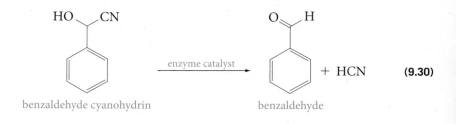

benzaldehyde cyanohydrin   benzaldehyde   (9.30)

9.11 / Addition of Nitrogen Nucleophiles

Ammonia, amines, and certain related compounds have an unshared electron pair on the nitrogen atom and act as nitrogen nucleophiles toward the carbonyl carbon atom. For example, primary amines react as follows:

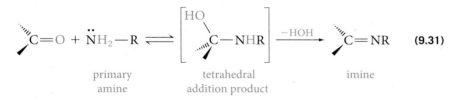

$$\underset{\substack{\text{primary} \\ \text{amine}}}{} \qquad \underset{\substack{\text{tetrahedral} \\ \text{addition product}}}{} \qquad \underset{\text{imine}}{} \qquad \textbf{(9.31)}$$

The tetrahedral addition product that is formed first is similar to a hemiacetal, but with an NH group in place of one of the oxygens. These addition products are normally not stable. They eliminate water to form a product with a carbon–nitrogen double bond. With primary amines, the products are called **imines**. Imines are like carbonyl compounds, except that the O is replaced by NR. They are important intermediates in some biochemical reactions, particularly in binding carbonyl compounds to the free amino groups that are present in most enzymes.

Imines are compounds containing a carbon–nitrogen double bond.

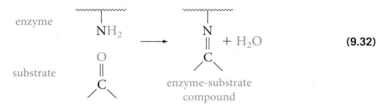

$$\qquad \qquad \qquad \qquad \qquad \qquad \qquad \qquad \qquad \textbf{(9.32)}$$

For example, retinal (see "A Word About . . . The Chemistry of Vision" in Chapter 3) binds to the protein opsin in this way to form rhodopsin.

> **PROBLEM 9.18** Write an equation for the reaction of benzaldehyde with aniline (the formula of which is $C_6H_5NH_2$).

Other ammonia derivatives containing an —NH_2 group react with carbonyl compounds similarly to primary amines. Table 9.1 lists some specific examples. Notice that in each of these reactions, the two hydrogens attached to nitrogen and the oxygen of the carbonyl group are eliminated as water.

Table 9.1 ■ Nitrogen Derivatives of Carbonyl Compounds

Formula of ammonia derivative	Name	Formula of carbonyl derivative	Name
RNH_2 or $ArNH_2$	primary amine	$C=NR$ or $C=NAr$	imine
NH_2OH	hydroxylamine	$C=NOH$	oxime
NH_2NH_2	hydrazine	$C=NNH_2$	hydrazone
$NH_2NHC_6H_5$	phenylhydrazine	$C=NNHC_6H_5$	phenylhydrazone

EXAMPLE 9.6

Using Table 9.1 as a guide, write an equation for the reaction of hydrazine with cyclohexanone.

Solution

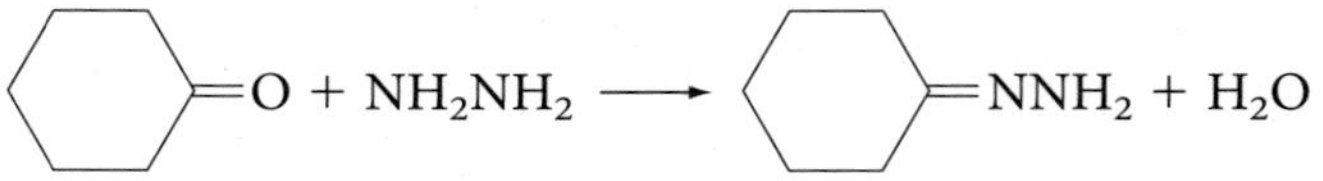

$$\text{(cyclohexanone)} =O + NH_2NH_2 \longrightarrow \text{(cyclohexanone)} =NNH_2 + H_2O$$

The product is a hydrazone.

PROBLEM 9.19 Using Table 9.1 as a guide, write an equation for the reaction of pentanal ($CH_3CH_2CH_2CH_2CH{=}O$) with

a. hydroxylamine (NH_2OH)
b. ethylamine ($CH_3CH_2NH_2$)
c. hydrazine (NH_2NH_2)
d. phenylhydrazine ($NH_2NHC_6H_5$)

9.12 Reduction of Carbonyl Compounds

Aldehydes and ketones are easily reduced to primary and secondary alcohols, respectively. Reduction can be accomplished in many ways, most commonly by metal hydrides.

The most common metal hydrides used to reduce carbonyl compounds are lithium aluminum hydride ($LiAlH_4$) and sodium borohydride ($NaBH_4$). The metal–hydride bond is polarized, with the metal positive and the hydrogen negative. Therefore, the reaction involves irreversible nucleophilic attack of the hydride (H^-) at the carbonyl carbon:

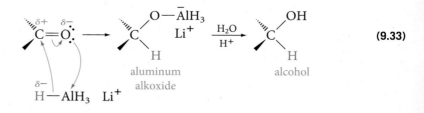

(9.33)

The initial product is an aluminum alkoxide, which is subsequently hydrolyzed by water and acid to give the alcohol. The net result is addition of hydrogen across the carbon–oxygen double bond. A specific example is

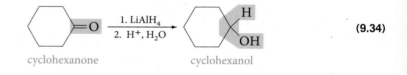

(9.34)

cyclohexanone   cyclohexanol

PROBLEM 9.20 Show how the following alcohols can be made from lithium aluminum hydride and a carbonyl compound:

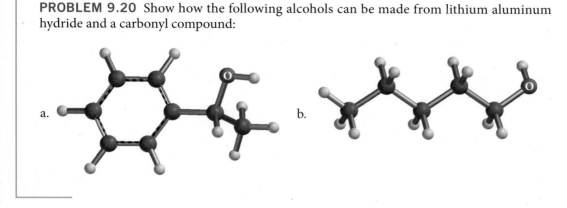

a. b.

Because a carbon–carbon double bond is not readily attacked by nucleophiles, metal hydrides can be used to reduce a carbon–oxygen double bond to the corresponding alcohol without reducing a carbon–carbon double bond present in the same compound.

$$CH_3{-}CH{=}CH{-}\overset{\overset{\displaystyle O}{\|}}{C}H \xrightarrow{\text{NaBH}_4} CH_3{-}CH{=}CH{-}CH_2OH \qquad \textbf{(9.35)}$$

2-butenal   2-buten-1-ol

PROBLEM 9.21 Show how

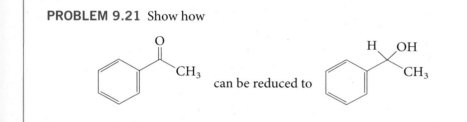

can be reduced to

9.13 Oxidation of Carbonyl Compounds

Aldehydes are more easily oxidized than ketones. Oxidation of an aldehyde gives a carboxylic acid with the same number of carbon atoms.

$$R{-}\overset{\overset{\displaystyle O}{\|}}{C}{-}H \xrightarrow[\text{agent}]{\text{oxidizing}} R{-}\overset{\overset{\displaystyle O}{\|}}{C}{-}OH \qquad \textbf{(9.36)}$$

aldehyde   acid

Because the reaction occurs easily, many oxidizing agents, such as $KMnO_4$, CrO_3, Ag_2O, and peracids (see eq. 8.18), will work. Specific examples are

$$CH_3(CH_2)_5CH{=}O \xrightarrow[\text{(Jones' reagent)}]{CrO_3,\ H^+} CH_3(CH_2)_5CO_2H \qquad \textbf{(9.37)}$$

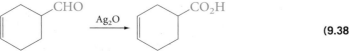

$$\qquad \textbf{(9.38)}$$

Silver ion as an oxidant is expensive but has the virtue that it selectively oxidizes aldehydes to carboxylic acids in the presence of alkenes (eq. 9.38).

A laboratory test that distinguishes aldehydes from ketones takes advantage of their different ease of oxidation. In the Tollens' silver mirror test, the silver–ammonia complex ion is reduced by aldehydes (but not by ketones) to metallic silver.* The equation for the reaction may be written as follows:

The symbol ↓ indicates formation of a precipitate; the symbol ↑ indicates the formation of a gas.

$$\underset{\text{aldehyde}}{\overset{\displaystyle\overset{O}{\|}}{RCH}} + \underset{\substack{\text{silver–ammonia}\\\text{complex ion}\\\text{(colorless)}}}{2\,Ag(NH_3)_2{}^+} + 3\,HO^- \longrightarrow \underset{\substack{\text{acid}\\\text{anion}}}{\overset{\displaystyle\overset{O}{\|}}{RC-O^-}} + \underset{\substack{\text{silver}\\\text{mirror}}}{2\,Ag\downarrow} + 4\,NH_3\uparrow + 2\,H_2O \qquad \textbf{(9.39)}$$

If the glass vessel in which the test is performed is thoroughly clean, the silver deposits as a mirror on the glass surface. This reaction is also employed to silver glass, using the inexpensive aldehyde formaldehyde.

> **PROBLEM 9.22** Write an equation for the formation of a silver mirror from formaldehyde and Tollens' reagent.

Aldehydes are so easily oxidized that stored samples usually contain some of the corresponding acid. This contamination is caused by air oxidation.

$$2\,RCHO + O_2 \longrightarrow 2\,RCO_2H \qquad \textbf{(9.40)}$$

Ketones also can be oxidized, but require special oxidizing conditions. For example, cyclohexanone is oxidized commercially to adipic acid, an important industrial chemical used to manufacture nylon. Over 5 billion pounds of adipic acid are produced each year.

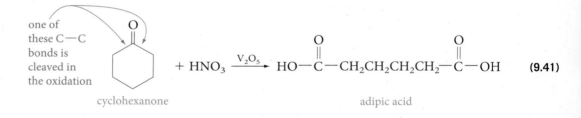

one of these C—C bonds is cleaved in the oxidation

$$+\ HNO_3 \xrightarrow{V_2O_5} \underset{\text{adipic acid}}{HO-\overset{\displaystyle\overset{O}{\|}}{C}-CH_2CH_2CH_2CH_2-\overset{\displaystyle\overset{O}{\|}}{C}-OH} \qquad \textbf{(9.41)}$$

cyclohexanone

9.14 Keto–Enol Tautomerism

Aldehydes and ketones may exist as an equilibrium mixture of two forms, called the **keto form** and the **enol form**. The two forms differ in the location of a proton and a double bond.

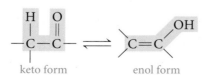

keto form   enol form   **(9.42)**

---

*Silver hydroxide is insoluble in water, so the silver ion must be complexed with ammonia to keep it in solution in a basic medium.

Tollens' silver mirror test (eq. 9.39).

© Martyn Chillmaid/Oxford Scientific/Photolibrary

This type of structural isomerism is called tautomerism (from the Greek *tauto,* the same, and *meros,* part). The two forms of the aldehyde or ketone are called **tautomers**.

Tautomers are structural isomers that differ in the location of a proton and a double bond. The **keto** and **enol** forms of an aldehyde or ketone are tautomers.

EXAMPLE 9.7

Write formulas for the keto and enol forms of acetone.

Solution

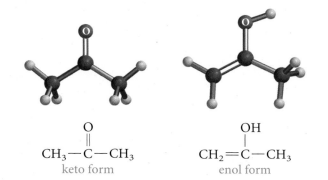

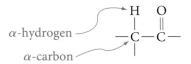

CH₃—C—CH₃   CH₂=C—CH₃
keto form   enol form

PROBLEM 9.23 Draw the structural formula for the enol form of

a. cyclohexanone
b. propanal (CH_3CH_2CHO)
c. 4-methoxycyclohexanone

Tautomers are structural isomers, *not* contributors to a resonance hybrid. They readily equilibrate, and we indicate that fact by using the equilibrium symbol ⇌ between their structures.

To be capable of existing in an enol form, a carbonyl compound must have a hydrogen atom attached to the carbon atom adjacent to the carbonyl group. This hydrogen is called an **α-hydrogen** and is attached to the **α-carbon atom** (from the first letter of the Greek alphabet, α, or alpha).

An **α-hydrogen** is attached to the **α-carbon atom**, the carbon atom adjacent to a carbonyl group.

Most simple aldehydes and ketones exist mainly in the keto form. Acetone, for example, is 99.9997% in the keto form, with only 0.0003% of the enol present. The main reason for the greater stability of the keto form is that the C=O plus C—H bond energy present in the keto form is greater than the C=C plus O—H bond energy of the enol form. We have already encountered some molecules, however, that have mainly the enol structure—the *phenols.* In this case, the resonance stabilization of the aromatic ring is greater than the usual energy difference that favors the keto over the enol form. Aromaticity would be destroyed if the molecule existed in the keto form; therefore, the enol form is preferred.

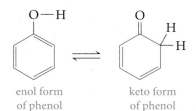

enol form   keto form
of phenol   of phenol

(9.43)

A WORD ABOUT...   Tautomerism and Photochromism

Some carbonyl compounds exist predominantly in the enol form due to favorable interactions between the tautomeric enol's OH group and an adjacent lone pair via a intermolecular hydrogen bond. For example, the equilibrium constant for 2,4-pentanedione in water lies in favor of the enol form and is about 4. Often, the equilibrium constant for the keto–enol tautomerism is very solvent dependent, and the keto form is more favored in less polar solvents, such as cyclohexane.

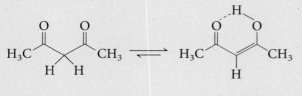

keto form   enol form

The concept of tautomerism can be expanded beyond keto and enol forms to include any pair or group of isomers that can be easily interconverted by the relocation of an atom and/or bonds. For example, imines and enamines (unsaturated amines) are tautomers whose relationship is similar to that of keto and enol forms.

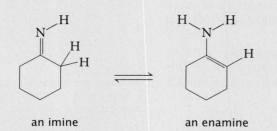

an imine   an enamine

For some pairs of tautomers, one can be converted to the other photochemically—that is, by the absorption of light. Irradiation of the following pale yellow phenol-imine causes the hydrogen atom to shift from the oxygen to the nitrogen, with appropriate rebonding.

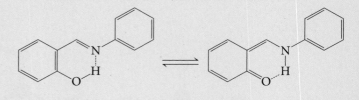

a phenol-imine   a keto-enamine
pale yellow   red
(both rings are aromatic)   (only one ring is aromatic)

If the keto-enamine product of this photochemical reaction is allowed to remain in the dark, it gradually changes back to the more stable phenol-imine.

Of what use can such a cycle of reactions, with no net change, possibly be? In this example, one tautomer is pale yellow, and the other is red. This phenomenon, in which two compounds undergo a reversible photochemical color change, is called **photochromism**. Photochromic substances have many practical uses. Glasses coated with these substances become darker when exposed to sunlight, because their lenses are impregnated with a photochromic material. When the sunlight dims or when taken indoors, the colored photochromic substance gradually changes back to its colorless form. Photochromic substances can also be used for data storage and display (as in digital watches), as second-order nonlinear optical materials in laser and telecommunication applications, as chemical switches in computers, for micro images (microfilm), for protection against sudden light flashes, and in many other creative ways. (See the special issue in "Photochromism: Memories and Switches," *Chemical Reviews*, **2000**, *100*, no. 5.)

See Problems 9.55 and 9.58.

Photochromism is the phenomenon in which two compounds undergo a reversible photochemical color change.

Carbonyl compounds that do not have an α-hydrogen cannot form enols and exist only in the keto form. Examples are

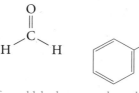

formaldehyde

benzaldehyde

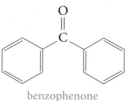

benzophenone

9.15 Acidity of α-Hydrogens; the Enolate Anion

The α-hydrogen in a carbonyl compound is more acidic than a normal hydrogen bonded to a carbon atom. Table 9.2 shows the pK_a values for a typical aldehyde and ketone as well as for reference compounds. The result of placing a carbonyl group adjacent to methyl protons is truly striking, an increase in their acidity of over 10^{30}! (Compare acetaldehyde or acetone with propane.) Indeed, these compounds are almost as acidic as the O—H protons in alcohols. Why is this?

There are two reasons. First, the carbonyl carbon carries a partial positive charge. Bonding electrons are displaced toward the carbonyl carbon and away from the α-hydrogen (shown by the red arrows below), making it easy for a base to remove the α-hydrogen as a proton (that is, without its bonding electrons).

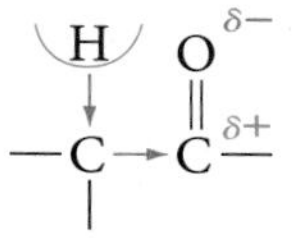

Second, the resulting anion is stabilized by resonance.

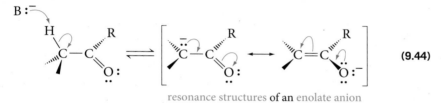

(9.44)

resonance structures of an enolate anion

The anion is called an **enolate anion**. Its negative charge is distributed between the α-carbon and the carbonyl oxygen atom.

An **enolate anion** is formed by removal of the α-hydrogen of a ketone or aldehyde.

Table 9.2 ◾ Acidity of α-Hydrogens		
Compound	**Name**	**pK_a**
$CH_3CH_2CH_3$	propane	~50
$CH_3\overset{O}{\overset{\|}{C}}CH_3$	acetone	19
$CH_3\overset{O}{\overset{\|}{C}}H$	acetaldehyde	17
CH_3CH_2OH	ethanol	16

EXAMPLE 9.8

Draw the formula for the enolate anion of acetone.

Solution

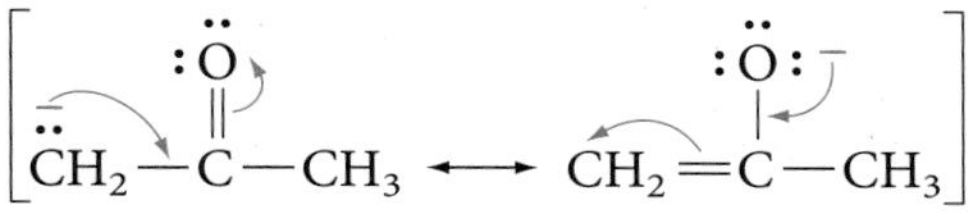

$$\left[\overset{\cdot\cdot}{\underset{\cdot\cdot}{C}}H_2 - \overset{\overset{\cdot\cdot}{\underset{\|}{O}}}{C} - CH_3 \longleftrightarrow CH_2 = \overset{\overset{\cdot\cdot}{\underset{\|}{O}:^-}}{C} - CH_3 \right]$$

An enolate anion is a resonance hybrid of two contributing structures that differ *only* in the arrangement of the electrons.

PROBLEM 9.24 Draw the resonance contributors to the enolate anion of

a. propanal   b. cyclopentanone

9.16 Deuterium Exchange in Carbonyl Compounds

Even though its concentration is very low, the presence of the enol form of ordinary aldehydes and ketones can be demonstrated experimentally. For example, the α-hydrogens can be exchanged for deuterium by placing the carbonyl compound in a solvent such as D_2O or CH_3OD. The exchange is catalyzed by acid or base. *Only the α-hydrogens exchange,* as illustrated by the following examples:

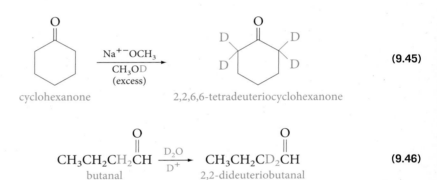

cyclohexanone   2,2,6,6-tetradeuteriocyclohexanone   (9.45)

$$CH_3CH_2CH_2CH \xrightarrow[D^+]{D_2O} CH_3CH_2CD_2CH$$

butanal   2,2-dideuteriobutanal   (9.46)

The mechanism of the base-catalyzed exchange of the α-hydrogens (eq. 9.45) involves two steps.

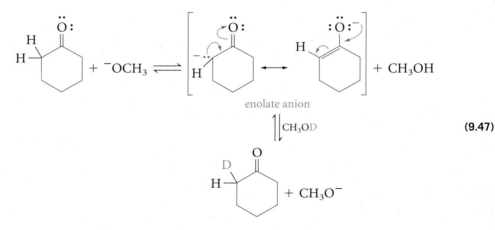

enolate anion

(9.47)

The base (methoxide ion) removes an α-proton to form the enolate anion. Reprotonation, but with CH_3OD, replaces the α-hydrogen with deuterium. With excess CH_3OD, all four α-hydrogens are eventually exchanged.

The mechanism of the acid-catalyzed exchange of the α-hydrogens (eq. 9.46) also involves several steps. The keto form is first protonated and, by loss of an α-hydrogen, converted to its enol.

$$CH_3CH_2CH_2CH \;\overset{D^+}{\rightleftharpoons}\; CH_3CH_2\overset{\displaystyle H}{\underset{\displaystyle H}{C}}\overset{+\ddot{O}-D}{\overset{\|}{-}}CH \;\overset{-H^+}{\rightleftharpoons}\; CH_3CH_2CH{=}CH \quad\quad \textbf{(9.48)}$$

keto form   enol form

In the reversal of these equilibria, the enol then adds D^+ at the α-carbon.

$$CH_3CH_2CH{=}CH \;\overset{\ddot{O}-D}{\underset{D^+}{\curvearrowright}} \;\rightleftharpoons\; CH_3CH_2\overset{\displaystyle D}{\underset{}{C}}H-\overset{\ddot{O}}{\overset{\|}{}}CH + D^+ \quad\quad \textbf{(9.49)}$$

Repetition of this sequence results in exchange of the other α-hydrogen.

PROBLEM 9.25 Identify the hydrogens that are readily exchanged for deuterium in

a. [structure: cyclopentanone with CH₂CH₃ substituent]

b. $(CH_3)_3CCCH_3$ with O (carbonyl)

9.17 | The Aldol Condensation

Enolate anions may act as carbon nucleophiles. They add reversibly to the carbonyl group of another aldehyde or ketone molecule in a reaction called the **aldol condensation**, an extremely useful carbon–carbon bond-forming reaction.

The simplest example of an aldol condensation is the combination of two acetaldehyde molecules, which occurs when a solution of acetaldehyde is treated with catalytic amounts of aqueous base.

An enolate anion adds to the carbonyl group of an aldehyde or ketone in an **aldol condensation**. An **aldol** is a 3-hydroxyaldehyde or 3-hydroxyketone.

$$\underset{\text{acetaldehyde}}{CH_3CH} + CH_3CH \;\overset{HO^-}{\rightleftharpoons}\; \underset{\substack{\text{3-hydroxybutanal}\\ \text{(an aldol)}}}{CH_3CH-CH_2CH} \quad\quad \textbf{(9.50)}$$

The product is called an **aldol** (so named because the product is both an *ald*ehyde and an alcoh*ol*).

The aldol condensation of acetaldehyde occurs according to the following three-step mechanism:

Step 1.
$$\overset{\alpha}{CH_3}-\overset{\ddot{O}}{\overset{\|}{C}}-H + HO^- \;\rightleftharpoons\; \underset{\text{enolate anion}}{\overset{-}{\ddot{C}}H_2-\overset{\ddot{O}}{\overset{\|}{C}}-H} + HOH \quad\quad \textbf{(9.51)}$$

Step 2.
$$CH_3-\overset{\ddot{O}}{\overset{\|}{C}}H + \underset{\text{nucleophile}}{\overset{-}{\ddot{C}}H_2-\overset{\ddot{O}}{\overset{\|}{C}}H} \;\rightleftharpoons\; \underset{\text{an alkoxide ion}}{CH_3\overset{:\ddot{O}:^-}{\overset{|}{C}}H-CH_2\overset{\ddot{O}}{\overset{\|}{C}}H} \quad\quad \textbf{(9.52)}$$

Step 3.

$$\text{CH}_3\overset{\overset{\displaystyle :\ddot{\text{O}}:^-}{|}}{\text{CH}}-\text{CH}_2\overset{\overset{\displaystyle \ddot{\text{O}}:}{\|}}{\text{CH}} + \text{HOH} \rightleftharpoons \text{CH}_3\overset{\overset{\displaystyle :\ddot{\text{O}}\text{H}}{|}}{\text{CH}}-\overset{\alpha}{\text{CH}_2}\overset{\overset{\displaystyle \ddot{\text{O}}:}{\|}}{\text{CH}} + \text{HO}^- \qquad (9.53)$$

$$\underset{\text{aldol}}{}$$

In step 1, the base removes an α-hydrogen to form the enolate anion. In step 2, this anion adds to the carbonyl carbon of *another* acetaldehyde molecule, forming a new carbon–carbon bond. Ordinary bases convert only a small fraction of the carbonyl compound to the enolate anion so that a substantial fraction of the aldehyde is still present in the un-ionized carbonyl form needed for this step. In step 3, the alkoxide ion formed in step 2 accepts a proton from the solvent, thus regenerating the hydroxide ion needed for the first step.

In the aldol condensation, the α-carbon of one aldehyde molecule becomes connected to the carbonyl carbon of another aldehyde molecule.

$$\text{RCH}_2\overset{\overset{\displaystyle O}{\|}}{\text{CH}} + \overset{\alpha}{\text{R}}\text{CH}_2\overset{\overset{\displaystyle O}{\|}}{\text{CH}} \xrightarrow[\text{H}_2\text{O}]{\text{HO}^-} \text{RCH}_2\overset{\overset{\displaystyle OH}{|}}{\underset{3}{\text{CH}}}-\overset{\alpha}{\underset{2}{\underset{|}{\text{CH}}}}\overset{\overset{\displaystyle O}{\|}}{\underset{1}{\text{CH}}} \qquad (9.54)$$

$$\underset{R}{}$$

$$\underset{\text{an aldol}}{}$$

Aldols are therefore 3-hydroxyaldehydes. *Since it is always the α-carbon that acts as a nucleophile, the product always has just one carbon atom between the aldehyde and alcohol carbons,* regardless of how long the carbon chain is in the starting aldehyde.

EXAMPLE 9.9

Give the structure of the aldol that is obtained by treating propanal ($\text{CH}_3\text{CH}_2\text{CH}{=}\text{O}$) with base.

Solution Rewriting eq. 9.54 with R = CH_3, the product is

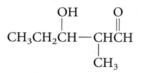

$$\text{CH}_3\text{CH}_2\overset{\overset{\displaystyle OH}{|}}{\text{CH}}-\overset{\overset{\displaystyle O}{\|}}{\underset{\overset{\displaystyle |}{\text{CH}_3}}{\text{CH}}}\text{CH}$$

PROBLEM 9.26 Write out the steps in the mechanism for formation of the product in Example 9.9.

9.18 The Mixed Aldol Condensation

The aldol condensation is versatile in that the enolate anion of *one* carbonyl compound can be made to add to the carbonyl carbon of *another,* provided that the reaction partners are carefully selected. Consider, for example, the reaction between acetaldehyde and benzaldehyde, when treated with base. Only acetaldehyde can form an enolate anion (benzaldehyde has no α-hydrogen). If the enolate ion of acetaldehyde adds to the benzaldehyde carbonyl group, a mixed aldol condensation occurs.

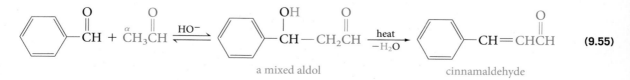

$$\underset{\text{a mixed aldol}}{} \qquad \qquad \underset{\text{cinnamaldehyde}}{} \qquad (9.55)$$

A WORD ABOUT... Water Treatment and the Chemistry of Enols/Enolates

In a city with a population of about 35,000, around 1.2 billion gallons of drinking water is delivered annually to homes. This water is usually purified before use to remove contaminants such as viruses and bacteria; organic chemicals, including pesticides and herbicides; and inorganic chemicals, including radioactive substances. These contaminants come from a variety of industrial and natural sources. The cleanup process involves several steps, including removal of water-insoluble material by sedimentation, coagulation, and filtration; softening of the water using lime (calcium oxide, CaO) and soda ash (sodium carbonate, Na_2CO_3); adjustment of the pH to 7.5–8.0 with carbon dioxide; and disinfection with chlorine (Cl_2). A typical water quality report will show that while the water delivered to homes is quite clean, α-halogenated ketones, halogenated carboxylic acids, and trihalomethanes (such as chloroform) are sometimes present at very low levels due to chemistry that occurs during the treatment process. What are these compounds, and how do they get into the water during the treatment process?

electrophile in this reaction. Repetition of this process several times provides polychlorinated compounds such as 1,1,1-trichloroacetone. Polychlorinated ketones can then undergo further reactions that provide chlorinated carboxylic acids and chloroform. Because acetone is a common water-soluble organic solvent and is also an end product of fat metabolism in humans and other animals, it is not surprising that it shows up in water treatment plants. The normal chemistry of ketones (via their enols/enolates) that takes place during the water treatment process, therefore, is responsible in part for the presence of low levels of chlorinated organic compounds in our drinking water. Whereas one could argue that water treatment introduces potentially toxic compounds into the drinking water supply, this is balanced by the removal of far more dangerous materials by the treatment process.

Some recent alternatives for water treatment include using the dissolved organic carbon, nitrates, and other components in the water as a food source to grow algae. Then such algal biomass can be harvested in order to capture the cell wall constituents, which include lipids and triglycerides (Chapter 15). The lipids can be converted

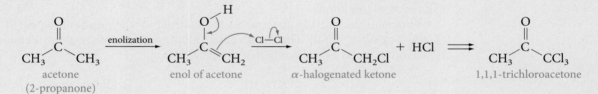

acetone (2-propanone)   enol of acetone α-halogenated ketone   1,1,1-trichloroacetone

When ketones are treated with halogens (Cl_2, Br_2, I_2), they undergo α-halogenation. This is illustrated above for acetone (2-propanone) and chlorine. Enolization of the acetone is followed by the reaction of enol with chlorine to provide α-chloroacetone. The enol (or enolate) of acetone behaves as a nucleophile and the chlorine behaves as an

to biodiesel and used as an alternative fuel source to petroleum-derived diesel (petrodiesel) in diesel-combustion engines (see Chapter 3 and "A Word About . . . Petroleum, Gasoline, and Octane Number," pages 102–103). For additional information, see http://www.nrel.gov/biomass/.
See Problem 9.52.

In this particular example, the resulting mixed aldol eliminates water on heating to give cinnamaldehyde (the flavor constituent of cinnamon).

EXAMPLE 9.10

Write the structure of the mixed aldol obtained from acetone and formaldehyde.

Solution Of the two reactants, only acetone has α-hydrogens.

$$H-\overset{O}{\overset{\|}{C}}-H \;+\; CH_3\overset{O}{\overset{\|}{C}}CH_3 \;\xrightarrow{\text{base}}\; H-\overset{OH}{\underset{H}{\overset{|}{C}}}-CH_2\overset{O}{\overset{\|}{C}}CH_3$$

PROBLEM 9.27 Using eqs. 9.51 through 9.53 as a guide, write out the steps in the mechanism for eq. 9.55.

PROBLEM 9.28 Write the structure of the mixed aldol obtained from propanal and benzaldehyde. What structure is obtained from dehydration of this mixed aldol?

9.19 Commercial Syntheses via the Aldol Condensation

Aldols are useful in synthesis. For example, acetaldehyde is converted commercially to crotonaldehyde, 1-butanol, and butanal using the aldol condensation.

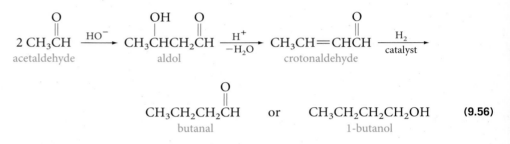

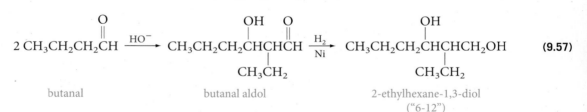

The particular product obtained in the hydrogenation step depends on the catalyst and reaction conditions.

Butanal is the starting material for the synthesis of the mosquito repellent "6-12" (2-ethylhexane-1,3-diol). The first step is an aldol condensation, and the second step is reduction of the aldehyde group to a primary alcohol.

The aldol condensation is also used in nature to build up (and, in the case of *reverse* aldol condensations, to break down) carbon chains.

PROBLEM 9.29 2-Ethylhexanol, used commercially in the manufacture of plasticizers and synthetic lubricants, is synthesized from butanal via its aldol product. Devise a route to it.

REACTION SUMMARY

1. Preparation of Aldehydes and Ketones

a. Oxidation of Alcohols (Sec. 9.3)

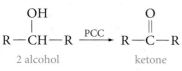

1 alcohol   aldehyde

2 alcohol   ketone

b. Friedel–Crafts Acylation (Sec. 9.3)

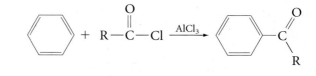

c. Hydration of Alkynes (Sec. 9.3)

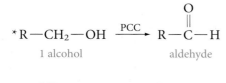

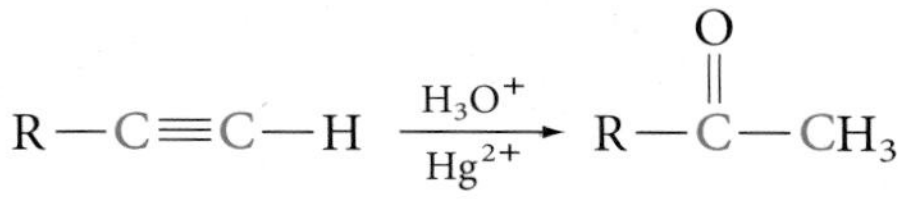

2. Reactions of Aldehydes and Ketones

a. Formation and Hydrolysis of Acetals (Sec. 9.7)

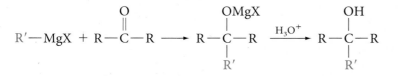

alcohol   carbonyl   hemiacetal   acetal

b. Addition of Grignard Reagents (Sec. 9.9)

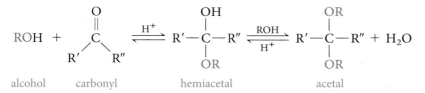

Formaldehyde gives 1° alcohols; other aldehydes give 2° alcohols; and ketones give 3° alcohols.

c. Formation of Cyanohydrins (Sec. 9.10)

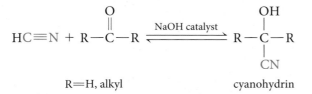

R=H, alkyl   cyanohydrin

---

*For all syntheses and reactions of carbonyl compounds in this summary, R can be alkyl or aryl.

d. Addition of Nitrogen Nucleophiles (Sec. 9.11 and Table 9.1)

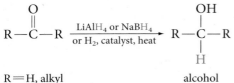

$$R'-\overset{..}{N}H_2 + R-\overset{\overset{\textstyle O}{\|}}{C}-R \longrightarrow R-\overset{\overset{\textstyle N-R'}{\|}}{C}-R + H_2O$$

$$R = H, \text{alkyl}$$

The product is an imine when R′ is an alkyl group.

e. Reduction to Alcohols (Sec. 9.12)

$$R-\overset{\overset{\textstyle O}{\|}}{C}-R \xrightarrow[\text{or } H_2,\ \text{catalyst, heat}]{\text{LiAlH}_4 \text{ or NaBH}_4} R-\overset{\overset{\textstyle OH}{|}}{\underset{\underset{\textstyle H}{|}}{C}}-R$$

R=H, alkyl   alcohol

f. Oxidation to Carboxylic Acids (Sec. 9.13)

$$R-\overset{\overset{\textstyle O}{\|}}{C}-H \xrightarrow[\text{O}_2,\ \text{or Ag}^{2+},\ \text{NaOH}]{\overset{\text{CrO}_3,\ \text{H}_2\text{SO}_4,\ \text{H}_2\text{O}}{\text{or}}} R-\overset{\overset{\textstyle O}{\|}}{C}-OH$$

aldehyde   carboxylic acid

g. Aldol condensation (Sec. 9.17)

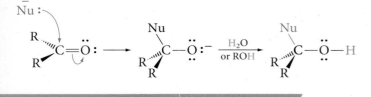

$$2\ RCH_2CH{=}O \xrightarrow{\text{base}} RCH_2\overset{\overset{\textstyle OH}{|}}{\underset{\underset{\textstyle R}{|}}{C}}HCHCH{=}O$$

aldehyde   aldol

MECHANISM SUMMARY

Nucleophilic Addition (Sec. 9.6)

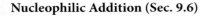

$$\overset{-}{Nu}:\!\curvearrowright \quad \overset{R}{\underset{R}{>}}C{=}\overset{..}{\underset{..}{O}}: \longrightarrow \overset{Nu}{\underset{R}{\overset{|}{\underset{R}{>}}}}C-\overset{..}{\underset{..}{O}}:^- \xrightarrow[\text{or ROH}]{H_2O} \overset{Nu}{\underset{R}{\overset{|}{\underset{R}{>}}}}C-\overset{..}{\underset{..}{O}}-H$$

ADDITIONAL PROBLEMS

⛎**WL** Interactive versions of these problems are assignable in OWL.

Nomenclature, Structure, and Properties of Aldehydes and Ketones

9.30 Name each of the following compounds.

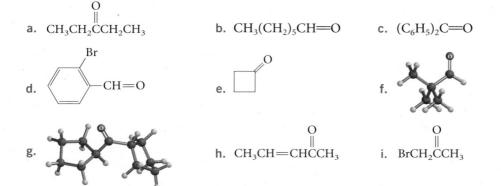

a. $CH_3CH_2\overset{\overset{\textstyle O}{\|}}{C}CH_2CH_3$

b. $CH_3(CH_2)_5CH{=}O$

c. $(C_6H_5)_2C{=}O$

d. (2-bromophenyl)—CH=O

e. (cyclobutanone structure)

f. (ball-and-stick structure)

g. (ball-and-stick structure)

h. $CH_3CH{=}CHCCH_3$ (with C=O)

i. $BrCH_2\overset{\overset{\textstyle O}{\|}}{C}CH_3$

9.31 Write a structural formula for each of the following:

a. 3-heptanone
c. *p*-bromobenzaldehyde
e. 3-hexenal
g. 2,2-dichlorohexanal
i. cyclobutanone

b. 3-isopropylheptanal
d. (*S*)-2-methylcyclohexanone
f. benzyl *p*-methylphenyl ketone
h. 4-phenyl-2-butanone
j. *p*-tolualdehyde

9.32 Give an example of each of the following:

a. acetal
c. cyanohydrin
e. oxime
g. enol
i. enolate

b. hemiacetal
d. imine
f. phenylhydrazone
h. aldehyde with no α-hydrogen
j. hydrazone

9.33 The boiling points of the isomeric carbonyl compounds heptanal, 4-heptanone, and 2,4-dimethyl-3-pentanone are 155°C, 144°C, and 124°C, respectively. Suggest a possible explanation for the observed order. (*Hint:* Recall the effect of chain branching on the boiling points of isomeric alkanes, and how steric effects can influence the association of the molecules.)

Synthesis of Ketones and Aldehydes

9.34 Write an equation for the synthesis of 2-octanone by

a. oxidation of an alcohol
b. hydration of an alkyne

9.35 Write an equation for the synthesis of hexanal from an alcohol.

9.36 Write an equation, using the Friedel–Crafts reaction, for the preparation of

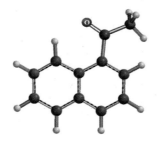

9.37 Using 1-hexyne as a starting reagent, suggest a synthesis of

a. 2-hexanone
c. a mixture of 1-hexene and 2-hexene

b. 2-hexyl alcohol
d. 1-hexene (and without 2-hexene present)

Reactions of Aldehydes and Ketones

9.38 Write an equation for the reaction, if any, of *p*-bromobenzaldehyde with each of the following reagents, and name the organic product.

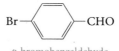

p-bromobenzaldehyde

a. methylmagnesium bromide, then H_3O^+
c. ethylene glycol, H^+
e. HCN (catalytic NaOH)

b. methylamine (CH_3NH_2)
d. phenylhydrazine
f. Tollens' reagent

g. CrO_3, H^+ h. phenylmagnesium bromide, then H_3O^+
i. excess methanol, dry HCl   j. hydroxylamine
k. sodium borohydride

9.39 What simple chemical test can distinguish between the members of the following pairs of compounds? (*Hint*: Think of a reaction that one compound will undergo and the other will not.)

a. pentanal and 2-pentanone
b. benzyl alcohol and benzaldehyde
c. cyclohexanone and 2-cyclohexenone

9.40 Use the structures shown in Figure 9.1 to write equations for the following reactions of natural products:

a. benzaldehyde + Jones' reagent   b. cinnamaldehyde + Tollens' reagent
c. vanillin + hydrazine   d. jasmone + sodium borohydride
e. carvone + lithium aluminum hydride   f. camphor + (1) methylmagnesium bromide and (2) H_3O^+
g. vanillin + excess methanol, dry HCl

9.41 Complete each of the following equations:

a. butanal + excess methanol, $H^+ \longrightarrow$ b. $CH_3CH(OCH_3)_2 + H_2O$, $H^+ \longrightarrow$

c. 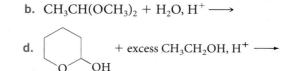 $+ H_2O$, $H^+ \longrightarrow$ d. $+ $ excess CH_3CH_2OH, $H^+ \longrightarrow$

9.42 Estrone (page 253) can be readily converted to ethynylestradiol:

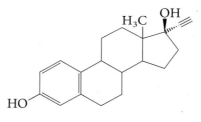

Ethynylestradiol was the first synthetic estrogen to be used in formulations of oral contraceptive pills. Suggest a synthesis of ethynylestradiol from estrone.

9.43. Two equivalents of phenol and one equivalent of acetone are reacted with an acid catalyst to yield bisphenol-A (eq. 9.4), which is used in a number of commercial applications. Bisphenol-A has been also shown to mimic estrogen biologically. Provide a mechanism for the formation of bisphenol-A from phenol and acetone. (*Hint*: See Sec. 4.9.d.)

Reactions with Grignard Reagents and Other Nucleophiles

9.44 Write an equation for the reaction of each of the following with ethylmagnesium bromide, followed by hydrolysis with aqueous acid:

a. formaldehyde   b. hexanal
c. acetophenone   d. ethylene oxide
e. cyclohexanone

9.45 Using a Grignard reagent and the appropriate aldehyde or ketone, show how each of the following can be prepared:

a. methylcyclohexanol   b. 3-octanol
c. 2-methyl-2-pentanol   d. 1-cyclopentylcyclopentanol
e. 1-phenyl-1-propanol   f. 3-butene-2-ol

9.46 Complete the equation for the reaction of

a. cyclohexanone + Na^{+-}C≡CH ⟶ $\xrightarrow{\text{H}_2\text{O}}{\text{H}^+}$

b. cyclopentanone + HCN $\xrightarrow{\text{KOH}}$

c. 2-butanone + NH$_2$OH $\xrightarrow{\text{H}^+}$

d. benzaldehyde + benzylamine ⟶

e. propanal + phenylhydrazine ⟶

9.47 The equilibrium constant for hydrate formation from acetaldehyde (CH$_3$CHO) is 1 (Sec. 9.8), and at equilibrium, there is an equal amount of acetaldehyde and its hydrate (CH$_3$CH(OH)$_2$) in solution. The equilibrium constant for forming the hydrate of chloral (Cl$_3$CCHO), however, is much larger, and at equilibrium, only the chloral hydrate (Cl$_3$CCH(OH)$_2$) is observed. As noted above, chloral hydrate has been used as an anesthetic and as a sedative (also, see "A Word About . . . Ether and Anesthesia," page 243). Provide an explanation for the difference in hydrate formation for acetaldehyde and chloral. (*Hint:* See Sec. 9.6.)

Oxidations and Reductions

9.48 Give the structure of each product.

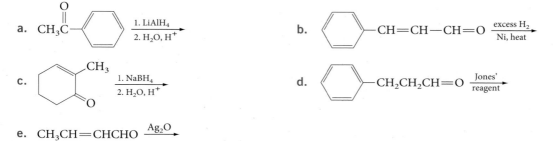

e. CH$_3$CH=CHCHO $\xrightarrow{\text{Ag}_2\text{O}}$

Enols, Enolates, and the Aldol Reaction

9.49 Write the structural formulas for all possible enols of

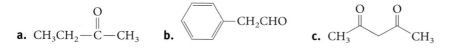

9.50 Complete the reaction shown below by drawing the structure of the product.

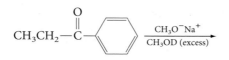

9.51 How many hydrogens are replaced by deuterium when each of the following compounds is treated with NaOD in D$_2$O?

a. 3-methylcyclopentanone

b. 3-methylhexanal

9.52 As described in "A Word About . . . Water Treatment and the Chemistry of Enols/Enolates," carbonyl compounds can become halogenated by treatment with a base and a halogen source, such as Cl$_2$. As shown on page 279, base-catalyzed chlorination of acetone leads to 1,1,1-trichloroacetone. For acetone, provide a mechanism that rationalizes the formation of 1,1,1-trichloroacetone vs. chlorination on both sides of the carbonyl group.

9.53 Write out the steps in the mechanism for the aldol condensation of butanal (the first step in the synthesis of the mosquito repellent "6-12," eq. 9.57).

9.54 Explain why the enol form of phenol is more stable than the keto form of phenol (eq. 9.43).

9.55 Draw the keto and enol tautomers of 1,3-diphenyl-1,3-propanedione.

9.56 Lily aldehyde, used in perfumes, can be made starting with a mixed aldol condensation between two different aldehydes. Provide their structures.

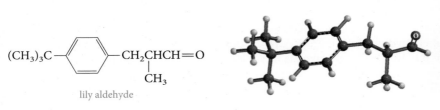

lily aldehyde

Puzzles

9.57 Excess benzaldehyde reacts with acetone and base to give a yellow crystalline product, $C_{17}H_{14}O$. Deduce its structure and explain how it is formed.

9.58 For the phenol-imine (pale yellow) and keto-enamine (red) compounds discussed in the "A Word About . . . Tautomerism and Photochromism," page 274, suggest what is unique about the two structures that would give each compound a unique color. (*Hint:* See Chapter 4.)

9.59 Vitamin B_6 (an aldehyde) reacts with an enzyme (partial structure shown below) to form a *coenzyme* that catalyzes the conversion of α-amino acids (Chapter 17) to α-keto acids.

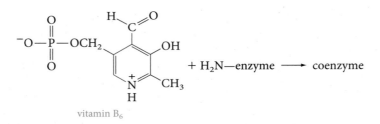

vitamin B_6

a. Draw the structure of the coenzyme.
b. α-Amino acids have the general structure shown below. Draw the structure of an α-keto acid.

$$
\underset{\underset{NH_2}{|}}{R-CH}-\overset{\overset{O}{\|}}{C}-OH \quad \text{α-amino acid}
$$

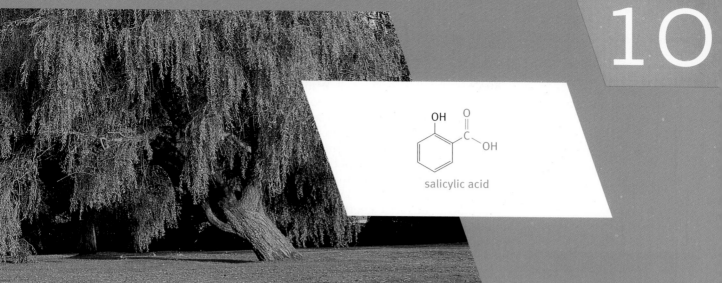

The bark of the white willow tree (*Salix alba*) is a source of salicylic acid, from which aspirin (acetylsalicylic acid) is made.

salicylic acid

© Geoff Kidd/Earth Scenes/Animals Animals

Carboxylic Acids and Their Derivatives

The taste of vinegar, the sting of an ant, the rancid smell of butter, and the relief derived from aspirin or ibuprofen—all of these are due to compounds that belong to the most important family of organic acids, the **carboxylic acids**. The resilience of polyester and nylon fabrics, the remarkable properties of Velcro, the softness of silk, the no-calorie sugar substitutes, the strength of bacterial cell walls, and the strength of our own cell membranes—all of these are due to properties of derivatives of carboxylic acids. The functional group common to all carboxylic acids is the **carboxyl group**. The name is a contraction of the parts: the *carb*onyl and hyd*roxyl* groups. The general formula for a carboxylic acid can be written in expanded or abbreviated forms.

In this chapter, we will describe the structures, properties, preparation, and reactions of carboxylic acids and will also discuss some common **carboxylic acid derivatives**, in which the hydroxyl group of an acid is replaced by other functional groups.

OWL

Online homework for this chapter can be assigned in OWL, an online homework assessment tool.

Carboxylic acids are organic acids that contain the carboxyl group. In carboxylic acid derivatives, the —OH group is replaced by other groups.

10.1 Nomenclature of Acids

Because of their abundance in nature, carboxylic acids were among the earliest classes of compounds studied by organic chemists. It is not surprising, then, that many of them have common names. These names usually come from some Latin or Greek word that indicates the original source of the acid. Table 10.1 lists the first ten unbranched carboxylic acids, with their common and IUPAC names. To obtain the IUPAC name of a carboxylic acid, we replace the final *e* in the name of the corresponding alkane with the suffix *-oic* and add the word *acid*. Substituted acids are named in two ways. In the IUPAC system, the chain is numbered beginning with the carboxyl carbon atom, and substituents are located in the usual way. If the common name of the acid is used, substituents are located with Greek letters, beginning with the α-carbon atom. IUPAC and common naming systems should not be mixed.

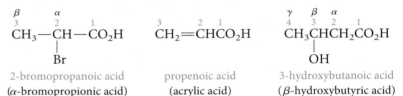

2-bromopropanoic acid
(α-bromopropionic acid)

propenoic acid
(acrylic acid)

3-hydroxybutanoic acid
(β-hydroxybutyric acid)

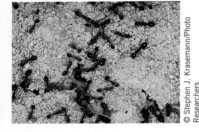

Stinging ants, source of formic acid, HCOOH.

The carboxyl group has priority over alcohol, aldehyde, or ketone functionality in naming. In the latter cases, the prefix *oxo-* is used to locate the carbonyl group of the aldehyde or ketone, as in these examples:

3-oxopropanoic acid

2-bromo-4-oxopentanoic acid

Table 10.1 ▪ Aliphatic Carboxylic Acids

Carbon atoms	Formula	Source	Common name	IUPAC name
1	HCOOH	ants (Latin, *formica*)	formic acid	methanoic acid
2	CH₃COOH	vinegar (Latin, *acetum*)	acetic acid	ethanoic acid
3	CH₃CH₂COOH	milk (Greek, *protos pion*, first fat)	propionic acid	propanoic acid
4	CH₃(CH₂)₂COOH	butter (Latin, *butyrum*)	butyric acid	butanoic acid
5	CH₃(CH₂)₃COOH	valerian root (Latin, *valere*, to be strong)	valeric acid	pentanoic acid
6	CH₃(CH₂)₄COOH	goats (Latin, *caper*)	caproic acid	hexanoic acid
7	CH₃(CH₂)₅COOH	vine blossom (Greek, *oenanthe*)	enanthic acid	heptanoic acid
8	CH₃(CH₂)₆COOH	goats (Latin, *caper*)	caprylic acid	octanoic acid
9	CH₃(CH₂)₇COOH	pelargonium (an herb with stork-shaped seed capsules; Greek, *pelargos*, stork)	pelargonic acid	nonanoic acid
10	CH₃(CH₂)₈COOH	goats (Latin, *caper*)	capric acid	decanoic acid

© Stephen J. Krasemann/Photo Researchers

PROBLEM 10.1 Write the structure for

a. 3-hydroxyhexanoic acid
c. 2-butynoic acid

b. 2-iodo-2-methyloctanoic acid
d. 5-ethyl-6-oxoheptanoic acid

PROBLEM 10.2 Give an IUPAC name for

a. 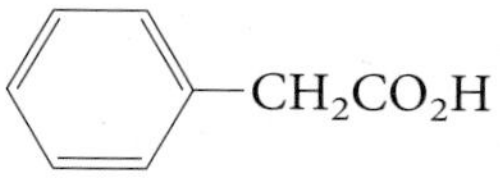 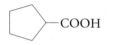—CH₂CO₂H

b. Br₂CHCH₂CO₂H

c. CH₃CH=CHCO₂H

d. (CH₃)₃CCH₂CH₂CO₂H

The root of Garden Heliotrope is a source of valeric acid, CH₃(CH₂)₃COOH.

When the carboxyl group is attached to a ring, the ending -*carboxylic acid* is added to the name of the parent cycloalkane.

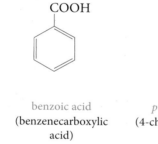

cyclopentanecarboxylic acid 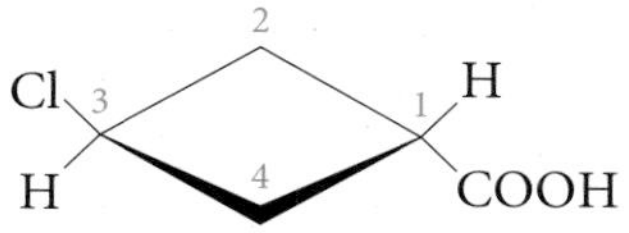   *trans*-3-chlorocyclobutanecarboxylic acid

Aromatic acids are named by attaching the suffix -*oic acid* or -*ic acid* to an appropriate prefix derived from the aromatic hydrocarbon.

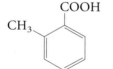

benzoic acid
(benzenecarboxylic
acid)

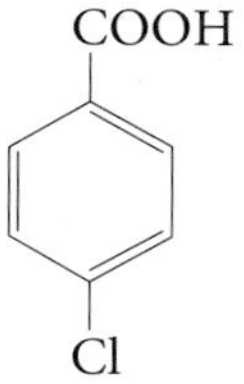

p-chlorobenzoic acid
(4-chlorobenzenecarboxylic
acid)

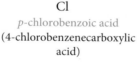

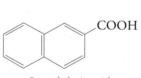

o-toluic acid
(2-methylbenzenecarboxylic
acid)

2-naphthoic acid
(2-naphthalenecarboxylic
acid)

Goats, source of caproic, caprylic, and capric acids: CH₃(CH₂)ₙCOOH, n = 4, 6, 8.

PROBLEM 10.3 Write the structure for

a. *cis*-3-isopropylcyclohexanecarboxylic acid

b. *o*-nitrobenzoic acid

PROBLEM 10.4 Give the correct name for

a.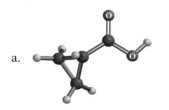

b.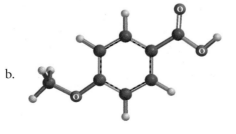

Table 10.2 ■ Aliphatic Dicarboxylic Acids

Formula	Common name	Source	IUPAC name
HOOC—COOH	oxalic acid	plants of the *oxalic* family (for example, sorrel)	ethanedioic acid
HOOC—CH$_2$—COOH	malonic acid	apple (Gk. *malon*)	propanedioic acid
HOOC—(CH$_2$)$_2$—COOH	succinic acid	amber (L. *succinum*)	butanedioic acid
HOOC—(CH$_2$)$_3$—COOH	glutaric acid	gluten	pentanedioic acid
HOOC—(CH$_2$)$_4$—COOH	adipic acid	fat (L. *adeps*)	hexanedioic acid
HOOC—(CH$_2$)$_5$—COOH	pimelic acid	fat (Gk. *pimele*)	heptanedioic acid

Rhubarb, a source of oxalic acid, HOOCCOOH.

Aliphatic dicarboxylic acids are given the suffix *-dioic acid* in the IUPAC system. For example,

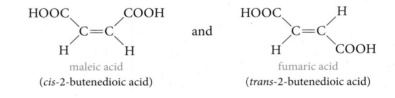

$$\overset{1}{HO_2C}—\overset{2}{CH_2}\overset{3}{CH_2}—\overset{4}{CO_2H} \qquad HO_2C—C\equiv C—CO_2H$$
butanedioic acid   butynedioic acid

Many dicarboxylic acids occur in nature and go by their common names, which are based on their source. Table 10.2 lists some common aliphatic diacids.* The most important commercial compound in this group is adipic acid, used to manufacture nylon.

The two butenedioic acids played a historic role in the discovery of *cis–trans* isomerism and are usually known by their common names maleic** and fumaric*** acid.

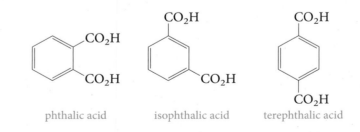

maleic acid   and   fumaric acid
(*cis*-2-butenedioic acid)   (*trans*-2-butenedioic acid)

The three benzenedicarboxylic acids are generally known by their common names.

phthalic acid   isophthalic acid   terephthalic acid

---

*The first letter of each word in the sentence "Oh my, such good apple pie" gives, in order, the first letters of the common names of these acids and can help you to remember them.

**From the Latin *malum* (apple). Malic acid (2-hydroxybutanedioic acid), found in apples, can be dehydrated on heating to give maleic acid.

***Found in fumitory, an herb of the genus *Fumaria*.

Juliette Wade/Garden Picture Library/Photolibrary

All three are important commercial chemicals, used to make polymers and other use-ful materials.

Finally, it is useful to have a name for an **acyl group**. Particular acyl groups are named from the corresponding acid by changing the *-ic* ending to *-yl*.

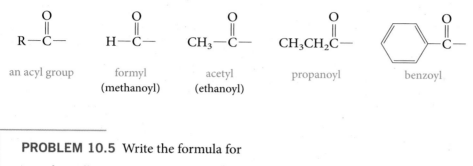

an acyl group	formyl	acetyl	propanoyl	benzoyl
	(methanoyl)	(ethanoyl)		

PROBLEM 10.5 Write the formula for

a. 4-formylbenzoic acid

b. benzoyl bromide

c. octanoyl bromide

d. acetylcyclopentane

10.2 Physical Properties of Acids

The first members of the carboxylic acid series are colorless liquids with sharp or unpleasant odors. Acetic acid, which constitutes about 4% to 5% of vinegar, provides the characteristic odor and flavor. Butyric acid gives rancid butter its disagreeable odor, and the goat acids (caproic, caprylic, and capric in Table 10.1) smell like goats. 3-Methyl-2-hexenoic acid, produced by bacteria, is responsible for the offensive odor of human armpits. Table 10.3 lists some physical properties of selected carboxylic acids.

Carboxylic acids are polar. Like alcohols, they form hydrogen bonds with themselves or with other molecules (Sec. 7.4). Therefore, they have high boiling points for their molecular weights—higher even than those of comparable alcohols. For example, acetic acid and propyl alcohol, which have the same formula weights (60 g/mol), boil at 118°C and 97°C, respectively. Carboxylic acids form dimers, with

Table 10.3 ■ Physical Properties of Some Carboxylic Acids

Name	bp, °C	mp, °C	Solubility, g/100 g H_2O at 25°C
formic acid	101	8	
acetic acid	118	17	
propanoic acid	141	−22	miscible (∞)
butanoic acid	164	−8	
hexanoic acid	205	−1.5	1.0
octanoic acid	240	17	0.06
decanoic acid	270	31	0.01
benzoic acid	249	122	0.4 (but 6.8 at 95°C)

the individual units neatly held together by *two* hydrogen bonds between the electron-rich oxygens and the electron-poor hydrogens (see Sec. 7.4).

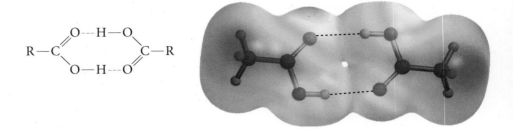

Hydrogen bonding also explains the water solubility of the lower molecular weight carboxylic acids.

10.3 / Acidity and Acidity Constants

Carboxylic acids (RCO_2H) dissociate in water, yielding a carboxylate anion (RCO_2^-) and a hydronium ion.

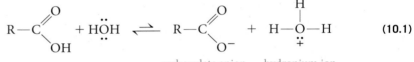

(10.1)

Their acidity constants K_a in water are given by the expression

$$K_a = \frac{[RCO_2^-][H_3O^+]}{[RCO_2H]}$$

(10.2)

(Before proceeding further, it would be a good idea for you to review Secs. 7.5 and 7.6.)

Table 10.4 lists the acidity constants for some carboxylic and other acids. In comparing data in this table, remember that the larger the value of K_a or the smaller the value of pK_a, the stronger the acid.

EXAMPLE 10.1

Which is the stronger acid, formic or acetic, and by how much?

Solution Formic acid is stronger; it has the larger K_a. The ratio of acidities is

$$\frac{2.1 \times 10^{-4}}{1.8 \times 10^{-5}} = 1.17 \times 10^1 = 11.7$$

This means that formic acid is 11.7 times stronger than acetic acid.

PROBLEM 10.6 Using the data given in Table 10.4, determine which is the stronger acid, acetic or dichloroacetic, and by how much.

Before we can explain the acidity differences in Table 10.4, we must examine the structural features that make carboxylic acids acidic.

Name	Formula	K_a	pK_a
Table 10.4 ▪ The Ionization Constants of Some Acids			
formic acid	HCOOH	2.1×10^{-4}	3.68
acetic acid	CH_3COOH	1.8×10^{-5}	4.74
propanoic acid	CH_3CH_2COOH	1.4×10^{-5}	4.85
butanoic acid	$CH_3CH_2CH_2COOH$	1.6×10^{-5}	4.80
chloroacetic acid	$ClCH_2COOH$	1.5×10^{-3}	2.82
dichloroacetic acid	$Cl_2CHCOOH$	5.0×10^{-2}	1.30
trichloroacetic acid	Cl_3CCOOH	2.0×10^{-1}	0.70
2-chlorobutanoic acid	$CH_3CH_2CHClCOOH$	1.4×10^{-3}	2.85
3-chlorobutanoic acid	$CH_3CHClCH_2COOH$	8.9×10^{-5}	4.05
benzoic acid	C_6H_5COOH	6.6×10^{-5}	4.18
o-chlorobenzoic acid	$o\text{-}Cl\text{—}C_6H_4COOH$	12.5×10^{-4}	2.90
m-chlorobenzoic acid	$m\text{-}Cl\text{—}C_6H_4COOH$	1.6×10^{-4}	3.80
p-chlorobenzoic acid	$p\text{-}Cl\text{—}C_6H_4COOH$	1.0×10^{-4}	4.00
p-nitrobenzoic acid	$p\text{-}NO_2\text{—}C_6H_4COOH$	4.0×10^{-4}	3.40
phenol	C_6H_5OH	1.0×10^{-10}	10.00
ethanol	CH_3CH_2OH	1.0×10^{-16}	16.00
water	HOH	1.8×10^{-16}	15.74

10.4 What Makes Carboxylic Acids Acidic?

You might wonder why carboxylic acids are so much more acidic than alcohols, since each class ionizes by losing H^+ from a hydroxyl group. There are two reasons, which can best be illustrated with a specific example.

From Table 10.4, we see that acetic acid is approximately 10^{11}, or 100,000 million, times stronger an acid than ethanol.

$$CH_3CH_2\overset{..}{\underset{..}{O}}H \;\rightleftharpoons\; CH_3CH_2\overset{..}{\underset{..}{O}}:^- + H^+ \qquad K_a = 10^{-16} \qquad \textbf{(10.3)}$$
ethoxide ion

$$CH_3\overset{\overset{\displaystyle\overset{\delta-}{:\!\overset{..}{O}\!:}}{\|}}{C}\text{—}\overset{..}{\underset{..}{O}}H \;\rightleftharpoons\; CH_3\overset{\overset{\displaystyle :O:}{\|}}{C}\text{—}\overset{..}{\underset{..}{O}}:^- + H^+ \qquad K_a = 10^{-5} \qquad \textbf{(10.4)}$$
acetate ion

The only difference between the structures of acetic acid and ethanol is the replacement of a CH_2 group (in ethanol) by a carbonyl group (in acetic acid). But we saw (Sec. 9.5) that a carbonyl carbon atom carries a substantial *positive* charge ($\delta+$). This charge makes it much easier to place a *negative* charge on the adjacent oxygen atom, which is exactly what happens when we ionize a proton from the hydroxyl group.

In ethoxide ion, *the negative charge is localized on a single oxygen atom.* In acetate ion, on the other hand, *the negative charge can be delocalized through resonance.*

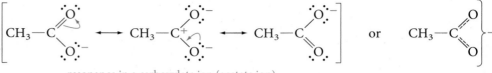

resonance in a carboxylate ion (acetate ion)

The negative charge is spread *equally* over the two oxygens so that each oxygen in the carboxylate ion carries only half the negative charge (Figure 10.1). The acetate ion is stabilized by resonance compared to the ethoxide ion, and this stabilization helps to drive the equilibrium more to the right in eq. 10.4 than in eq. 10.3. Consequently, more H^+ is formed from acetic acid than from ethanol.

▪ Figure 10.1

Electrostatic potential map of (a) acetate ion and (b) ethoxide ion. Note the negative (red) character for both oxygens in (a).

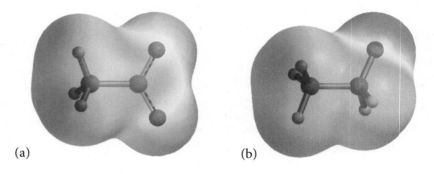

(a)   (b)

For both these reasons, the positive charge on the carbonyl carbon and delocalization of the carboxylate ion, carboxylic acids are much more acidic than alcohols.

EXAMPLE 10.2

Phenoxide ions are also stabilized by resonance (Sec. 7.6). Why are phenols weaker acids than carboxylic acids?

Solution First, the carbon atom to which the hydroxyl group is attached in a phenol is not as positive as a carbonyl carbon. Second, charge delocalization is not as great in phenoxide ions as in carboxylate ions because the contributors to the resonance hybrid are not equivalent. Some of them put the negative charge on carbon instead of on oxygen and disrupt aromaticity.

PROBLEM 10.7 Write two resonance structures for the benzoate ion ($C_6H_5CO_2^-$) that show how the negative charge is delocalized over the two oxygens. Can the negative charge in the benzoate ion be delocalized into the aromatic ring?

Physical data support the importance of resonance in carboxylate ions. In formic acid molecules, the two carbon–oxygen bonds have different lengths. But in sodium formate, both carbon–oxygen bonds of the formate ion are identical, and their length is between those of normal double and single carbon–oxygen bonds.

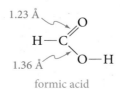

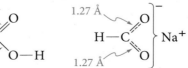

formic acid   sodium formate

Effect of Structure on Acidity; the Inductive Effect Revisited

The data in Table 10.4 show that even among carboxylic acids (where the ionizing functional group is kept constant), acidities can vary depending on what other groups are attached to the molecule. Compare, for example, the K_a of acetic acid with those of mono-, di-, and trichloroacetic acids, and note that the acidity varies by a factor of 10,000.

The most important factor operating here is the inductive effect of the groups close to the carboxyl group. This effect relays charge through bonds, by displacing bonding electrons toward electronegative atoms, or away from electropositive atoms. Recall that *electron-withdrawing groups enhance acidity, and electron-releasing groups reduce acidity* (see Sec. 7.6).

Let us examine the carboxylate ions formed when acetic acid and its chloro derivatives ionize:

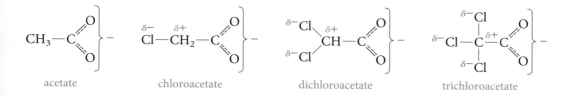

| acetate | chloroacetate | dichloroacetate | trichloroacetate |

Because chlorine is more electronegative than carbon, the C—Cl bond is polarized with the chlorine partially negative and the carbon partially positive. Thus, electrons are pulled away from the carboxylate end of the ion toward the chlorine. The effect tends to spread the negative charge over more atoms than in acetate ion itself and thus stabilizes the ion. The more chlorines, the greater the effect and the greater the strength of the acid.

EXAMPLE 10.3

Explain the acidity order in Table 10.4 for butanoic acid and its 2- and 3-chloro derivatives.

Solution The 2-chloro substituent increases the acidity of butanoic acid substantially, due to its inductive effect. In fact, the effect is about the same as for chloroacetic and acetic acids. The 3-chloro substituent exerts a similar *but much smaller* effect, because the C—Cl bond is now farther away from the carboxylate group. *Inductive effects fall off rapidly with distance.*

PROBLEM 10.8 Account for the relative acidities of benzoic acid and its *ortho, meta,* and *para* chloro derivatives (Table 10.4).

We saw in Example 10.1 that formic acid is a substantially stronger acid than acetic acid. This suggests that the methyl group is more electron-releasing (hence anion-destabilizing and acidity-reducing) than hydrogen. This observation is consistent with what we have already learned about carbocation stabilities—that alkyl groups are more effective than hydrogen atoms at releasing electrons to, and therefore stabilizing, a positive carbon atom (see Sec. 3.10). A similar effect was seen for the relative acidity of ethanol and *t*-butanol in water (see Sec. 7.6).

10.6 Conversion of Acids to Salts

Carboxylic acids, when treated with a strong base, form carboxylate salts. For example,

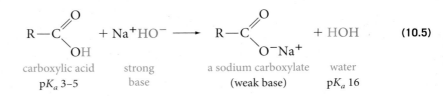

$$R-C\overset{O}{\underset{OH}{\Big\langle}} + Na^+HO^- \longrightarrow R-C\overset{O}{\underset{O^-Na^+}{\Big\langle}} + HOH \qquad \textbf{(10.5)}$$

carboxylic acid | strong | a sodium carboxylate | water
pK_a 3–5 | base | (weak base) | pK$_a$ 16

The salt can be isolated by evaporating the water. As we will see in Chapter 15, carboxylate salts of certain acids are useful as soaps and detergents.

Carboxylate salts are named as shown in the following examples:

$$CH_3-C\overset{O}{\underset{O^-Na^+}{\Big\langle}} \qquad \underset{}{\text{C}_6H_5}-C\overset{O}{\underset{O^-K^+}{\Big\langle}} \qquad \left(CH_3CH_2C\overset{O}{\underset{O^-}{\Big\langle}}\right)_2 Ca^{2+}$$

sodium acetate | potassium benzoate | calcium propanoate
(sodium ethanoate)

The cation is named first, followed by the name of the carboxylate ion, which is obtained by changing the *-ic* ending of the acid to *-ate*.

EXAMPLE 10.4

Name the following carboxylate salt:

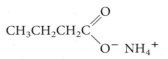

$$CH_3CH_2CH_2C\overset{O}{\underset{O^-\ NH_4^+}{\Big\langle}}$$

Solution The salt is ammonium butanoate (IUPAC) or ammonium butyrate (common).

PROBLEM 10.9 Write an equation, analogous to eq. 10.5, for the preparation of potassium 3-bromooctanoate from the corresponding acid.

10.7 Preparation of Acids

Organic acids can be prepared in many ways, four of which are described here: (1) oxidation of primary alcohols or aldehydes, (2) oxidation of alkyl side chains on aromatic rings, (3) reaction of Grignard reagents with carbon dioxide, and (4) hydrolysis of alkyl cyanides (nitriles).

10.7.a Oxidation of Primary Alcohols and Aldehydes

The oxidation of primary alcohols (Sec. 7.12) and aldehydes (Sec. 9.13) to carboxylic acids has already been mentioned. It is easy to see that these are oxidation reactions because going from an alcohol to an aldehyde to an acid requires replacement of C—H bonds by C—O bonds.

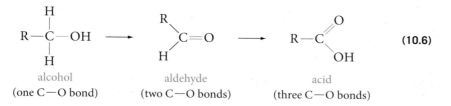

(10.6)

alcohol   aldehyde   acid

(one C—O bond)   (two C—O bonds)   (three C—O bonds)

The most commonly used oxidizing agents for these purposes are potassium permanganate ($KMnO_4$), chromic acid anhydride (CrO_3), nitric acid (HNO_3), and, with aldehydes only, silver oxide (Ag_2O). For specific examples, see eqs. 7.37, 9.37, 9.38, and 9.41.

10.7.b Oxidation of Aromatic Side Chains

Aromatic acids can be prepared by oxidizing an alkyl side chain on an aromatic ring.

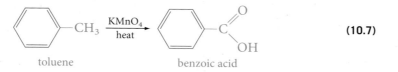

(10.7)

toluene   benzoic acid

This reaction illustrates the striking stability of aromatic rings; it is the alkane-like methyl group, not the aromatic ring, that is oxidized. The reaction involves attack of the oxidant at a C—H bond adjacent to the benzene ring. Longer side chains are also oxidized to a carboxyl group.

(10.8)

If no C—H bond is in the benzylic position, however, the aromatic ring is oxidized, although only under severe reaction conditions.

$$(CH_3)_3C \overset{}{\underset{}{\bigcirc}} \xrightarrow[\text{heat}]{KMnO_4} (CH_3)_3CCO_2H \qquad (10.9)$$

With oxidants other than potassium permanganate, this reaction is commercially important. For example, terephthalic acid (Sec. 10.1), one of the two raw materials needed to manufacture Dacron, is produced in this way, using a cobalt catalyst and air for the oxidation.

(10.10)

p-xylene   terephthalic acid

Phthalic acid, used for making plasticizers, resins, and dyestuffs, is manufactured by similar oxidations, starting with *o*-xylene.

$$\overset{CH_3}{\underset{CH_3}{\bigcirc}} \xrightarrow[CH_3CO_2H]{O_2,\ Co(III)} \overset{COOH}{\underset{COOH}{\bigcirc}} \qquad (10.11)$$

o-xylene   phthalic acid

10.7.c Reaction of Grignard Reagents with Carbon Dioxide

As we saw previously, Grignard reagents add to the carbonyl groups of aldehydes or ketones to give alcohols. In a similar way, they add irreversibly to the carbonyl group of carbon dioxide to give acids, after protonation of the intermediate carboxylate salt with a mineral acid like aqueous HCl.

$$\underset{\substack{R-MgX \\ \delta- \quad \delta+}}{\overset{\substack{\delta+ \quad \delta- \\ O=C=O}}{}} \longrightarrow R-\overset{O}{\overset{\|}{C}}-O^-\overset{+}{M}gX \xrightarrow{H_3O^+} R-\overset{O}{\overset{\|}{C}}-OH + H_2O \qquad (10.12)$$

This reaction gives good yields and is an excellent laboratory method for preparing both aliphatic and aromatic acids. Note that the acid obtained has one more carbon atom than the alkyl or aryl halide from which the Grignard reagent is prepared, so the reaction provides a way to increase the length of a carbon chain.

EXAMPLE 10.5

Show how $(CH_3)_3CBr$ can be converted to $(CH_3)_3CCO_2H$.

Solution $(CH_3)_3CBr \xrightarrow[\text{ether}]{Mg} (CH_3)_3CMgBr \xrightarrow[\text{2. }H_3O^+]{\text{1. }CO_2} (CH_3)_3CCO_2H$

PROBLEM 10.10 Show how 4-methylcyclohexyl chloride can be converted to 4-methylcyclohexanecarboxylic acid.

PROBLEM 10.11 Devise a synthesis of butanoic acid $(CH_3CH_2CH_2CO_2H)$ from 1-propanol $(CH_3CH_2CH_2OH)$.

10.7.d Hydrolysis of Cyanides (Nitriles)

The carbon–nitrogen triple bond of organic cyanides can be hydrolyzed to a carboxyl group. The reaction requires either acid or base. In acid, the nitrogen atom of the cyanide is converted to an ammonium ion.

$$\underset{\substack{\text{a cyanide,} \\ \text{or nitrile}}}{R-C\equiv N} + 2\,H_2O \xrightarrow{HCl} \underset{\text{an acid}}{R-\overset{O}{\overset{\|}{C}}-OH} + \underset{\substack{\text{ammonium} \\ \text{ion}}}{\overset{+}{N}H_4} + Cl^- \qquad (10.13)$$

In base, the nitrogen is converted to ammonia and the organic product is the carboxylate salt, which must be neutralized in a separate step to give the acid.

$$R-C\equiv N + 2\,H_2O \xrightarrow{NaOH} \underset{\text{a carboxylate salt}}{R-\overset{O}{\overset{\|}{C}}-O^-Na^+} + \underset{\text{ammonia}}{NH_3} \qquad (10.14)$$

$$\downarrow H^+$$

$$R-\overset{O}{\overset{\|}{C}}-OH$$

A WORD ABOUT...   Green Chemistry and Ibuprofen: A Case Study

From our increasing need to respect nature and protect our environment has come a new field of chemistry—"green chemistry"—the design and development of chemistry that is environmentally friendly, chemistry that avoids pollution. This presents many challenges to organic synthesis. One notion of an ideal synthesis is one that provides a useful compound in one step with formation of no disposable by-products by a process that consumes little energy. Such a synthesis would certainly be environmentally friendly! This goal is seldom met, but general principles can be applied to try to approach this ideal.

First let us consider some reactions we have learned. Addition reactions (catalytic hydrogenation and Diels–Alder reactions, for example) do not create any by-products. The same can be said for isomerization reactions. Such reactions are said to be "atom economical"—all of the atoms in the reactants appear in the product.* On the other hand, elimination reactions and substitution reactions necessarily produce by-products. This does not mean that they are bad, but if a synthesis can be devised that focuses on addition and isomerization reactions, less attention will have to be devoted to disposing of, or developing uses for, by-products.

Some other general strategies for the development of green chemistry are to use catalysts to accomplish reactions (rather than stoichiometric reagents), to minimize the use of heavy metals as stoichiometric oxidants (for

have been developed, and several of these have been commercialized. The following synthesis begins with the reaction of isobutylbenzene with acetic anhydride using HF as the solvent. This is a variation of the Friedel–Crafts acylation in which the anhydride serves as the source of an acylium ion (see Sec. 4.9.d). Through clever engineering processes, the reaction solvent (HF) serves as both the acid catalyst and solvent (recyclable) for the reaction, and water is the only major reaction by-product. The second step is an addition reaction, catalytic hydrogenation of a ketone to an alcohol (see eq. 9.57). The final step is a reaction we have not discussed that involves palladium-catalyzed "insertion" of carbon monoxide into a benzylic C—O bond to give the carboxylic acid (ibuprofen). This reaction is clearly atom economical. Finally, the chemical yields of all of these reactions are very high, and very little chemical waste is produced.** Although this synthesis is an excellent example of green chemistry in action, there is room for improvement. For example, this produces a racemic mixture of ibuprofen, whereas only the (S)-enantiomer is biologically active (see "A Word About . . . Enantiomers and Biological Activity" in Chapter 5).

It is clear that green chemistry will play an important role in the twenty-first century. This has been recognized by the Presidential Green Chemistry Challenge, initiated by President Clinton in 1995 to reward the development of environmentally benign chemistry. Although biological

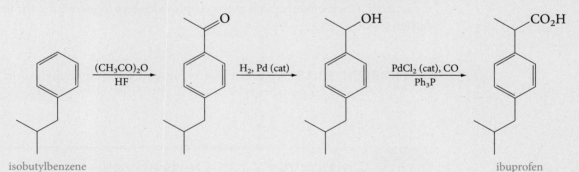

isobutylbenzene

ibuprofen

example, chromium), to focus on the use of molecular oxygen and hydrogen peroxide as oxidants, and to minimize the use of solvents in reactions.

Let us examine a synthesis that does a good job of meeting the goals of green chemistry. Ibuprofen is a very important anti-inflammatory drug. It is the active ingredient of many over-the-counter drugs used to relieve pain from headaches and arthritis. Approximately 25 million pounds of this simple carboxylic acid were produced by synthesis in 2000! A large number of ibuprofen syntheses

processes seldom meet the notion of an ideal synthesis, to strive for this ideal can only lead to new and better chemistry.

See Problem 10.63.

---

*For more on "atom economy," see B. M. Trost, *Angew. Chem. Int. Ed. Engl.* **1995**, *34*, 259. For more on green chemistry, see W. Leiner, *Science* **1999**, *284*, 1780, and visit the following Web site: http://www.epa.gov/greenchemistry.

**For an overview of other syntheses of ibuprofen, consult B. G. Reuben and H. A. Wittcoff, *Pharmaceutical Chemicals in Perspective,* John Wiley and Sons, New York, 1989.

The mechanism of nitrile hydrolysis involves acid or base promoted addition of water across the triple bond. This gives an intermediate imidate that tautomerizes to an amide. The amide is then hydrolyzed to the carboxylic acid. The addition of water to the nitrile resembles the hydration of an alkyne (eq. 3.52). The oxygen of water behaves as a nucleophile and bonds to the electrophilic carbon of the nitrile. Amide hydrolysis will be discussed in Section 10.20.

$$
\underset{\text{nitrile}}{R\overset{\delta+}{-}C\overset{\delta-}{\equiv}N} \xrightarrow[\text{H}^+ \text{ or HO}^-]{\text{H}_2\text{O}} \underset{\text{imidate}}{R\overset{\overset{\displaystyle OH}{|}}{-}C=NH} \xrightarrow{\text{tautomerization}} \underset{\text{amide}}{R\overset{\overset{\displaystyle O}{\|}}{-}C-NH_2} \xrightarrow[\text{H}^+ \text{ or HO}^-]{\text{hydrolysis}} \underset{\text{acid}}{R\overset{\overset{\displaystyle O}{\|}}{-}C-OH} \qquad \textbf{(10.15)}
$$

Alkyl cyanides are generally made from the corresponding alkyl halide (usually primary) and sodium cyanide by an S_N2 displacement, as shown in this synthesis of an acid:

$$
\underset{\substack{\text{propyl bromide}\\ \text{(1-bromopropane)}}}{CH_3CH_2CH_2Br} \xrightarrow{\text{NaCN}} \underset{\substack{\text{butyronitrile}\\ \text{(butanenitrile)}}}{CH_3CH_2CH_2CN} \xrightarrow[\text{H}^+]{\text{H}_2\text{O}} \underset{\substack{\text{butyric acid}\\ \text{(butanoic acid)}}}{CH_3CH_2CH_2CO_2H} + NH_4^+ \qquad \textbf{(10.16)}
$$

> **PROBLEM 10.12** Why is it *not* possible to convert bromobenzene to benzoic acid by the nitrile method? Instead, how could this conversion be accomplished?

Organic cyanides are commonly named after the corresponding acid, by changing the *-ic* or *-oic* suffix to *-onitrile* (hence, butyronitrile in eq. 10.16). In the IUPAC system, the suffix *-nitrile* is added to the name of the hydrocarbon with the same number of carbon atoms (hence butanenitrile in eq. 10.16).

Note that with the hydrolysis of nitriles, as with the Grignard method, the acid obtained has one more carbon atom than the alkyl halide from which the cyanide is prepared. Consequently, both methods provide ways of increasing the length of a carbon chain.

> **PROBLEM 10.13** Write equations for synthesizing phenylacetic acid ($C_6H_5CH_2CO_2H$) from benzyl bromide ($C_6H_5CH_2Br$) by two routes.

10.8 Carboxylic Acid Derivatives

Carboxylic acid derivatives are compounds in which the hydroxyl part of the carboxyl group is replaced by various other groups. All acid derivatives can be hydrolyzed to the corresponding carboxylic acid. In the remainder of this chapter, we will consider the preparation and reactions of the more important of these acid derivatives. Their general formulas are as follows:

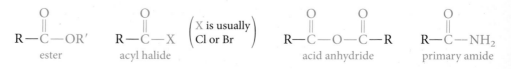

Esters and amides occur widely in nature. Anhydrides, however, are uncommon in nature, and acyl halides are strictly creatures of the laboratory.

10.9 Esters

Esters are derived from acids by replacing the —OH group by an —OR group. They are named in a manner analogous to carboxylic acid salts. The R part of the —OR group is named first, followed by the name of the acid, with the *-ic* ending changed to *-ate.*

An **ester** is a carboxylic acid derivative in which the O—H group is replaced by an —OR group.

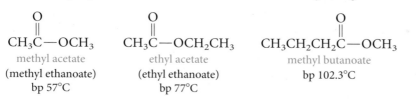

CH₃C—OCH₃ methyl acetate (methyl ethanoate) bp 57°C

CH₃C—OCH₂CH₃ ethyl acetate (ethyl ethanoate) bp 77°C

CH₃CH₂CH₂C—OCH₃ methyl butanoate bp 102.3°C

Notice the different names of the following pair of isomeric esters, where the R and R′ groups are interchanged.

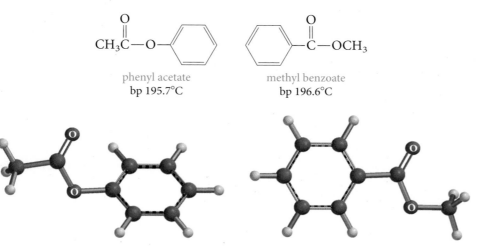

CH₃C—O— phenyl acetate bp 195.7°C

—C—OCH₃ methyl benzoate bp 196.6°C

Esters are named as two words that are *not* run together.

EXAMPLE 10.6

Name CH₃CH₂CO₂CH(CH₃)₂.

Solution The related acid is CH₃CH₂CO₂H, so the last part of the name is *propanoate* (change the *-ic* of propanoic to *-ate*). The alkyl group that replaces the hydrogen is *isopropyl,* or *2-propyl,* so the correct name is *isopropyl propanoate,* or *2-propyl propanoate.*

PROBLEM 10.14 Write the IUPAC name for

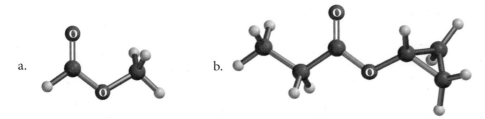

a.   b.

PROBLEM 10.15 Write the structure of

a. 3-pentyl butanoate   b. methyl 2-methylhexanoate

Female elephants release the ester (Z)-7-dodecen-1-yl acetate to attract mates.

Many esters are rather pleasant-smelling substances and are responsible for the flavor and fragrance of many fruits and flowers. Among the more common are pentyl acetate (bananas), octyl acetate (oranges), ethyl butanoate (pineapples), and pentyl butanoate (apricots). Natural flavors can be exceedingly complex. For example, no fewer than 53 esters have been identified among the volatile constituents of Bartlett pears! Mixtures of esters are used as perfumes and artificial flavors. Low-molecular-weight esters are also used by insects and animals to transmit signals. Female elephants release (Z)-7-dodecen-1-yl acetate to signal their readiness to mate. Many moths release the same ester to attract mates.

10.10 Preparation of Esters; Fischer Esterification

When a carboxylic acid and an alcohol are heated in the presence of an acid catalyst (usually HCl or H_2SO_4), an equilibrium is established with the ester and water.

$$\underset{\text{acid}}{R-\overset{\overset{\displaystyle O}{\|}}{C}-OH} + \underset{\text{alcohol}}{HO-R'} \underset{}{\overset{H^+}{\rightleftharpoons}} \underset{\text{ester}}{R-\overset{\overset{\displaystyle O}{\|}}{C}-OR'} + H_2O \qquad \textbf{(10.17)}$$

Fischer esterification is the acid-catalyzed condensation of a carboxylic acid and an alcohol.

The process is called **Fischer esterification** after Emil Fischer (page 163), who developed the method. Although the reaction is an equilibrium, it can be shifted to the right in several ways. If either the alcohol or the acid is inexpensive, a large excess can be used. Alternatively, the ester and/or water may be removed as formed (by distillation, for example), thus driving the reaction forward.

> **PROBLEM 10.16** Following eq. 10.17, write an equation for the preparation of ethyl pentanoate from the correct acid and alcohol.

10.11 The Mechanism of Acid-Catalyzed Esterification; Nucleophilic Acyl Substitution

We can ask the following simple mechanistic question about Fischer esterification: Is the water molecule formed from the hydroxyl group of the acid and the hydrogen of the alcohol (as shown in color in eq. 10.17) or from the hydrogen of the acid and the hydroxyl group of the alcohol? This question may seem rather trivial, but the answer provides a key to understanding much of the chemistry of acids, esters, and their derivatives.

This question was resolved using isotopic labeling. For example, Fischer esterification of benzoic acid with methanol that had been enriched with the ^{18}O isotope of oxygen gave labeled methyl benzoate.*

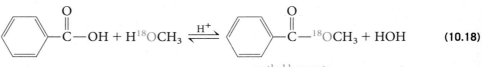

$$\text{methyl benzoate}$$

$$\qquad \textbf{(10.18)}$$

---

*^{18}O is oxygen with two additional neutrons in its nucleus. It is two mass units heavier than ^{16}O. ^{18}O can be distinguished from ^{16}O by mass spectrometry (see Chapter 12).

None of the ^{18}O appeared in the water. Thus it is clear that *the water was formed using the hydroxyl group of the acid and the hydrogen of the alcohol.* In other words, in Fischer esterification, the —OR group of the alcohol replaces the —OH group of the acid.

How can we explain this experimental fact? A mechanism consistent with this result is as follows (the oxygen atom of the alcohol is shown in color so that its path can be traced):

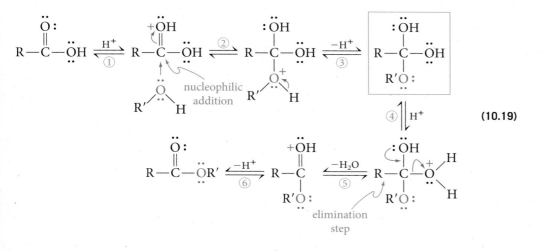

(10.19)

Let us go through this mechanism, which looks more complicated than it really is, one step at a time.

Step 1. The carbonyl group of the acid is reversibly protonated. This step explains how the acid catalyst works. Protonation increases the positive charge on the carboxyl carbon and enhances its reactivity toward nucleophiles (recall the similar effect of acid catalysts with aldehydes and ketones, eq. 9.9). Note that the carbonyl oxygen gets protonated because it is the more basic oxygen.

Step 2. *This is the crucial step.* The alcohol, as a nucleophile, attacks the carbonyl carbon of the protonated acid. This is the step in which the new C—O bond (the ester bond) is formed.

Steps 3 and 4. These steps are equilibria in which oxygens lose or gain a proton. Such acid–base equilibria are reversible and rapid and go on constantly in any acidic solution of an oxygen-containing compound. In step 4, it does not matter which —OH group is protonated since these groups are equivalent.

Step 5. This is the step in which water, one product of the overall reaction, is formed. For this step to occur, an —OH group must be protonated to improve its leaving-group capacity. (This step is similar to the reverse of step 2.)

Step 6. This deprotonation step gives the ester and regenerates the acid catalyst. (This step is similar to the reverse of step 1.)

Some other features of the mechanism in eq. 10.19 are worth examining. The reaction begins with a carboxylic acid, in which the carboxyl carbon is trigonal and sp^2-hybridized. The end product is an ester; the ester carbon is also trigonal and sp^2-hybridized. However, the reaction proceeds through a neutral **tetrahedral intermediate** (shown in a box in eq. 10.19 and in color in eq. 10.20), in which the carbon atom has

A **tetrahedral intermediate** has an sp^3-hybridized carbon atom.

four groups attached to it and is thus sp^3-hybridized. If we omit all of the proton-transfer steps in eq. 10.19, we can focus on this feature of the reaction:

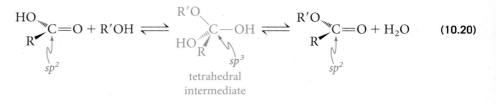

$$(10.20)$$

The net result of this process is substitution of the —OR′ group of the alcohol for the —OH group of the acid. Hence the reaction is referred to as **nucleophilic acyl substitution**. But the reaction is not a direct substitution. Instead, it occurs in two steps: (1) nucleophilic addition, followed by (2) elimination. We will see in the next and subsequent sections of this chapter that this is a general mechanism for nucleophilic substitutions at the carbonyl carbon atoms of carboxylic acid derivatives.

Nucleophilic acyl substitution is substitution of another group for the —OH group of a carboxylic acid.

> **PROBLEM 10.17** Following eq. 10.19, write out the steps in the mechanism for the acid-catalyzed preparation of ethyl acetate from ethanol and acetic acid. In the United States, this method is used commercially to produce more than 100 million pounds of ethyl acetate annually, mainly for use as a solvent in the paint industry, but also as a solvent for nail polish and various glues.

10.12 Lactones

Hydroxy acids contain a hydroxyl group and a carboxyl group.

Lactones are **cyclic esters**.

Hydroxy acids contain both functional groups required for ester formation. If these groups can come in contact through bending of the chain, they may react with one another to form **cyclic esters** called **lactones**. For example,

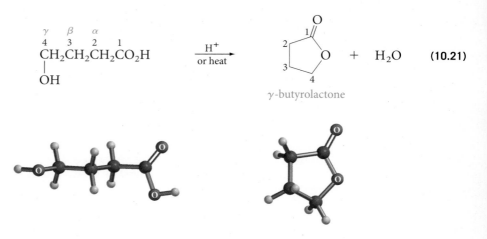

$$(10.21)$$

Most common lactones have five- or six-membered rings, although lactones with smaller or larger rings are known. Two examples of six-membered lactones from nature are coumarin, which is responsible for the pleasant odor of newly mown hay, and nepetalactone, the compound in catnip that excites cats. Erythromycin, widely used as an antibiotic, is an example of a macrocyclic lactone.*

---

*The R and R′ groups in erythromycin are carbohydrate units (see Chapter 16).

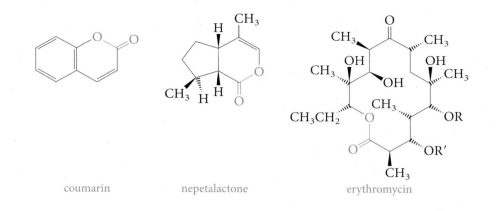

coumarin   nepetalactone   erythromycin

PROBLEM 10.18 Write the steps in the mechanism for the acid-catalyzed reaction in eq. 10.21.

10.13 Saponification of Esters

Esters are commonly hydrolyzed with base. The reaction is called **saponification** (from the Latin *sapon,* soap) because this type of reaction is used to make soaps from fats (Chapter 15). The general reaction is as follows:

Saponification is the hydrolysis of an ester with a base.

$$R-C\overset{O}{\underset{OR'}{}} + Na^+HO^- \xrightarrow[\text{H}_2\text{O}]{\text{heat}} R-C\overset{O}{\underset{O^-Na^+}{}} + R'OH \qquad (10.22)$$

ester   nucleophile   salt of an acid   alcohol

The mechanism is another example of a nucleophilic acyl substitution. It involves nucleophilic attack by hydroxide ion, a strong nucleophile, on the carbonyl carbon of the ester.

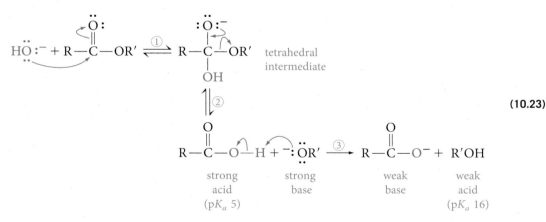

(10.23)

strong   strong   weak   weak
acid   base   base   acid
(pK_a 5)   (pK_a 16)

The key step is nucleophilic addition to the carbonyl group (step 1). The reaction proceeds via a tetrahedral intermediate, but the reactant and the product are trigonal. *Saponification is not reversible;* in the final step (3), the strongly basic alkoxide ion removes a proton from the acid to form a carboxylate ion and an alcohol molecule—a step that proceeds completely in the forward direction.

Saponification is especially useful for breaking down an unknown ester, perhaps isolated from a natural source, into its component acid and alcohol for structural determination.

> **PROBLEM 10.19** Following eq. 10.22, write an equation for the saponification of methyl benzoate.

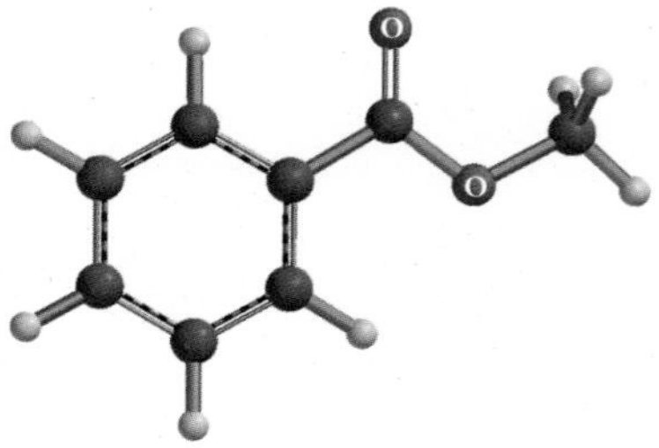

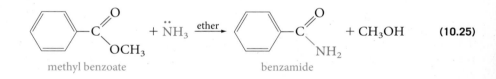

10.14 Ammonolysis of Esters

Ammonia converts esters to amides.

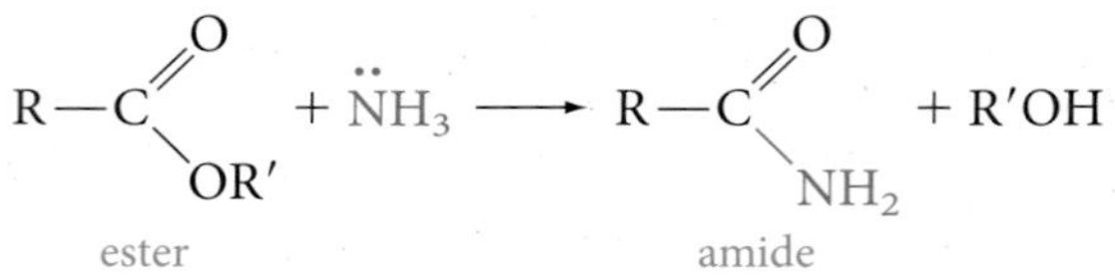

$$R-C{\overset{O}{\underset{OR'}{\big|}}} + \overset{..}{N}H_3 \longrightarrow R-C{\overset{O}{\underset{NH_2}{\big|}}} + R'OH \qquad (10.24)$$

ester   amide

For example,

$$\text{C}{\overset{O}{\underset{OCH_3}{\big|}}} + \overset{..}{N}H_3 \xrightarrow{\text{ether}} \text{C}{\overset{O}{\underset{NH_2}{\big|}}} + CH_3OH \qquad (10.25)$$

methyl benzoate   benzamide

The reaction mechanism is very much like that of saponification. The unshared electron pair on the ammonia nitrogen initiates nucleophilic attack on the ester carbonyl group.

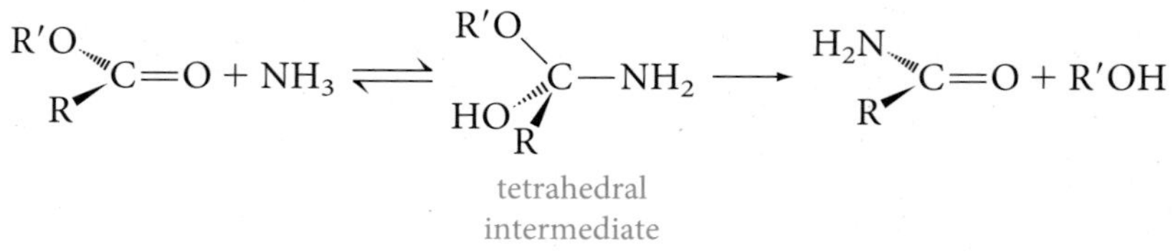

$$\underset{R}{\overset{R'O}{>}}C=O + NH_3 \; \rightleftharpoons \; \underset{HO}{\overset{R'O}{>}}\underset{R}{\overset{|}{C}}-NH_2 \longrightarrow \underset{R}{\overset{H_2N}{>}}C=O + R'OH \qquad (10.26)$$

tetrahedral
intermediate

> **PROBLEM 10.20** The first step in eq. 10.26 really involves two reactions, *addition* of ammonia to the carbonyl carbon to form an ammonium alkoxide followed by a *proton transfer* from the nitrogen to the alkoxide oxygen. Illustrate this process with equations using the arrow-pushing formalism. The second step in eq. 10.26 also involves two steps, *elimination* of an alkoxide $(R'O^-)$ followed by deprotonation of the hydroxyl group. Write a detailed mechanism for these steps.

10.15 Reaction of Esters with Grignard Reagents

Esters react with two equivalents of a Grignard reagent to give tertiary alcohols. The reaction proceeds by *irreversible* nucleophilic attack of the Grignard reagent on the ester carbonyl group. The initial product, a ketone, reacts further in the usual way to give the tertiary alcohol.

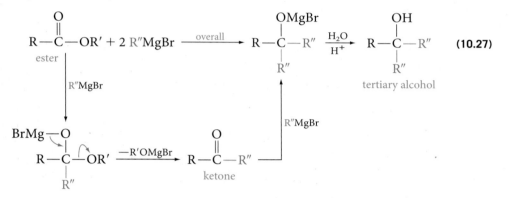

This method is useful for making tertiary alcohols in which at least two of three alkyl groups attached to the hydroxyl-bearing carbon atom are identical.

PROBLEM 10.21 Using eq. 10.27 as a guide, write the structure of the tertiary alcohol that is obtained from

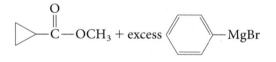

10.16 Reduction of Esters

Esters can be reduced to primary alcohols by lithium aluminum hydride ($LiAlH_4$).

$$R-\overset{\overset{O}{\|}}{C}-OR' \xrightarrow[\text{ether}]{LiAlH_4} RCH_2OH + R'OH \qquad \textbf{(10.28)}$$

ester   primary alcohol

The mechanism is similar to the hydride reduction of aldehydes and ketones (eq. 9.33).

$$R-\overset{\overset{O}{\|}}{C}-OR' \xrightarrow{H-\bar{A}lH_3} R-\overset{\overset{O-\bar{A}lH_3}{|}}{\underset{H}{C}}-OR' \xrightarrow{-\bar{A}lH_3(OR')} R-\overset{\overset{O}{\|}}{C}-H \xrightarrow{H-\bar{A}lH_2(OR')}$$

ester   aldehyde

$$R-\overset{\overset{O-\bar{A}lH_2(OR')}{|}}{\underset{H}{C}}-H \xrightarrow[H^+]{H_2O} RCH_2OH + R'OH \qquad \textbf{(10.29)}$$

                                    1° alcohol

The intermediate aldehyde is not usually isolable and reacts rapidly with additional hydride to produce the alcohol.

Thus, with $LiAlH_4$, it is possible to reduce the carbonyl group of an ester without reducing a C=C bond in the same molecule. For example,

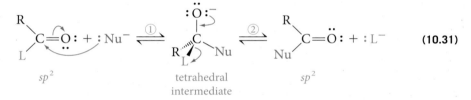

$$CH_3CH{=}CHC{-}OCH_2CH_3 \xrightarrow[\text{2. } H_2O, H^+]{\text{1. } LiAlH_4} CH_3CH{=}CHCH_2OH + CH_3CH_2OH \qquad \textbf{(10.30)}$$

ethyl 2-butenoate   2-buten-1-ol

10.17 The Need for Activated Acyl Compounds

As we have seen, most reactions of carboxylic acids, esters, and related compounds involve, as the first step, nucleophilic attack on the carbonyl carbon atom. Examples are Fischer esterification, saponification and ammonolysis of esters, and the first stage of the reaction of esters with Grignard reagents or lithium aluminum hydride. All of these reactions can be summarized by a single mechanistic equation:

$$
\underset{sp^2}{\overset{R}{\underset{L}{\bigg\backslash}}C{=}\overset{..}{\underset{..}{O}}{:} + {:}Nu^-} \underset{①}{\rightleftharpoons} \underset{\substack{\text{tetrahedral}\\\text{intermediate}}}{\overset{:\overset{..}{O}{:}^-}{\underset{R\overset{\text{\tiny''}}{/}\diagdown Nu}{\underset{L}{\overset{|}{C}}}}} \underset{②}{\rightleftharpoons} \underset{sp^2}{\overset{R}{\underset{Nu}{\bigg\backslash}}C{=}\overset{..}{\underset{..}{O}}{:} + {:}L^-} \qquad \textbf{(10.31)}
$$

The carbonyl carbon, initially trigonal, is attacked by a nucleophile $Nu{:}^-$ to form a tetrahedral intermediate (step 1). Loss of a leaving group $:L^-$ (step 2) then regenerates the carbonyl group with its trigonal carbon atom. The net result is the replacement of L by Nu.

Biochemists look at eq. 10.31 in a slightly different way. They refer to the overall reaction as an **acyl transfer**. The acyl group is transferred from L in the starting material to Nu in the product.

Regardless of how we consider the reaction, one important feature that can affect the rate of both steps is the nature of the leaving group. *The rates of both steps in a nucleophilic acyl substitution reaction are enhanced by increasing the electron-withdrawing properties of the leaving group.* Step 1 is favored because the more electronegative L is, the more positive the carbonyl carbon becomes, and therefore the more susceptible the carbonyl carbon is to nucleophilic attack. Step 2 is also facilitated because the more electronegative L is, the better leaving group it becomes.

In general, esters are *less* reactive toward nucleophiles than are aldehydes or ketones because the positive charge on the carbonyl carbon in esters can be delocalized to the oxygen atom. Consequently, the ester is more stable and less prone to attack.

> An **acyl transfer** is the transfer of an acyl group from a leaving group to a nucleophile.

The carbonyl carbon has a partial positive charge.

The positive charge can be delocalized to the oxygen.

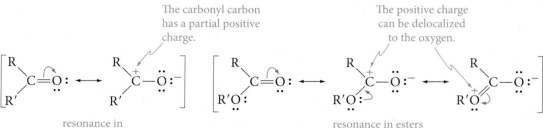

resonance in aldehydes and ketones   resonance in esters

Now let us examine some of the ways in which the carboxyl group can be modified to *increase* its reactivity toward nucleophiles.

10.18 Acyl Halides

Acyl halides are among the most reactive of carboxylic acid derivatives. *Acyl chlorides* are more common and less expensive than bromides or iodides. They can be prepared from acids by reaction with thionyl chloride.

> An **acyl halide** is a carboxylic acid derivative in which the —OH group is replaced by a halogen atom.

$$R-\overset{\overset{\displaystyle O}{\|}}{C}-OH + SOCl_2 \longrightarrow R-\overset{\overset{\displaystyle O}{\|}}{C}-Cl + HCl + SO_2 \qquad \textbf{(10.32)}$$

The mechanism is similar to that for the formation of chlorides from alcohols and thionyl chloride. The hydroxyl group is converted to a good leaving group by thionyl chloride, followed by a nucleophilic acyl substitution in which chloride is the nucleophile (compare with Sec. 7.10). Phosphorus pentachloride and other reagents can also be used to prepare acyl chlorides from carboxylic acids.

$$R-\overset{\overset{\displaystyle O}{\|}}{C}-OH + PCl_5 \longrightarrow R-\overset{\overset{\displaystyle O}{\|}}{C}-Cl + HCl + POCl_3 \qquad \textbf{(10.33)}$$

Acyl halides react rapidly with most nucleophiles. For example, they are rapidly hydrolyzed by water.

$$CH_3-\overset{\overset{\displaystyle O}{\|}}{C}-Cl + HOH \xrightarrow{\text{rapid}} CH_3-\overset{\overset{\displaystyle O}{\|}}{C}-OH + HCl \qquad \textbf{(10.34)}$$

acetyl chloride   acetic acid   (fumes)

For this reason, acyl halides have irritating odors. Benzoyl chloride (eq. 10.35), for example, is a lachrymator (tear gas).

EXAMPLE 10.7

Write a mechanism for the reaction shown in eq. 10.34.

Solution Nucleophilic addition of water to the carbonyl group, followed by proton transfer and elimination of HCl from the tetrahedral intermediate, gives the observed products.

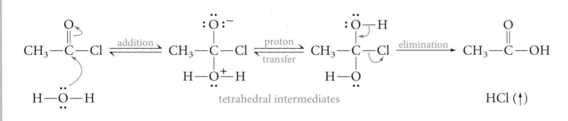

Acyl halides react rapidly with alcohols to form esters.

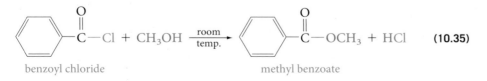

benzoyl chloride   methyl benzoate

Indeed, the most common way to prepare an ester *in the laboratory* is to convert an acid to its acid chloride, then react the latter with an alcohol. Even though two steps are necessary (compared with one step for Fischer esterification), the method may be preferable, especially if either the acid or the alcohol is expensive. (Recall that Fischer esterification is an equilibrium reaction and must often be carried out with a large excess of one of the reactants.)

> **PROBLEM 10.22** Rewrite eq. 10.32 to show the preparation of benzoyl chloride (see eq. 10.35).
>
> **PROBLEM 10.23** Explain why acyl halides may be irritating to the nose.
>
> **PROBLEM 10.24** Write a mechanism for the reaction shown in eq. 10.35.

Acyl halides react rapidly with ammonia to form amides.

$$CH_3\overset{\overset{\displaystyle O}{\|}}{C}\!-\!Cl \;+\; 2\,NH_3 \;\longrightarrow\; CH_3\overset{\overset{\displaystyle O}{\|}}{C}\!-\!NH_2 \;+\; NH_4^+\; Cl^- \qquad \textbf{(10.36)}$$

acetyl chloride   acetamide

The reaction is much more rapid than the ammonolysis of esters. Two equivalents of ammonia are required, however—one to form the amide and one to neutralize the hydrogen chloride.

Acyl halides are used to synthesize aromatic ketones, through Friedel–Crafts acylation of aromatic rings (review Sec. 4.9.d).

> **PROBLEM 10.25** Devise a synthesis of 4-methylphenyl propyl ketone from toluene and butanoic acid as starting materials.

10.19 Acid Anhydrides

Acid anhydrides are carboxylic acid derivatives formed by condensing two carboxylic acid molecules.

Acid anhydrides are derived from acids by removing water from two carboxyl groups and connecting the fragments.

two acid molecules   an acid anhydride

The most important commercial aliphatic anhydride is acetic anhydride ($R=CH_3$). About 1 million tons are manufactured annually, mainly to react with alcohols to form acetates. The two most common uses are in making cellulose acetate (rayon) and aspirin (acetylsalicylic acid).

The name of an anhydride is obtained by naming the acid from which it is derived and replacing the word *acid* with *anhydride*.

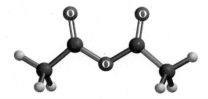

$$CH_3\!-\!\overset{\overset{\displaystyle O}{\|}}{C}\!-\!O\!-\!\overset{\overset{\displaystyle O}{\|}}{C}\!-\!CH_3$$

ethanoic anhydride or acetic anhydride

> **PROBLEM 10.26** Write the structural formula for
>
> a. butanoic anhydride   b. benzoic anhydride

Anhydrides are prepared by dehydration of acids. Dicarboxylic acids with appropriately spaced carboxyl groups lose water on heating to form cyclic anhydrides with five- and six-membered rings. For example,

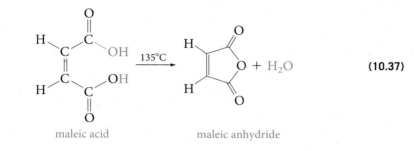

maleic acid   maleic anhydride

(10.37)

PROBLEM 10.27 Predict and name the product of the following reaction:

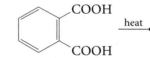

COOH

heat →

COOH

PROBLEM 10.28 Do you expect fumaric acid (page 290) to form a cyclic anhydride on heating? Explain.

Anhydrides can also be prepared from acid chlorides and carboxylate salts in a reaction that occurs by a nucleophilic acyl substitution mechanism. This is a good method for preparing anhydrides derived from two different carboxylic acids, called **mixed anhydrides**.

Mixed anhydrides are prepared from two different carboxylic acids.

$$CH_3CH_2CH_2 - \overset{\overset{\displaystyle O}{\|}}{C} - Cl + Na^{+-}O - \overset{\overset{\displaystyle O}{\|}}{C} - CH_3 \longrightarrow$$

$$CH_3CH_2CH_2 - \overset{\overset{\displaystyle O}{\|}}{C} - O - \overset{\overset{\displaystyle O}{\|}}{C} - CH_3 + NaCl \qquad \textbf{(10.38)}$$

butanoic ethanoic anhydride

Anhydrides undergo nucleophilic acyl substitution reactions. They are more reactive than esters, but less reactive than acyl halides, toward nucleophiles. Some typical reactions of acetic anhydride follow:

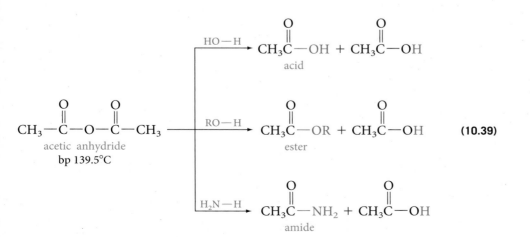

A WORD ABOUT... Thioesters, Nature's Acyl-Activating Groups

Acyl transfer plays an important role in many biochemical processes. However, acyl halides and anhydrides are far too corrosive to be cell constituents—they are hydrolyzed quite rapidly by water and are therefore incompatible with cellular fluid. Most ordinary esters, on the other hand, react too slowly with nucleophiles for acyl transfer to be carried out efficiently at body temperatures. Consequently, other functional groups have evolved to activate acyl groups in the cell. The most important of these is **coenzyme A** (the A stands for acetylation, one of the functions of this enzyme). Coenzyme A is a complex *thiol* (Figure 10.2). It is usually abbreviated by the symbol **CoA—SH**. Though its structure is made up of three parts—adenosine diphosphate (ADP), pantothenic acid (a vitamin), and 2-aminoethanethiol—it is the thiol group that gives coenzyme A its most important functions.

Coenzyme A can be converted to **thioesters**, the active acyl-transfer agents in the cell. Of the thioesters that coenzyme A forms, the acetyl ester, called **acetyl-coenzyme A** and abbreviated as

$$CH_3\overset{\overset{O}{\|}}{C}-S-CoA$$

is the most important. Acetyl-CoA reacts with many nucleophiles to transfer the acetyl group.

$$CH_3\overset{\overset{O}{\|}}{C}-S-CoA + Nu: \xrightarrow[enzyme]{H_2O}$$

acetyl-CoA

$$CH_3\overset{\overset{O}{\|}}{C}-Nu + CoA-SH$$

The reactions are usually enzyme-mediated and occur rapidly at ordinary cell temperatures.

Why are thioesters superior to ordinary esters as acyl-transfer agents? Part of the answer lies in the acidity difference between alcohols and thiols (Sec. 7.17). Since thiols are much stronger acids than are alcohols, their conjugate bases, ⁻SR, are much weaker bases than ⁻OR. Thus, the —SR group of thioesters is a much better leaving group, in nucleophilic substitution reactions, than is the —OR group of ordinary esters. Thioesters are not so reactive that they hydrolyze in cellular fluid, but they are appreciably more reactive than simple esters. Nature makes use of this feature.

See Problem 10.64.

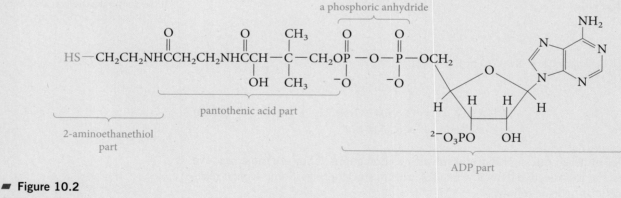

■ **Figure 10.2**
Coenzyme A.

Water hydrolyzes an anhydride to the corresponding acid. Alcohols give esters, and ammonia gives amides. In each case, one equivalent of acid is also produced.

PROBLEM 10.29 Write an equation for the reaction of acetic anhydride with 1-pentanol ($CH_3CH_2CH_2CH_2CH_2OH$).

PROBLEM 10.30 Write equations for the reactions of maleic anhydride (see eq. 10.37) with

a. water   b. 1-propanol   c. ammonia

The reaction of acetic anhydride with salicylic acid (*o*-hydroxybenzoic acid) is used to synthesize aspirin. In this reaction, the phenolic hydroxyl group is **acetylated** (converted to its acetate ester).

Annual aspirin production in the United States is more than 24 million pounds, enough to produce over 30 billion standard 5-grain (325 mg) tablets. Aspirin is widely used, either by itself or mixed with other drugs, as an analgesic and antipyretic. It is not without dangers, however. Repeated use may cause gastrointestinal bleeding, and a large single dose (10 to 20 g) can cause death.

An alcohol is said to be **acetylated** when converted to its acetate ester.

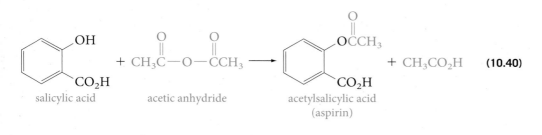

salicylic acid   acetic anhydride   acetylsalicylic acid
(aspirin)   **(10.40)**

10.20 Amides

Amides are the least reactive of the common carboxylic acid derivatives. They occur widely in nature. The most important amides are the proteins, whose chemistry we will discuss in Chapter 17. Here we will concentrate on just a few properties of simple amides.

Amides are carboxylic acid derivatives in which the —OH group is replaced by —NH_2, —NHR, or —NR_2.

Primary amides have the general formula $RCONH_2$. They can be prepared by the reaction of ammonia with esters (eq. 10.24), with acyl halides (eq. 10.36), or with acid anhydrides (eq. 10.39). Amides can also be prepared by heating the ammonium salts of acids.

$$R-\overset{O}{\overset{\|}{C}}-OH + NH_3 \longrightarrow R-\overset{O}{\overset{\|}{C}}-O^-NH_4^+ \xrightarrow{heat} R-\overset{O}{\overset{\|}{C}}-NH_2 + H_2O \quad \textbf{(10.41)}$$

ammonium salt   amide

Amides are named by replacing the *-ic* or *-oic* ending of the acid name, either the common or the IUPAC name, with the *-amide* ending.

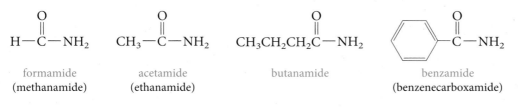

formamide   acetamide   butanamide   benzamide
(methanamide)   (ethanamide)   (benzenecarboxamide)

PROBLEM 10.31

a. Name $(CH_3)_2CHCH_2CONH_2$
b. Write the structure of 1-phenylcyclopentanecarboxamide

The above examples are all primary amides. Secondary and tertiary amides, in which one or both of the hydrogens on the nitrogen atom are replaced by organic groups, are described in the next chapter.

Amides have a planar geometry. Even though the carbon–nitrogen bond is normally written as a single bond, rotation around that bond is restricted because of resonance.

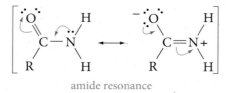

amide resonance

The dipolar contributor is so important that the carbon–nitrogen bond behaves much like a double bond. Consequently, the nitrogen and the carbonyl carbon, and the two atoms attached to each of them, lie in the same plane, and rotation at the C—N bond is restricted. Indeed, the C—N bond in amides is only 1.32 Å long—much shorter than the usual carbon–nitrogen single bond length (which is about 1.47 Å).

As the dipolar resonance contributor suggests, amides are highly polar and form strong hydrogen bonds.

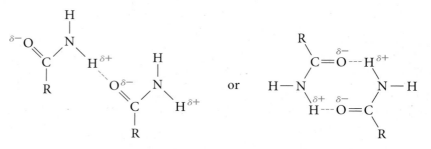

Amides have exceptionally high boiling points for their molecular weights, although alkyl substitution on the nitrogen lowers the boiling and melting points by decreasing the hydrogen-bonding possibilities, as shown in the following two pairs of compounds:

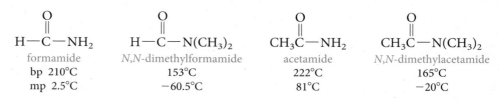

formamide	*N,N*-dimethylformamide	acetamide	*N,N*-dimethylacetamide
bp 210°C	153°C	222°C	165°C
mp 2.5°C	−60.5°C	81°C	−20°C

PROBLEM 10.32 Show that hydrogen bonding is possible for acetamide, but not for *N,N*-dimethylacetamide.

Like other acid derivatives, amides react with nucleophiles. For example, they can be hydrolyzed by water.

$$\underset{\text{amide}}{R-\overset{\overset{\textstyle O}{\|}}{C}-NH_2} + H-OH \xrightarrow[\text{HO}^-]{\text{H}^+ \text{ or}} \underset{\text{acid}}{R-\overset{\overset{\textstyle O}{\|}}{C}-OH} + NH_3 \qquad \textbf{(10.42)}$$

The reactions are slow, and prolonged heating or acid or base catalysis is usually necessary.

PROBLEM 10.33 Using eq. 10.42 as a model, write an equation for the hydrolysis of acetamide.

Amides can be reduced by lithium aluminum hydride to give amines.

$$\underset{\text{amide}}{R-\overset{\overset{\displaystyle O}{\|}}{C}-NH_2} \xrightarrow[\text{ether}]{\text{LiAlH}_4} \underset{\text{amine}}{RCH_2NH_2} \qquad \qquad \textbf{(10.43)}$$

This is an excellent way to make primary amines, whose chemistry is discussed in the next chapter.

> **PROBLEM 10.34** Using eq. 10.43 as a model, write an equation for the reduction of acetamide with LiAlH$_4$.

Urea is a special amide, a diamide of carbonic acid. A colorless, water-soluble, crystalline solid, urea is the normal end product of protein metabolism. An average adult excretes approximately 30 g of urea in his or her urine daily. Urea is produced commercially from carbon dioxide and ammonia, mainly for use as a fertilizer.

$$\underset{\text{carbonic acid}}{HO-\overset{\overset{\displaystyle O}{\|}}{C}-OH} \qquad \underset{\substack{\text{urea}\\\text{mp 133°C}}}{H_2N-\overset{\overset{\displaystyle O}{\|}}{C}-NH_2}$$

10.21 / A Summary of Carboxylic Acid Derivatives

We have studied a rather large number of reactions in this chapter. However, most of them can be summarized in a single chart, shown in Table 10.5, and visually presented in Figure 10.3.

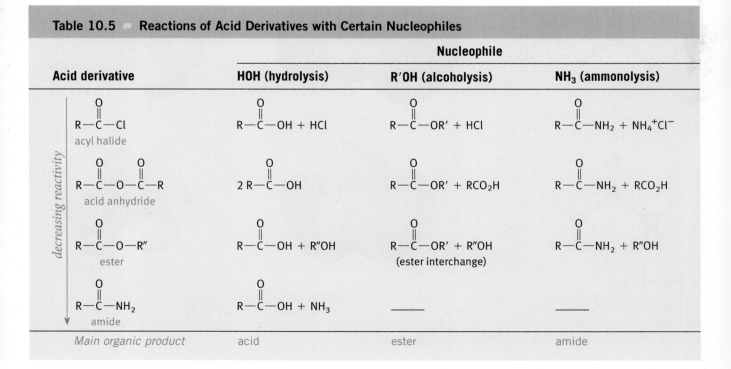

Table 10.5 ▬ Reactions of Acid Derivatives with Certain Nucleophiles

Acid derivative	Nucleophile		
	HOH (hydrolysis)	R'OH (alcoholysis)	NH$_3$ (ammonolysis)
$R-\overset{O}{\underset{\|}{C}}-Cl$ acyl halide	$R-\overset{O}{\underset{\|}{C}}-OH$ + HCl	$R-\overset{O}{\underset{\|}{C}}-OR'$ + HCl	$R-\overset{O}{\underset{\|}{C}}-NH_2$ + NH$_4^+$Cl$^-$
$R-\overset{O}{\underset{\|}{C}}-O-\overset{O}{\underset{\|}{C}}-R$ acid anhydride	$2\,R-\overset{O}{\underset{\|}{C}}-OH$	$R-\overset{O}{\underset{\|}{C}}-OR'$ + RCO$_2$H	$R-\overset{O}{\underset{\|}{C}}-NH_2$ + RCO$_2$H
$R-\overset{O}{\underset{\|}{C}}-O-R''$ ester	$R-\overset{O}{\underset{\|}{C}}-OH$ + R''OH	$R-\overset{O}{\underset{\|}{C}}-OR'$ + R''OH (ester interchange)	$R-\overset{O}{\underset{\|}{C}}-NH_2$ + R''OH
$R-\overset{O}{\underset{\|}{C}}-NH_2$ amide	$R-\overset{O}{\underset{\|}{C}}-OH$ + NH$_3$	_____	_____
Main organic product	acid	ester	amide

decreasing reactivity (left margin, pointing downward)

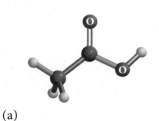

(a)

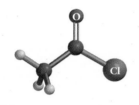
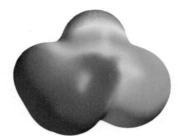

(b)

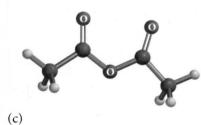
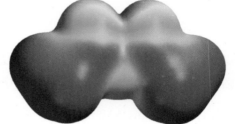

(c)

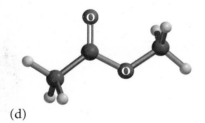
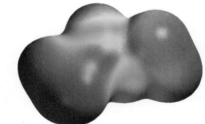

(d)

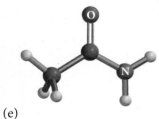

(e)

▬ Figure 10.3

Three-dimensional representations and electrostatic potential maps of representative carboxylic acid derivatives. Ball-and-stick structures are provided on the left, electrostatic potential maps in the center, and space-filling models on the right for (a) acetic acid (CH_3CO_2H); (b) acetyl chloride ($CH_3C(=O)Cl$); (c) acetic anhydride ($CH_3C(=O)-O-C(=O)CH_3$); (d) methyl acetate ($CH_3C(=O)OCH_3$); and (e) acetamide ($CH_3C(=O)NH_2$).

The four types of acid derivatives are listed at the left of the chart in order of decreasing reactivity toward nucleophiles. Three common nucleophiles are listed across the top. Note that the main organic product in each column is the same, regardless of which type of carboxylic acid derivative we start with. For example, hydrolysis gives the corresponding organic acid, whether we start with an acyl halide, acid anhydride, ester, or amide. Similarly, alcoholysis gives an ester, and ammonolysis gives an amide. Note also that the *other* reaction product is generally the same from a given carboxylic acid derivative (horizontally across the table), regardless of the nucleophile. For example, starting with an ester, RCO_2R'', we obtain as the second product the alcohol $R''OH$, regardless of whether the reaction type is hydrolysis, alcoholysis, or ammonolysis.

All of the reactions in Table 10.5 take place via attack of the nucleophile on the carbonyl carbon of the carboxylic acid derivative, as described in eq. 10.31. Indeed, most of the reactions from Sections 10.10 through 10.19 occur by that same mechanism. We can sometimes use this idea to predict new reactions.

For example, the reaction of esters with Grignard reagents (eq. 10.27) involves nucleophilic attack of the Grignard reagent on the ester's carbonyl group. Keeping in mind that all carboxylic acid derivatives are susceptible to nucleophilic attack, it is understandable that acyl halides also react with Grignard reagents to give tertiary alcohols. The first steps involve ketone formation as follows:

$$R-\overset{\overset{\displaystyle O}{\|}}{C}-Cl + R'MgX \longrightarrow R-\overset{\overset{\displaystyle O^-MgX}{|}}{\underset{\underset{\displaystyle R'}{|}}{C}}-Cl \longrightarrow R-\overset{\overset{\displaystyle O}{\|}}{C}-R' + MgXCl \qquad (10.44)$$

The ketone can sometimes be isolated, but usually it reacts with a second mole of Grignard reagent to give a tertiary alcohol.

$$R-\overset{\overset{\displaystyle O}{\|}}{C}-R' + R'MgX \longrightarrow R-\overset{\overset{\displaystyle O^-MgX}{|}}{\underset{\underset{\displaystyle R'}{|}}{C}}-R' \xrightarrow{H_3O^+} R-\overset{\overset{\displaystyle OH}{|}}{\underset{\underset{\displaystyle R'}{|}}{C}}-R' \qquad (10.45)$$

> **PROBLEM 10.35** Predict the product from the reaction of phenylmagnesium bromide (C_6H_5MgBr) with benzoyl chloride (C_6H_5COCl).

10.22 The α-Hydrogen of Esters; the Claisen Condensation

In this final section, we describe an important reaction of esters that resembles the aldol condensation of aldehydes and ketones (Sec. 9.17). It makes use of the α-hydrogen (see pages 272–275) of an ester.

An **ester enolate** is the anion
formed by removing the α-hydrogen
of an ester.

Being adjacent to a carbonyl group, the α-hydrogens of an ester are weakly acidic ($pK_a \sim 23$) and can be removed by a *strong base*. The product is an **ester enolate**.

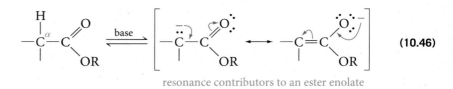

resonance contributors to an ester enolate   **(10.46)**

Common bases used for this purpose are sodium alkoxides or sodium hydride. The ester enolate, once formed, can act as a carbon nucleophile and add to the carbonyl group of another ester molecule. This reaction is called the Claisen condensation. It is a way of making β-keto esters. We will use ethyl acetate as an example to see how the reaction works.

Treatment of ethyl acetate with sodium ethoxide in ethanol produces the β-keto ester, ethyl acetoacetate:

$$CH_3\overset{\overset{O}{\|}}{C}-OCH_2CH_3 + H-\overset{\alpha}{CH_2}-\overset{\overset{O}{\|}}{C}-OCH_2CH_3 \xrightarrow[\substack{\text{in ethanol} \\ \text{2. } H_3O^+}]{\text{1. NaOCH}_2CH_3}$$

ethyl acetate   ethyl acetate

$$CH_3\overset{\overset{O}{\|}}{C}-CH_2-\overset{\overset{O}{\|}}{C}-OCH_2CH_3 + CH_3CH_2OH \quad \textbf{(10.47)}$$

ethyl acetoacetate
(ethyl 3-oxobutanoate)

The Claisen condensation takes place in three steps.

Step 1. $\;CH_3\overset{\overset{O}{\|}}{C}-OCH_2CH_3 + Na^{+-}OCH_2CH_3 \rightleftharpoons$

sodium ethoxide

$$Na^{+-}CH_2\overset{\overset{O}{\|}}{C}OCH_2CH_3 + CH_3CH_2OH \quad \textbf{(10.48)}$$

ester enolate

Step 2. $\;CH_3\overset{\overset{O}{\|}}{C}-OCH_2CH_3 + {}^-CH_2\overset{\overset{O}{\|}}{C}OCH_2CH_3 \rightleftharpoons$

$$CH_3\overset{\overset{\overline{O}}{|}}{\underset{\underset{O}{\|}}{\underset{CH_2C-OCH_2CH_3}{C}}}OCH_2CH_3 \rightleftharpoons CH_3\overset{\overset{O}{\|}}{C}CH_2\overset{\overset{O}{\|}}{C}OCH_2CH_3 + {}^-OCH_2CH_3 \quad \textbf{(10.49)}$$

β-keto ester

Step 3. $\;CH_3\overset{\overset{O}{\|}}{C}CH_2\overset{\overset{O}{\|}}{C}OCH_2CH_3 + {}^-OCH_2CH_3 \longrightarrow$

$$CH_3\overset{\overset{O}{\|}}{C}-\overset{-}{C}H-\overset{\overset{O}{\|}}{C}OCH_2CH_3 + CH_3CH_2OH \quad \textbf{(10.50)}$$

enolate ion of a β-keto ester

In step 1, the base (sodium ethoxide) removes an α-hydrogen from the ester to form an ester enolate. In step 2, this ester enolate, acting as a nucleophile, adds to the carbonyl group of a second ester molecule, displacing ethoxide ion. This step follows the mechanism in eq. 10.31 and proceeds through a tetrahedral intermediate. These first two steps of the reaction are completely reversible.

Step 3 drives the equilibrium forward. In this step, the β-keto ester is converted to *its* enolate anion. The methylene (CH_2) hydrogens in ethyl acetoacetate are α *to two carbonyl groups* and hence are appreciably more acidic than ordinary α-hydrogens. They have a pK_a of 12 and are easily removed by the base (ethoxide ion) to form a resonance-stabilized β-keto enolate ion, *with the negative charge delocalized to both carbonyl oxygen atoms.*

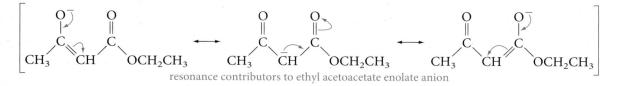

resonance contributors to ethyl acetoacetate enolate anion

To complete the Claisen condensation, the solution is acidified, to regenerate the β-keto ester from its enolate anion.

EXAMPLE 10.8

Identify the product of the Claisen condensation of ethyl propanoate:

$$CH_3CH_2\overset{\displaystyle O}{\overset{\|}{C}}-OCH_2CH_3$$

Solution The product is

$$CH_3CH_2\overset{\displaystyle O}{\overset{\|}{\underset{\beta}{C}}}-\underset{\underset{\displaystyle CH_3}{|}}{\overset{\alpha}{C}H}-\overset{\displaystyle O}{\overset{\|}{C}}OCH_2CH_3$$

The α-carbon of one ester molecule displaces the —OR group and becomes joined to the carbonyl carbon of the other ester. The product is always a β-keto ester.

PROBLEM 10.36 Using eqs. 10.48 through 10.50 as a model, write out the steps in the mechanism for the Claisen condensation of ethyl propanoate.

The Claisen condensation, like the aldol condensation (Sec. 9.17), is useful for making new carbon–carbon bonds. The resulting β-keto esters can be converted to a variety of useful products. For example, ethyl acetate can be converted to ethyl butanoate by the following sequence.

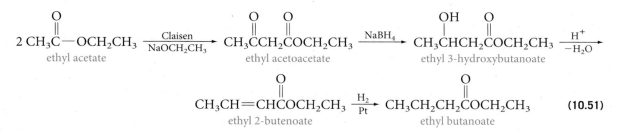

In this way, the acetate chain is lengthened by two carbon atoms. Nature makes use of a similar process, catalyzed by various enzymes, to construct the long-chain carboxylic acids that are components of fats and oils (Chapter 15).

REACTION SUMMARY

1. Preparation of Acids

a. From Alcohols or Aldehydes (Sec. 10.7)

$$RCH_2OH \xrightarrow{CrO_3,\ H_2SO_4,\ H_2O} RCO_2H \xleftarrow[\text{or } O_2 \text{ or } Ag^+]{CrO_3,\ H_2SO_4,\ H_2O} RCH{=}O$$

b. From Alkylbenzenes (Sec. 10.7)

$$ArCH_3 \xrightarrow[\text{or } O_2,\ Co^{+3}]{KMnO_4} ArCO_2H$$

c. From Grignard Reagents (Sec. 10.7)

$$RMgX + CO_2 \longrightarrow RCO_2MgX \xrightarrow{H_3O^+} RCO_2H$$

d. From Nitriles (Sec. 10.7)

$$RC{\equiv}N + 2\,H_2O \xrightarrow{H^+ \text{ or } HO^-} RCO_2H + NH_3$$

2. Reactions of Acids

a. Acid–Base (Secs. 10.4 and 10.6)

$$RCO_2H \rightleftharpoons RCO_2^- + H^+ \quad \text{(ionization)}$$
$$RCO_2H + NaOH \longrightarrow RCO_2^-Na^+ + H_2O \quad \text{(salt formation)}$$

b. Preparation of Esters (Secs. 10.10 and 10.12)

$$RCO_2H + R'OH \xrightarrow{H^+} RCO_2R' + H_2O$$

c. Preparation of Acid Chlorides (Sec. 10.18)

$$RCO_2H + SOCl_2 \longrightarrow RCOCl + HCl + SO_2$$
$$RCO_2H + PCl_5 \longrightarrow RCOCl + HCl + POCl_3$$

d. Preparation of Anhydrides (Sec. 10.19)

$$
\underset{\displaystyle R-\overset{\textstyle O}{\overset{\|}{C}}-Cl}{} + Na^{+-}O-\overset{\textstyle O}{\overset{\|}{C}}-R' \longrightarrow R-\overset{\textstyle O}{\overset{\|}{C}}-O-\overset{\textstyle O}{\overset{\|}{C}}-R' + NaCl
$$

e. Preparation of Amides (Sec. 10.20)

$$RCO_2^-NH_4^+ \xrightarrow{\text{heat}} RCONH_2 + H_2O$$

Also see reactions of esters, acid chlorides, and anhydrides in Section 10.21.

3. Reactions of Carboxylic Acid Derivatives

a. Saponification of Esters (Sec. 10.13)

$$RCO_2R' + NaOH \longrightarrow RCO_2^-Na^+ + R'OH$$

b. Ammonolysis of Esters (Sec. 10.14)

$$RCO_2R' + NH_3 \longrightarrow RCONH_2 + R'OH$$

c. Esters with Grignard Reagents (Sec. 10.15)

$$RCO_2R' \xrightarrow{2\ R''MgX} R-\overset{\displaystyle R''}{\underset{\displaystyle R''}{C}}-OMgX \xrightarrow{H_3O^+} R-\overset{\displaystyle R''}{\underset{\displaystyle R''}{C}}-OH$$
$$+ R'OH$$

d. Reduction of Esters (Sec. 10.16)

$$RCO_2R' + LiAlH_4 \longrightarrow RCH_2OH + R'OH$$

e. Nucleophilic Acyl Substitution Reactions of Acid Chlorides and Anhydrides (Secs. 10.18 and 10.19)

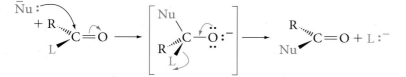

f. Hydrolysis of Amides (Sec. 10.20)

$$RCONH_2 + H_2O \xrightarrow{H^+ \text{ or } HO^-} RCO_2H + NH_3$$

g. Reduction of Amides (Sec. 10.20)

$$RCONH_2 \xrightarrow{LiAlH_4} RCH_2NH_2$$

h. Claisen Condensation (Sec. 10.22)

$$2\ RCH_2CO_2R' \xrightarrow[\text{2. } H_3O^+]{\text{1. } R'O^-Na^+} \underset{\overset{|}{R}}{RCH_2\overset{\overset{O}{\|}}{C}CHCO_2R'} + R'OH$$

MECHANISM SUMMARY

Nucleophilic Acyl Substitution (Secs. 10.11 and 10.17)

ADDITIONAL PROBLEMS

⊍WL Interactive versions of these problems are assignable in OWL.

Nomenclature and Structure of Carboxylic Acids

10.37 Write a structural formula for each of the following acids:

  a. 4-ethylhexanoic acid
  d. cyclopentanecarboxylic acid
  g. *p*-toluic acid
  j. 1-naphthoic acid

  b. 2-bromobutanoic acid
  e. 2-isopropylbenzoic acid
  h. 2-ethylbutanedioic acid
  k. 2,3-dimethyl-3-butenoic acid

  c. 3-chlorohexanoic acid
  f. 3-oxooctanoic acid
  i. *p*-methoxyphenylacetic acid

10.38 Name each of the following acids:

a. $(CH_3)_2C(Br)CH_2CH_2COOH$ b. $CH_3CH(OCH_3)CH(CH_3)COOH$

c.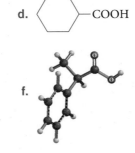

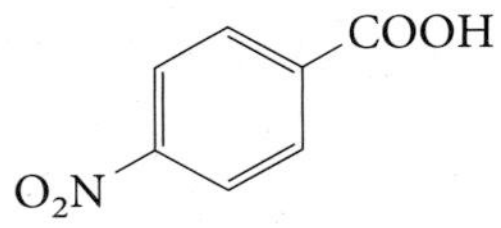

d. ⬡—COOH

e. $CH_2{=}CHCOOH$ f.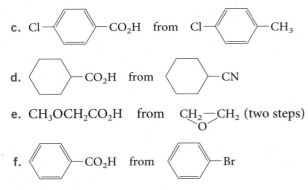

g. CH_3CF_2COOH h. $HC{\equiv}CCH_2CO_2H$

Synthesis and Properties of Carboxylic Acids

10.39 Which will have the higher boiling point? Explain your reasoning.

a. CH_3CH_2COOH or $CH_3CH_2CH_2CH_2OH$
b. $CH_3CH_2CH_2CH_2COOH$ or $(CH_3)_3CCOOH$

10.40 In each of the following pairs of acids, which would be expected to be the stronger acid, and why?

a. $ClCH_2CO_2H$ and $BrCH_2CO_2H$ b. $o\text{-}BrC_6H_4CO_2H$ and $m\text{-}BrC_6H_4CO_2H$
c. Cl_3CCO_2H and F_3CCO_2H d. $C_6H_5CO_2H$ and $p\text{-}CH_3OC_6H_4CO_2H$
e. $ClCH_2CH_2CO_2H$ and $CH_3CHClCO_2H$

10.41 Write a balanced equation for the reaction of

a. $ClCH_2CH_2CO_2H$ with KOH   b. $CH_3(CH_2)_4CO_2H$ with $Ca(OH)_2$

10.42 Give equations for the synthesis of

a. $CH_3CH_2CH_2CO_2H$ from $CH_3CH_2CH_2CH_2OH$
b. $CH_3CH_2CH_2CO_2H$ from $CH_3CH_2CH_2OH$ (two ways)

c. Cl—⬡—CO_2H from   Cl—⬡—CH_3

d. ⬡—CO_2H from   ⬡—CN

e. $CH_3OCH_2CO_2H$ from $CH_2{-}CH_2$ (two steps)
       with O bridge below

f. ⬡—CO_2H from   ⬡—Br

10.43 The Grignard route for the synthesis of $(CH_3)_3CCO_2H$ from $(CH_3)_3CBr$ (Example 10.5) is far superior to the nitrile route. Explain why.

Nomenclature and Structure of Carboxylic Acid Derivatives

10.44 Write a structure for each of the following compounds:

a. isobutyl acetate
c. sodium 2-chlorobutanoate
e. phenyl benzoate
g. 2-methoxybutanoyl chloride
i. propanoic anhydride
k. α-methyl-γ-butyrolactone

b. isopropyl formate
d. calcium acetate
f. *o*-toluamide
h. benzonitrile
j. 2-acetylcyclohexanecarboxylic acid

10.45 Name each of the following compounds:

a. Br—⟨benzene ring⟩—COO$^-$ NH$_4^+$

b. $[CH_3(CH_2)_2CO_2^-]_2Ca^{2+}$

c. $(CH_3)_2CHCH_2CH_2COOC_6H_5$

d. $CF_3CO_2CH_3$

e. $HCONH_2$

f. $CH_3(CH_2)_2 \overset{\overset{\displaystyle O}{\|}}{C} - O - \overset{\overset{\displaystyle O}{\|}}{C} (CH_2)_2CH_3$

10.46 Draw the structure of the mating pheromone of the female elephant, (*Z*)-7-dodecen-1-yl acetate (see page 302).

10.47 Organic emissions from mobile sources (cars, trucks, planes, and so on) become oxidized in the troposphere and can then assist the formation of particulate secondary organic aerosols. Such small particulate matter can penetrate deep into our lungs and cause acute irritations. It has been reported that carboxylic acids, such as benzoic acid, can form stable complexes with sulfuric acid (H_2SO_4) in a similar manner that carboxylic acids can form dimers (Sec. 10.2). Suggest a structure for a stable complex between benzoic acid and sulfuric acid.

Synthesis and Reactions of Esters

10.48 Write an equation for the Fischer esterification of butanoic acid ($CH_3CH_2CH_2CO_2H$) with ethanol.

10.49 Write out each step in the Fischer esterification of benzoic acid with methanol. (You may wish to use eq. 10.19 as a model.)

10.50 Starting from bromobenzene, provide a short synthesis of methyl benzoate ($C_6H_5CO_2CH_3$).

10.51 Write an equation for the reaction of propyl benzoate with

a. hot aqueous sodium hydroxide
b. ammonia (heat)
c. phenylmagnesium iodide (two equivalents), then H_3O^+
d. lithium aluminum hydride (two equivalents), then H_3O^+

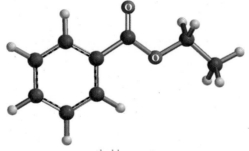

ethyl benzoate

10.52 Write out all of the steps in the mechanism for

    a. saponification of $CH_3CH_2CO_2CH_2CH_3$ **b.** ammonolysis of $CH_3CH_2CO_2CH_2CH_3$

10.53 Identify the Grignard reagent and the ester that would be used to prepare

$$\text{a.} \quad CH_3CH_2-\overset{\overset{\displaystyle OH}{|}}{\underset{\underset{\displaystyle C_6H_5}{|}}{C}}-CH_2CH_3 \qquad\qquad \text{b.} \quad CH_3CH_2CH_2C(C_6H_5)_2OH$$

Reactions of Carboxylic Acid Derivatives

10.54 Explain each difference in reactivity toward nucleophiles.

    a. Esters are less reactive than ketones.
    b. Benzoyl chloride is less reactive than cyclohexanecarbonyl chloride.

10.55 Write an equation for

    a. hydrolysis of butanoyl chloride   **b.** ammonolysis of butanoyl bromide
    c. 2-methylpropanoyl chloride + ethylbenzene + $AlCl_3$ **d.** succinic acid + heat (235°C)
    e. benzoyl chloride with ethanol   **f.** esterification of 1-pentanol with acetic anhydride
    g. phthalic anhydride + ethanol (1 equiv.) + H^+ **h.** phthalic anhydride + ethanol (excess) + H^+
    i. adipoyl chloride + ammonia (excess)

10.56 Complete the equation for each of the following reactions:

    a. $CH_3CH_2CH_2CO_2H + PCl_5 \longrightarrow$ **b.** $CH_3(CH_2)_6CO_2H + SOCl_2 \longrightarrow$

    c. (o-xylene) $+ KMnO_4 \longrightarrow$ **d.** (benzene ring)$-CO_2^-NH_4^+ + \text{heat} \longrightarrow$

    e. $CH_3(CH_2)_5CONH_2 + LiAlH_4 \longrightarrow$ **f.** (cyclopentane)$-CO_2CH_2CH_3 + LiAlH_4 \longrightarrow$

10.57 Considering the relative reactivities of ketones and esters toward nucleophiles, which of the following products seems the more likely?

$$\underset{CH_3\overset{\overset{\displaystyle O}{||}}{C}CH_2CH_2CO_2CH_3}{} \xrightarrow{NaBH_4} \underset{CH_3\overset{\overset{\displaystyle O}{||}}{C}CH_2CH_2CH_2OH}{} \quad \text{or} \quad \underset{CH_3\overset{\overset{\displaystyle OH}{|}}{C}HCH_2CH_2CO_2CH_3}{}$$

10.58 Mandelic acid, which has the formula $C_6H_5CH(OH)COOH$, can be isolated from bitter almonds (called *mandel* in German). It is sometimes used in medicine to treat urinary infections. Devise a two-step synthesis of mandelic acid from benzaldehyde, using the latter's cyanohydrin (see Sec. 9.10) as an intermediate.

The Claisen Condensation

10.59 Write the structure of the Claisen condensation product of methyl 3-phenylpropanoate ($C_6H_5CH_2CH_2CO_2CH_3$), and show the steps in its formation.

10.60 Diethyl adipate, when heated with sodium ethoxide, gives the product shown, by an *intra*molecular Claisen condensation:

$$\underset{\text{diethyl adipate}}{CH_3CH_2O\overset{\overset{\displaystyle O}{||}}{C}-(CH_2)_4-\overset{\overset{\displaystyle O}{||}}{C}OCH_2CH_3} \xrightarrow[\text{2. } H_3O^+]{\text{1. NaOCH}_2CH_3} \underset{\text{ethyl 2-oxocyclopentanecarboxylate}}{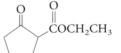}$$

Write out the steps in a plausible mechanism for the reaction.

10.61 Analogous to the mixed aldol condensation (Sec. 9.18), mixed Claisen condensations are possible. Predict the structure of the product obtained when a mixture of ethyl benzoate and ethyl acetate is heated with sodium ethoxide in ethanol.

Miscellaneous Problems

10.62 Write the important resonance contributors to the structure of acetamide and tell which atoms lie in a single plane.

10.63 On page 299, "A Word About . . . Green Chemistry and Ibuprofen: A Case Study" showed how efficiently ibuprofen can be prepared on a large scale. Another nonsteroidal, anti-inflammatory drug (NSAID) is acetaminophen. Suggest a short synthesis of acetaminophen from *p*-hydroxyaniline.

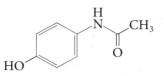

10.64 As noted in the "A Word About . . . Thioesters, Nature's Acyl-Activating Groups" on page 312, biological systems rely on thioesters for acyl transfer, but thioesters can be exploited in the laboratory as well. Provide the product for the treatment of

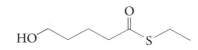

with catalytic NaOH.

10.65 Consider the structure of the catnip ingredient nepetalactone (page 305).

   a. Show with dotted lines that the structure is composed of two isoprene units.
   b. Circle the stereogenic centers and determine their configurations (*R* or *S*).

10.66 The lactone shown below, known as *wine lactone*, is a sweet and coconut-like smelling odorant isolated recently from white wines such as Gewürztraminer.

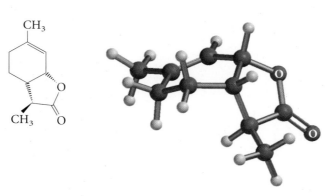

How many stereocenters are present, and what is the configuration (*R* or *S*) at each?

10.67 Provide a short synthesis of the ester-acid below, starting from maleic acid; see Section 10.1 for a structure of maleic acid. (Note, an ideal synthesis would avoid creating a mixture.)

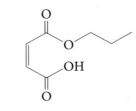

10.68 (5R,6S)-6-Acetoxy-5-hexadecanolide is a pheromone that attracts certain disease-carrying mosquitoes to sites where they like to lay their eggs. Such compounds might be used to lure these insects away from populated areas to locations where they can be destroyed. The last two steps in a recent synthesis of this compound are shown below. Provide reagents that would accomplish these transformations.

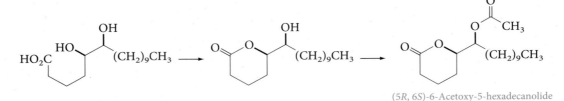

(5R, 6S)-6-Acetoxy-5-hexadecanolide

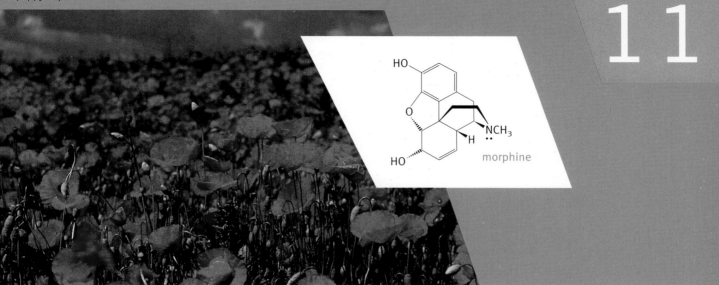

The painkiller morphine is obtained from opium, the dried sap of the unripe seed of the poppy *Papaver somniferum*.

© Darek Karp / Animals Animals

Amines and Related Nitrogen Compounds

In this chapter, we will discuss the last of the major families of simple organic compounds—the amines. **Amines** are relatives of ammonia that abound in nature and play an important role in many modern technologies. Examples of important amines are the painkiller morphine, found in poppy seeds, and putrescine, one of several polyamines responsible for the unpleasant odor of decaying flesh. A diamine that is largely the creation of humans is 1,6-diaminohexane, used in the synthesis of nylon. Amine derivatives, known as quaternary ammonium salts, also touch our daily lives in the form of synthetic detergents. Several neurotoxins also belong to this family of compounds. They are toxic because they interfere with the key role that acetylcholine, also a quaternary ammonium salt, plays in the transmission of nerve impulses.

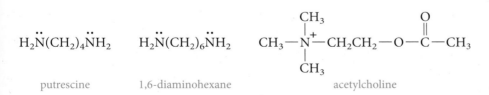

putrescine   1,6-diaminohexane   acetylcholine

In this chapter, we will first describe the structure, preparation, chemical properties, and uses of some simple amines. Later in the chapter, we will discuss a few natural and synthetic amines with important biological properties.

UWL

Online homework for this chapter can be assigned in OWL, an online homework assessment tool.

11.1 Classification and Structure of Amines

Amines are organic bases derived from ammonia.

The relation between ammonia and amines is illustrated by the following structures:

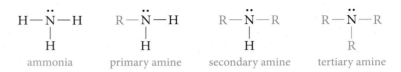

ammonia   primary amine   secondary amine   tertiary amine

Primary amines have one organic group attached to nitrogen, **secondary** amines have two, and **tertiary** amines have three.

For convenience, amines are classified as **primary**, **secondary**, or **tertiary**, depending on whether one, two, or three organic groups are attached to the nitrogen. The *R* groups in these structures may be alkyl or aryl, and when two or more *R* groups are present, they may be identical to or different from one another. In some secondary and tertiary amines, the nitrogen may be part of a ring.

> **PROBLEM 11.1** Classify each of the following amines as primary, secondary, or tertiary:
>
> a. $(CH_3)_3CCH_2NH_2$
>
> b.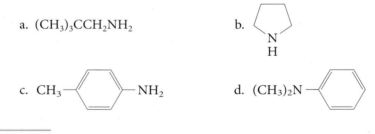
>
> c. CH_3—⟨ ⟩—NH_2
>
> d. $(CH_3)_2N$—⟨ ⟩

The nitrogen atom in amines is trivalent. Moreover, the nitrogen carries an unshared electron pair. Therefore, the nitrogen orbitals are sp^3-hybridized, and the overall geometry is pyramidal (nearly tetrahedral), as shown for trimethylamine in Figure 11.1. From this geometry, one might think that an amine with three different groups attached to the nitrogen would be chiral, with the unshared electron pair acting as the fourth group. This is true in principle, but in practice, the two enantiomers usually interconvert rapidly through inversion, via an "umbrella-in-the-wind" type of process, and are not resolvable.

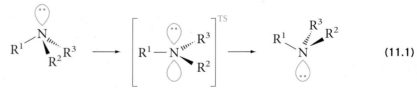

planar transition state

(11.1)

■ Figure 11.1

(a) An orbital view of the pyramidal bonding in trimethylamine.
(b) Top view of a space-filling model of trimethylamine. The center ball represents the orbital with the unshared electron pair.

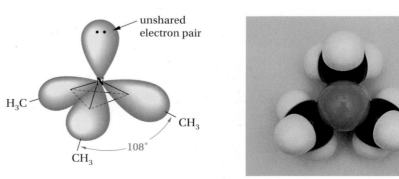

(a)   (b)

© Tom Pantages

11.2 / Nomenclature of Amines

Amines can be named in several different ways. Commonly, simple amines are named by specifying the alkyl groups attached to the nitrogen and adding the suffix -*amine*.

$$CH_3CH_2NH_2 \qquad (CH_3CH_2)_2NH \qquad (CH_3CH_2)_3N$$

ethylamine   diethylamine   triethylamine
(primary)   (secondary)   (tertiary)

In the IUPAC system, the amino group, —NH_2, is named as a substituent, as in the following examples:

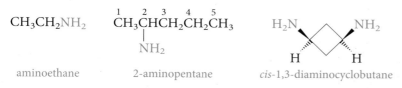

aminoethane   2-aminopentane   *cis*-1,3-diaminocyclobutane

In this system, secondary or tertiary amines are named by using a prefix that includes all but the longest carbon chain, as in

$$\overset{1}{C}H_3NH\overset{2}{C}H_2\overset{3}{C}H_2CH_3$$
1-methylamino**propane**

$$CH_3\overset{|}{N}\overset{CH_2CH_3}{-}\overset{1}{C}H_2\overset{2}{C}H_2\overset{3}{C}H_3$$
1-(ethylmethylamino)**propane**

dimethylamino**cyclohexane**

Recently, *Chemical Abstracts* (CA) introduced a system for naming amines that is rational and easy to use. In this system, amines are named as **alkanamines**. For example,

$$CH_3CH_2CH_2NH_2$$
propanamine

$$CH_3\overset{|}{C}HCH_3 \\ NH_2$$
2-propanamine

$$CH_3CHCH_2CH_2CH_3 \\ NHCH_3$$
N-methyl-2-pentanamine

> Amines are named as **alkanamines** in the CA system.

EXAMPLE 11.1

Name ⟨hexagon⟩— $N(CH_3)_2$ by the CA system.

Solution The largest alkyl group attached to nitrogen is used as the root of the name. The compound is *N,N*-dimethylcyclohexanamine.

PROBLEM 11.2 Name $CH_3CH_2CHCH_2CH_3$ by the CA system.
$$\overset{|}{N}(CH_3)_2$$

When other functional groups are present, the amino group is named as a substituent:

3-aminobutanoic acid   1-amino-3-pentanone   2-methylaminoethanol

Aromatic amines are named as derivatives of aniline. In the CA system, aniline is called benzenamine; these CA names are shown in parentheses.

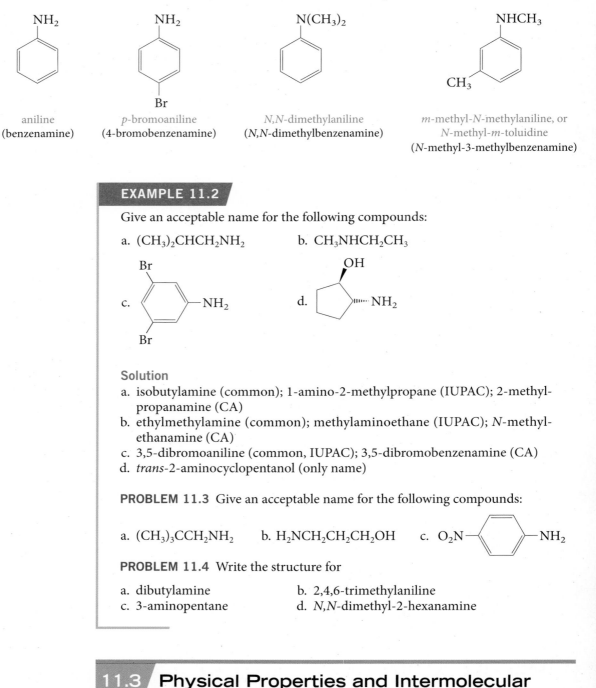

aniline
(benzenamine)

p-bromoaniline
(4-bromobenzenamine)

N,N-dimethylaniline
(*N,N*-dimethylbenzenamine)

m-methyl-*N*-methylaniline, or
N-methyl-*m*-toluidine
(*N*-methyl-3-methylbenzenamine)

EXAMPLE 11.2

Give an acceptable name for the following compounds:

a. $(CH_3)_2CHCH_2NH_2$ b. $CH_3NHCH_2CH_3$

c.

d.

Solution

a. isobutylamine (common); 1-amino-2-methylpropane (IUPAC); 2-methyl-propanamine (CA)
b. ethylmethylamine (common); methylaminoethane (IUPAC); *N*-methyl-ethanamine (CA)
c. 3,5-dibromoaniline (common, IUPAC); 3,5-dibromobenzenamine (CA)
d. *trans*-2-aminocyclopentanol (only name)

PROBLEM 11.3 Give an acceptable name for the following compounds:

a. $(CH_3)_3CCH_2NH_2$ b. $H_2NCH_2CH_2CH_2OH$ c. O_2N—⟨ ⟩—NH_2

PROBLEM 11.4 Write the structure for

a. dibutylamine   b. 2,4,6-trimethylaniline
c. 3-aminopentane   d. *N,N*-dimethyl-2-hexanamine

11.3   Physical Properties and Intermolecular Interactions of Amines

Table 11.1 lists the boiling points of some common amines. Methylamine and ethylamine are gases, but primary amines with three or more carbons are liquids. Primary amines boil well above alkanes with comparable molecular weights, but below comparable alcohols, as shown in Table 11.2. Intermolecular N—H· · ·N hydrogen bonds are important and raise the boiling points of primary and secondary amines but are not as strong as the O—H· · ·O bonds of alcohols (see Sec. 7.4). The reason for this is that nitrogen is not as electronegative as oxygen (see Table 1.4).

Table 11.1 ■ The Boiling Points of Some Simple Amines		
Name	**Formula**	**bp, °C**
ammonia	NH_3	−33.4
methylamine	CH_3NH_2	−6.3
dimethylamine	$(CH_3)_2NH$	7.4
trimethylamine	$(CH_3)_3N$	2.9
ethylamine	$CH_3CH_2NH_2$	16.6
propylamine	$CH_3CH_2CH_2NH_2$	48.7
butylamine	$CH_3CH_2CH_2CH_2NH_2$	77.8
aniline	$C_6H_5NH_2$	184.0

Table 11.2 ■ A Comparison of Alkane, Amine, and Alcohol Boiling Points*		
alkane	CH_3CH_3 (30) bp −88.6°C	$CH_3CH_2CH_3$ (44) bp −42.1°C
amine	CH_3NH_2 (31) bp −6.3°C	$CH_3CH_2NH_2$ (45) bp +16.6°C
alcohol	CH_3OH (32) bp +65.0°C	CH_3CH_2OH (46) bp +78.5°C

*Molecular weights (in g/mol) are given in parentheses.

PROBLEM 11.5 Explain why the tertiary amine $(CH_3)_3N$ boils so much lower than its primary isomer $CH_3CH_2CH_2NH_2$.

All three classes of amines can form hydrogen bonds with the —OH group of water (that is, O—H· · ·N). Primary and secondary amines can also form hydrogen bonds with the oxygen atom in water: N—H· · ·O. Thus, most simple amines with up to five or six carbon atoms are either completely or appreciably soluble in water.

Now we will describe some ways in which amines can be prepared.

11.4 Preparation of Amines; Alkylation of Ammonia and Amines

Ammonia reacts with alkyl halides to give amines via a two-step process. The first step is a nucleophilic substitution reaction (S_N2).

$$H_3N\colon + R-X \longrightarrow R-\overset{+}{N}H_3 \ X^-$$

ammonia　　　　　　　　alkylammonium
halide

(11.2)

The free amine can then be obtained from its salt by treatment with a strong base.

$$R - \overset{+}{N}H_3\ X^- + NaOH \longrightarrow \underset{\substack{\text{primary} \\ \text{amine}}}{RNH_2} + H_2O + Na^+X^- \tag{11.3}$$

Primary, secondary, and tertiary amines can be similarly alkylated.

$$\underset{\substack{\text{primary} \\ \text{amine}}}{R\ddot{N}H_2} + R - X \longrightarrow R_2\overset{+}{N}H_2\ X^- \xrightarrow{\text{NaOH}} \underset{\substack{\text{secondary} \\ \text{amine}}}{R_2NH} \tag{11.4}$$

$$\underset{\substack{\text{secondary} \\ \text{amine}}}{R_2\ddot{N}H} + R - X \longrightarrow R_3\overset{+}{N}H\ X^- \xrightarrow{\text{NaOH}} \underset{\substack{\text{tertiary} \\ \text{amine}}}{R_3N} \tag{11.5}$$

$$\underset{\substack{\text{tertiary} \\ \text{amine}}}{R_3\ddot{N}} + R - X \longrightarrow \underset{\substack{\text{quaternary} \\ \text{ammonium salt}}}{R_4N^+\ X^-} \tag{11.6}$$

Unfortunately, mixtures of products are often obtained in these reactions because the starting ammonia or amine and the alkylammonium ion formed in the S_N2 step can equilibrate, as in the following equation:

$$NH_3 + R\overset{+}{N}H_3\ X^- \rightleftharpoons NH_4^+X^- + RNH_2 \tag{11.7}$$

So, in the reaction of ammonia with an alkyl halide (eq. 11.2), some primary amine is formed (eq. 11.7), and it may be further alkylated (eq. 11.4) to give a secondary amine, and so on. By adjusting the ratio of the reactants, however, a good yield of one desired amine may be obtained. For example, with a large excess of ammonia, the primary amine is the major product.

Aromatic amines can often be alkylated selectively.

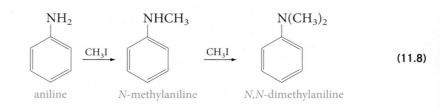

$$\underset{\text{aniline}}{} \xrightarrow{CH_3I} \underset{\text{N-methylaniline}}{} \xrightarrow{CH_3I} \underset{\text{N,N-dimethylaniline}}{} \tag{11.8}$$

The alkylation can be intramolecular, as in the following final step in a laboratory synthesis of nicotine:

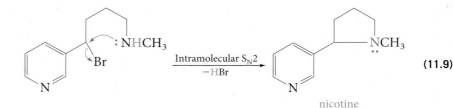

$$\xrightarrow[-\text{HBr}]{\text{Intramolecular } S_N2} \underset{\text{nicotine}}{} \tag{11.9}$$

Tobacco plant.

© Bill Beatty/Animals Animals

EXAMPLE 11.3

Write an equation for the synthesis of benzylamine, ⬡—CH_2NH_2.

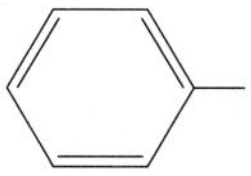

Solution

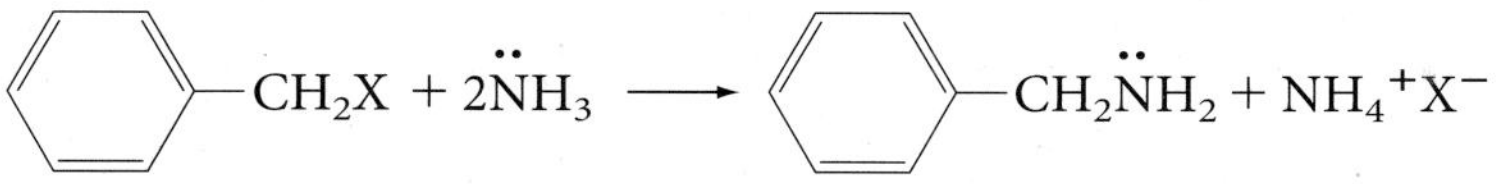

⬡—CH_2X + 2$\ddot{N}H_3$ $\longrightarrow$ ⬡—$CH_2\ddot{N}H_2$ + $NH_4{}^+X^-$

(X = Cl, Br, or I)

Use of excess ammonia helps prevent further substitution.

PROBLEM 11.6 Complete equations for the following reactions:

a. $CH_3CH_2CH_2CH_2Br$ + 2 NH_3 $\longrightarrow$

b. CH_3CH_2I + 2$(CH_3CH_2)_2NH$ $\longrightarrow$

c. $(CH_3)_3N$ + CH_3I $\longrightarrow$

d. $CH_3CH_2CH_2NH_2$ + ⬡—CH_2Br $\longrightarrow$

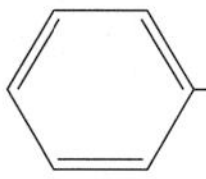

PROBLEM 11.7 Give a synthesis of ⬡—$NHCH_2CH_3$ from aniline.

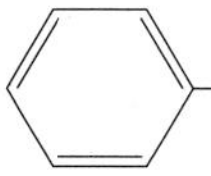

11.5 Preparation of Amines; Reduction of Nitrogen Compounds

All bonds to the nitrogen atom in amines are either N—H or N—C bonds. Nitrogen in ammonia or amines is therefore in a reduced form. It is not surprising, then, that organic compounds in which a nitrogen atom is present in a more oxidized form can be reduced to amines by appropriate reducing agents. Several examples of this useful synthetic approach to amines are described here.

The best route to *aromatic primary amines* is by *reduction of the corresponding nitro compounds,* which are in turn prepared by electrophilic aromatic nitration. The nitro group is easily reduced, either catalytically with hydrogen or by chemical-reducing agents.

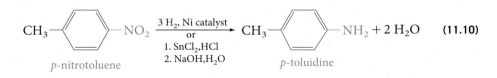

CH_3—⬡—NO_2 $\xrightarrow[\substack{\text{or} \\ \text{1. SnCl}_2,\text{HCl} \\ \text{2. NaOH,H}_2\text{O}}]{\text{3 H}_2,\text{ Ni catalyst}}$ CH_3—⬡—NH_2 + 2 H_2O **(11.10)**

p-nitrotoluene   *p*-toluidine

EXAMPLE 11.4

Devise a synthesis of *p*-chloroaniline, Cl—⬡—NH_2, from chloro-benzene.

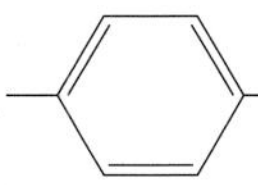

Solution Chlorobenzene is first nitrated; —Cl is an *o,p*-directing group, so the major product is *p*-chloronitrobenzene. This product is then reduced.

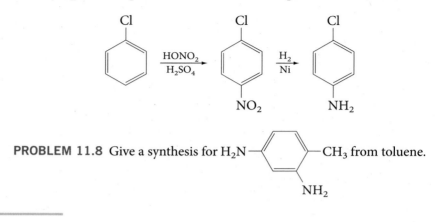

PROBLEM 11.8 Give a synthesis for H$_2$N—⟨benzene ring⟩—CH$_3$ from toluene.

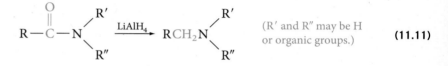

As described in the previous chapter (eq. 10.43), *amides can be reduced to amines* with lithium aluminum hydride.

$$\underset{\substack{\| \\ O}}{R-C-N}\overset{R'}{\underset{R''}{}} \xrightarrow{\text{LiAlH}_4} RCH_2N\overset{R'}{\underset{R''}{}} \qquad \text{(R' and R'' may be H or organic groups.)} \qquad (11.11)$$

Depending on the structures of R′ and R″, we can obtain primary, secondary, or tertiary amines in this way.

EXAMPLE 11.5

Complete the equation $\underset{\substack{\| \\ O}}{CH_3C}NHCH_2CH_3 \xrightarrow{\text{LiAlH}_4}$.

Solution The C=O group is reduced to CH$_2$. The product is the secondary amine CH$_3$CH$_2$NHCH$_2$CH$_3$.

PROBLEM 11.9 Show how CH$_3$CH$_2$N(CH$_3$)$_2$ can be synthesized from an amide.

Reduction of nitriles (cyanides) gives *primary amines.*

$$R-C\equiv N \xrightarrow[\text{or H}_2,\text{ Ni}]{\text{LiAlH}_4} RCH_2NH_2 \qquad (11.12)$$

EXAMPLE 11.6

Complete the equation NCCH$_2$CH$_2$CH$_2$CH$_2$CN $\xrightarrow[\text{Ni catalyst}]{\text{excess H}_2}$.

Solution Both CN groups are reduced. The product H_2N—$(CH_2)_6$—NH_2, or 1,6-diaminohexane, is one of two raw materials for the manufacture of nylon (page 412).

PROBLEM 11.10 Devise a synthesis of

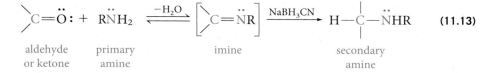

Aldehydes and ketones undergo **reductive amination** when treated with ammonia, primary, or secondary amines, to give primary, secondary, or tertiary amines, respectively. The most commonly used laboratory reducing agent for this purpose is the metal hydride sodium cyanoborohydride, $NaBH_3CN$.

Aldehydes and ketones undergo **reductive amination** when treated with amines in the presence of $NaBH_3CN$.

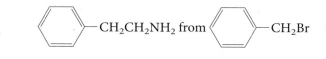

aldehyde or ketone	primary amine	imine	secondary amine

The reaction involves nucleophilic attack on the carbonyl group, leading to an imine (in the case of ammonia or primary amines; compare with eq. 9.31) or an iminium ion with secondary amines. The reducing agent then reduces the C=N bond.

PROBLEM 11.11 Using eq. 11.13 as a guide, devise a synthesis of 2-aminopentane, shown below, from 2-pentanone.

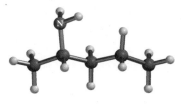

Now that we know several ways to make amines, let us examine some of their properties.

11.6 The Basicity of Amines

The unshared pair of electrons on the nitrogen atom dominates the chemistry of amines. Because of this electron pair, amines are both basic and nucleophilic.

Aqueous solutions of amines are basic because of the following equilibrium:

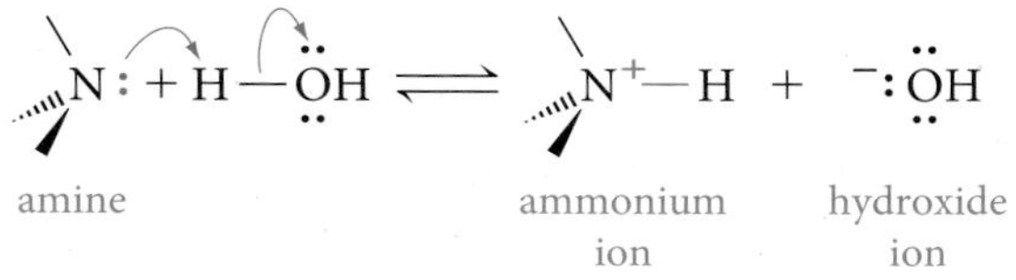

$$\underset{\text{amine}}{\overset{|}{\underset{}{\diagdown}}N\colon} + H\!-\!\ddot{O}H \rightleftharpoons \underset{\substack{\text{ammonium}\\\text{ion}}}{\overset{|}{\underset{}{\diagdown}}N^{+}\!-\!H} + \underset{\substack{\text{hydroxide}\\\text{ion}}}{^{-}\!\colon\!\ddot{O}H} \qquad \textbf{(11.14)}$$

EXAMPLE 11.7

Write an equation that shows why aqueous solutions of ethylamine are basic.

Solution $CH_3CH_2\overset{..}{N}H_2 + H_2O \rightleftharpoons CH_3CH_2\overset{+}{N}H_3 + HO^-$
ethylamine   ethylammonium
ion

Amines are more basic than water. They accept a proton from water, producing hydroxide ion, so their solutions are basic.

PROBLEM 11.12 Write an equation representing the equilibrium in an aqueous solution of trimethylamine, $(CH_3)_3N$.

An *amine* and its *ammonium ion* (eq. 11.14) are related as a *base* and its *conjugate acid*. For example, RNH_3^+ is the conjugate acid of the primary amine RNH_2. It is convenient, when comparing basicities of different amines, to compare instead the acidity constants (pK_a's) of their conjugate acids in water. Equation 11.15 expresses this acidity for a primary alkylammonium ion.

$$\overset{+}{R}NH_3 + H_2O \rightleftharpoons RNH_2 + H_3O^+ \qquad (11.15)$$
conjugate   base
acid

$$K_a = \frac{[RNH_2][H_3O^+]}{[RNH_3^+]}$$

The larger the K_a (or the smaller the pK_a), the stronger $R\overset{+}{N}H_3$ is as an acid, or the weaker RNH_2 is as a base.

EXAMPLE 11.8

The pK_a's of NH_4^+ and $CH_3\overset{+}{N}H_3$ are 9.30 and 10.64, respectively. Which is the stronger base, NH_3 or CH_3NH_2?

Solution NH_4^+ is the stronger acid (lower pK_a). Therefore, NH_3 is the *weaker* base, and CH_3NH_2 is the *stronger* base.

Table 11.3 lists some amine basicities. Alkylamines are approximately 10 times as basic as ammonia. Recall that alkyl groups are electron-donating relative to hydrogen. This electron-donating effect stabilizes the ammonium ion (positive charge) relative to the free amine (eq. 11.14). Hence it decreases the acidity of the ammonium ion, or increases the basicity of the amine. In general, *electron-donating groups increase the basicity of amines, and electron-withdrawing groups decrease their basicity.*

PROBLEM 11.13 Do you expect $ClCH_2CH_2NH_2$ to be a stronger or weaker base than $CH_3CH_2NH_2$? Explain.

Table 11.3 ▬ Basicities of Some Common Amines, Expressed as pK_a of the Corresponding Ammonium Ions			
	Formula		
Name	Amine	Ammonium ion	pK_a of the ammonium ion
ammonia	$\overset{..}{N}H_3$	$\overset{+}{N}H_4$	9.30
methylamine	$CH_3\overset{..}{N}H_2$	$CH_3\overset{+}{N}H_3$	10.64
dimethylamine	$(CH_3)_2\overset{..}{N}H$	$(CH_3)_2\overset{+}{N}H_2$	10.71
trimethylamine	$(CH_3)_3\overset{..}{N}$	$(CH_3)_3\overset{+}{N}H$	9.77
ethylamine	$CH_3CH_2\overset{..}{N}H_2$	$CH_3CH_2\overset{+}{N}H_3$	10.67
propylamine	$CH_3CH_2CH_2\overset{..}{N}H_2$	$CH_3CH_2CH_2\overset{+}{N}H_3$	10.58
aniline	$C_6H_5\overset{..}{N}H_2$	$C_6H_5\overset{+}{N}H_3$	4.62
N-methylaniline	$C_6H_5\overset{..}{N}HCH_3$	$C_6H_5\overset{+}{N}H_2(CH_3)$	4.85
N,N-dimethylaniline	$C_6H_5\overset{..}{N}(CH_3)_2$	$C_6H_5\overset{+}{N}H(CH_3)_2$	5.04
p-chloroaniline	$p\text{-}ClC_6H_4\overset{..}{N}H_2$	$p\text{-}ClC_6H_4\overset{+}{N}H_3$	3.98

Aromatic amines are much weaker bases than aliphatic amines or ammonia. For example, aniline is less basic than cyclohexylamine by nearly a million times.

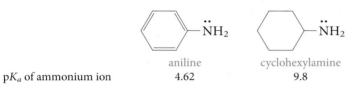

	aniline	cyclohexylamine
pK_a of ammonium ion	4.62	9.8

The reason for this huge difference is the resonance delocalization of the unshared electron pair that is possible in aniline, but not in cyclohexylamine (Figure 11.2).

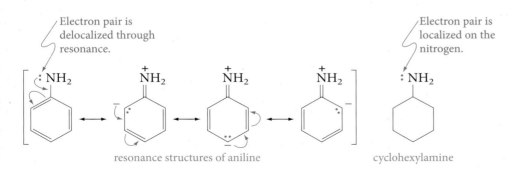

Electron pair is delocalized through resonance.

Electron pair is localized on the nitrogen.

resonance structures of aniline

cyclohexylamine

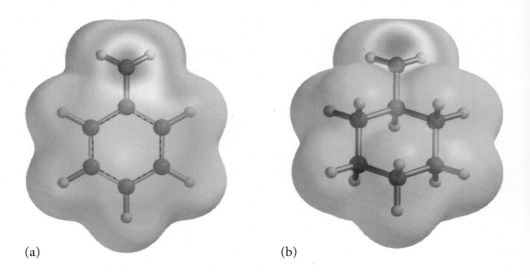

(a)   (b)

Resonance stabilizes the unprotonated form of aniline. This shifts the equilibrium in eq. 11.15 to the right, increasing the acidity of the anilinium ion or decreasing the basicity of aniline. Another way to describe the situation is to say that the unshared electron pair in aniline is delocalized and therefore less available for donation to a proton than is the electron pair in cyclohexylamine.

PROBLEM 11.14 Compare the basicities of the last four amines in Table 11.3, and explain the reasons for the observed basicity order.

PROBLEM 11.15 Place aniline, *p*-toluidine, and *p*-nitroaniline in order of increasing basicity.

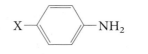

$$X = H \quad \text{aniline}$$
$$X = CH_3 \quad \textit{p}\text{-toluidine}$$
$$X = NO_2 \quad \textit{p}\text{-nitroaniline}$$

11.7 / Comparison of the Basicity and Acidity of Amines and Amides

Amines and amides each have nitrogens with an unshared electron pair. There is a huge difference, however, in their basicities. Aqueous solutions of *amines* are *basic*; aqueous solutions of *amides* are essentially *neutral*. Why this striking difference?

The answer lies in their structures, as illustrated in the following comparison of a primary amine with a primary amide:

localized; available
for protonation

delocalized; less available
for protonation

$$R-\overset{\cdot\cdot}{N}H_2$$
amine

$$\left[R-\overset{\overset{\displaystyle\cdot\cdot}{\overset{\displaystyle O:}{\|}}}{C}-\overset{\cdot\cdot}{N}H_2 \longleftrightarrow R-\overset{\overset{\displaystyle :\overset{\cdot\cdot}{O}:^-}{|}}{C}=\overset{+}{N}H_2 \right]$$
amide

In the amine, the electron pair is mainly localized on the nitrogen. In the amide, the electron pair is delocalized to the carbonyl oxygen. The effect of this delocalization is seen in the low pK_a values for the conjugate acids of amides, compared with those for the conjugate acids of amines, for example:

$$\overset{+}{:O}-H$$
$$\parallel \; ..$$
$$CH_3CH_2\overset{+}{N}H_3 \qquad CH_3CNH_2$$

conjugate acid of:	ethylamine	acetamide
pK_a:	10.67	−0.6

Notice that amides are not protonated on nitrogen, but instead on the carbonyl oxygen. This is because protonation on oxygen gives a resonance-stabilized cation, while protonation on nitrogen does not.

Primary and secondary amines and amides have N—H bonds, and one might expect that they could on occasion behave as acids (proton donors).

$$R-\overset{..}{N}H_2 \;\rightleftharpoons\; R-\overset{..}{\underset{..}{N}}H^- + H^+ \qquad K_a \cong 10^{-40} \qquad \textbf{(11.16)}$$

Primary amines are exceedingly weak acids, much weaker than alcohols. Their pK_a is about 40, compared with about 16 for alcohols. The main reason for the difference is that nitrogen is much less electronegative than oxygen and thus cannot stabilize a negative charge nearly as well.

Amides, on the other hand, are *much stronger acids than amines;* in fact, their pK_a (about 15) is comparable to that of alcohols:

$$\underset{\substack{\\ R-C-\overset{..}{N}H_2}}{\overset{O}{\parallel}} \;\rightleftharpoons\; \left[\underset{\substack{\\ R-C-\overset{..}{\underset{..}{N}}H}}{\overset{\overset{..}{O}:}{\parallel}} \;\longleftrightarrow\; \underset{\substack{\\ R-C=\overset{..}{N}H}}{\overset{:\overset{..}{O}:^-}{\mid}} \right] + H^+ \qquad K_a \cong 10^{-15} \qquad \textbf{(11.17)}$$

amidate anion

One reason is that the negative charge of the **amidate anion** can be delocalized through resonance. Another reason is that the nitrogen in an amide carries a partial positive charge (see page 338), making it easy to lose the attached proton, which is also positive.

It is important to understand these differences between amines and amides, not only because they involve important chemical principles, but also because they help us understand the chemistry of certain natural products, such as peptides and proteins.

The **amidate anion** is formed by removal of a proton from the amide nitrogen.

PROBLEM 11.16 Place the following compounds (a) in order of increasing basicity and (b) in order of increasing acidity.

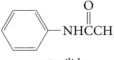

| acetanilide | cyclohexylamine | aniline |

11.8 Reaction of Amines with Strong Acids; Amine Salts

Alkylamines react with strong acids to form **alkylammonium salts**.

Amines react with strong acids to form **alkylammonium salts**. An example of this reaction for a primary amine and HCl is as follows:

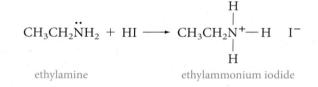

$$R-\overset{..}{N}H_2 \; + \; HCl \longrightarrow \; R\overset{+}{N}H_3 \quad Cl^- \qquad \text{(11.18)}$$

primary amine   an alkylammonium chloride

EXAMPLE 11.9

Complete the following acid–base reaction, and name the product.

$$CH_3CH_2NH_2 + HI \longrightarrow$$

Solution

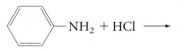

$$CH_3CH_2\overset{..}{N}H_2 \; + \; HI \longrightarrow \; CH_3CH_2\overset{\overset{\displaystyle H}{|}}{\underset{\underset{\displaystyle H}{|}}{N^+}}-H \quad I^-$$

ethylamine   ethylammonium iodide

PROBLEM 11.17 Complete the following equation, and name the product:

$$\bigcirc\!\!-NH_2 + HCl \longrightarrow$$

This type of reaction is used to separate or extract amines from neutral or acidic water-insoluble substances. Consider, for example, a mixture of *p*-toluidine and *p*-nitrotoluene, which might arise from a preparation of the amine that for some reason does not go to completion (eq. 11.10). The amine can be separated from the unreduced nitro compound by the following scheme:

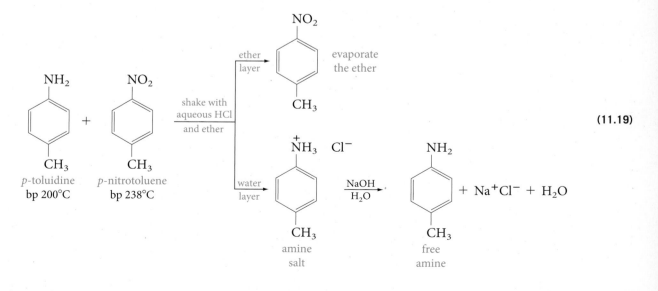

(11.19)

A WORD ABOUT... Alkaloids and the Dart-Poison Frogs

Anyka/Shutterstock

A dart-poison frog.

Alkaloids are basic, nitrogen-containing compounds of plant or animal origin, often having complex structures and significant pharmacological properties. Nicotine (from tobacco) and the amine obtained by deprotonation of squalamine (from sharks) are examples of alkaloids already mentioned in this chapter. Several more will appear in Chapter 13.

One prolific producer of alkaloids is the *dart-poison frogs,* a family of colorful and petite amphibians native to Costa Rica, Panama, Ecuador, and Colombia. The intense coloration of these frogs serves as a warning to potential predators who would have an unpleasant experience if they tried to make a meal of one of these tiny creatures. This is because the frogs secrete toxic alkaloids from glands on the surface of their skin. These secretions are so toxic that they have been used by locals to poison blowgun darts used in hunting; hence the name *dart-poison frogs.*

Scientists from the National Institutes of Health have isolated and determined the structures of many of the compounds present in these skin secretions using the techniques of mass spectrometry and NMR spectroscopy (Chapter 12). Thus far, the structures of close to 200 different alkaloids have been determined. The most potent of these toxins is batrachotoxin (from *Phyllobates terribilis*), an example of a steroidal alkaloid. Other toxins include

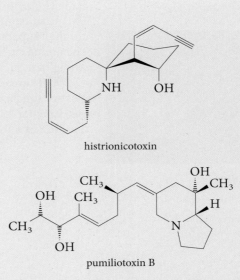

histrionicotoxin

pumiliotoxin B

histrionicotoxin (from *Dendrobates histrionicus*) and pumiliotoxin B (from *Dendrobates pumilio*).

Because many of these compounds are produced in only microgram quantities by the frogs, laboratory syntheses have often been developed to confirm structures and also to provide a supply of material for pharmacological studies. It turns out that most of these toxins act on the nervous system by affecting the manner in which ions are transported across cell membranes. As a result of this property, several of these alkaloids are now used as research tools in the field of neuroscience.

In 1992, an alkaloid with painkilling properties far greater than that of morphine was isolated from the Ecuadorian frog *Epipedobates tricolor*. Named epibatidine, it was hoped that this simple alkaloid would be a lead compound for the development of a new family of painkillers. Whether or not epibatidine or related synthetic materials will eventually result in new painkillers remains to be determined, but epibatidine is already being marketed in the form of its tartrate salt for use in biomedical research. Research in this interesting area of natural product chemistry once again confirms that big things can come in small packages.

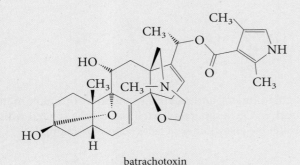

batrachotoxin

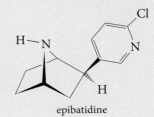

epibatidine

See Problems 11.37 and 11.38.

The mixture, neither component of which is water soluble, is dissolved in an inert, low-boiling solvent such as diethyl ether and is shaken with aqueous hydrochloric acid. The amine reacts to form a salt, which is ionic and dissolves in the water layer. The nitro compound does not react and remains in the ether layer. The two layers are then separated. The nitro compound can be recovered by evaporating the ether. The amine can be recovered from its salt by making the aqueous layer alkaline with a strong base such as NaOH.

There are many natural and synthetic amine salts of biological interest. Two examples are squalamine, an antimicrobial steroid recently isolated from the dogfish shark (see Chapter 15 for more about steroids), and (+)-methamphetamine hydrochloride, the addictive and toxic stimulant commonly known as "ice" or "meth."

Dogfish shark.

© Joyce Photographics/Photo Researchers

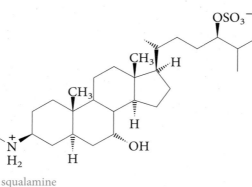

squalamine   methamphetamine hydrochloride

11.9 / Chiral Amines as Resolving Agents

Amines also form salts with organic acids. This reaction is used to resolve enantiomeric acids (Sec. 5.12). For example, (R)- and (S)-lactic acids can be resolved by reaction with a chiral amine such as (S)-1-phenylethylamine:

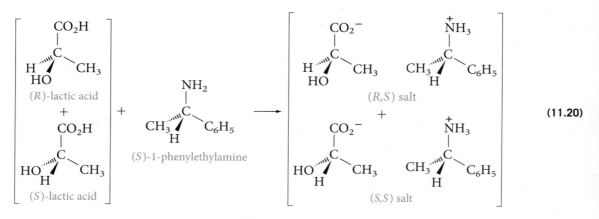

(11.20)

The salts are *diastereomers*, not enantiomers, and can be separated by ordinary methods, such as fractional crystallization. Once separated, each salt can be treated with a strong acid, such as HCl, to liberate one enantiomer of lactic acid. For example,

(R,S) salt + HCl ⟶   (11.21)

(R)-lactic acid   (S)-1-phenylethyl-
                    ammonium chloride

The chiral amine can be recovered for reuse by treating its salt with sodium hydroxide (as in the last step of eq. 11.19).

Numerous chiral amines are available from natural products and can be used to resolve acids. Conversely, some chiral acids are available to resolve amine enantiomers.

So far, we have considered reactions in which amines act as bases. Now we will examine some reactions in which they act as nucleophiles.

11.10 Acylation of Amines with Acid Derivatives

Amines are nitrogen nucleophiles. They react with the carbonyl group of carboxylic acid derivatives (acyl halides, anhydrides, and esters) by nucleophilic acyl substitution (Sec. 10.11).

Looked at from the viewpoint of the amine, we can say that the N—H bond in primary and secondary amines can be *acylated* by acid derivatives. For example, primary and secondary amines react with acyl halides to form amides (compare with eq. 10.36).

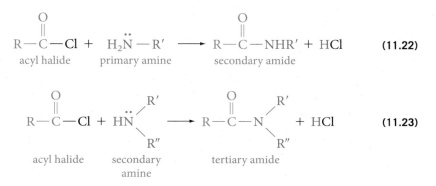

If the amine is inexpensive, two equivalents are used—one to form the amide and the second to neutralize the HCl. Alternatively, an inexpensive base may be added for the latter purpose. This can be sodium hydroxide (especially if R is *aromatic*) or a tertiary amine; having no N—H bonds, tertiary amines cannot be acylated, but they can neutralize the HCl.

EXAMPLE 11.10

Using eq. 10.31 as a guide, write out the steps in the mechanism for eq. 11.22.

Solution

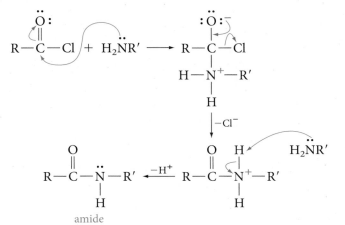

The first step involves nucleophilic addition to the carbonyl group. Elimination of HCl completes the substitution reaction.

Acylation of amines is often put to practical use. For example, the insect repellent OFF® is the amide formed in the reaction of *m*-toluyl chloride and diethylamine.

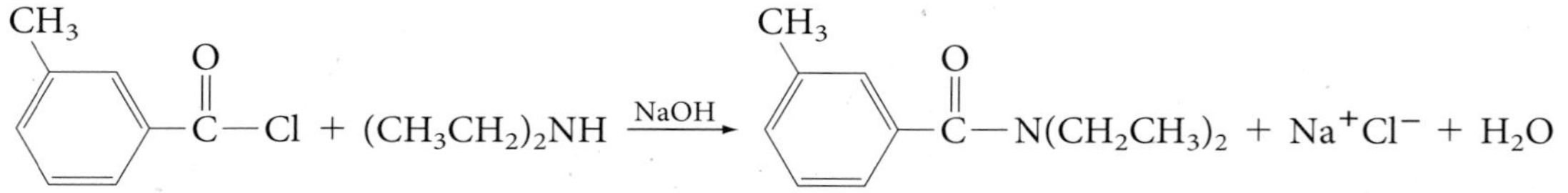

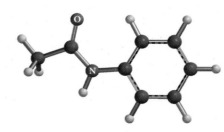

$$\text{(11.24)}$$

m-toluyl chloride   diethylamine   *N,N*-diethyl-*m*-toluamide (the insect repellent OFF®)

> **PROBLEM 11.18** Write out the steps in the mechanism for the synthesis of OFF® (eq. 11.24).

The antipyretic (fever-reducing substance) acetanilide is an amide prepared from aniline and acetic anhydride.

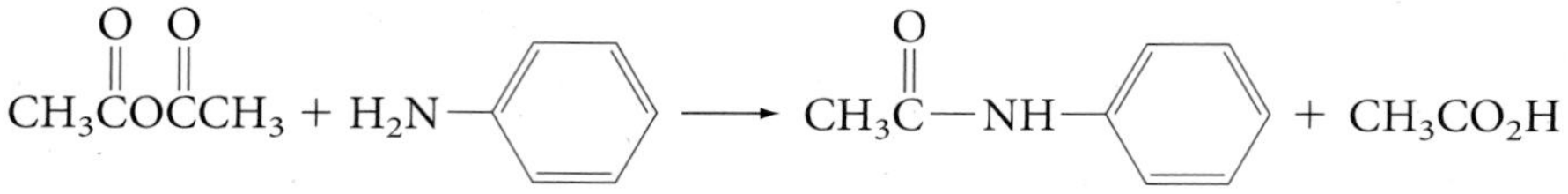

$$\text{(11.25)}$$

acetic anhydride   aniline   acetanilide

> **PROBLEM 11.19** Provide the structures of the amides obtained from reaction of acetic anhydride with
>
> a. $(CH_3CH_2)_2NH$ b. $CH_3CH_2NH_2$

11.11   Quaternary Ammonium Compounds

In **quaternary ammonium salts**, all four hydrogens of the ammonium ion are replaced by organic groups.

Tertiary amines react with primary or secondary alkyl halides by an S_N2 mechanism (eq. 11.6). The products are **quaternary ammonium salts**, in which all four hydrogens of the ammonium ion are replaced by organic groups. For example,

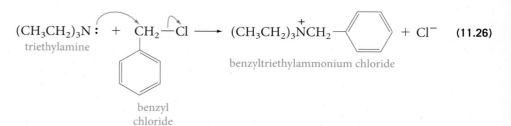

$$\text{(11.26)}$$

triethylamine

benzyltriethylammonium chloride

benzyl chloride

Quaternary ammonium compounds are important in biological processes. One of the most common natural quaternary ammonium ions is **choline**, which is present in phospholipids (Sec. 15.6).

Choline and **acetylcholine** are important quaternary ammonium ions in biological processes.

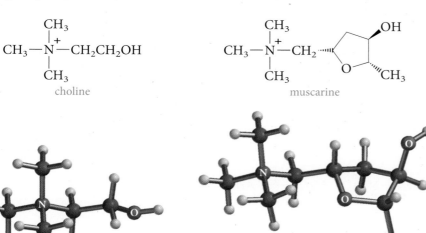

choline   muscarine

***Amanita muscaria*, a source of muscarine.**

Choline is not only involved in various metabolic processes, but is also the precursor of **acetylcholine** (page 327), a compound that plays a key role in the transmission of nerve impulses. The mushroom *Amanita muscaria* contains the deadly neurotoxin muscarine, which structurally resembles acetylcholine and probably interferes with the function of this neurotransmitter.

11.12 Aromatic Diazonium Compounds

Primary aromatic amines react with nitrous acid at 0°C to yield **aryldiazonium ions**. The process is called **diazotization**.

In **diazotization**, primary aromatic amines react with nitrous acid to form **aryldiazonium ions**.

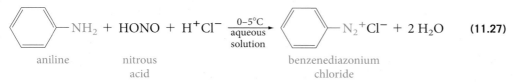

$$\text{aniline} + \text{HONO} + \text{H}^+\text{Cl}^- \xrightarrow[\substack{\text{aqueous}\\\text{solution}}]{0\text{–}5°\text{C}} \text{benzenediazonium chloride} \quad N_2{}^+\text{Cl}^- + 2\,H_2O \qquad (11.27)$$

aniline   nitrous acid   benzenediazonium chloride

Diazonium compounds are extremely useful synthetic intermediates. Before we describe their chemistry, let us try to understand the steps in eq. 11.27. First, we need to examine the structure of nitrous acid.

Nitrous acid decomposes rather rapidly at room temperature. It is therefore prepared as needed by treating an aqueous solution of sodium nitrite with a strong acid at ice temperature. At that temperature, nitrous acid solutions are reasonably stable.

$$\underset{\text{sodium nitrite}}{Na^+NO_2{}^-} + H^+Cl^- \xrightarrow{0\text{–}5°\text{C}} \underset{\text{nitrous acid}}{H-\overset{..}{\underset{..}{O}}-\overset{..}{N}=\overset{..}{\underset{..}{O}}:} + Na^+Cl^- \qquad (11.28)$$

The reactive species in reactions of nitrous acid is the nitrosonium ion (NO^+). It is formed by protonation of the nitrous acid, followed by loss of water (compare with eq. 4.18):

$$\overset{..}{\underset{..}{HO}}-\overset{..}{N}=\overset{..}{\underset{..}{O}}: + H^+ \rightleftharpoons \overset{+}{\underset{\underset{H}{|}}{HO}}-\overset{..}{N}=\overset{..}{\underset{..}{O}}: \rightleftharpoons H_2O + :\overset{+}{N}=\overset{..}{\underset{..}{O}}: \qquad (11.29)$$

nitrosonium ion

How do the two nitrogens, one from the amine and one from the nitrous acid, become bonded to one another, as they appear in diazonium ions? This happens in the first step of diazotization (eq. 11.30), which involves nucleophilic attack of the primary amine on the nitrosonium ion, followed by proton loss.

$$ArNH_2 + :\overset{+}{N}=\overset{..}{\underset{..}{O}}: \longrightarrow ArN^+\!\!-\!\!N=\overset{..}{\underset{..}{O}}: \rightleftharpoons ArN\!\!-\!\!N=\overset{..}{\underset{..}{O}}: + H^+ \qquad (11.30)$$

a primary nitrosamine

Protonation of the oxygen in the resulting nitrosamine, followed by elimination of water, then gives the aromatic diazonium ion.

$$ArN\!-\!N=\overset{..}{\underset{..}{O}}: + H^+ \longrightarrow ArN=\overset{+}{N}\!-\!\overset{..}{\underset{..}{O}}H \xrightarrow{-H_2O} Ar\overset{+}{N}\equiv N: \qquad (11.31)$$

aryldiazonium ion

Notice that in the final product, there are no N—H bonds; both hydrogens of the amino group are lost, the first in eq. 11.30 and the second in eq. 11.31. Therefore, *only primary amines can be diazotized*. (Secondary and tertiary amines do react with nitrous acid, but their reactions are different and less important in synthesis.)

Solutions of aryldiazonium ions are moderately stable and can be kept at 0°C for several hours. They are useful in synthesis because the diazonio group ($—N_2^+$) can be replaced by nucleophiles; the other product is nitrogen gas.

$$Ar\!-\!\overset{+}{N}\equiv N: + Nu:^- \longrightarrow Ar\!-\!Nu + N_2 \qquad (11.32)$$

Specific useful examples are shown in eq. 11.33. The nucleophile always takes the position on the benzene ring that was occupied by the diazonio group.

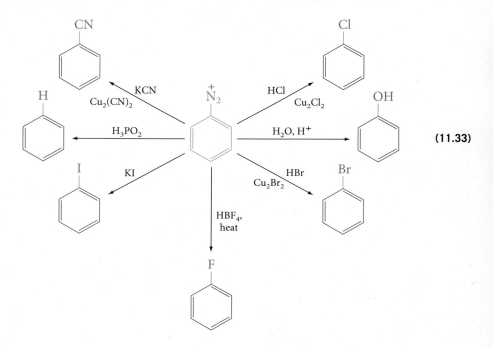

(11.33)

Conversion of diazonium compounds to aryl chlorides, bromides, or cyanides is usually accomplished using cuprous salts, and is known as the **Sandmeyer reaction**. Since a CN group is easily converted to a CO_2H group (eq. 10.13), this provides another route to aromatic carboxylic acids. The reaction with KI gives aryl iodides, usually not easily accessible by direct electrophilic iodination. Similarly, direct aromatic fluorination is difficult, but aromatic fluorides can be prepared from diazonium compounds and tetrafluoroboric acid, HBF_4.

In the **Sandmeyer reaction**, diazonium ions react with cuprous salts to form aryl chlorides, bromides, or cyanides.

Phenols can be prepared by adding diazonium compounds to hot aqueous acid. This reaction is important because there are not many ways to introduce an —OH group directly on an aromatic ring.

Finally, we sometimes use the orienting effect of a nitro or amino group and afterwards remove this substituent from the aromatic ring. This can be done by diazotization followed by reduction. A common reducing agent for this purpose is **hypophosphorous acid**, H_3PO_2.

Hypophosphorous acid is used to reduce the diazonio group to H.

Here are some examples of ways that diazonium compounds can be used in synthesis:

EXAMPLE 11.11

How can *m*-dibromobenzene be prepared?

Solution It *cannot* be prepared by direct electrophilic bromination of bromobenzene, because the Br group is *o,p*-directing (Sec. 4.11). But we can take advantage of the *m*-directing effect of a nitro group and then convert the nitro group to a bromine atom, as follows:

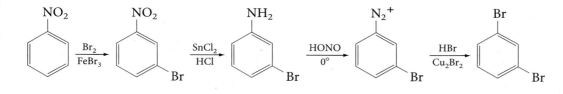

EXAMPLE 11.12

How can *o*-toluic (*o*-methylbenzoic) acid be prepared from *o*-toluidine (*o*-methylaniline)?

Solution

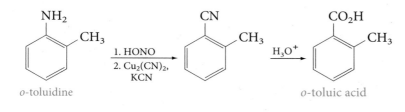

EXAMPLE 11.13

Design a route to 1,3,5-tribromobenzene from aniline.

Solution First brominate; the amino group is *o,p*-directing and ring-activating. Then remove the amino group by diazotization and reduction.

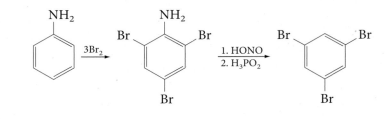

PROBLEM 11.20 Design a synthesis of each of the following compounds, using a diazonium ion intermediate.

a. *m*-chlorofluorobenzene from benzene
b. *m*-nitrophenol from *m*-nitroaniline
c. 3,5-dibromotoluene from *p*-toluidine
d. 2,4-difluorotoluene from toluene

11.13 Diazo Coupling; Azo Dyes

Being positively charged, aryldiazonium ions are electrophiles. They are *weak* electrophiles, however, because the positive charge can be delocalized through resonance.

EXAMPLE 11.14

Write the resonance contributors for the benzenediazonium ion that show how the nitrogen farthest from the benzene ring can become electrophilic.

Solution

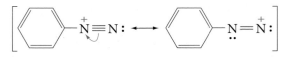

In the second contributor, the nitrogen at the right has only six electrons; it can react as an electrophile.

PROBLEM 11.21 Draw resonance contributors that show that the positive charge in benzenediazonium ion can also be delocalized to the *ortho* and *para* carbons of the benzene ring. (CAREFUL! These contributors have two positive charges and one negative charge.)

Aryldiazonium ions react with strongly activated aromatic rings (phenols and aromatic amines) to give **azo compounds**. For example,

Azo compounds contain the azo group, —N=N—.

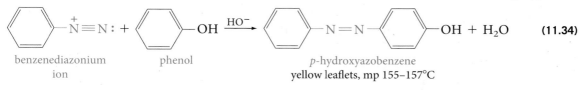

p-hydroxyazobenzene
yellow leaflets, mp 155–157°C

The nitrogen atoms are retained in the product. This electrophilic aromatic substitution reaction is called **diazo coupling**, because in the product, two aromatic rings are coupled by the azo, or —N=N—, group. *Para* coupling is preferred, as in eq. 11.34, but if the *para* position is blocked by another substituent, *ortho* coupling can occur. *All azo compounds are colored,* and many are used commercially as dyes for cloth and in (film-based) color photography.*

Diazo coupling is an electrophilic aromatic substitution reaction in which phenols and aromatic amines react with aryldiazonium electrophiles to give azo compounds.

PROBLEM 11.22 Methyl orange is an azo dye used as an indicator in acid–base titrations. (It is yellow–orange above pH 4.5 and red below pH 3.) Show how it can be synthesized from *p*-aminobenzenesulfonic acid (sulfanilic acid) and *N,N*-dimethylaniline.

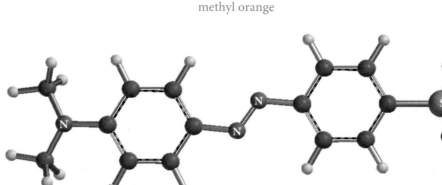

methyl orange

At this point, we have completed a survey of the main functional groups in organic chemistry. By now, all of the structures in the table inside the front cover of this book should seem familiar to you. In the next chapter, we will describe some modern techniques that help us to assign a structure to a particular molecule. After that, we will conclude with a series of chapters on important commercial and biological applications of organic chemistry.

Andrew Lambert Photography/Photo Researchers Inc.

Methyl orange indicator in basic solution (right) and in acidic solution (left).

---

*For an interesting discussion of the diazo copying process, see the article by B. Osterby, *J. Chem. Educ.* **1989**, *66*, 1206–1208.

REACTION SUMMARY

1. Alkylation of Ammonia and Amines to Form Amines (Sec. 11.4)

$$R{-}X + 2\,NH_3 \longrightarrow R{-}NH_2 + NH_4{}^+\,X^-$$

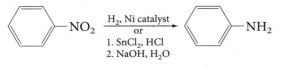

2. Reduction Routes to Amines (Sec. 11.5)

a. Catalytic or Chemical Reduction of the Nitro Group

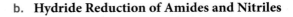

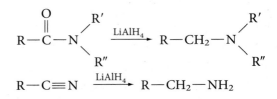

b. Hydride Reduction of Amides and Nitriles

c. Reductive Amination of Aldehydes and Ketones

3. Amines as Bases (Secs. 11.6 and 11.8)

$$R{-}NH_2 + H{-}OH \longrightarrow R{-}\overset{+}{N}H_3 + {}^-OH \qquad\qquad R{-}NH_2 + H{-}Cl \longrightarrow R{-}\overset{+}{N}H_3 + Cl^-$$

4. Amines as Nucleophiles

a. Acylation of Amines (Sec. 11.10)

Secondary and Tertiary Amides from Primary and Secondary Amines

b. Alkylation of Amines: Quaternary Ammonium Salts (Sec. 11.11)

$$R_3N + R'X \longrightarrow R_3\overset{+}{N}{-}R'\,X^-$$

5. Aryldiazonium Salts: Formation and Reactions (Secs. 11.12 and 11.13)

a. Formation from Aniline and Nitrous Acid (Sec. 11.12)

$$ArNH_2 \ + \ HONO \ \xrightarrow{HX} \ ArN_2^+ \ X^-$$
$$\text{(aryldiazonium salt)}$$

b. Reactions to Form Substituted Benzenes (Sec. 11.12)

$$ArN_2^+ \ + \ H_2O \ \xrightarrow{heat} \ ArOH \ + \ N_2 \ + \ H^+$$
$$\text{(phenols)}$$

$$ArN_2^+ \ + \ HX \ \xrightarrow{Cu_2X_2} \ ArX \ \ (X{=}Cl, Br)$$

$$ArN_2^+ \ + \ KI \ \longrightarrow \ ArI$$

$$ArN_2^+ \ + \ KCN \ \xrightarrow{Cu_2(CN)_2} \ ArCN$$

$$ArN_2^+ \ + \ HBF_4 \ \longrightarrow \ ArF$$

$$ArN_2^+ \ + \ H_3PO_2 \ \longrightarrow \ ArH$$

c. Diazo Coupling (Sec. 11.13)

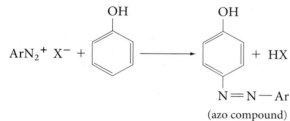

$$\text{(azo compound)}$$

MECHANISM SUMMARY

Diazotization (Sec. 11.12)

$$\left[\overset{Ar}{\underset{H}{\diagdown}}\ddot{N}{-}\ddot{N}{=}\ddot{O}: \right] \ \rightleftharpoons \ Ar{-}\ddot{N}{=}N{-}\ddot{O}{-}H \ \xrightarrow{H^+} \ Ar{-}\ddot{N}{=}N{-}\overset{+}{\ddot{O}}{-}H \ \longrightarrow \ Ar{-}\overset{+}{N}{\equiv}N: \ + \ H_2O$$
$$\overset{\phantom{Ar{-}\ddot{N}{=}N{-}\overset{+}{\ddot{O}}}}{\underset{H}{\phantom{{|}}}}$$

ADDITIONAL PROBLEMS

⏺**WL** Interactive versions of these problems are assignable in OWL.

Nomenclature and Structure of Amines

11.23 Give an example of each of the following:

    a. a primary amine   **b.** a cyclic tertiary amine   **c.** a secondary aromatic amine

    d. a quaternary ammonium salt   **e.** an aryldiazonium salt   **f.** an azo compound

    g. a primary amide

11.24 Write a structural formula for each of the following compounds:

    a. diethylpropylamine   **b.** *N*-methylbenzylamine   **c.** *sec*-butylamine

    d. 1,5-diaminopentane   **e.** *N,N*-dimethylaminocyclopentane   **f.** *N,N*-dimethyl-3-hexanamine

    g. tetraethylammonium chloride   **h.** *p*-nitroaniline   **i.** 2-aminohexane

    j. diphenylamine   **k.** *o*-toluidine   **l.** 3-methyl-2-pentanamine

11.25 Write a correct name for each of the following compounds:

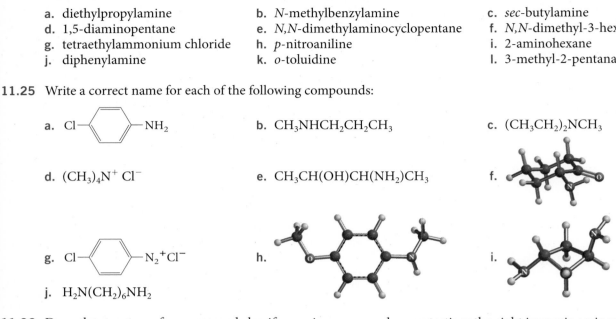

    b. $CH_3NHCH_2CH_2CH_3$

    c. $(CH_3CH_2)_2NCH_3$

    d. $(CH_3)_4N^+ Cl^-$

    e. $CH_3CH(OH)CH(NH_2)CH_3$

    g. $Cl-\!\!\!\bigcirc\!\!\!-N_2{}^+Cl^-$

    j. $H_2N(CH_2)_6NH_2$

11.26 Draw the structures for, name, and classify as primary, secondary, or tertiary the eight isomeric amines with the molecular formula $C_4H_{11}N$.

Properties of Amines and Quaternary Ammonium Salts

11.27 Tell which is the stronger base and why.

    a. aniline or *p*-cyanoaniline   **b.** aniline or diphenylamine

11.28 Write out a scheme similar to eq. 11.19 to show how you could separate a mixture of *p*-toluidine, *p*-methyl-phenol, and *p*-xylene.

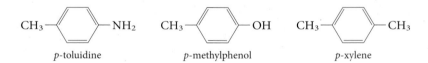

                      p-toluidine   *p*-methylphenol   *p*-xylene

11.29 Draw the important contributors to the resonance hybrid structure of *p*-nitroaniline (page 338).

11.30 Place the following substances, which have nearly identical formula weights, in order of increasing boiling point: $CH_3CH_2CH_2CH_2NH_2$, $CH_3CH_2CH_2CH_2OH$, $CH_3CH_2CH_2OCH_3$, and $CH_3CH_2CH_2CH_2CH_3$.

11.31 Explain why compound A can be separated into its *R*- and *S*-enantiomers, but compound B cannot.

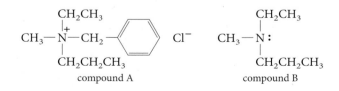

                              compound A   compound B

11.32 Give the priority order of groups in compound A (Problem 11.31), and draw a dash-wedge formula for its *R*-isomer.

Preparation and Reactions of Amines

11.33 Give equations for the preparation of the following amines from the indicated precursor:

    a. *N,N*-diethylaniline from aniline   **b.** *m*-bromoaniline from benzene

    c. *p*-bromoaniline from benzene   **d.** 1-aminohexane from 1-bromopentane

11.34 Complete the following equations:

    a. (cyclopentyl)—NH_2 + CH_2=$CHCH_2Br$ $\xrightarrow{\text{heat}}$

    b. $CH_3\overset{\text{O}}{\overset{\|}{C}}Cl$ + $H_2NCH_2CH_2CH(CH_3)_2$ $\longrightarrow$ A $\xrightarrow{\text{LiAlH}_4}$ B

    c. $CH_3O\overset{\text{O}}{\overset{\|}{C}}$—(phenyl) $\xrightarrow[\text{H}^+]{\text{HONO}_2}$ C $\xrightarrow[\text{excess}]{\text{LiAlH}_4}$ D

    d. (phenyl)—CH_2Br $\xrightarrow{\text{NaCN}}$ E $\xrightarrow{\text{LiAlH}_4}$ F $\xrightarrow{(CH_3\overset{\text{O}}{\overset{\|}{C}})_2O}$ G

    e. (cyclohexyl)=O + $(CH_3)_2CHNH_2$ $\xrightarrow{\text{NaBH}_3\text{CN}}$ H

11.35 Write an equation for the reaction of

    a. *p*-toluidine (page 338) with hydrochloric acid

    b. triethylamine, $(CH_3CH_2)_3N$, with sulfuric acid

    c. dimethylammonium chloride, $(CH_3)_2\overset{+}{N}H_2Cl^-$, with sodium hydroxide

    d. *N,N*-dimethylaniline (page 330) with methyl iodide

    e. cyclohexylamine (page 337) with acetic anhydride

11.36 Write out the steps in the mechanism for the following reaction:

$$CH_3CH_2NH_2 + CH_3\overset{\text{O}}{\overset{\|}{C}}O\overset{\text{O}}{\overset{\|}{C}}CH_3 \longrightarrow CH_3CH_2NH\overset{\text{O}}{\overset{\|}{C}}CH_3 + CH_3COOH.$$

Explain why only one of the hydrogens of the amine is replaced by an acetyl group, even if a large excess of acetic anhydride is used.

Synthetic and Biological Applications of Amine Chemistry

11.37 As noted in the "A Word About … Alkaloids and the Dart-Poison Frogs" on page 341, many alkaloids have potent efficacy with regard to disrupting neurological function. Methamphetamine hydrochloride is an addictive and toxic stimulant.

    a. Outline a synthesis of methamphetamine hydrochloride (shown below) that uses 1-phenyl-2-propanone (phenylacetone) and methylamine as carbon sources.

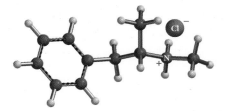

    b. Will the product of your proposed synthesis be optically active or racemic? Explain why.

11.38 New evidence has been presented that dart-poison frogs partially obtain the bioactive alkaloids secreted on their skin from their diet. For example, ants found in the tropics generate alkaloid toxins that are very similar to those found in poison frogs.

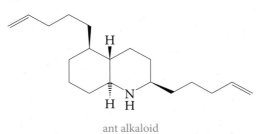

ant alkaloid

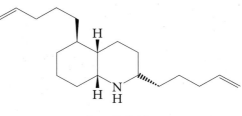

frog alkaloid

How many stereogenic centers are present in these alkaloids?

11.39 Decamethonium bromide is used in surgery as a muscle relaxant. It acts by preventing the enzyme acetylcholine esterase from destroying acetylcholine (see page 327), a necessary step in the transmission of nerve impulses. Show how decamethonium bromide can be synthesized from a diamine and an alkyl halide.

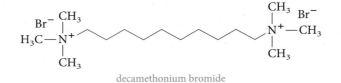

decamethonium bromide

11.40 Choline (Sec. 11.11) can be prepared by the reaction of trimethylamine with ethylene oxide. Write an equation for the reaction, and show its mechanism.

11.41 Acetylcholine (Sec. 11.11) is synthesized in the body's neurons. The enzyme choline acetyltransferase catalyzes its synthesis from acetyl-CoA (see "A Word About...Thioesters, Nature's Acyl-Activating Groups" on page 312) and choline. Write an equation for the reaction, using the formula $CH_3\overset{\|}{\underset{O}{C}}-S-CoA$ for acetyl-CoA.

Formation and Reactions of Aryldiazonium Ions

11.42 Primary aliphatic amines (RNH_2) react with nitrous acid in the same way that primary arylamines ($ArNH_2$) do, to form diazonium ions. But alkyldiazonium ions RN_2^+ are much less stable than aryldiazonium ions ArN_2^+ and readily lose nitrogen even at 0°C. Explain the difference.

11.43 Write an equation for the reaction of CH_3—⟨benzene⟩—N_2^+ HSO_4^- with

   a. HBF_4, then heat   **b.** aqueous acid, heat   **c.** KCN and cuprous cyanide
   d. *p*-methoxyphenol and HO^- **e.** HCl and cuprous chloride   **f.** *N,N*-dimethylaniline and base
   g. hypophosphorous acid   **h.** KI

11.44 Show how diazonium ions could be used to synthesize

   a. *p*-chlorobenzoic acid from *p*-chloroaniline   **b.** *m*-iodochlorobenzene from benzene
   c. *m*-iodoacetophenone from benzene   **d.** 3-cyano-4-methylbenzenesulfonic acid from toluene

11.45 Congo red is used as a direct dye for cotton. Write equations to show how it can be synthesized from benzidine and 1-aminonaphthalene-4-sulfonic acid.

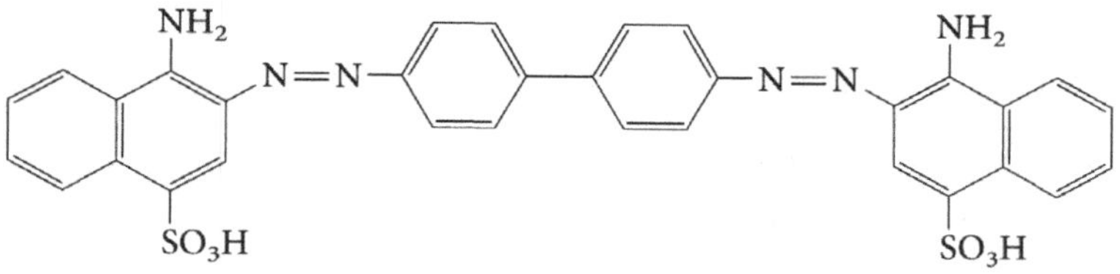

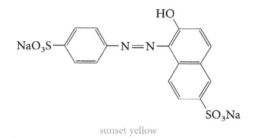

Congo red

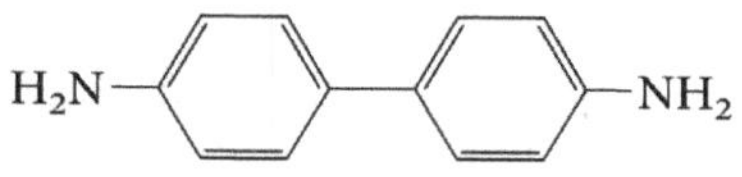

benzidine 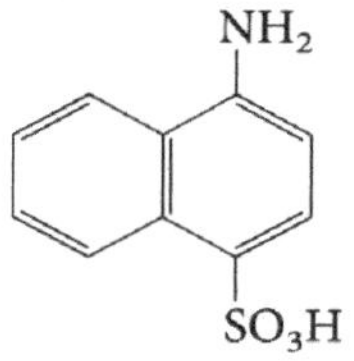   1-aminonaphthalene-4-sulfonic acid

11.46 Sunset yellow is a food dye that can be used to color Easter eggs. Write an equation for an azo coupling reaction that will give this dye.

sunset yellow

Appendix

Table A — Bond Energies for the Dissociation of Selected Bonds in the Reaction
$A—X \rightarrow A\cdot + X\cdot$ (in kcal/mol)

I. Single bonds — Bond energies (kcal/mol)

A—X	X = H	F	Cl	Br	I	OH	NH₂	CH₃	CN
$CH_3—X$	105	108	84	70	57	92	85	90	122
$CH_3CH_2—X$	100	108	80	68	53	94	84	88	
$(CH_3)_2CH—X$	96	107	81	68	54	94	84	86	
$(CH_3)_3C—X$	96		82	68	51	93	82	84	
H—X	104	136	103	88	71	119	107	105	124
X—X	104	38	59	46	36			90	
Ph—X	111	126	96	81	65	111	102	101	
$CH_3C(O)—X$	86	119	81	67	50	106	96	81	
$H_2C=CH—X$	106								
$HC\equiv C—X$	132								

II. Multiple bonds — Bond energies (kcal/mol)

$H_2C=CH_2$	163
$HC\equiv CH$	230
$H_2C=NH$	154
$HC\equiv N$	224
$H_2C=O$	175
$C\equiv O$	257

Table B — Bond Lengths of Selected Bonds (in angstroms, Å)

I. Single bonds

Bond	Length (Å)	Bond	Length (Å)
H—H	0.74	H—C=	1.08
H—F	0.92	H—Ph	1.08
H—Cl	1.27	H—C≡	1.06
H—Br	1.41	C—C	1.54
H—I	1.61	C—N	1.47
H—OH	0.96	C—O	1.43
H—NH₂	1.01	C—F	1.38
H—CH₃	1.09	C—Cl	1.77
F—F	1.42	C—Br	1.94
Cl—Cl	1.98	C—I	2.21
Br—Br	2.29		
I—I	2.66		

II. Double bonds

Bond	Length (Å)
C=C	1.33
C=O	1.21

III. Triple bonds

Bond	Length (Å)
C≡C	1.20
C≡N	1.16
C≡O	1.13

Table C Typical Acidities of Organic Functional Groups

Name and Example*	pK_a	Conjugate Base
Hydrochloric acid, **HCl**	−7	Cl^-
Sulfuric acid, H_2SO_4	−3	HSO_4^-
Sulfonic acid	−2–0	
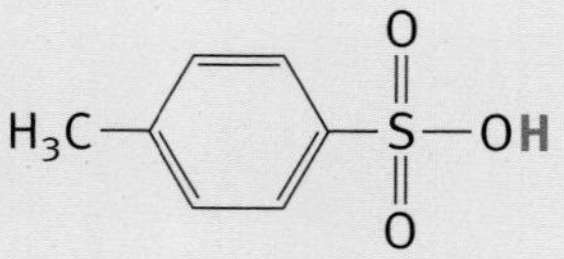	−1	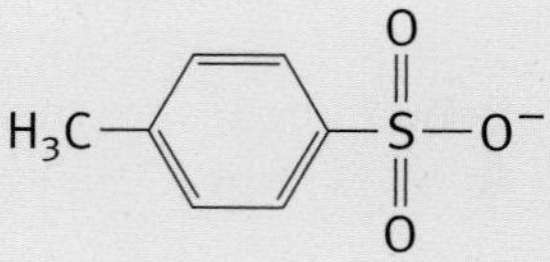
Carboxylic acid	3–5	
$CH_3—C(=O)—OH$	4.74	$CH_3—C(=O)—O^-$
Arylammonium ion	4–5	
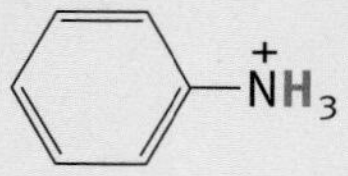	4.6	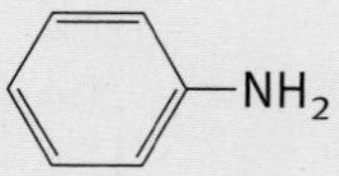
Ammonium ion, $\overset{+}{N}H_4$	9.3	NH_3
Phenol	9–10	
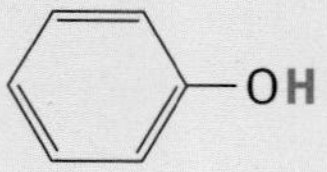	10	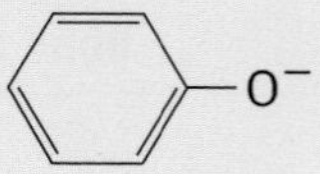
β-diketone	9–10	
$CH_3—C(=O)—CH_2—C(=O)—CH_3$	9	$CH_3—C(=O)—\bar{C}H—C(=O)—CH_3$
Thiol	8–12	
CH_3CH_2SH	10.6	$CH_3CH_2S^-$
β-ketoester	10–11	
$CH_3—C(=O)—CH_2—C(=O)—OCH_2CH_3$	10.7	$CH_3—C(=O)—\bar{C}H—C(=O)—OCH_2CH_3$
Alkylammonium ion	10–12	
$CH_3CH_2\overset{+}{N}H_3$	10.7	$CH_3CH_2NH_2$
Water, H_2O	15.7	HO^-

Strong Acid → Weak Acid; Weak Base → Strong Base

Table C ▬ Typical Acidities of Organic Functional Groups (continued)

Name and Example*	pK_a	Conjugate Base
Alcohol	15–19	
CH_3CH_2OH	15.9	$CH_3CH_2O^-$
Amide	15–19	
$CH_3-\overset{\overset{\displaystyle O}{\|}}{C}-NH_2$	15	$CH_3-\overset{\overset{\displaystyle O}{\|}}{C}-\bar{N}H$
Aldehyde, ketone	17–20	
$CH_3-\overset{\overset{\displaystyle O}{\|}}{C}-CH_3$	19	$CH_3-\overset{\overset{\displaystyle O}{\|}}{C}-\bar{C}H_2$
Ester	23–25	
$CH_3-\overset{\overset{\displaystyle O}{\|}}{C}-OCH_2CH_3$	24.5	$\bar{C}H_2-\overset{\overset{\displaystyle O}{\|}}{C}-OCH_2CH_3$
Alkyne	23–25	
$H-C\equiv C-H$	24	$H-C\equiv C^-$
Ammonia, NH_3	33	$\bar{N}H_2$
Hydrogen, H_2	35	H^-
Alkylamine	~40	
(cyclohexyl)$-NH_2$	42	(cyclohexyl)$-\bar{N}H$
Alkene	~45	
$H_2C{=}CH_2$	44	$H_2C{=}\bar{C}H$
Aromatic hydrocarbon	41–43	
(benzene)$-H$	43	(benzene)$^-$
Alkane	50–60	
CH_4	50	$\bar{C}H_3$

*Some inorganic acids are included for comparison.

Strong Acid ↑ ... Weak Acid (left margin)

Weak Base ↑ ... Strong Base (right margin)

Key terms that appear in **boldface** are followed by their definitions in *italics*. Page numbers followed by *n* refer to notes.

cumulated, 69
facts about, 73
infrared stretching frequencies of, 372
    (Table 12.4)
isolated, 69
orbital model of, 74–76
rotation of, 74
Double-headed straight arrow, 22, 85
Double helix, 535–537
Du Vigneaud, Vincent, 512*n*
Dyes, 256, 349, 447, 501
Dynamite, 223

E1 mechanism   *An elimination reaction
    mechanism: a two-step process in
    which a leaving group departs from
    the substrate, followed by loss of a
    proton from the carbon adjacent to
    the resulting carbocation with overall
    formation of a C═C,* 196
E2 mechanism   *An elimination reaction
    mechanism: a one-step process in which
    a hydrogen atom and leaving group are
    eliminated from adjacent carbon atoms
    and a carbon-carbon double bond is
    formed,* 195
Eclipsed conformation, 48, 170
Edman degradation, 507, 508, 522
Edman, Pehr, 507
Edman's reagent, 507
Eigen, Manfred, 543*n*
Elastomers, 423
Electromagnetic spectrum, types of, 358
    (Table 12.1)
Electron-donating groups, 214, 295
Electron-dot structure, limitations of, 23
Electronegativity   *The tendency of atoms to
    accept electrons and form anions; the
    greater the electronegativity, the more
    the atom accepts electrons,* 4, 7, 10
    (Table 1.4)
Electronic transitions, 375
Electron pairs, 9, 11
Electrons   *Negatively charged particles
    that surround the nucleus of an
    atom,* 2–3
    arrangement of, in atoms, 3 (Table 1.2)
    in covalent bonds, 5–6, 7, 9, 10–11
    in ionic compounds, 4
    in molecular orbital, 23–24
    nonbonding, 11
    number of, in first three shells, 2 (Table 1.1)
    unshared, 11
    valence, 7, 8 (Table 1.3), 7
Electron-transfer reaction, 4
Electron-withdrawing groups, 94, 214, 295, 363
Electrophiles   *Electron-poor reactants:
    they seek electrons and form bonds to
    nucleophiles,* 82. See also Nucleophile
    strong electrophile, 123
Electrophilic addition reaction   *A reaction
    in which an electrophile adds to a
    carbon-carbon multiple bond,* 83–84
    to alkenes, 82–86, 107
    to conjugated dienes, 92–93, 106
    regioselectivity of, 89
Electrophilic aromatic nitration, 333
Electrophilic aromatic substitution   *A
    reaction of an aromatic compound with
    an electrophile that gives a substituted*

aromatic compound, 122–123,
    140–141, 392, 395, 407, 408
    acylation (*see* Acylation)
    alkylation (*see* Alkylation)
    directing effects in synthesis, 134
    in furan, pyrrole, and thiophene, 400
    halogenation (*see* Halogenation)
    mechanism of, 123–128
    meta-directing groups, 130, 132–134
    nitration, 122, 126, 140
    ortho,para-directing groups, 130–132
    in phenols, 224
    of polycyclic aromatic heterocycles, 395,
        407, 408
    of pyridine, 392, 408
    sulfonation, 122, 126–127, 140, 416–417
Electrophoresis   *A method for separating
    amino acids and proteins based on
    their charge differences and direction
    of migration in an electric field at
    controlled pH,* 500
Electropositivity   *The tendency of atoms to
    give up electrons and form cations; the
    greater the electropositivity, the more
    easily the atom gives up electrons,* 4, 7
Electrospray ionization (ESI), 380
Electrostatic potential maps, 26–27
    acetamide, 316
    acetate, 294
    acetic acid, 316
    acetic anhydride, 316
    acetyl chloride, 316
    acetylene, 101
    aniline, 338
    benzene, 123, 129
    carbonyl carbon, 259
    cyclohexylamine, 338
    dimethyl ether, 242
    ethoxide, 294
    ethylene, 76
    ethylene oxide, 242
    furan, 399
    hydrogen bonding between thymine and
        adenine, cytosine, and guanine, 537
    methyl acetate, 316
    nitrobenzene, 129
    1-propanol, 210
    pyrrole, 399
    stearate, 444
    sucrose, 477
    toluene, 129
    water molecule, 45
Elemental analysis, 356
Elements. *See* Chemical elements
Elimination reactions, 195–196, 202
    alkenes from, 216–217, 229
    of alkyl halides, 195, 196–198
    bimolecular, 195–196, 202
    dehydrohalogenation and, 195–196
    E1 and E2 mechanisms of, 195–196
    unimolecular, 195–196, 202
Elion, Gertrude B., 543*n*, 544
Enanthic acid, 288 (Table 10.1)
Enantiomeric acids, 342
Enantiomers, 175
Enantiomers   *A pair of molecules that are
    nonsuperimposable mirror images of
    one another,* 149, 153, 160, 169
    biological activity and, 172–173
    of 2-butanol, 165

diastereomers vs., 167
    of glyceraldehydes, 462
    of 3-methylhexane, 152, 156
    properties of, 162–163
    resolution of
        chiral amines, 342–343
        racemic mixtures, 173–174
    R-S convention, 153–157
    stereochemistry of, 170–172
Endings, of chemical names. *See* Nomenclature
Endothermic reaction   *A reaction that
    requires the intake of heat,* 86, 88
Enediol, 486
Energy
    activation, 87
    bond, 6, 554 (Table A)
    of light, 357
    resonance, 121–122
        of benzenes, 121–122
    stabilization, 122
Enflurane, 243
Enolate anion   *The anion formed by removal
    of the a-hydrogen of a carbonyl
    compound by a base,* 275–276
Enols/enolates, 104, 272
    chemistry of, 279
    water treatment and, 279
Enthalpy (ΔH), 86
Entropy, 86*n*
Environmental issues
    automobile exhaust, 57
    biodegradable polymers, 426
    CFCs, 199–200
Enzymatic oxidation, 136
Enzyme inhibitors, 450
Enzymes, 518
    chirality and action of, 163
    in detergents, 447
    for digesting cellulose, 482
Epibatidine, 341
Epichlorohydrin, 432
Epimers   *Diastereomers that differ in
    configuration at only one stereogenic
    center,* 465
Epoxides   *Cyclic three-membered ring ethers,*
    235, 412*n*
    from alkenes, 99, 244–245, 249
    gypsy moths and, 245
    reactions of, 245–247, 249
Epoxy resins, 432
Equatorial   *The six positions parallel to the
    mean plane of the ring in the chair
    conformation of a six-membered
    ring—for example, in cyclohexane,*
    51–52
Equilibrium constant (Keq)   *A constant that
    indicates the direction that is favored
    for a given reaction; the greater the
    equilibrium constant, the more product
    formation is favored,* 86
Erythromycin, 305
Erythrose, 463, 464, 465
Eschenmoser, A., 548
ESI. *See* Electrospray ionization (ESI)
Essential amino acids   *Amino acids that
    cannot be synthesized by adult humans
    and therefore must be included in the
    diet in the form of proteins,* 495
Essential oils, 452
Ester enolate, 317–318